Basic Skills in English

Purple Level

Yellow Level

Blue Level

Orange Level

Green Level

Red Level

Basic Skills in English

Orange Level

Joy Littell, EDITORIAL DIRECTOR

McDougal, Littell & Company
Evanston, Illinois
New York   Dallas   Sacramento

AUTHORS

Joy Littell, Editorial Director, McDougal, Littell & Company

The Editorial Staff of McDougal, Littell & Company

Kraft and Kraft, Developers of Educational Materials, Newburyport, Massachusetts

CONSULTANTS

Carole B. Bencich, Coordinator of Secondary Language Arts, Brevard County School Board, Rockledge, Florida

Dr. Sheila F. S. Ford, Coordinator for Secondary Language Arts, Spring Branch Independent School District, Houston, Texas

Marietta H. Hickman, English Department Chairman, Wake Forest-Rolesville High School, Wake Forest, North Carolina

Mary Evans Roberts, Supervisor of English and Language Arts, Savannah-Chatham Public Schools, Savannah, Georgia

ISBN: 0-86609-488-1   TE ISBN: 0-86609-490-3

Acknowledgments

Simon & Schuster: for entries from *Webster's New World Dictionary,* Students Edition; copyright © 1981 by Simon & Schuster, Inc. Macmillan Publishing Company: the Handbook section contains, in revised form, some materials that appeared originally in *The Macmillan English Series, Grade 7,* by Thomas Clark Pollock et. al., © 1963 by Macmillan Company. Used by arrangement. (Acknowledgments are continued on page 730.)

86 87 88 / 12 11 10 9 8 7 6 5 4

Composition

WRITING SECTION 1
Building Your Vocabulary 1

Part 1 **It's Alive** Learning About Language 2
Part 2 **Speaking of the Future** New Language for Special Fields 4
Part 3 **Direct Answers** Context: Definition and Restatement 6
Part 4 **Ample Examples** Context Clues: Examples 8
Part 5 **Drawing Parallels** Context Clues: Comparison and Contrast 10
Part 6 **Between the Lines** Inferring Word Meanings 12
Part 7 **Words of a Feather** Using Synonyms and Antonyms 14
Part 8 **Base Hit** Learning Word Parts: Base Words 16
Part 9 **In First Place** Learning Word Parts: Prefixes 18
Part 10 **End of the Line** Learning Word Parts: Suffixes 20

WRITING SECTION 2
Using a Dictionary 23

Part 1 **In So Many Words** How to Use a Dictionary 24
Part 2 **Lead the Way** How To Use Guide Words 26
Part 3 **Upon My Word!** How To Read a Dictionary Entry 28
Part 4 **A Number of Choices** How To Find the Meaning of a Word 31

WRITING SECTION 3
The Right Language at the Right Time 35

Part 1 **A Proper Time** Using Standard and Nonstandard English 36
Part 2 **Here Today** Using and Misusing Slang 38
Part 3 **A Way of Speaking** Using and Misusing Jargon 40

WRITING SECTION 4
Writing Effective Sentences 43

Part 1 **Make Your Point** Writing Sentences 44
Part 2 **Running on Empty** Avoiding Empty Sentences 46
Part 3 **Slim Down** Avoiding Padded Sentences 48
Part 4 **Slow Down** Avoiding Overloaded Sentences 50

WRITING SECTION 5

Sentence Combining 53

Part 1 **Join the Crowd** Combining Sentences 54

Part 2 **Taking Part** Combining Sentence Parts 56

Part 3 **In Addition** Combining by Adding Single Words 58

Part 4 **A Winning Combination** Using Combining Skills in Writing 60

WRITING SECTION 6

A Look at Paragraphs 63

Part 1 **Group Work** Defining a Paragraph 64

Part 2 **All for One** Recognizing Unity in a Paragraph 66

Part 3 **One for All** Using a Topic Sentence 68

Part 4 **An Idea Takes Shape** Developing a Paragraph 70

Part 5 **Read the Labels** Recognizing Three Kinds of Paragraphs 72

WRITING SECTION 7

Writing a Paragraph 75

Part 1 **Paragraph in Progress** Writing as a Process 76

Part 2 **Something To Say** Pre-Writing: Choosing Subjects 78

Part 3 **Zero In** Pre-Writing: Narrowing a Topic 80

Part 4 **What's the Point?** Pre-Writing: Purpose and Audience 82

Part 5 **Make It Direct** Pre-Writing: Topic Sentences 84

Part 6 **Now What?** Pre-Writing: Developing a Paragraph 86

Part 7 **Make Arrangements** Pre-Writing: Organizing a Paragraph 88

Part 8 **Discovery** Writing the First Draft 90

Part 9 **Finish It Off** The First Draft: Ending a Paragraph 92

Part 10 **Polishing Up** Revising Your Paragraph 94

WRITING SECTION 8

The Process of Writing 97

WRITING SECTION 9

The Narrative Paragraph 105

Part 1 **The Big Event** Pre-Writing: Developing a Narrative 106

Part 2 **Time Will Tell** Pre-Writing: Using Chronological Order 108

Part 3 **Insiders and Outsiders** Pre-Writing: Choosing a Point of View 110

Part 4 **Good Timing** Writing the First Draft 112

Part 5 **Instant Replay** Revising Your Narrative Paragraph 114

WRITING SECTION 10

The Descriptive Paragraph 117

Part 1 **In a Sense**   Pre-Writing: Gathering Sensory Details 118
Part 2 **Words in Space**   Pre-Writing: Using Spatial Order 120
Part 3 **In the Mood**   Pre-Writing: Creating Mood 122
Part 4 **In Place**   Writing the First Draft 124
Part 5 **Share the Experience**   Revising Your Descriptive Paragraph 126

WRITING SECTION 11

The Explanatory Paragraph   Telling *How* 129

Part 1 **Get into It**   Pre-Writing: Explaining a Process 130
Part 2 **One, Two, Three**   Pre-Writing: Using Step-by-Step Order 132
Part 3 **Follow the Plan**   Writing the First Draft 134
Part 4 **Clearing Things Up**   Revising Your Explanatory *How* Paragraph 136

WRITING SECTION 12

The Explanatory Paragraph   Telling *Why* 139

Part 1 **A Matter of Opinion**   Pre-Writing: Developing an Opinion 140
Part 2 **For What Reasons?**   Pre-Writing: Organizing an Opinion 142
Part 3 **Tryout**   Writing the First Draft 144
Part 4 **A Good Look**   Revising Your Explanatory *Why* Paragraph 146

WRITING SECTION 13

The Explanatory Paragraph   Telling *What* 149

Part 1 **What's the Point?**   Pre-Writing: Learning About Definitions 150
Part 2 **What Do You Say?**   Pre-Writing: Developing a Definition 152
Part 3 **The Plain Truth**   Writing the First Draft 154
Part 4 **Checkpoint**   Revising Your Definition 156

WRITING SECTION 14

A Look at Compositions 159

Part 1 **Compose Yourself**   Learning About Compositions 160
Part 2 **First Steps**   Pre-Writing: Developing a Composition 162
Part 3 **Group Effort**   Pre-Writing: Organizing a Composition 164
Part 4 **Experiment!**   Writing the First Draft 166

Part 5 **Fine-Tuning** Revising Your Composition 168

Part 6 **Name Game** Writing a Title 170

Part 7 **Home Free** The Final Copy 172

Part 8 **Don't Forget** Guidelines for Writing a Composition 174

WRITING SECTION 15
The Narrative Composition 177

Part 1 **Have You Heard?** Pre-Writing: Planning a Story 178

Part 2 **I Can See It Now** Pre-Writing: Plotting a Story 180

Part 3 **What a View!** Pre-Writing: Choosing a Point of View 182

Part 4 **It Goes Like This** Writing the First Draft 184

Part 5 **Speak Up** The First Draft: Dialogue 186

Part 6 **The Time Is Right** The First Draft: Transitions 188

Part 7 **The Grand Finale** Revising Your Narrative Composition 190

WRITING SECTION 16
The Descriptive Composition 193

Part 1 **Show and Tell** Pre-Writing: Using Sensory Details 194

Part 2 **Paint a Picture** Writing the First Draft 196

Part 3 **See It Through** The First Draft: Ending a Description 198

Part 4 **The Final Picture** Revising Your Descriptive Composition 200

WRITING SECTION 17
The Explanatory Composition Telling *How* 203

Part 1 **Talent Show** Pre-Writing: Planning an Explanation 204

Part 2 **Follow Me** Pre-Writing: Using Step-by-Step Order 206

Part 3 **Marking Time** Writing the First Draft 208

Part 4 **Getting It Right** Revising Your Explanation 210

WRITING SECTION 18
The Explanatory Composition Telling *Why* 213

Part 1 **Why, Oh Why?** Pre-Writing: Developing an Opinion 214

Part 2 **Saving the Best** Pre-Writing: Organizing Your Details 216

Part 3 **It Stands to Reason** Writing the First Draft 218

Part 4 **The Final Lap** Revising Your Explanation 220

WRITING SECTION 19

The Explanatory Composition   Telling *What*   223

Part 1 **A Chance To Explain**   Pre-Writing: Developing a Definition   224
Part 2 **Exactly So**   Pre-Writing: Organizing a Definition   226
Part 3 **Which Way Is Best?**   Writing the First Draft   228
Part 4 **Clean-Up**   Revising Your Definition   230

WRITING SECTION 20

Writing a Report   233

Part 1 **Get the Facts**   Learning About Reports   234
Part 2 **Take Note**   Gathering Information   236
Part 3 **Sorting It Out**   Organizing Your Notes   238
Part 4 **Get It on Paper**   Writing the First Draft   240
Part 5 **The Last Detail**   Revising Your Report   242
Part 6 **Where Credit Is Due**   Preparing a Bibliography   244

WRITING SECTION 21

Clear Thinking   247

Part 1 **Nothing but the Facts**   Identifying Facts   248
Part 2 **Says Who?**   Using Good Sources   250
Part 3 **Prove It!**   Distinguishing Fact and Opinion   252
Part 4 **The Reasons Why**   Supporting Opinions   254
Part 5 **Spinning Wheels**   Circular Reasoning   256
Part 6 **Snarl and Purr**   Recognizing Loaded Language   258

WRITING SECTION 22

Using the Library   261

Part 1 **One for the Books**   How To Use the Library   262
Part 2 **It's in the Cards**   How To Use the Card Catalog   265
Part 3 **First Stop**   How To Use an Encyclopedia   268
Part 4 **Fact Finding**   How To Use Reference Works   271

WRITING SECTION 23

Study and Research Skills   275

Part 1   **Note Well**   Understanding the Assignment   276
Part 2   **This Way, Please**   Following Directions   278
Part 3   **A Quiet Place**   A Time and a Place for Studying   280
Part 4   **Making the Most of It**   The SQ3R Study Method   282
Part 5   **Remember This**   Taking Notes   284
Part 6   **One Way or Another**   Adjusting Your Reading Rate   286
Part 7   **Seeing Is Believing**   Using Graphic Aids   288
Part 8   **Graphic Descriptions**   Reading Graphs   290
Part 9   **Testing, Testing**   Preparing for and Taking Tests   292
Part 10   **The Answer Key**   Answering Objective Test Questions   294
Part 11   **Get It in Writing**   Answering Written Test Questions   296

WRITING SECTION 24

Letters, Forms, and Applications   299

Part 1   **Mail Call**   How To Write a Friendly Letter   300
Part 2   **A Proper Send-off**   How To Prepare Letters for the Mail   303
Part 3   **Thanks So Much**   How To Write Social Notes   305
Part 4   **Be Businesslike**   How To Write a Business Letter   307
Part 5   **Help!**   How To Write a Letter of Request   310
Part 6   **Letters That Work**   How To Write Letters of Application   313
Part 7   **Apply Yourself**   How To Complete a Job Application   316
Part 8   **Paperwork**   How To Complete Work-Related Forms   319

WRITING SECTION 25

Preparing a Talk   323

Part 1   **A Manner of Speaking**   Formal and Informal Talks   324
Part 2   **Look Before You Leap**   Preparing an Informal Talk   326
Part 3   **A Formal Engagement**   Preparing a Formal Talk   328
Part 4   **Source Sorcery**   Gathering and Organizing Information   330
Part 5   **Together at Last**   Writing a Formal Talk   332
Part 6   **Special Delivery**   Presenting Yourself to an Audience   334
Part 7   **Mirror, Mirror**   Practicing a Talk   336
Part 8   **Have You Heard?**   Listening to and Judging Talks   338

Handbook

HANDBOOK SECTION 1

The Sentence and Its Parts   343

Part	1	**The Parts of a Sentence**	344
Part	2	**Kinds of Sentences**	346
Part	3	**Simple Subjects and Predicates**	348
Part	4	**Main Verbs and Helping Verbs**	351
Part	5	**Compound Subjects and Compound Verbs**	354
Part	6	**Subjects in Unusual Order**	356
Part	7	**Subjects and Verbs in Questions and Exclamations**	358
Part	8	**Sentences That Begin with *There***	360
Part	9	**Subjects and Verbs in Imperative Sentences**	362
		Additional Exercises	364
		Mixed Review	369
		Using Grammar in Writing	371

HANDBOOK SECTION 2

Avoiding Fragments and Run-on Sentences   372

Part	1	**Avoiding Sentence Fragments**	373
Part	2	**Avoiding Run-on Sentences**	374
		Additional Exercises	376
		Mixed Review	378
		Using Grammar in Writing	379

HANDBOOK SECTION 3

Using Verbs   380

Part 1   **The Work of Verbs**   381

Part 2   **Parts of the Verb**   383

Part 3   **Verbs and Direct Objects**   384

Part 4   **Transitive and Intransitive Verbs**   387

Part 5   **Linking Verbs**   390

Part 6   **Tenses of Verbs**   392

Part 7   **The Principal Parts of Verbs**   394

Additional Exercises   397

Mixed Review   400

Using Grammar in Writing   402

HANDBOOK SECTION 4

Using Irregular Verbs   403

Additional Exercises   416

Mixed Review   417

Using Grammar in Writing   418

HANDBOOK SECTION 5

Using Troublesome Pairs of Verbs   419

Part 1   **Using *Learn* and *Teach***   420

Part 2   **Using *Let* and *Leave***   421

Part 3   **Using *Lie* and *Lay***   422

Part 4   **Using *May* and *Can***   423

Part 5   **Using *Rise* and *Raise***   424

Part 6   **Using *Sit* and *Set***   425

Additional Exercises   426

Mixed Review   427

Using Grammar in Writing   428

HANDBOOK SECTION 6

Using Nouns   429

Part 1   **What Are Nouns?**   429

Part 2   **Common Nouns and Proper Nouns**   431

Part	3	**Nouns Used as Subjects**	433
Part	4	**Nouns Used as Direct Objects**	434
Part	5	**Nouns Used as Indirect Objects**	437
Part	6	**Predicate Nouns**	439
Part	7	**The Plurals of Nouns**	441
Part	8	**Possessive Nouns**	444
		Additional Exercises	446
		Mixed Review	450
		Using Grammar in Writing	452

HANDBOOK SECTION 7

Using Pronouns — 453

Part	1	**What Are Pronouns?**	453
Part	2	**Subject Forms of Pronouns**	456
Part	3	**Object Forms of Pronouns**	458
Part	4	***We Girls* or *Us Girls; We Boys* or *Us Boys***	459
Part	5	**Possessive Forms of Pronouns**	461
Part	6	**Pronouns and Antecedents**	462
Part	7	**Compound Personal Pronouns**	464
Part	8	**Demonstrative Pronouns**	465
Part	9	**Interrogative Pronouns**	466
Part	10	**Indefinite Pronouns**	468
		Additional Exercises	470
		Mixed Review	475
		Using Grammar in Writing	477

HANDBOOK SECTION 8

Using Adjectives — 478

Part	1	**What Are Adjectives?**	478
Part	2	**Predicate Adjectives**	481
Part	3	**Pronouns Used as Adjectives**	484
Part	4	**Demonstrative Adjectives**	485

Part 5   **Adjectives in Comparisons**   486

Part 6   **Special Problems with Modifiers**   489

Additional Exercises   491

Mixed Review   494

Using Grammar in Writing   495

HANDBOOK SECTION 9

Using Adverbs   496

Part 1   **What Are Adverbs?**   496

Part 2   **Adverbs in Comparisons**   501

Part 3   **Adjective or Adverb?**   504

Part 4   **Special Problems with Modifiers**   507

Additional Exercises   510

Mixed Review   512

Using Grammar in Writing   513

HANDBOOK SECTION 10

Using Prepositions   514

Part 1   **What Are Prepositions?**   515

Part 2   **Objects of Prepositions**   517

Part 3   **Prepositional Phrases as Modifiers**   520

Part 4   **Putting Prepositional Phrases in the Right Place**   523

Part 5   **Preposition or Adverb?**   525

Additional Exercises   527

Mixed Review   530

Using Grammar in Writing   531

HANDBOOK SECTION 11

Using Conjunctions   532

Additional Exercises   535

Mixed Review   536

Using Grammar in Writing   537

HANDBOOK SECTION 12
Using the Parts of Speech 538

Part 1 **The Parts of Speech** 538
Part 2 **Words Used as Different Parts of Speech** 540
Additional Exercises 542
Mixed Review 543
Using Grammar in Writing 544

HANDBOOK SECTION 13
Sentence Patterns 545

Part 1 **Word Order and Meaning** 545
Part 2 **The N V Pattern** 546
Part 3 **The N V N Pattern** 547
Part 4 **The N V N N Pattern** 548
Part 5 **The N LV N Pattern** 549
Part 6 **The N LV Adj Pattern** 550
Additional Exercises 552
Mixed Review 553
Using Grammar in Writing 554

HANDBOOK SECTION 14
Using Verbals 555

Part 1 **Gerunds** 556
Part 2 **Participles** 558
Part 3 **Infinitives** 561
Part 4 **A Review of Verbals** 565
Additional Exercises 567
Mixed Review 570
Using Grammar in Writing 571
Cumulative Review 572

HANDBOOK SECTION 15

Making Subjects and Verbs Agree 574

Part 1   **Singular and Plural Forms**   575
Part 2   **Agreement of Subject and Verb**   576
Part 3   **Verbs with Compound Subjects**   578
Part 4   **Agreement in Inverted Sentences**   580
Part 5   **Verbs with *There***   581
Part 6   **Indefinite Pronouns**   583
     Additional Exercises   585
     Mixed Review   588
     Using Grammar in Writing   589
     Cumulative Review   590

HANDBOOK SECTION 16

Using Compound Sentences 592

Part 1   **Review of the Sentence**   593
Part 2   **What Is a Compound Sentence?**   595
     Additional Exercises   604
     Mixed Review   605
     Using Grammar in Writing   606

HANDBOOK SECTION 17

Using Complex Sentences 607

Part 1   **What Is a Complex Sentence?**   608
Part 2   **Adverb Clauses**   612
Part 3   **Adjective Clauses**   614
Part 4   **Noun Clauses**   616
Part 5   **A Review of Subordinate Clauses**   618
Part 6   **More About Sentence Fragments**   619
Part 7   **A Review of Sentences**   621
     Additional Exercises   623
     Mixed Review   625
     Using Grammar in Writing   627
     Cumulative Review   628

HANDBOOK SECTION 18

Capitalization 631

Proper Nouns and Adjectives 632
First Words 641
Additional Exercises 646
Mixed Review 649
Using Mechanics in Writing 650

HANDBOOK SECTION 19

Punctuation 651

End Marks 652
The Comma 656
The Semicolon 669
The Colon 670
The Hyphen 671
The Apostrophe 672
Quotation Marks 676
Additional Exercises 683
Mixed Review 690
Using Mechanics in Writing 691

HANDBOOK SECTION 20

Spelling 692

A General Method of Attack on Spelling 693
A Method of Attack on Specific Words 694
Rules for Spelling 695
Words Often Confused 700
Additional Exercises 706
Mixed Review 707
Using Mechanics in Writing 708
Cumulative Review 709

Building Your Vocabulary

Part 1 **It's Alive!**
Learning About Language

Part 2 **Speaking of the Future**
New Language for Special Fields

Part 3 **Direct Answers**
Context: Definition and Restatement

Part 4 **Ample Examples**
Context Clues: Examples

Part 5 **Drawing Parallels**
Context Clues: Comparison and Contrast

Part 6 **Between the Lines**
Inferring Word Meanings

Part 7 **Words of a Feather**
Using Synonyms and Antonyms

Part 8 **Base Hit**
Learning Word Parts: Base Words

Part 9 **In First Place**
Learning Word Parts: Prefixes

Part 10 **End of the Line**
Learning Word Parts: Suffixes

It's Alive!

Learning About Language

Here's the Idea   English is a living language. It keeps growing and changing. In the process of change, some words are
dropped from common use. Others are added. Words are
added to the English language in several ways.

One major way in which English grows is by **borrowing.** Many
words used in the United States are not native English words.
They come from other languages. Borrowed words include
American Indian words, like *pecan;* French words, like *bureau;*
Spanish words, like *tornado;* and Italian words, like *pizza.*

Another way English gains new words is by making **words
from people's names.** For instance, a person named Louis Braille
was blinded in an accident in 1812 when he was three years old.
When he was fifteen years old, Braille invented a language
system based on raised dots that the blind could read. *Braille*
later became the word naming this system.

English also grows when a new word is made from part of
another word. This process is called **clipping.** Clipping creates
the word *auto* from *automobile.* It creates *fan* from *fanatic.*

Can you see how English is enriched by the addition of new
words? As you add words to your own vocabulary, you will be
able to express ideas in interesting and more precise ways.

Check It Out   Read the following examples.

1. The word *cole slaw* is borrowed from Dutch, *plaza* from
Spanish, and *yogurt* from Turkish.

2. The word *bowie* knife is made from the name of Colonel
James Bowie, *Morse* code from Samuel Morse, and *pasteurize* from
Louis Pasteur.

3. The word *flu* is clipped from *influenza, gym* from *gymnasium,* and *jet* from *jet airplane.*

- Do you see how the English language is enriched by new words?
- What does your dictionary tell you about these examples?

Try Your Skill   Can you guess where each of the following words came from? Use a dictionary to help you find the answers.

ranch	dorm
shampoo	lab
skunk	math
wagon	sub

Use a dictionary to answer the following questions.

1. For whom was the Franklin stove named?
2. For whom was the poinsettia named?
3. For whom is the month of August named?

Keep This in Mind

- English is a living language. It changes continually.
- New words are added by borrowing, by making words from people's names, and by clipping.

Now Write   Use a dictionary to help you find out how each of these words came into English. Write your answers in complete sentences. Label your paper **It's Alive!** and put it into your folder.

cotton	Bunsen burner	bus
laugh	marathon	memo
train	saxophone	taxi

Speaking of the Future

New Language for Special Fields

Here's the Idea   You live in a time of rapid change. Every day brings new discoveries, inventions, fashions, and fads. As the world changes, your language changes with it. New words are created to describe new ideas. Old words are given new meanings. In short, your language grows and develops like a living thing.

Most of the new words that enter your language are from the fields of science and technology. The word *quasar,* for example, was created in 1965. It describes a new kind of object in space discovered by astronomers. The word *memory* was given a new meaning by computer scientists in the 1950's. They used the word to describe the part of a computer that stores information. To understand the world of the future, you will have to understand many new words. Whenever you read or hear one of these new words, try to find out its meaning. Then try to use the word in your own speech and writing. This will help to prepare you for life in this modern age.

Check It Out   Read the following list of recently-created words.

Computer Science	Space Science	Entertainment
debugging	light-year	video-cassette
hardware	black hole	pay television
terminal	space shuttle	video-disc
microcomputer	nebula	music video

- Which of these terms are made from previously-existing words? What were their original meanings?
- Which of these words are brand new?

Try Your Skill   Using a dictionary, answer the following questions.

   1. What does the word *fault* mean to a geologist? To a tennis pro?
   2. What is a *printout*? What existing words were used to make this new term?
   3. What is a *bug* to a computer scientist?
   4. What are the various meanings of the word *magnitude*? What does this word mean to an astronomer?
   5. What does *video* mean in such words as *video-cassette, video game,* and *videotape*?

Keep This in Mind

- Your language changes as the world changes.
- New words are created, and existing words take on new meanings to describe the world today.

Now Write   Look through some magazines dealing with science and computers. Make a list of ten new terms from these fields. Using a dictionary, write the meaning of each new term. Then, use each term in a sentence that shows your understanding of its meaning. Label your paper **Speaking of the Future.** Save it in your folder.

Direct Answers

Context: Definition and Restatement

Here's the Idea When you see an unfamiliar word, do you look it up in a dictionary? Do you ask someone for the definition? There is another method that you can use. You can try to learn the meaning of an unfamiliar word by thinking about the context. **Context** means the words and sentences around a word. The most direct context clues to the meaning of a word are definition and restatement.

When **definition** is used, the meaning of a new word is stated in a direct way.

> Jamie placed the bowl inside the *kiln*. A *kiln* is an oven for baking pottery.

When **restatement** is used, the meaning of a new word is usually signaled by key words, like *or, is called, that is, which is,* or *in other words.* A comma or a pair of commas may also be used to signal the meaning of the new word.

> The sailboat *careened,* or leaned sideways, in the storm.
> Shakespeare was a master at exposing the *foibles,* or minor weaknesses, of the characters in his plays.

Do you see how helpful these context clues are? As you read, look for similar clues. You will be able to add many new words to your vocabulary.

Check It Out Read these examples.

  1. Have you used an *almanac?* An almanac is a book published each year that lists facts about many subjects.

  2. A Channel 5 *editorial,* a statement of opinion made by the station manager, criticized the new mayor.

3. We learned about the Ming *dynasty,* which is the series of Chinese rulers from the Ming family.

4. World leaders met recently to discuss *disarmament.* Disarmament is the reduction of military forces and equipment.

5. In the future many homes may be heated by *solar* energy; that is, energy that comes from the sun.

- What clues indicate definition or restatement?
- What is the meaning of each italicized word?

Try Your Skill   Use context clues to find the meanings of the italicized words. Then write definitions for these words.

1. The doctor charged only a *nominal,* or very small, fee.

2. The *marimba,* a kind of xylophone, makes lovely, ringing sounds.

3. As a hockey player Dave was *aggressive;* that is, he was bold and forceful.

4. The government sent troops after the *insurgents.* An insurgent is a rebel.

5. A *southpaw,* or left-handed pitcher, has the advantage when facing a left-handed batter.

Keep This in Mind

- You can often learn the meanings of unfamiliar words by thinking about their context.
- The most direct context clues are definition and restatement.

Now Write   Imagine that you are writing for young readers. You want to use the following words: *cheetah, drum, landlubber, marathon, oxygen,* and *volunteer.* Check the meanings of the words in a dictionary. Then use each word in a sentence, using a definition or restatement to give the meaning of the word. Label your paper **Direct Answers**. Put it into your folder.

Ample Examples

Context Clues: Examples

Here's the Idea   Writers may supply the meanings of unfamiliar words by giving **examples** in the context. A familiar example may give you the clue you need to define a word you do not know. For instance, do you know what a *pugilist* is? Read the following sentence.

> America's great *pugilists,* like Rocky Marciano and Muhammad Ali, shared the qualities of determination and discipline.

Do you recognize the names of famous boxers? If so, you know that the word *pugilist* must mean "professional boxer." From this sentence you can see that examples do not always tell you exactly what an unfamiliar word means. However, they do give you a general idea of the word.

Several key words and phrases alert you to the use of examples. Here are some of the more common ones:

like	for example
other	for instance
this, these	such as
especially	

When you see an unfamiliar word, check the context for any of these key words and phrases.

Check It Out   Read the following sentences.

1. Alexis collects foreign *currencies,* such as pounds, pesos, francs, yen, and lira.
2. *Carbonated* beverages, such as ginger ale and root beer, give Kate the hiccups.

3. Hawaii, Samoa, Tahiti, and other *Polynesian* islands are located in the Pacific.

4. Many chemical elements, such as *neon* or hydrogen, exist in the form of gas.

- What words or phrases indicate that examples are used?
- What is the meaning of each italicized word?

Try Your Skill   As you read the following sentences, write what you think each italicized word means.

1. The planets bear the names of *Neptune, Mars,* and other Roman gods.

2. *Mesquite,* like many thorny trees, grows in desert areas of the southwestern U.S.

3. On a clear night, *constellations,* such as the Big Dipper and Little Dipper, can be seen in the sky.

4. Some parts of an automobile engine, the *carburetor* for example, may need adjustment from time to time.

5. Some *tubers,* especially potatoes and yams, are grown on this farm.

Keep This in Mind

- Examples in context help you to learn the meaning of an unfamiliar word. Such key words as *like, other,* and *for example* signal the use of examples.

Now Write   Choose three of these words: *cotton, dolphins, peaches, softball.* Write a sentence for each, using an example to explain the word. Be sure to include key words that signal examples. Use a dictionary to help you. Label your paper **Ample Examples.** Put your work into your folder.

Drawing Parallels

Context Clues: Comparison and Contrast

Here's the Idea   Two other kinds of context clues can help you figure out the meanings of unfamiliar words. They are comparison and contrast. These context clues will tell you what an unfamiliar word is like or unlike.

When **comparison** is used, an unfamiliar word is compared with a similar word that is known to you. Look at this sentence:

> The cat's *amber* eyes were like the color of honey.

You may not know exactly what *amber* means, but through comparison you know it is like the color of honey.

When **contrast** is used, an unfamiliar word is compared with an opposite word that is known to you. Read this sentence:

> Unlike Jill, who is very talkative, Monica is *laconic.*

The word *laconic* may be unfamiliar to you. However, from the context, key words and phrases help give you the meaning. These are the most common context clues:

Comparison: as, like, in the same way, just as, similar to
Contrast: although, but, unlike, on the contrary, on the other hand, however

Check It Out   As you read the following sentences, use the context clues to find the meanings of the italicized words.

1. Although driver education is not required in some states, it is *mandatory* in this state.
2. No scent is as *tantalizing* as the sweet aroma of homemade apple pie.
3. The sound of the rain was as *persistent* as the ticking of the clock on the mantle.

4. In contrast to how depressed they had been after four straight losses, the players were *jubilant* after their victory.

- What key words signal that comparison is used?
- What key words signal that contrast is used?

Try Your Skill Write what you think the italicized words mean according to the context clues.

1. The *discordant* music sounded like pots and pans clanging together.
2. Unlike a pullover sweater, which must be pulled on over the head, a *cardigan* can be unbuttoned and put on like a shirt.
3. Although Kim gave us enthusiastic praise for our work on the play, Jean's remarks were *perfunctory.*
4. The *desolate* house looked as though it were haunted.
5. Although Roy is careful about spending money, his brother Andy is *extravagant.*

Keep This in Mind

- Comparison is a context clue that shows how things are similar. Such key words as *like* and *as* signal comparison.
- Contrast is a context clue that shows how things are different. Such key words as *but, unlike,* and *on the contrary* signal contrast.

Now Write Choose four of these words: *sour, transparent, enormous, miniscule, lively, ridiculous.* Write a sentence for each, using a comparison or contrast to explain the word. Use a dictionary if necessary. Use key words to signal each context clue. Label your paper **Drawing Parallels.** Keep your work in your folder.

Between the Lines

Inferring Word Meanings

Here's the Idea Sometimes the context in which an unfamiliar word appears does not give direct clues to the meaning of the word. The context may only hint at the meaning of an unfamiliar word. You must read between the lines to find clues. Then you draw a conclusion about what the word means. This process of reading between the lines to reach a conclusion is called **inference.**

The main idea of a whole paragraph can center on the meaning of an unfamiliar word. For example, as you read the following paragraph, try to **infer** the meaning of *kibitzer.*

> When you are playing cards, there are few things more irritating than a *kibitzer.* Kibitzers love to stand behind you and smile or groan as you pick up your cards. By doing this, they manage to give the other players a clear idea of your hand. Kibitzers also love to give you advice. In fact, they will criticize you if you don't follow their suggestions.

From this paragraph you can infer that a kibitzer is a person who bothers people, in this case cardplayers, by offering unwanted advice.

Check It Out Read the following paragraph.

> My friend Mark is a *gourmet.* Mark says that good food is one of life's greatest pleasures. He does not care for most of the food I usually eat. Yesterday, for example, Mark turned down a peanut butter and jelly sandwich I offered him. He also refused a bologna sandwich. I think Mark would rather go hungry than eat something that is not carefully prepared and that he does not completely enjoy eating.

- What can you infer about the meaning of *gourmet?*

Try Your Skill   As you read the following paragraphs, try to infer the meanings of the italicized words. Then, write definitions for them.

1. My brother is an *avid* reader. He is like my mother; they would both rather read than eat or sleep. I suspect that if nothing else were available, my brother would probably read the phone book.

2. Sally is far more *gregarious* than her two older sisters. They are quiet girls who seldom go out. Sally considers it a waste of time to stay home when she could be out with her friends.

3. My sister is much more *frugal* than I am. She carries a little notebook in her purse and keeps track of every penny she spends. She never buys anything without checking to see if she can buy it cheaper at another store. Each month her bank account grows. I don't think she ever buys anything without giving it long and careful thought.

Keep This in Mind

- Inference is the process of reading between the lines to draw a conclusion about the meaning of a word. Sometimes inferences can be drawn from the main idea of a paragraph.

Now Write   Imagine that you are writing for young readers about daydreams. You want to hint at the meaning of the word *daydream* without defining it directly. Write three or four sentences about daydreaming. Label your paper **Between the Lines** and put your work into your folder.

Words of a Feather

Using Synonyms and Antonyms

Here's the Idea   Many English words have similar meanings. They are called **synonyms.** Examples are *pick, choose,* and *select.* Sometimes there is only a slight difference between the meanings of synonyms. However, because of that slight difference, one word will fit into the context of a sentence better than its synonyms. For example, you might *pick* a card, *choose* a partner, and *select* the best answer.

Each synonym has its own meaning. Here are three synonyms: *slip, err,* and *blunder.* They all mean "to do something incorrectly." But are they exactly the same? Read these examples.

> I *slipped* in calling him by my brother's name.
> The report *erred* in calling Columbus a Spaniard.
> Henry *blundered* by failing to stop at the stop sign.

From these examples, you can see that *slipped* suggests that a person made a minor, unintentional mistake. *Erred* suggests that a person overlooked or misunderstood something. *Blundered* suggests that a person made a careless mistake, perhaps a serious mistake.

Using the correct word is important. The wrong word will give the wrong idea. The more synonyms you know, the more exact your writing will be.

Antonyms are words with opposite meanings. They include such pairs of words as *fast—slow, in—out, loud—soft,* and *strong—weak.* Antonyms serve several useful functions. They, too, add precision to your writing. They can also serve to point out contrasts. For example, "The basketball player was so tall that he made his six-foot-tall coach look short."

14

Check It Out   Read the following sentences.

   1. The fruit salad was so *good,* I had a second helping.
     helpful   proper   pleasant   delicious
   2. Barbara is a cheerful person. Jim, on the other hand, is usually *sad.*
     heartbroken   gloomy   grave   displeased

- Which is the best synonym for *good?* Why?
- Which antonym for *cheerful* is more appropriate than *sad?* Why?

Try Your Skill   Each of the following sentences contains an italicized word that does not quite fit the context of the sentence. Below each sentence are four synonyms. On your paper, write the sentence, using the most appropriate synonym.

   1. Tim answered the question in a *small* voice.
     ordinary   humble   soft   tiny
   2. The lifeguard *moved* into the water when she heard a cry.
     leaped   skipped   walked   wandered
   3. The pilot tested his instruments to be sure they were *right.*
     accurate   suitable   fitting   true

Keep This in Mind

- Synonyms are words with nearly the same meaning.
- Antonyms are words with opposite meanings. Antonyms, as well as synonyms, help you write precisely.

Now Write   Choose two of the italicized words in **Try Your Skill.** Check their meanings in the dictionary. Use each word correctly in a sentence of your own. Then use an antonym of *small* or *right* in a sentence. Label your paper **Words of a Feather** and put your work into your folder.

Base Hit

Learning Word Parts: Base Words

Here's the Idea   A **base word** is a word on which other words are based. Word parts may be added at the beginning of a base word or at the end. Sometimes word parts are added at both places. For instance, *misuse, useful,* and *reusable* are all formed by adding word parts to the base word *use.*

Often the base word is clear, as it is in the word *misprint.* Here the base word is clearly *print.* In some words, though, you may have to look more carefully. Can you find the base word in *indirectness?* To find it, you have to remove a word part from each end of the base word. Then you see that *direct* is the base word.

Being aware of base words helps you to enlarge your vocabulary. You can look at an unfamiliar word and recognize within it a word you already know. This gives you some idea of what the unfamiliar word means.

Check It Out   Look at each group of words below.

believe	reader	helpful
unbelievable	readable	helpless
disbelieving	misread	helper
uncaring	misunderstand	unreasonable
careful	understandable	reasonable
careless	misunderstanding	reasonably

• What is the base word in each group of words?

Try Your Skill   Read each word below and determine what the base word is. Number your paper from 1 to 20 and write the correct base word.

1. washable
2. extraordinary
3. misfortune
4. heater
5. misspell
6. thoughtless
7. harmful
8. review
9. improvement
10. actor
11. foreground
12. enjoyment
13. remake
14. interaction
15. joyful
16. nonbreakable
17. mispronounce
18. sickness
19. fearless
20. renew

Keep This in Mind

- A base word is a word on which other words are based. Word parts may be added at the beginning of a base word, at the end, or at both places. Recognizing base words will help you to determine the meaning of longer, unfamiliar words.

Now Write   Using any newspaper or magazine available to you, find ten words that contain base words. Copy each word as it appears in context. Then write the base word. You may want to use a dictionary to help you. Label your paper **Base Hit** and keep it in your folder.

In First Place

Learning Word Parts: Prefixes

Here's the Idea A **prefix** is a word part added to the beginning of a base word. The word part *re-* is a prefix in *rebuild* and *recall.* A prefix has its own meaning that changes the meaning of the base word. Some prefixes may have more than one meaning. The prefix *re-* means "again" or "back." *Rebuild* means "to build again," while *recall* means "to call back."

Watch out for words that seem to begin with a prefix but really do not. The word *reason,* for example, does not contain the prefix *re-.* To determine whether a word has a prefix, look at what remains if you omit the prefix. *Reorder* becomes *order,* a base word, and "to order again" makes sense. *Reason,* however, becomes *ason,* which is not a word. Not all words contain prefixes.

Here is a list of common prefixes, their meanings, and examples of each. When you know these six prefixes, you can figure out the meanings of hundreds of English words.

Prefix	Meaning	Example
extra-	"outside, beyond"	extraordinary
fore-	"before, front"	forehead
inter-	"between, among"	international
mis-	"wrong, bad"	misplace
non-	"not"	nonstop
re-	"again" or "back"	rerun, repay

Check It Out Read the following words and their definitions. Notice how the meanings of the prefix and base word combine to create a new word with a new meaning.

extracurricular—"outside the regular courses offered by a school"
forewarn—"to warn before"
interplanetary—"between planets"
misdeed—"a wrong act, a crime"
nonfiction—"not imaginary, real"
redo—"to do again"
replace—"to put back"

- What is the prefix in each example? What is the base word?

Try Your Skill   Many of the words below have prefixes. Some do not. For each word that has a prefix, write the meaning of the prefix plus the base word. For example, for the word *retype* you would write: again + type.

1. misfit	6. foreign	11. nonactive
2. interstate	7. replay	12. misfortune
3. ready	8. none	13. extrasensory
4. reschedule	9. extralegal	14. forerunner
5. foresee	10. miserable	15. return

Keep This in Mind

- A prefix is a word part that is added to the beginning of a base word. Each prefix has a meaning of its own that changes the meaning of a base word.

Now Write   Use a dictionary to find six words, each containing one of the six prefixes you have learned. List new words and define them. As a final step, study the words and make them part of your vocabulary. Label your paper **In First Place.** Put your work into your folder.

End of the Line

Learning Words Parts: Suffixes

Here's the Idea A word part that is added at the end of a word is called a **suffix**. In *wonderful,* the suffix is *-ful.* Suffixes change the meanings of words just as prefixes do.

Sometimes the spelling of a base word changes when a suffix is added. For example, a letter may be dropped from the base word. *Love* becomes *lovable.* Sometimes the final consonant may be doubled. *Win* becomes *winner.* At other times, the final letter of the base word may be changed. *Happy* becomes *happiness.*

The following list shows seven common suffixes with their meanings. Examples are also given.

Suffix	Meaning	Example
-able or **-ible**	"can be, having this quality"	movable, sensible
-er or **-or**	"a person or thing that does something"	leader, generator
-less	"without"	helpless
-ful	"full of"	joyful
-ous	"full of"	mysterious
-ment	"the state or quality of being"	movement
-ness	"the state or quality of being"	sadness

Check It Out Read the following words and their definitions. Notice how the meanings of the suffix and base word combine to create a new word with a new meaning.

20

BUSINESS REPLY MAIL
FIRST CLASS MAIL PERMIT NO. 22, TAMPA FL

POSTAGE WILL BE PAID BY ADDRESSEE

TIME

PO BOX 61192
TAMPA FL 33661-1192

SEASONS GREETINGS FROM TIME

A
Desk Calendar
and Executive Pen

FREE

when you give a gift of
TIME

Send a one-year (52 issues) gift subscription
in my name to:

NAME _____ (please print)

ADDRESS _____ APT. _____

CITY _____ STATE ____ ZIP _____

Cover price: $2.95. Rate good in
U.S. for new gifts only. For additional
gifts, include a separate list of
names and addresses.

Send me my FREE Desk Calendar and
Executive Pen. Bill me only $1.09 an issue
(over 63% off TIME's cover price) for my gift
subscription:

MY NAME _____ (please print)

ADDRESS _____ APT. _____

CITY _____ STATE ____ ZIP _____

☐ Payment enclosed ☐ Bill me in full
☐ Bill me in three equal monthly installments

TDBP5D9

FREE!

washable—"can be washed"
survivor—"a person who survives"
valueless—"without value or worth"
harmful—"full of harm"
envious—"full of envy"
contentment—"the state of being content, satisfied"
greediness—"the quality of being greedy"

- What is the suffix in each word? In which words is the spelling of the base word changed?

Try Your Skill Number your paper from 1 to 16. Find the suffix in each word below. Then write the base word and the meaning of the suffix for each word. For example, for the word *sensible* you would write: sense + having this quality.

1. driver
2. deafness
3. useful
4. famous
5. improvement
6. taxable
7. operator
8. thoughtless
9. glamorous
10. waiter
11. gentleness
12. returnable
13. director
14. doubtful
15. studious
16. thankful

Keep This in Mind

- A suffix is a word part added to the end of a base word. A suffix has a meaning of its own that changes the meaning of a base word. Sometimes the spelling of a base word is changed when a suffix is added.

Now Write Use a dictionary to find seven words, each containing one of the seven suffixes you have learned. List the words and define them. Label your paper **End of the Line** and keep it in your folder.

Using a Dictionary

Part 1 **In So Many Words**
How To Use a Dictionary

Part 2 **Lead the Way**
How To Use Guide Words

Part 3 **Upon My Word!**
How To Read a Dictionary Entry

Part 4 **A Number of Choices**
How To Find the Meaning of a Word

In So Many Words

How To Use a Dictionary

Here's the Idea A dictionary is a useful tool. This handy reference book contains lists of words and information about the words. When you read, you will see unfamiliar words. A dictionary will help you understand the meanings of these words. When you write, you may be unsure about the spelling or usage of some words. A dictionary helps then, too.

There are many kinds of dictionaries. Some are written for people of certain age groups. Some dictionaries cover only one major subject. Even general dictionaries differ. Some are unabridged, or complete. Many are abridged, or shortened. Each dictionary has its own terms, symbols, abbreviations, and organization. It is important, then, to become familiar with the dictionary you use.

All dictionaries have one thing in common, however. Words are always arranged in alphabetical order, which allows you to find a word quickly. Words beginning with *a* come before words beginning with *b*. If two words begin with the same letter, they are alphabetized by the second letter. If the first two letters are the same, look at the third letter, and so on. The following sequence of words is in alphabetical order: *transfer, transistor, translate, transmission, transparent,* and *transplant.*

Check It Out Look at the bottom portion of a dictionary page shown on the next page.

- How is each column of words listed? What words are new to you?
- What special symbols are used in this dictionary?

he·red·i·ty (ha red′a tē) *n.,* *pl.* **-ties** [< Fr. < L. *hereditas.* heirship < *heres,* heir: for IE. base see GO] **1.** the transmission of characteristics from parents to offspring by means of genes in the chromosomes **2.** all the characteristics that one inherits genetically

Her·e·ford (hur′fard, her′a-) *n.* [orig. bred in *Herefordshire,* England] any of a breed of beef cattle having a white face and a red body with white markings

here·in (hir in′) *adv.* **1.** in here; in or into this place **2.** in this writing [her name is listed *herein*] **3.** in this matter, detail, etc. [you don't speak clearly and *herein* you are at fault]

here·in·a·bove (hir′in a buv′) *adv.* in the preceding part (of this document, speech, etc.): also **here′in·be·fore′** (-bi fôr′)

here·in·af·ter (-af′tar) *adv.* in the following part (of this document, speech, etc.): also **here′in·be·low′** (-bi lō′)

HEREFORD COW

her·mit (hur′mit) *n.* [< OFr. < LL. < LGr. < Gr. *erēmitēs* < *erēmos,* solitary] a person who lives by himself away from others, often for religious reasons; recluse **her·mit′ic, her·mit′i·cal** *adj.* **—her′mit·like′** *adj.*

her·mit·age (-ij) *n.* **1.** the place where a hermit lives **2.** a place where a person can live away from other people; retreat

hermit crab any of various soft-bellied crabs that live in the empty shells of certain mollusks, as snails

☆**hermit thrush** a N. American thrush with a brown body, spotted breast, and reddish-brown tail

Her·mon (hur′man), **Mount** mountain on the border between Syria & Lebanon

Her·mo·sil·lo (er′mô sē′yô) city in NW Mexico: pop. 197,000

her·ni·a (hur′nē a) *n., pl.* **-ni·as, -ni·ae′** (-ē′) [L.: for IE. base see CORD] the sticking out of all or part of an organ, esp. a part of the intestine, through a tear in the wall of the surrounding structure; rupture **—her′ni·al** *adj.*

HERMIT CRAB
(to 18 in. long)

---

fat, āpe, cär; ten, ēven; is, bīte; gō, hôrn, tōōl, look; oil, out; up, fur; get; joy; yet; chin; she; thin, then; zh, leisure; ŋ, ring; ə for *a* in *ago, e* in *agent, i* in *sanity, o* in *comply, u* in *focus;* ' as in *able* (ā′b'l); Fr. bál; ë, Fr. coeur; ö, Fr. feu; Fr. mon; ô, Fr. coq; ü, Fr. duc; r, Fr. cri; H, G. ich; kh, G. doch; ‡foreign; ☆ Americanism; < derived from. See inside front cover.

Try Your Skill

Arrange the following list of words in alphabetical order: *tie, mill, soft, art, article, brook, tiger, tight, sofa, softly, milk, bronze, soggy, artificial, tie-dye, tile.*

Keep This in Mind

- A dictionary is a reference book that lists words alphabetically and gives an explanation for each word.
- Become familiar with the abbreviations, symbols, and organization of the dictionary you use.

Now Write

Think of ten words that begin with the same letter and arrange the words in alphabetical order. Write a definition for each word. Use a dictionary to help you. Label your paper **In So Many Words** and keep it in your folder.

Lead the Way

How To Use Guide Words

Here's the Idea Most dictionaries have two **guide words** on each page. The guide words appear in large, bold print at the top of the page. Guide words tell you at a glance the range of words on each page. The guide word on the left is the same as the first entry word on the page. The guide word on the right is the same as the last entry word on the page. Every other word on the page is somewhere between the two words in alphabetical order. Look at this top portion of a dictionary page.

Maxine   593   **meager**

Max·ine (mak sēn′) [fem. of *Max:* see MAXIMILIAN] a feminine name
Max·well (maks′wel, -wəl), **James Clerk** (klärk) 1831–79; Scot. physicist
May¹ (mā) *n.* [OFr. < L. < *Maia,* goddess of increase] **1.** the fifth month of the year, having 31 days **2.** the springtime of life; youth
May² (mā) [contr. of MARY, MARGARET] a feminine name
may (mā) *v.aux. pt.* **might** [OE. *mæg* < IE. base *magh-,* to be able] a helping verb followed by an infinitive (without *to*) and meaning: **1.** to be possible or likely to *[it may rain]* **2.** to be allowed or have permission to *[you may go]* **3.** to be able to as a result *[they died that we may be free]* **4.** it is to be wished or hoped that *[may he rest in peace]* —see SYN. at CAN¹
Ma·ya (mä′yə) *n.* **1.** *pl.* **Ma′yas, Ma′ya** a member of a tribe of Indians in SE Mexico and Central America, who had a highly developed civilization **2.** their language —*adj.* of the Mayas — **Ma′yan** *adj., n.*
Ma·ya·güez (mä′yä gwes′) seaport in W Puerto Rico: pop. 69,000
☆ **May apple** **1.** a woodland plant with shield-shaped leaves and a single large, white flower, found in the eastern U.S. **2.** its yellow, oval fruit
may·be (mā′bē) *adv.* [ME. (for *it may be*)] perhaps
May·day (mā′dā′) *n.* [< Fr. (*venez*) *m'aider,* (come) help me] the international radiotelephone signal for help, used by ships and aircraft in distress
May Day May 1: as a traditional spring festival, often celebrated by dancing, crowning a May queen, etc.; as an international labor holiday, observed in many countries by parades, demonstrations, etc.

maze (māz) *n.* [< OE. *amasian,* to amaze & pp. *amasod,* puzzled] **1.** a confusing, intricate network of winding pathways; labyrinth, specif. one used in psychological experiments and tests **2.** a state of confusion or bewilderment — **ma′zy** *adj.* **-zi·er, -zi·est** —**ma′zi·ly** *adv.* —**ma′zi·ness** *n.*
ma·zur·ka, ma·zour·ka (mə·zur′kə, -zoor′-) *n.* [Pol. *mazurka,* woman from Mazovia, region of C Poland] **1.** a lively Polish dance like the polka **2.** music for this, generally in 3/4 or 3/8 time

MAZE

Maz·zi·ni (mät tsē′nē, mäd dzē′nē), **Giu·sep·pe** (jōō zep′pe) 1805–72; It. patriot & revolutionist
M.B.A. Master of Business Administration
M-ba·ba·ne ('m bä bä′nä) capital of Swaziland: pop. 14,000
MBS Mutual Broadcasting System
Mc-, Mᶜ- *same as* MAC-
M.C. **1.** Master of Ceremonies **2.** Member of Congress
☆ **Mc·Car·thy·ism** (mə kär′thē iz'm) *n.* [after J. *McCarthy,* U.S. senator (1946–57)] the use of careless, often false, accusations and methods of investigating that violate civil liberties
Mc·Clel·lan (mə klel′ən), **George Brin·ton** (brin′t'n) 1826–85; Union general in the Civil War
Mc·Cor·mick (mə kôr′mik), **Cyrus Hall** (hôl) 1809–84; U.S. inventor of the reaping machine
Mc·Coy (mə koi′), **the** (**real**) [Slang] the real person or thing, not a substitute

Dictionary guide words help you find the word you need. First look for guide words that have the same first letter as the word you need. Then look for guide words having the same second letter. Keep looking for guide words that are more and more like the word you want.

Check It Out   Look at the top portion of a dictionary page shown on the facing page.

- What are the guide words for this page? Would you find the word *meager* on this page? Which way would you turn to find the word *maximum? meal? mature? meaning?*

Try Your Skill   Write the following sets of guide words on your paper: *raga/raise, raised/Ramses, seal/seating, seatmate/ second nature*. Write each of the following words under the appropriate set of guide words. Then arrange each list in alphabetical order.

rain	raid	search	ramp
rally	ragged	seat	second cousin
Seattle	ram	raisin	ramble
seam	second base	second	raise
seaport	railroad	season	seaweed

Keep This in Mind

- Guide words show the alphabetical range of words on each page of the dictionary. The left guide word is the same as the first word on the page. The right guide word is the same as the last word on the page.

Now Write   If you were writing a composition about musical instruments, you might have to look up the following words: *kettledrum, lute, mandolin, oboe, sitar, sousaphone, viola,* and *zither*. Find each word in a dictionary. On your paper, list each word and write the guide words that appear on the page where the word is found. Choose four of the words and write four sentences. Use one of the words in each sentence. Label your paper **Lead the Way** and put it into your folder.

Upon My Word!

How To Read a Dictionary Entry

Here's the Idea   A dictionary entry explains the meaning of a word. In addition, an entry contains much other information that is useful. All of the information will not be contained in every entry. Also, the information will not be arranged in the same order in every dictionary. Most dictionaries, however, will give you the following information.

The **entry word** itself is shown in bold type and divided. For example, the word *vacation* is entered as **va·ca·tion.** When writing, you may have to divide a word at the end of a line. Use the dictionary to find the correct division.

The **pronunciation** of a word is usually given within parentheses. Special symbols help you to sound out the word. The word is divided into syllables, and an accent mark tells you which syllable to stress. For example, *auditorium* appears as ⟨ô′ də tôr′ ē əm⟩.

The **part of speech** is given by an abbreviation in bold print. For example, *noun* is abbreviated **n.** Usually you will find a list of abbreviations in the front of your dictionary.

Sometimes a word can be used as more than one part of speech. If so, the other parts of speech will also be given.

If a word has **special forms** or **endings,** they will be included next in the entry. For example, the entry for the irregular verb *do* includes the forms **did, done,** and **doing.** Plural endings of some nouns are also given. For the noun *potato,* for instance, the plural ending **-toes** is given.

The **origin,** or **history,** of a word is next, usually in brackets. Symbols are used. The symbol < means "came from." The abbreviations *OE., Fr.,* and *L.* stand for "Old English," "French," and "Latin." Look up unfamiliar abbreviations.

Definitions are given in a numbered list. Usually the most common definition is first. If a word has a special meaning in a particular field, the dictionary mentions the field. For example, one definition of *love* is "*Tennis*—a score of zero."

A word may have a meaning that is generally used informally. This is a colloquial meaning. The dictionary indicates this by using an abbreviation. For example, one definition of *buzz* is "[Colloq.] a telephone call." The dictionary also indicates slang, which is very informal, popular language. For example, one definition of *bread* is "[Slang] money."

Synonyms and **antonyms** may also be listed. Some entries may include a *synonymy*—a group of synonyms and their shades of meaning. Sometimes, the notation "*see* **SYN.** *at*" may direct you to a synonymy under a different entry.

Do you see how helpful a dictionary can be? Be familiar with the way an entry is given in the dictionaries you use.

Check It Out   Read this dictionary entry.

> **con·di·tion** (kən dish′ən) *n.* [< OFr. < L. *condicio*, agreement < *com-*, together + *dicere*, to speak] **1.** anything required before the performance or completion of something else; provision; stipulation *[conditions* set for a cease-fire*]* **2.** prerequisite *[some consider wealth a *condition* of happiness]* **3.** anything that has an effect on the nature of something else; circumstance *[conditions* were favorable for business*]* **4.** manner or state of being *[a house in a dilapidated *condition]* **5.** *a)* state of health *[the patient's *condition]* *b)* [Colloq.] an illness; ailment *[a lung *condition]* **6.** a proper or healthy state *[athletes out of *condition]* **7.** social position; rank; station ☆**8.** the requirement that a student make up deficiencies in a subject in order to pass it **9.** *Law* a clause in a contract, will, etc. that revokes or modifies all or part of it if a certain thing happens —*vt.* **1.** to impose a condition or conditions on **2.** to be a condition of; determine, modify, or influence *[factors which *condition* our lives]* **3.** to bring into a proper or desired condition *[training camps help to *condition* a team]* **4.** *Psychol.* *a)* to develop a conditioned reflex or behavior pattern in *b)* to cause to become accustomed (*to*) *[to *condition* women to annual fashion changes]* —*see* **SYN.** at STATE —**on condition that** provided that —**con·di′tion·er** *n.*

- How many syllables are there in *condition*? Where is the pronunciation given? What part of speech is *condi-*

tion? Is it used as any other part of speech? From what languages did the word come? What is the most common definition? Are there any definitions used in special fields? Are any synonyms mentioned?

Try Your Skill Read the following dictionary entry.

scene (sēn) *n.* [< MFr. < L. < Gr. *skene*, tent, stage: for IE. base see SHINE] **1.** the place in which any event occurs *[the scene of the crime]* **2.** the setting of the action of a play, story, etc. *[the scene of Hamlet is Denmark]* **3.** a division of a play, usually part of an act **4.** a part of a play, story, etc. that is a single, continuous unit of action *[a deathbed scene]* **5.** *same as* SCENERY (sense 1) **6.** a view, landscape, etc. *[a peaceful autumn scene]* **7.** a show of strong feeling before others *[she made a scene in court]* **8.** a real or imaginary event, esp. as described *[she witnessed a distressing scene on her way home]* **9.** [Colloq.] a particular area of interest or activity *[the poetry scene]* —see *SYN.* at VIEW —**behind the scenes 1.** backstage **2.** in private or in secrecy —☆**make the scene** [Slang] **1.** to be present **2.** to participate actively or successfully

1. How is the word *scene* pronounced?
2. What part of speech is it?
3. What is the most common meaning?
4. What is a synonym for *scene?*
5. What slang phrase includes the word *scene?*

Keep This in Mind

- A dictionary entry contains the meanings of a word and other helpful information. Entries may differ in different dictionaries.

Now Write Use a dictionary to find words with these characteristics. Each word should have one characteristic.

1. has two pronunciations
2. has three parts of speech
3. has come from Spanish
4. has an informal meaning
5. has an antonym
6. has a synonym

A Number of Choices

How To Find the Meaning of a Word

Here's the Idea   When you see an unfamiliar word, you look it up in a dictionary. What do you do if the word has several meanings? How can you tell which is the right one? Most of the time the context will help you find the right meaning.

For example, the simple word *run* has a surprising number of meanings. *Webster's New World Dictionary, Students Edition,* gives forty-nine meanings for *run* as a verb. The same entry lists twenty meanings for *run* as a noun, two for *run* as an adjective, and twenty phrases that include *run*. In each sentence below, the context helps you to determine the meaning of *run*.

   1. I had to *run* to catch the bus this morning.
(In this context, *run* means "move swiftly.")
   2. The Mississippi River *runs* into the Gulf of Mexico.
(In this context, *runs* means "flows.")
   3. Red hair and freckles *run* in our family.
(In this context, *run* means "continue to occur.")
   4. Jim Rice's double brought in the winning *run*.
(In this context, *run* means "scoring point.")

You can see that a single entry can contain many different meanings for a word.

Sometimes, however, the same word seems to appear in more than one entry. You will find the word *bat*, for example, entered three times: *bat*[1], a noun, means "a club used to hit a ball"; *bat*[2], also a noun, means "a mouselike mammal that flies at night"; and *bat*[3], a verb, means "to blink, as to *bat an eye*." In each of the three entries, the word *bat* has a different meaning and a different origin. Such a word is called a *homograph*. A homograph has the same spelling, but it may have different pronunciations. You can see that each entry is not a shade of meaning of the same word, but it is really a different word. If you see a word with more than one entry, read all the entries to find the meaning you want.

Check It Out   Read the dictionary entries below.

> **school**¹ (skool) *n.* [OE. *scol* < L. *schola* < Gr. *schole*, leisure (esp. as used for study), school < IE. base *segh-*, to hold] **1.** a place or institution for teaching and learning *[a public school,* dancing *school]* **2.** *a)* the building or buildings, classrooms, etc. of a school   *b)* all of its students and teachers *[most of the school* attends the games*]*   *c)* a regular session of teaching at a school *[school* begins next week*]* **3.** *a)* attendance at a school *[to miss school* for a week*]*   *b)* the process of being educated at a school *[he finished school* at seventeen*]* **4.** any situation or experience through which one gains knowledge, training, etc. *[the school* of hard knocks*]* **5.** a particular division of an institution of learning, esp. of a university *[the school* of law*]*   **6.** a group following the same teachings, beliefs, methods, etc. *[the Impressionist school]* **7.** a way of life *[a gentleman of the old school]* —*vt.* **1.** to teach; instruct; educate *[he was schooled* in the old methods*]* **2.** to discipline or control *[to school* oneself to be patient*]* —*adj.* of a school or schools —see *SYN.* at TEACH
> **school**² (skool) *n.* [Du., a crowd] a large number of fish or water animals of the same kind swimming or feeding together —*vi.* to move together in such a school —see *SYN.* at GROUP

- Which definition of *school*¹ fits the context of the following sentence? I missed *school* last Monday.
- From what language did *school*¹ come? *school*²? What parts of speech is *school*¹ used as? *school*²? Under what word would you find a synonym for *school*¹? *school*²?

Try Your Skill   Read the following dictionary entries. Then read the five sentences. Decide which meaning of *shock* fits the context of each sentence. Write your answer.

> **shock**¹ (shäk) *n.* [< Fr. < MFr. *choquer*, prob. < MDu. *schokken*, to collide] **1.** a sudden, powerful blow, shake, disturbance, etc. *[the shock* of an earthquake*]* **2.** *a)* a sudden and strong upsetting of the mind or feelings   *b)* something causing this *[her accident was a shock* to us*]* **3.** the violent effect on the body of an electric current passed through it

4. [Colloq.] *short for* SHOCK ABSORBER: *used in pl.* **5.** *Med.* a disorder caused by severe injury or damage to the body, loss of blood, etc., and marked by a sharp drop in blood pressure, a rapid pulse, etc. —*vt.* **1.** to disturb emotionally; astonish, horrify, etc. *[her words shocked us]* **2.** to cause a physical shock to **3.** to produce electric shock in —*vi.* to be shocked, distressed, etc. *[one who does not shock easily]* —**shock′er** *n.*

SYN.—**shock** suggests a violent disturbance of the mind or emotions caused by an unexpected, overwhelming event that comes as a blow *[shocked by her sudden death]*; **startle** implies a slight shock of surprise or alarm, often one that causes a person to jump or flinch *[startled by the clap of thunder]*; **paralyze** suggests such extreme shock as to make one unable to move for a time *[paralyzed with fear]*; to **stun** is to shock with such force as to make one numb, dazed, or speechless *[stunned by the disaster]*

shock² (shak) *n.* [prob. via MDu. or MLowG. *schok*] a number of sheaves of grain, as corn or wheat, stacked together on end to cure and dry —*vt., vi.* to gather in shocks

shock³ (shak) *n.* [< ? SHOCK²] a thick, bushy or tangled mass, as of hair

1. I was *shocked* by the violence in the TV movie.
2. The *shocks* of wheat cast long shadows across the field.
3. A *shock* of hair kept falling in Betsy's eyes as she wrote.
4. The mechanic replaced the worn *shocks* in the Chevy.
5. Grandpa Willie is in Forbes Hospital suffering from *shock*.

Keep This in Mind

- When you look up an unfamiliar word in the dictionary, decide which meaning fits the context.
- Sometimes a word has more than one entry, with a different origin and meaning for each. Again, use the context to help you find the meaning.

Now Write Look up two of the following words in the dictionary: *bark, lean, part,* and *sound.* If the word appears in more than one entry, read through all the entries. Write three definitions for each of the two words. Then write a sentence using each of the meanings you have written. Label your paper **A Number of Choices** and put it into your folder.

The Right Language at the Right Time

Part 1 **A Proper Time**
Using Standard and Nonstandard English

Part 2 **Here Today**
Using and Misusing Slang

Part 3 **A Way of Speaking**
Using and Misusing Jargon

A Proper Time

Using Standard and Nonstandard English

Here's the Idea You wouldn't wear a bathing suit to a concert. Neither would you get all dressed up to go to the beach. Similarly, different types of language are suitable for different situations. There are two types, or levels, of language from which you can choose. They are called **standard English** and **nonstandard English.** These two types of language are described in the following chart:

Two Levels of Language

	Standard English	Nonstandard English
Definition	Standard English is language that follows the rules of good grammar and usage.	Nonstandard English is language that does not follow the rules of good grammar and usage.
Use	Standard English is acceptable in all situations.	Nonstandard English is unacceptable in all situations except very casual conversation with friends.
Examples	1. He doesn't care. 2. Those chairs are broken. 3. I'm not going.	1. He don't care. 2. Them chairs is broke. 3. I ain't going.

Notice that nonstandard English is unacceptable in most situations. Get into the habit of using standard English.

Check It Out   Read the following pairs of sentences.

Standard	Nonstandard
1. We are done with our work.	1. We done with our work.
2. She didn't say anything.	2. She didn't say nothing.
3. We saw those photo-graphs.	3. We seen them photo-graphs.
4. He and I are brothers.	4. Him and me are brothers.
5. Are you the winner?	5. Is you the winner?

- What is nonstandard about the second sentence in each pair?

Try Your Skill   From each pair, choose the sentence that is written in standard English.

1. I don't know if she like you, but I think she do.
   I don't know if she likes you, but I think she does.
2. John and me went to the bake sale.
   John and I went to the bake sale.
3. I want to know where he went.
   I want to know where he gone.
4. We couldn't figure out why he did it.
   We couldn't figure out why he done it.

Keep This in Mind

- Standard English is appropriate in any situation.
- Use standard English when you speak or write.

Now Write   Write a short description of a movie, concert, or sports event. Exchange your paper with a classmate. Circle any examples of nonstandard English in your classmate's paper. Then, take back your own paper and revise it. Replace any nonstandard English with standard English. Save your work.

Here Today

Using and Misusing Slang

Here's the Idea   **Slang** is a type of nonstandard English made up of fad words and phrases. Most slang is temporary. It lives a brief, colorful life. Then, it disappears and is replaced by newer slang. For example, the following slang terms were popular during the 1950's:

> cool cat   hep   wowsville

Today these terms sound dated. They have been replaced by the slang of the 1980's.

You are probably familiar with many slang words and phrases in use today. Some of these terms may even be part of your everyday speech. If you do use slang terms regularly, be aware that slang is not acceptable in most formal situations. Slang should never be used in compositions, reports, business letters, or talks. Slang may be used in casual conversation with friends. It may also be used to make dialogue in a short story sound realistic.

If you do not know whether a particular word is slang, look it up in a dictionary. If the word is not in the dictionary, or if it is labeled *slang,* avoid using it in formal speech and writing.

Check It Out   The following slang terms all have the same meaning. However, each term was popular at a different time during the past seventy years. Read this list of terms.

the cat's pajamas	out of sight
the bee's knees	groovy
swell	neat
peachy	far out

- Can you guess the meaning shared by these terms?
- Are any of these terms popular today? What does this tell you about the nature of slang?

Try Your Skill   Identify the slang terms in the following sentences. Then, rewrite each sentence. Replace each slang term with a standard word or phrase.

1. The accident was a real bummer.
2. Don't be so uptight. Try to relax.
3. Your performance will be fine if you just play it cool.
4. These new fashions have a lot of pizazz.
5. Some guy left a package for you.

Keep This in Mind

- Slang is a type of nonstandard English made of fad words and phrases.
- Use slang only in casual conversation or when writing dialogue for a short story.
- Do not use slang in compositions, reports, business letters, or talks.

Now Write   Working with a partner, make a list of slang terms that are now popular. Write the definition of each term. Then, ask some older people to tell you what slang terms they used when they were young. Make a list of these terms and define them. Label your paper **Here Today.** Save it in your folder.

A Way of Speaking

Using and Misusing Jargon

Here's the Idea   Many activities have their own special vocabularies. These special vocabularies are called **jargon.** People who work in specialized fields use jargon to communicate with one another quickly. For example, when one auto mechanic talks to another, he or she will use words like *rings, manifold, lifters, catalytic converter,* and *headers.* The mechanics understand one another because they are speaking the jargon of their own field. A person who doesn't know anything about cars will be mystified by such language.

Whenever you speak or write about a specialized activity, be careful about the use of jargon. If you know that your audience is familiar with the activity, you can use as much jargon as you want. However, if your audience is not familiar with the activity, you should avoid jargon completely. If you must use a jargon word, define it right away. Otherwise, your reader or listener will not understand what you are saying.

Check It Out   Read the following words from the jargon of basketball:

> center court
> foul
> double-dribble
> rim shot
> zone defense
> forward

- How many of these words do you know?
- Which of these words would be understood only by someone who knows a great deal about basketball?

- Which of these words have other meanings outside of basketball?

Try Your Skill   The following words are from the jargon of the theatre. Look up each word in the dictionary. Find out how this word is used by theater people. Then, write two sentences. In the first sentence, make a statement using the word. In the second sentence, define the word.

> Example: *teasers*
> > a. The lights were hidden behind *teasers*.
> > b. *Teasers* are rows of very short curtains that hang above the stage.

1. blocking
2. scrim
3. book
4. properties
5. proscenium

Keep This in Mind

- Many activities have their own special vocabulary called *jargon.*
- Use jargon only when you are sure your audience is familiar with it.

Now Write   Choose a special activity that you enjoy a great deal. This may be a sport, a hobby, or a class in school. Make a list of the jargon words that are used by people who perform this activity. Then, write a paragraph describing the activity. When you use a jargon word in the paragraph, make sure you define it. Label your paper **A Way of Speaking.** Save it in your folder.

Writing Effective Sentences

Part 1 **Make Your Point**
Writing Sentences

Part 2 **Running on Empty**
Avoiding Empty Sentences

Part 3 **Slim Down**
Avoiding Padded Sentences

Part 4 **Slow Down**
Avoiding Overloaded Sentences

Make Your Point

Writing Sentences

Here's the Idea   You have seen how important it is to choose words carefully in order to express an idea. The next step is to learn to make your words work together in sentences. A **sentence** is a group of words that expresses a complete thought.

A good sentence makes a point. It expresses an idea in a direct, clear, fresh way. A single sentence can be imaginative and powerful.

Some sentences express an idea particularly well. Consider the examples below:

> Dogs do not dislike poor families.—CHINESE PROVERB

> A thought comes when it wishes, not when I wish.
> —FRIEDRICH NIETZSCHE

> Courage is the price that life exacts for granting peace.
> —AMELIA EARHART

> Some books are to be tasted, others to be swallowed, and some few to be chewed and digested.—FRANCIS BACON

Sentences such as these have been remembered because each makes a point in a lively and original way. When you write a sentence, you will also want to express your idea in a clear and interesting way.

Check It Out   Read the following sentences.

1. Lee walked slowly to the end of the diving board and stared down at the water.
2. Police sirens wailed through the night.
3. In the winter, thermostats should be set at sixty-eight degrees to conserve fuel.

4. Do you know how to write a check?

5. An oboe is a musical instrument that makes a high, sad sound.

- Does each sentence express a single complete thought? Is each sentence clear and direct?

Try Your Skill   Write one sentence in response to each direction below. Make your sentences clear and interesting. Use real or imaginary details.

1. Tell one thing you enjoy doing.
2. Describe a pet you'd like to own.
3. Explain how you travel to school.
4. Explain why everyone should vote in an election.
5. Explain what a sister is.
6. Describe your favorite article of clothing.
7. Tell one event that made you feel like a success.
8. Explain why you like a certain friend.

Keep This in Mind

- A sentence is a group of words that expresses a complete thought. A good sentence is clear and interesting.

Now Write   Write one sentence that tells an event that happened. Write one sentence that describes something. Write one that explains how something is made. Write one that explains why something should be done. Write one that explains what something is. Your sentences may tell only part of a larger idea. However, the point of each sentence should be clear to a reader. Choose your words carefully. Include real or imaginary details. When you are finished, read and revise your work until you are satisfied with it. Label your paper **Make Your Point.** Put your work into your folder.

Running on Empty

Avoiding Empty Sentences

Here's the Idea   Some sentences do not express an idea clearly or completely. They are called **empty sentences.** One type of empty sentence repeats an idea.

> Chuck has a huge appetite, and he always wants to eat.

Appetite means "the desire to eat," so the second part of the sentence is unnecessary. Avoid repetition. Make the sentence simpler or add more information.

> Chuck has a huge appetite.
> Chuck has a huge appetite, especially for sweets.

Another type of empty sentence makes a statement or offers an opinion without supplying facts, reasons, or examples to back it up. Readers are left hanging. Read the example below:

> The movie rating system should be eliminated.

Such a strong statement is empty of meaning for a reader unless it is explained. Supporting evidence may be given in the same sentence or in another sentence.

> The movie rating system should be eliminated so that movies, like other forms of entertainment, are open to everyone.
> The movie rating system should be eliminated. Like other forms of entertainment, movies should be open to everyone.

In some instances, a strong opinion may be developed in a longer piece of writing, such as a paragraph or a composition.

Check It Out   Read the following empty sentences.

1. Bicycling is the best form of exercise.
2. I paid a great deal for this watch, which was very expensive.

3. Everyone should have a hobby.

4. A motorcycle offers an exciting ride, and I'd like to ride a motorcycle.

5. Everyone should be required to pass a basic skills test in order to earn a high school diploma.

- Which sentences repeat an idea? Which sentences offer an unsupported opinion?
- How would you improve these empty sentences?

Try Your Skill   Rewrite each of these empty sentences.

1. My tooth aches and I am in pain.
2. It is a good book because I like it.
3. Every citizen should be required to serve his or her country for one year.
4. The loggers chopped down all the trees, and none were left standing.
5. All licensed drivers should have to take a driving test every five years.

Keep This in Mind

- Sentences that repeat ideas or offer unsupported opinions are empty sentences.
- Improve a sentence that repeats an idea by making it simpler or by adding information. Improve a sentence with an unsupported opinion by including reasons or facts that support the opinion.

Now Write   Label your paper *Empty Sentences.* Find, or write, two examples of each kind of empty sentence. Improve the sentences by avoiding repetition or by including reasons or facts. Keep your work in your folder.

Slim Down

Avoiding Padded Sentences

Here's the Idea   Some sentences do not make a point directly. They contain useless words and phrases that bury the main idea. Such sentences are called **padded sentences.**

There are several common phrases that add nothing to the meaning of a sentence and should be avoided. Here are some of these expressions that pad a sentence.

because of the fact that	what I mean is
due to the fact that	what I believe is
on account of the fact that	what I'm saying is
the thing is	I mean
my feeling is	you see
I am going to write about	well

You can usually improve a padded sentence by omitting the useless expressions. Sometimes, however, you have to rewrite the sentence completely.

Padded: I couldn't go out on Thursday because of the fact that I had a report to write.

Improved: I couldn't go out on Thursday because I had a report to write.

Padded: On account of the fact that he is a good cook, Jack wanted to get a job in a restaurant after school.

Improved: Jack, a good cook, wanted to work in a restaurant after school.

Check It Out   Read the following padded sentences.

1. What I'm trying to say is that my drawings are of places in my neighborhood.

2. Betty was late for school because, you know, she forgot to set her alarm clock.

3. I'm going to write about what happened the week I cooked dinner for my family.

4. Because of the fact that it rained, the class picnic was postponed.

- How would you improve each of these padded sentences?

Try Your Skill Improve the padded sentences below. Either eliminate any unnecessary words and phrases, or rewrite the entire sentence.

1. My feeling is that this chair is very comfortable.

2. I'm upset due to the fact that I have three tests this week.

3. The thing is that my older sister never wants to hear my opinions.

4. Owing to the fact that this book is overdue, I should return it to the library immediately.

5. The point is that the prices of food, clothing, and housing are rising steadily.

Keep This in Mind

- Sentences containing unnecessary words are padded sentences. Improve a padded sentence by omitting the useless expressions or by revising the sentence.

Now Write Label your paper *Padded Sentences*. Find, or write, four examples of padded sentences. Improve the sentences. Eliminate unnecessary phrases or rewrite the sentence. Keep your paper in your folder.

Slow Down

Avoiding Overloaded Sentences

Here's the Idea   Padded sentences contain too many words. **Overloaded sentences** contain too many ideas. Read the overloaded sentences below.

> It was a snowstorm, and the black and white cat sat on the porch and watched as a flock of birds came to the feeder, and the cat waited, ready to pounce.

From this example, you can see that in an overloaded sentence, too many ideas run together. Confusion results. You cannot tell which of the many ideas is the main one. The best way to avoid overloaded sentences is to separate each main idea into its own sentence.

Look at the example sentence again. Notice that *and* is used much too often. *And* is a useful word, but it can be overused. When *and* is used to connect two equal parts of one idea, it is being used correctly. When *and* is used to connect different ideas or ideas that are not equally important, it confuses readers. It leads them to believe that there is a connection when there is none.

A sentence usually contains only one main idea. You can improve an overloaded sentence by breaking it into several shorter sentences.

> During the snowstorm, the black and white cat sat on the porch. As a flock of birds came to the feeder, the cat watched and waited. It was ready to pounce.

Check It Out   Read the following overloaded sentence.

Overloaded: I explained to Marlene and Richard how I do my
                      homework and I said that I do my science first,

and then I concentrate on math and French, and once I start I don't stop until it's finished.

Improved: I explained to Marlene and Richard how I do my homework. I said that I do my science first, and then I concentrate on math and French. Once I start, I don't stop until it's finished.

• How has this overloaded sentence been improved?

Try Your Skill Improve the following overloaded sentences.

1. One play turned Sunday's football game around. Two of the Dallas Cowboys tackled the Green Bay Packers' quarterback, and his pass went right into the hands of one of the Cowboys, and the crowd roared, and the Cowboy who intercepted the pass ran it seventy-three yards for a touchdown.

2. My brother is in a rock group. He has an electric guitar, with two amplifiers, and he plays it every day, and the sounds he gets from it are amazing, and his group is going to play at a school dance on Friday.

3. It was the day before the wedding, and the bride and groom sat together in the kitchen, and the refrigerator hummed, and the television screamed in the next room, and they didn't say a word to each other.

Keep This in Mind

• Sentences that contain too many ideas are overloaded sentences. Improve an overloaded sentence by breaking it into several shorter sentences.

Now Write Label your paper *Overloaded Sentences*. Find or write three examples of overloaded sentences. Improve the sentences by breaking them into several shorter sentences. Keep your paper in your folder.

Sentence Combining

Part 1 **Join the Crowd**
Combining Sentences

Part 2 **Taking Part**
Combining Sentence Parts

Part 3 **In Addition**
Combining by Adding Single Words

Part 4 **A Winning Combination**
Using Combining Skills in Writing

Join the Crowd

Combining Sentences

Here's the Idea One way to make your writing interesting is to vary the length of your sentences. Too many short, simple sentences can make your writing sound choppy and dull. You can often combine two short sentences into one longer sentence.

Sometimes two sentences state similar ideas. Both ideas are equally important. Such sentences can usually be joined by a comma and the word *and*.

> Karen played the piano. Felipe sang.
>
> Karen played the piano, **and** Felipe sang.

At other times, two sentences state contrasting ideas of equal importance. Sentences like these can usually be joined with a comma and the word *but*.

> Bill fed the cat. She wasn't hungry.
>
> Bill fed the cat, **but** she wasn't hungry.

Occasionally, two sentences offer a choice between ideas of equal importance. Such sentences can usually be joined with a comma and the word *or*.

> Will Sheila play on the varsity team this year? Will she play on the junior varsity again?
>
> Will Sheila play on the varsity team this year, **or** will she play on the junior varsity again?

Check It Out Study the following sentences.

1. Melinda attended the meeting, but Alice did not.
2. You can use a calculator, or you can add the figures yourself.
3. The thunder rumbled, and lightning filled the sky.

- Which sentence combines similar ideas of equal importance?
- Which sentence combines contrasting ideas of equal importance?
- Which sentence combines ideas of equal importance and offers a choice between them?

Try Your Skill Combine each pair of sentences. Follow the directions in parentheses.

1. Should we go on ahead? Should we wait for the rest of the campers? (Join with **, or.**)

2. The lights dimmed. A hush fell over the audience. (Join with **, and.**)

3. Strange sounds came from the woods. I wasn't afraid. (Join with **, but.**)

4. Mark wants to become an actor. Rosa wants to skate in the Olympics. (Join with **, and.**)

Keep This in Mind

- Use a comma and *and* to combine sentences that state similar ideas of equal importance.
- Use a comma and *but* to combine sentences that state contrasting ideas of equal importance.
- Use a comma and *or* to combine sentences that offer a choice between ideas of equal importance.

Now Write Combine each pair of sentences using **, and** or **, but** or **, or.**

1. Ted arrived on flight 112. His father met him at the airport.
2. Lightning struck a generator. The city went dark.
3. An eclipse will occur next month. It won't be total.
4. Did you correct the problem? Is the engine still stalling?

Label your paper **Join the Crowd.** Save it in your folder.

Taking Part

Combining Sentence Parts

Here's the Idea   Sometimes two sentences contain many of the same words. This is usually a sign of dull writing. You can improve these weak sentences by combining them. To do this, take part of one sentence and join it to the other sentence.

Sentence parts that state similar ideas of equal importance can usually be joined with *and.*

> Mark repairs automobiles. *Mark repairs* motorcycles.

> Mark repairs automobiles **and** motorcycles.

Notice that the repeated words in italics were dropped in the combined sentence.

Sentence parts that state contrasting ideas can usually be joined with *but.*

> Joan loves science fiction movies. Joan hates horror films.

> Joan loves science fiction movies **but** hates horror films.

Sentence parts that offer a choice between ideas of equal importance can usually be joined with *or.*

> Will you vote for Enrico? *Will you vote for* Melinda?

> Will you vote for Enrico **or** Melinda?

Check It Out   Study the following examples.

1. Her voice was strong. *Her voice was* unsteady.
   Her voice was strong but unsteady.
2. Will we meet tomorrow? *Will we meet* Friday?
   Will we meet tomorrow or Friday?
3. Buses are not permitted on the bridge. Trucks *are not permitted on the bridge.*
   Buses and trucks are not permitted on the bridge.

- Which example combines similar sentence parts of equal importance?
- Which example combines contrasting sentence parts of equal importance?
- Which example combines sentence parts that offer a contrast between ideas of equal importance?

Try Your Skill   Join each pair of sentences according to the directions in parentheses. Leave out the italicized words.

1. Betty enjoys science fiction. *Betty enjoys* mysteries. (Join with **and.**)

2. We can hold a book sale. *We can hold* a car wash. (Join with **or.**)

3. The rolls were crispy outside. *The rolls were* chewy inside. (Join with **but.**)

4. Hiking boots must be sturdy. *Hiking boots must be* comfortable. (Join with **and.**)

Keep This in Mind

- Use *and* to join sentence parts that state similar ideas of equal importance.
- Use *but* to join sentence parts that state contrasting ideas of equal importance.
- Use *or* to join sentence parts that offer a choice between ideas of equal importance.

Now Write   Join each pair of sentences. Use *and, but,* or *or.*

1. Did you buy a paperback copy? Did you buy the hardback edition?

2. The bears found the honey. The bears ate it eagerly.

3. Ted located the fuse box. Ted couldn't find a fuse.

4. We could go to a movie. We could stay at home.

Label your paper **Taking Part.** Save it in your folder.

In Addition

Combining by Adding Single Words

Here's the Idea   Sometimes the second sentence in a pair contains only one important word. All the other words in the sentence are unnecessary. In such cases, the one important word can be added to the first sentence.

> The jugglers were followed by a trapeze act. *The trapeze act was daring.*
>
> The jugglers were followed by a **daring** trapeze act.

Notice that the words in italics were dropped. The word *daring* was then added to the first sentence.

Sometimes the form of the important word must be changed before it is added to another sentence. You may have to change the ending of the word by adding *-ing, -ed,* or *-ly.*

> A police officer stopped the car. *The car was traveling at great speed.*
>
> A police officer stopped the **speeding** car.
>
> The paper is on the teacher's desk. *The paper is* complete.
>
> The **completed** paper is on the teacher's desk.
>
> Susan sang. *It was* beautiful.
>
> Susan sang **beautifully.**

Check It Out   Study the following examples.

1. Marsha discarded some of her records. *They were* old.
   Marsha discarded some of her old records.

2. The sidewalk was covered with pigeons. *The pigeons* cooed.
   The sidewalk was covered with cooing pigeons.

3. The doctor rushed to the quarterback. *He was in a* daze.
   The doctor rushed to the dazed quarterback.

4. The candidate spoke to the press. *The candidate was* brief.
   The candidate spoke briefly to the press.

- What words were added to make the combined sentences?
- What words had to change form?

Try Your Skill   Combine each pair of sentences. Leave out the words in italics. Remember that the word you add to the first sentence may have to change form.

1. Crustaceans have shells. *Their shells are* hard.
2. The campers built a fire. *The fire* blazed.
3. The scientist examined the moon rocks. *The scientist was* careful.
4. Ramon could not work in the room. *There was too much* clutter *in the room.*

Keep This in Mind

- Some sentences can be combined by adding a single word from one sentence to the other.
- When adding a word to a sentence, you may have to change the ending of the word to *-ing*, *-ed*, or *-ly*.

Now Write   Combine each group of sentences by adding a word to the first sentence. Leave out the words in italics.

1. Nitrogen is a gas. *It is* colorless.
2. The captain told us a tale. *The tale* frightened *us.*
3. We bought some popcorn. *The popcorn had* butter *on it.*
4. The astronauts opened the hatch. *They were* cautious.

Label your paper **In Addition.** Save it in your folder.

A Winning Combination

Using Combining Skills in Writing

Here's the Idea   Sometimes two sentences state closely-related ideas. A reader may better understand how the ideas are related if the sentences are combined. You have learned several ways to combine related ideas in sentences.

1. You can combine two sentences by using a comma and the words *and, but,* or *or.*
2. You can join parts of sentences by using just the words *and, but,* or *or.*
3. You can combine sentences by adding an important word from one sentence to the other. To do this, you sometimes must change the form of the added word by adding *-ing, -ed,* or *-ly.*

   Use the combining skills you have learned whenever you revise your writing. Combining sentences will help you to show how your ideas are related. It will also add variety to your sentences.

Check It Out   Read the following paragraph.

   1. The pilot glanced at his instrument panel. The pilot's glance was quick. 2. His fuel was low. One of his engines had been struck by lightning. 3. The pilot could ditch the plane in the lake. He could try to make an emergency landing on the highway. 4. He decided to send a distress signal. He decided to make an emergency landing.

   · Would this be a better paragraph if some of the sentences were combined? Explain your answer.

Try Your Skill Rewrite the paragraph given in **Check It Out.** Follow these directions:

1. Combine the first pair of sentences. Add *-ly* to the important word in the second sentence. Take out the repeated words.
2. Combine the second pair of sentences by using a comma and *and.*
3. Combine the third pair of sentences by using a comma and *or.*
4. Combine the fourth pair of sentences by using just the word *and* to join together sentence parts.

Keep This in Mind

- Use sentence combining when you revise your writing.
- Combine sentences to show relationships between ideas.
- Combine sentences to add variety to your writing.

Now Write Read the following paragraph. Then revise it, using the sentence combining techniques you have learned. Follow the directions in parentheses.

Gorillas look mean. They are actually very gentle. (Join the two sentences with a comma and the word *but.*) Most gorillas are friendly. Most gorillas are shy. (Combine sentence parts with the word *but.*) They need companionship. They prefer to live in groups. (Join the sentence parts with the word *and.*) Gorillas sometimes act fierce. Gorillas act fierce if something frightens them. (Change the form of the word *frightens* by adding *-ed.* Then, add this word to the first sentence.) They stand on their hind legs. They beat their chests. (Join the sentence parts with the word *and.*) They do this out of fear. Human beings need not worry about being attacked. (Join the two sentences with *and.*)

Label your paper **A Winning Combination.** Save it in your folder.

A Look at Paragraphs

Part 1 **Group Work**
Defining a Paragraph

Part 2 **All for One**
Recognizing Unity in a Paragraph

Part 3 **One for All**
Using a Topic Sentence

Part 4 **An Idea Takes Shape**
Developing a Paragraph

Part 5 **Read the Labels**
Recognizing Three Kinds of Paragraphs

Group Work

Defining a Paragraph

Here's the Idea   A **paragraph** is a group of sentences that develop one main idea. All the sentences in a paragraph should work together to make that one idea clear.

As you read the following groups of sentences, notice how sentences in each group work together.

1   Neither the mist nor the strange moans of nighttime desert dwellers troubled Artoo Detoo. He made his careful way up the rocky gully. He was hunting for the easiest pathway to the top. His squarish, broad footpads made clicking sounds. The sounds seemed loud in the evening light as the sand underfoot gave way to gravel.   —GEORGE LUCAS

2   Holmes was certainly not a difficult man to live with. He was quiet in his ways, and his habits were regular. It was rare for him to be up after ten at night, and he had invariably breakfasted and gone out before I rose in the morning. Sometimes he spent his day at the chemical laboratory, sometimes in the dissecting rooms, and occasionally in long walks, which appeared to take him into the lowest portions of the city.

—SIR ARTHUR CONAN DOYLE

3   Melons were gathered as they were consumed. In the autumn pumpkins and beans were gathered and placed in bags or baskets; ears of corn were tied together by the husks, and then the harvest was carried on the backs of ponies up to our homes. Here the corn was shelled, and all the harvest stored away in caves or other secluded places to be used in winter.

—GERONIMO

Check It Out   Take another look at the three groups of sentences. The first group tells part of a story. The second group describes a person. The third group describes one aspect of Apache Indian life. Are these groups of sentences paragraphs?

- Does each group of sentences deal with one main idea? Does every sentence in a group say something about the main idea?

Try Your Skill   Read the groups of sentences below. One of them is a paragraph. One is not. For the group that is a paragraph, write the main idea. For the group that is not a paragraph, explain why it is not.

1   Insects that live together in large colonies are called social insects. Ants and bees are both social insects. Each of these insects has one particular job to do that helps to keep the whole society alive. These insects live in large groups because there are so many different jobs required. All the members must do their own jobs well and must cooperate with the others.

2   Television is a relaxing form of entertainment. Dancing and sports require you to move around a lot. You can watch television while lying down. Most people need to lie down after they've played a strenuous game. Basketball can be especially tiring, unless of course you're watching it on TV.

Keep This in Mind

- A paragraph is a group of sentences that develop one main idea. Every sentence in the group should deal with that idea.

Now Write   Look again at the group of sentences in **Try Your Skill** that do not make a good paragraph. Write the first sentence of that paragraph. Then write several more sentences that help to explain the first sentence. Label your paper **Group Work** and put it into your folder.

All for One

Recognizing Unity in a Paragraph

Here's the Idea A paragraph should develop one idea. All the sentences in a paragraph should tell something about that main idea. When they do, a paragraph has **unity.**

Look at the following paragraph. Notice how all the sentences tell something about a family trip that was rained out.

> Huddled together, the Robb family viewed their soggy surroundings. Tiny rivers of rain trickled through the holes in their canvas tent. The once-fluffy sleeping bags had absorbed a great deal of water. They were like enormous sponges. Soaked bits of twigs and pine needles clung to everyone's wet clothes. In miserable agreement, the entire Robb family vowed never to go camping again.

Check It Out Now read the following paragraph.

> It is often said that necessity is the mother of invention. That was certainly true just before Christmas in 1818. A mouse had chewed a hole in the bellows of a church organ in Oberndorf, Austria. The organ would not play. Quickly, Franz Gruber wrote a song that could be played on a guitar instead. On Christmas Eve he played the guitar, and the choir sang the new carol. Because of a hungry mouse, "Silent Night" is now sung all over the world every Christmas Eve.

- Do all of the sentences relate to one main idea? Does the paragraph have unity?

Try Your Skill Each paragraph below has at least one sentence that is not related to the main idea. Such sentences prevent the paragraph from having unity. For each paragraph, write the sentence or sentences that do not belong.

1   Solving word problems in math is not so hard. First, you have to figure out what question you are trying to answer. Then you must decide what figuring you need to do. Next, see which numbers and facts are necessary for the solution and which are thrown in to trick you. Some people have trouble with math, while others just breeze through it. Following these steps will help you to solve word problems more easily.

2   The legend of Johnny Appleseed is based on the life of a real person. His name was John Chapman. He was born in 1775. He died in 1845. Because of Johnny Appleseed, apples are now an important crop. They are grown from coast to coast. The state of Washington produces more apples than any other state.

3   Physical education classes in school teach more than just team sports. They teach individual sports as well, such as running, swimming, and tennis. A person can continue these individual sports for life. Team sports, however, may be hard to keep up with outside of school. People should organize teams where they work.

Keep This in Mind

- All the sentences in a paragraph should develop one main idea. Then a paragraph has unity.

Now Write   Label your paper **All for One.** Write the name of a person whom you admire, a place you have visited, or a sport that you enjoy. Number your paper from 1 to 5. Then write five sentences that say something about your topic. Keep your work in your folder.

One for All

Using a Topic Sentence

Here's the Idea You know that a good paragraph develops just one main idea. How do you express one idea briefly and clearly? The best way is to write a topic sentence. The **topic sentence** of a paragraph states the main idea. The rest of the sentences should support the idea expressed in the topic sentence.

A topic sentence often begins a paragraph. This helps the writer and the reader. First, the topic sentence helps the writer to keep in mind what it is that he or she wants to say. Second, the topic sentence tells the reader what the paragraph is going to be about.

Check It Out Read the paragraph below.

Many animals need the companionship of other animals. In fact, some animals suffer without it. A race horse, for instance, often has an animal companion that shares its stall. This companion might be a dog, a cat, or even a goat. As long as its companion is around, the race horse will perform well. If the companion leaves or dies, though, the horse may lose all its spirit.

- Which sentence is the topic sentence? What is the main idea of this paragraph?

Try Your Skill Read the groups of sentences below. Each group has one sentence in it that states the main idea of the whole group. This sentence is the topic sentence. On a piece of paper, write the topic sentence of each group.

1. (a) It continued for several decades.
   (b) Those from Europe arrived on the East Coast, while the Japanese landed in California.

(c) In 1890, a new wave of immigration into this country began.

(d) People poured in from Europe, Russia, and Japan.

(e) The immigrants helped each other adjust to their new home.

2. (a) Others, like bats, use a kind of radar to keep them safe and help them locate prey.

(b) They are especially adapted to night life.

(c) Some animals, like cats, have other features like long whiskers that keep them from bumping into things.

(d) Nocturnal animals sleep by day and hunt by night.

(e) They usually have very keen vision and extra sharp hearing.

3. (a) This happened right after the new music teacher came.

(b) Now it plays rock music, jazz, and country and western as well.

(c) All these changes have made it one of the most popular after-school activities.

(d) The school band has really changed.

(e) The band used to play only marching music and school songs.

Keep This in Mind

- A topic sentence often begins a paragraph. The topic sentence states the main idea of the paragraph.

Now Write   Think of three topics that you might want to write a paragraph about. You might want to write about something that happened to you. You might want to write about some place you enjoy. Decide what the main idea of each paragraph would be. Then write a topic sentence for each paragraph that states that main idea. Write the title of this lesson, **One for All,** at the top of your paper. Then put your work into your folder.

An Idea Takes Shape

Developing a Paragraph

Here's the Idea A topic sentence presents the main idea of a paragraph. This idea is developed with sensory details, examples, facts and statistics, or incidents or anecdotes.

Sensory details are details that appeal to the senses of sight, sound, hearing, touch, or taste.

> Miss Adela Strangeworth came daintily along Main Street on her way to the grocery. The sun was shining, the air was fresh and clear after the night's heavy rain, and everything in Miss Strangeworth's little town looked washed and bright. Miss Strangeworth took deep breaths and thought that there was nothing in the world like a fragrant summer day.
>
> —SHIRLEY JACKSON

One or more **examples** can be used to develop a paragraph that begins with a general statement.

> Many nationalities have a starchy food that they use as a base for most meals. People in many Oriental countries use rice. South Americans and Mexicans eat many foods with a corn-meal base. A basic starch, in some form, is used all over the world.

Facts and statistics can prove a point or make an idea clear.

> A person's life expectancy depends on the country where the person lives. Australian men have a life expectancy of 67.6 years. Men in Peru can expect to live only 52.6 years. People in Chad have the lowest life expectancies. For men, it is only 29 years. For women, it is 35 years. Women in Norway have the highest life expectancy. They can expect to live 78.7 years.

Incidents or anecdotes (very short stories) can be used to illustrate a point.

> Chris was always there when I needed him. I remember how awful I felt after the Centerville game last year. We had played

terribly. We looked like a bunch of kindergarten kids out on the field. After the game, Chris met me outside the locker room. All the way home, he didn't say a word. He knew I didn't want to talk. When we got to my house, he smiled and said, "Hey, it's only a game." I needed to hear that then. Chris understood.

Check It Out   Read the following paragraph.

When the fog rolls in, the harbor is veiled in mystery. All the warehouses look haunted. Fishermen appear ghostly as they wend their way along hidden piers to invisible boats. The powerful beam from the lighthouse pierces the thick white curtain, warning ships of danger. Most eerie of all is a mournful voice that seems to come from nowhere—the foghorn.

- Is the topic sentence developed by sensory details? examples? facts and statistics? incidents or anecdotes?

Try Your Skill   Read the topics listed below and decide how you might develop each of them. Write *Sensory Details, Specific Examples, Facts and Statistics,* or *Incidents or Anedotes.*

1. the most popular video games
2. a perfect summer day
3. the costs of running this school
4. incredible feats of strength

Keep This in Mind

- The main idea of a paragraph may be developed by sensory details, by specific examples, by facts and statistics, or by incidents or anecdotes.

Now Write   Choose one of the four topics in **Try Your Skill.** Write a topic sentence. List sensory details, examples, facts and statistics, or an incident or anecdote that you could use to develop it. Label your paper **An Idea Takes Shape.** Keep your work.

Read the Labels

Recognizing Three Kinds of Paragraphs

Here's the Idea A paragraph may tell a story, describe something, or explain something. Each kind of paragraph has a different name and presents an idea in a different way.

Narrative paragraphs tell a story or tell about something that happened. The events may be real or imaginary.

Descriptive paragraphs use words to create pictures. Descriptions appeal to all the senses.

Explanatory paragraphs may tell *how* to do something, or *how* something happens or works. They can also tell *why* something is or should be done, or *what* something is.

Check It Out Notice how the subject of dogs is presented in three different ways in three different kinds of paragraphs.

1   The dog waited until everyone was out of the apartment, and then jumped up to sleep on Ben's bed. Later in the afternoon, however, footsteps sounded in the hall and a key turned in the lock. The dog reacted quickly. It leaped from the bed immediately. When Ben came into his room, the dog was lying quietly curled up on the rug. However, Ben could see from the rumpled blankets where the dog had been.

2   The dog looked like a miniature wolf. It had stiff, grey fur that formed a thick mat on its back and soft tufts on its legs. The dog's ears were pointed. Its eyes were shiny and black. The animal made no sound as it entered the room.

3   When you train a dog to come to you, don't give it a chance to make a wrong move. Instead, put it on a long leash or rope. Then stand a few feet from the dog and say "Come" in a friendly voice. Tug gently on the rope as you do this. When the dog gets up close to you, reward it so that it knows it has done the right thing.

- Which paragraph is narrative? Which is descriptive? Which is explanatory?

Try Your Skill As you read these topic sentences, decide what kind of paragraph they would probably be part of. Write *Narrative*, *Descriptive*, or *Explanatory*.

1. The streets were covered by a soft carpet of snow that muffled all sounds.
2. One morning right after breakfast, the phone rang.
3. My first subway trip was a disaster.
4. The best way to lift something heavy without straining your back is to start with the proper posture.
5. An abacus is a frame containing movable beads that is used for teaching arithmetic.
6. I believe that the Walker School should not be closed.

Keep This in Mind

- Narrative paragraphs tell a story or relate events.
- Descriptive paragraphs create word pictures by appealing to the senses.
- Explanatory paragraphs tell *how* to do something, *how* something happens or works, *why* something is or should be done, or *what* something is.

Now Write Read over your topic sentence and list of related sentences from **Now Write** in **An Idea Takes Shape**. Which of the three types of paragraphs would you use for your topic? Write the name for that type of paragraph on your paper. Explain why it is the best type to use with your topic. Label your paper **Read the Labels** and keep it in your folder.

Writing
a Paragraph

Part 1 **Paragraph in Progress**
Writing as a Process

Part 2 **Something To Say**
Pre-Writing: Choosing Subjects

Part 3 **Zero In**
Pre-Writing: Narrowing a Topic

Part 4 **What's the Point?**
Pre-Writing: Purpose and Audience

Part 5 **Make It Direct**
Pre-Writing: Topic Sentences

Part 6 **Now What?**
Pre-Writing: Developing a Paragraph

Part 7 **Make Arrangements**
Pre-Writing: Organizing a Paragraph

Part 8 **Discovery**
Writing the First Draft

Part 9 **Finish It Off**
The First Draft: Ending a Paragraph

Part 10 **Polishing Up**
Revising Your Paragraph

Paragraph in Progress

Writing as a Process

Here's the Idea   You have learned what a paragraph is and how a paragraph can be developed. Now you are ready to learn how to write a paragraph of your own.

If you are going to complete any task successfully, you must think it out carefully. Writing is no exception. The best way to be sure that your writing is clear, well-developed, and lively is to follow a step-by-step process called the **process of writing.**

The process of writing has three main stages. The first stage is called **pre-writing.** It includes all of the planning that you do before you write. During this stage, you will choose and narrow a topic. Then you will gather details to develop your topic. Finally, you will arrange your ideas in a logical order.

The second stage is called **writing the first draft.** At this stage in the process, you turn your pre-writing notes into a paragraph. You let your thoughts flow freely. You write your ideas in good order. You needn't worry about grammar and mechanics at this point. You will have time later to correct your mistakes.

The third stage in the process of writing is called **revising.** During this stage you will improve your ideas and your writing style. You will also proofread your first draft to find and correct any errors in grammar and mechanics.

Use the process of writing whenever you write. It will help to make you a better writer.

Check It Out   Read the following notes and paragraph.

General Topic: a summer adventure
Narrowed Topic: a weekend in Wisconsin
Pre-Writing Notes: swimming, water skiing, fishing for trout, no TV—didn't miss it, cabin on lake, sandy beach, blackberry pie

First Draft: Our weekend at the lake was great. We swam all the time and water skied. One day we went fishing I caught a trout. There wasnt any TV. We didn't even notice. The cabin was right on Lake Michigan. The beach was sandy. At night we ate on the porch. There was blackberries by the cabin. Mom made a pie. Next year I hope we go back.

- What two steps in the process of writing did this writer complete? What step hasn't been done yet?

Try Your Skill   Here is the revised paragraph about a weekend in Wisconsin. Correct the two errors that remain.

Our weekend *in a cabin* at the lake was great. We swam all the time and water-skied *every day.* One day we went fishing *and* I caught a trout. *We ate it for supper.* There wasnt any TV *but* We didn't even notice. The cabin was right on *a sandy beach at* Lake Michigan. The beach was sandy. At night we ate on the *screened-in* porch. There was *wild* blackberries *growing* by the cabin. Mom made a pie. *On Sunday,* Next year I hope we go back.

Now Write   A journal can help you become a better writer. Get a notebook and try to write in it every day. For today, write about something interesting that you saw or read about recently.

Something To Say

Pre-Writing: Choosing Subjects

Here's the Idea Students often wonder what makes a subject worth writing about. In general, the best topics are those that a writer is most interested in. To write well about a topic, you must feel that you really have something important to say.

Where do you find these kinds of topics? You might be surprised to learn that the best topics are already right in your head. You have many ideas, feelings, and memories of past experiences that would be interesting for others to read about. To discover these topics, try using one of these methods:

Look in your journal. Your journal contains your thoughts and feelings about people, places, and events. If they interest you, you can make them interesting for your reader.

Brainstorm. Brainstorming is a word game that can lead to interesting writing ideas. You can brainstorm by yourself or with friends. Start with a word or a general idea such as *the park*. List everything that comes into your mind when you think of the park. You could come up with writing ideas such as "weekend ice hockey games," or "the botanical gardens." Each of those ideas could lead to writing possibilities.

Read. Browse through some books, magazines, and newspapers that interest you. Read some articles, stories, or poems. Look at some photographs. These are all good sources of ideas.

Check It Out Imagine that one student started a class brainstorming session with the word *animals*. Look at the "idea tree" that the class brainstormed from that one word.

- What ideas could you add to this idea tree?
- What possible writing ideas can you find in the idea tree?

vets   obedience   dolphin

racing   school   monkey

"Lassie"   good friends

horses   dogs   shows

cages

pets   zoo

animals

Try Your Skill   Here are five broad topics that one student came up with. She looked in her journal and leafed through a book of photographs. Choose one of these subjects and do some brainstorming. When you are finished, look over your notes. In your journal, write down at least three possible writing ideas.

heroes   fashions   holidays   winning   my sister/brother

Keep This in Mind

- Choose a topic that interests you and that you know something about.
- You can find writing ideas in your journal, by brainstorming, and by reading.

Now Write   Make a list of topics that interest you and that you know something about. Use the methods you learned about in this lesson. Come up with at least five or six writing ideas. Save your list in your folder.

Zero In

Pre-Writing: Narrowing a Topic

Here's the Idea If you write a paragraph about a topic that is too general, you will probably find it hard to say anything interesting. Some subjects are too broad to write about in a paragraph. If you started with a general topic like "recreation," you might end up with a dull paragraph like this:

> Recreation is as important as work. I enjoy cooking out of doors with my family. I like to swim, skate, and play soccer. There is never enough time to do all the things I enjoy.

If you narrowed the topic, however, you could focus on just one recreational activity. One good way to narrow a topic is to ask questions about it. Such questions might begin with *who, what, when, where, why,* and *how.*

For instance, if your general subject is recreation, you might ask *What?* about it, to get a list of activities you enjoy.

swimming   skating   soccer   outdoor cooking

Now you would choose one of these activities to explore further. Suppose you choose *outdoor cooking.* Begin asking other questions about it, like these:

When? summers, weekends, holidays (July 4, Labor Day)
Who? me, my family, friends
Where? backyard, park, beach

As you make your notes, you will probably remember specific times when you cooked outdoors. You might remember the Fourth of July cookout you planned for your family—the time when a thunderstorm struck just as you got everything ready. Now you have discovered a topic that can be covered well in one paragraph: an Independence Day cookout disaster.

Check It Out   Read this paragraph.

My Independence Day cookout for my family turned into a disaster. When it was time to start the fire, I discovered we were out of charcoal. Wondering why I hadn't checked this detail sooner, I ran to the store and bought more. After several starts, I finally had a strong fire going. Then I hauled dishes, silverware, napkins, and extra chairs out onto the lawn. I brought out creamy cole slaw, hot German potato salad, mustard, ketchup, and platters of sliced tomatoes and sweet onions. Just as I was putting the first hot dogs and hamburgers on the grill, I felt several drops of rain splatter on my arm. The drops of rain soon became a downpour. Screaming for help, I began grabbing the water-logged food. The next time I plan a cookout, I'll check the weather forecast first.

- What makes this paragraph more interesting than the one in **Here's the Idea?** What does this tell you about the importance of narrowing a topic?

Try Your Skill   Choose one of these general topics. Ask *Who? What? When? Where? Why?* or *How?* Use your answers to develop a topic that could be covered in one paragraph.

travel   television   music   friends   art   hobbies

Keep This in Mind

- Narrow a general topic by asking *who, what, when, where, why, and how* questions. Be sure that your narrowed topic can be covered well in one paragraph.

Now Write   Look at your list of topics from the last lesson. Choose one topic. Ask *who, what, when, where, why,* and *how* questions about it. Use your answers to narrow the topic so that it can be covered well in one paragraph. Save your work.

What's the Point?

Pre-Writing: Purpose and Audience

Here's the Idea   Now that you have a topic to write about, you should stop to consider two important questions: "What is the purpose of my paragraph?" and "For whom am I writing?"

Anything you write has a **purpose.** The purpose of your paragraph is what you hope to accomplish with your writing. Your purpose might be to tell a story or to describe someone or something. Your purpose might also be to define a word, explain a process, or express an opinion. If you know your purpose *before* you begin writing, you will write a better paragraph. Knowing your purpose will help you to see your topic more clearly. It will also help you to choose the right kinds of details to develop your topic.

The readers you have in mind are called your **audience.** As you continue planning your paragraph, ask yourself what your audience is like. What age are your readers? Knowing this will help you choose the right vocabulary for your paragraph. What are your audience's interests and opinions? Answering this question will tell you whether you have chosen a topic that your audience is likely to enjoy. Consider whether your audience knows a little, a lot, or nothing at all about your chosen topic. Then you will know how detailed your information should be. Learn as much as you can about your readers. Then you can write a paragraph just for them.

Check It Out   Look over these possible purposes and audiences for a paragraph about dancing.

	Topic:	dancing
Possible Purposes:		to tell about my first high-school dance
		to describe the grace of a ballet dancer
		to define a dancing term
		to explain how to do a new dance
		to explain why I like or dislike dancing
Possible Audiences:		a teacher who likes to dance
		a classmate
		a friend I am writing a letter to
		someone who disapproves of dancing

- How would these different purposes and audiences change the way you developed this paragraph?

Try Your Skill   Choose one of the purposes listed in **Check It Out** and one of the possible audiences. Then explain how you would develop a paragraph for that purpose and audience. What vocabulary would you use? How detailed would your information have to be?

Keep This in Mind

- Your purpose is your reason for writing.
- Your audience is the person or persons for whom you are writing.
- Knowing your purpose and your audience will help you to write a better paragraph.

Now Write   Look at the topic you chose in **Zero In**. Decide what your purpose is. Name your audience and write a brief description of them. Save your paper in your folder.

Make It Direct

Pre-Writing: Topic Sentences

Here's the Idea   Narrowing a topic gives you a clear idea of your subject. Writing a clear topic sentence helps you to make your subject clear for your audience.

   A good topic sentence states the main idea of your paragraph. In other words, it tells the reader what your paragraph is about.

   A well-written topic sentence is direct and interesting. It should introduce the topic, not *you*. Don't write a topic sentence like this one:

> In this paragraph I will explain why women live longer than men.

This sentence takes too long to get to the point. It contains unnecessary words. Look at this revised topic sentence.

> Women live longer than men for three important reasons.

This sentence is direct. It gets right to the point. Furthermore, it is interesting. It makes the reader want to read on to discover *why* women live longer than men.

   A well-written topic sentence is informative. It gives specific information about a paragraph. Don't write a general statement like this one.

> Swimming regularly is good for you.

This sentence is not specific enough. It doesn't say *how* or *why* swimming is good for you. Read the revised topic sentence.

> Swimming regularly improves physical fitness in two important ways.

This sentence tells the reader exactly what your paragraph is about.

Check It Out Read the topic sentences below.

1. My paragraph is about the day of my history exam.
2. Learning to roller skate requires practice, patience, and padding.
3. The city of Los Angeles is nice.
4. Bees live in a highly organized society where every bee has a specific job to do.

- Which sentences are well-written topic sentences? Which ones are not? Give reasons for your answers.

Try Your Skill Below are five poorly written topic sentences. Rewrite each of the sentences. Make each rewritten sentence direct, interesting, and informative.

1. There is an animal that is the biggest land animal in the world, and it is an African elephant.
2. When I look around me at everyone else in school, it seems as if every person I see is wearing some kind of ring.
3. It is easy to learn how to juggle.
4. I have a cousin named Bobby who is a nice person and has a hobby that I'm sure will be interesting to you.
5. I like to watch game shows.

Keep This in Mind

- A topic sentence states the main idea of a paragraph.
- A topic sentence should be direct, interesting, and informative.

Now Write Look at the topic you narrowed in Part 3, **Zero In.** Write two or three different topic sentences that state the main idea of your topic. Write sentences that are direct, interesting, and informative. Save your topic sentences in your folder.

Now What?

Pre-Writing: Developing a Paragraph

Here's the Idea   You have chosen and narrowed a topic for a paragraph. You have identified your purpose and your audience. You have written an interesting and informative topic sentence. Now you are ready to develop your topic. In Section 6, you learned that you can develop a paragraph in four ways. You can use sensory details, specific examples, facts and statistics, or incidents or anecdotes. The type of development you use depends on your topic and your purpose.

One way to gather information is through **observation.** If you are planning a description, you can observe your subject firsthand, and write down all of the sensory details you notice.

You can also gather information by **brainstorming.** Think about your subject. Write down all of the details and examples that come to mind.

Another way to find information for your paragraph is by doing **research.** If you need facts and statistics, the library is the place to go. Read about your subject in books, magazines, newspapers, and encyclopedias. Take notes as you read.

Finally, you can gather information by searching your own **experiences.** The incidents and anecdotes that you need to illustrate a point can come from day-to-day experiences.

Check It Out   Here is a list of pre-writing notes that one student made for a paragraph. The broad topic was *Nursing*. The narrowed topic was *A Candy-Striper's Day*.

Saturday afternoons
Dad drives Ken to band practice
Dad drives me to the hospital
Uniform must be clean

Some unpleasant jobs
Ms. Kim—my supervisor
Hospital is brand new
Make patients comfortable
Difficult patients
Serve meals, change beds, talk to patients
Favorite patient—Mr. Francesco
Want to be a doctor
Best job—feeding babies in nursery

- Do all the student's notes develop the narrowed topic? Which details do not?
- What methods do you think the student used to gather the information? Explain your answer.

Try Your Skill   Here is a narrowed topic for a paragraph. Make a list of details, examples, or facts and figures that you might use to develop the topic. Compare your pre-writing notes with those of your classmates.

the kitchen: the activity center of our home

Keep This in Mind

- The type of information you look for depends on your topic and your purpose.
- You can gather information for your paragraph through observation, by brainstorming, through research, and from your experiences.

Now Write   Review the topic you narrowed in **Zero In**. Decide what type of information you need to develop your paragraph. Use one or more of the methods described in this lesson to gather your information. Save your pre-writing notes in your folder.

Make Arrangements

Pre-Writing: Organizing a Paragraph

Here's the Idea   After you have gathered details to develop your main idea, you are ready for the next pre-writing step. Now you have to organize your notes by arranging them in an order that makes sense.

What is a logical order? The type of paragraph you are planning will give you a clue. Different types of paragraphs are organized in different ways.

If you are writing a paragraph that tells a story, you will arrange your pre-writing notes in **chronological order.** This is the order in which events happened or should happen. Chronological order is also the best way to organize an explanation that tells how to do something or how something happens or works.

A paragraph that describes someone or something calls for a different kind of organization. You would present your details in the order that you want your reader to notice them. This is called **spatial order.**

The pre-writing notes for a paragraph that explains *why* something is or should be are best arranged in the **order of their importance.** You begin with the least important reason and build toward the most important.

If you are writing a paragraph that defines a word or an idea, you would organize your details from the **general to the specific.**

Check It Out   Here is a poorly organized paragraph.

> When you start jogging, take it easy. Switch between running and walking. Even Olympic runners had to begin somewhere. Be sure to limber up first. Don't get discouraged. Your muscles may be tight. Soon you will be able to run a mile or more. Your strength and energy will gradually increase.

- What is the writer trying to do in this paragraph?
- Why is the organization confusing?
- What kind of organization would be best for this paragraph?

Explain your answers.

Try Your Skill   This paragraph is not well organized. Rearrange the sentences in a logical order. Tell what order you used.

Monday was a disaster. I walked into my math class twenty minutes late . On my long walk to school, I lost my pen. I missed my bus. On the bus going home, I realized I had forgotten to buy a ticket to the conference basketball game. Now I would have to pay full price at the door. After lunch, I found out that I had read the wrong story for English. Tuesday has got to be better! I had forgotten to set my alarm before I went to sleep. My lunch was left on the kitchen table, next to my math homework.

Keep This in Mind

- Pre-writing notes can be arranged in chronological order, spatial order, the order of importance, or general to specific order.
- Choose the kind of organization that best suits the type of paragraph you are writing.

Now Write   Look at the pre-writing notes that you wrote in **Now What?** Arrange your notes in an order that makes sense for the type of paragraph you are writing. Save your notes in your folder.

Part 8

Discovery

Writing the First Draft

Here's the Idea All of the planning you have been doing in pre-writing is about to pay off. Now you are ready to write the first draft of your paragraph.

A first draft is sometimes called a discovery draft. Discovering new ideas, better ways to use language, and different types of organization are all part of writing a first draft.

At this important stage in the process of writing, try to write freely. Concentrate on discovering what it is that you want to say. Don't worry about making errors in punctuation or spelling. There will be time later to find and correct these mistakes. To give yourself room to make corrections later, write your first draft on every other line of your paper.

As you write, refer to your pre-writing notes. You may discover some details that do not help you to develop your topic or to accomplish your purpose. These details should be left out of your paragraph. At the same time, new ideas and details may also occur to you. You may also realize that the organization of your ideas could be improved. You might want to change the order of your sentences to make your ideas clearer.

Keep in mind that your first draft is not the final copy of your paragraph. Making changes is an important part of writing a first draft. Use this draft to experiment and discover.

Check It Out Read the following first draft. It was written from the pre-writing notes in Part 6. Look back at those notes to see how the writer used them to write this paragraph.

> Being a Candy Striper is a good experience. Every Saturday, my dad drives my brother to band practice. Then he drops me off at the county hospital. I check in with my supervisor, Ms. Kim. She assigns us our jobs for the day. I like feeding the babies

in the nursery. I want to be a doctor someday. Some patients are difficult. One of my favorite patients is Mr. Francesco. Our main job is to make patients comfortable. We change sheets deliver meals and do other things. Some jobs aren't the greatest. Ms. Kim reminds us that everything we do is important.

- Are there any details in the pre-writing notes on pages 86–87 that were left out of the first draft? Why?
- Did the writer add any new ideas that weren't in the pre-writing notes?

Try Your Skill   Write a brief first draft from these pre-writing notes. You may change the order of details. You may leave out some ideas if you wish. You will want to add other details that occur to you. Before you begin writing, decide on your purpose and your audience.

Topic: Heroes and heroines are an important part of our lives.
Notes: Cartoon characters—Spider Man, Wonder Woman
          Sports heroes—baseball, football, Olympics
          People who risk their lives—police, firefighters
          Historical figures—political figures, war heroes, doctors
          and scientists

Keep This in Mind

- The first draft is the first written version of your paragraph.
- Use the first draft to experiment with your ideas and to discover new ones.
- Write freely without worrying about making errors in grammar or mechanics.

Now Write   Reread the pre-writing notes that you organized in Part 7. Write the first draft of your paragraph. Use the guidelines in this lesson as you write. Save your first draft.

Finish It Off

The First Draft: Ending a Paragraph

Here's the Idea The last step in writing the first draft of a paragraph is coming up with an ending sentence. What does a good ending sentence do? It sums up in an interesting way what has been said in the paragraph.

An ending sentence should not add any new information to a paragraph. Suppose you wrote a paragraph about how to polish gemstones to make jewelry. Your last sentence should not be about how to clean silver jewelry. Instead, your concluding sentence should sum up what you said about polishing stones.

An ending sentence should also be interesting. If it is, your reader will be more likely to remember what your paragraph was about.

If you are having difficulty writing a concluding sentence, look at your topic sentence. What is the main idea? Your ending sentence should sum up that main idea in different words.

Check It Out Read the following paragraph.

Sometimes when I'm in shop class I look like a creature from outer space. My safety goggles and respirator make it hard to tell that I'm human. The goggles cover the whole top half of my face. The respirator covers most of the lower half. Sometimes I am covered with sawdust. I certainly do not look as if I belong on this earth.

- Does the ending sentence sum up the main idea of the paragraph? Is the ending sentence interesting?

Try Your Skill Read these three paragraphs. Rewrite the poorly written ending sentences. Try to make your ending sentences interesting. Be sure that they sum up the main ideas.

1   The new band uniforms are designed to be neat and trim. They are fashioned from a soft navy blue material that refuses to wrinkle. The jackets have white collars, white cuffs, and a white pocket. The pants have a broad white stripe down each leg. *I have been in the band for two years.*

2   The bleachers were bursting with eager baseball fans. Many waved Cubs pennants or wore Cubs T-Shirts. One young man organized a cheering section. People discussed the players and the standings. *Everyone agreed that it was a warm day.*

3   The only time I had ever ridden a horse, I felt like a character in a comedy. First, the saddle slid off when I tried to mount the horse. Then my boot stuck in the stirrup. Worst of all, the horse ignored me completely. As my friends rode out of sight, the horse lowered its head and nibbled the grass. *My horse was obviously hungry.*

Keep This in Mind

- A good ending sentence should sum up the main idea of the paragraph in an interesting way.

Now Write   Write a strong ending sentence for your paragraph. First, read your paragraph to yourself. Then write an ending that sums up the main idea. Make the ending interesting. Save your work in your folder.

Polishing Up

Revising Your Paragraph

Here's the Idea Revising is the final step in the process of writing. The purpose of revision is to make your writing the best it can be. Revision is your chance to see what is good about your paragraph and what should be improved.

First you will revise the ideas in your paragraph. Be sure that your topic sentence is direct, interesting, and informative. Keep in mind your purpose for writing. Does your paragraph do what you set out to do? Remember your audience. Is your paragraph right for the people who will be reading it?

Fine-tune the ideas that you used to develop your paragraph. Ask yourself whether all of the details develop the main idea. Cross out any ideas that do not develop your topic sentence.

Carefully go over the organization of your paragraph. Does the order of your details make sense? Would using a different method of organization make your ideas clearer?

When you are satisfied with your ideas and your organization, look at the language you have used. Is it lively and interesting? Have you used strong, specific verbs? Are your adjectives vivid? Is your word choice suitable for your audience? Add or change words until you are satisfied.

Finally, proofread your paragraph for errors in grammar, capitalization, punctuation, and spelling. When you have revised your paragraph completely, make a final copy of it. Proofread and correct this final copy.

Check It Out Read this revised paragraph.

- Name some specific ways the writer has changed and improved this paragraph.

Check It Out   Read this revised paragraph.

My volunteer work as
great
~~Being~~ a Candy Striper ~~is~~ a ~~good~~ experience. Every Saturday,
has been
my dad ~~drives my brother to hockey practice. Then he~~ drops me
First,
off at the county hospital. I check in with my supervisor, Ms.
My favorite job is
Kim. She assigns us our jobs for the day. ~~I like~~ feeding the babies
in the nursery. ~~I want to be a doctor someday.~~ Some patients are
Other patients are a joy.   *He is always telling*
difficult. One of my favorite older patients is Mr. Francesco. *stories*
and joking
Our main job is to make the patients comfortable. We change *around.*
work   *like*
sheets, deliver meals, and do other things. Some jobs aren't the *cleaning*
up after
greatest. Ms. Kim reminds us that everything we do is important. *sick*
always   *patients,*
Being a candy
striper has taught me many
lessons about people and life.

Try Your Skill   Read this first draft. Use the guidelines in
this lesson to revise it.

> Fads are hear today and gone tomorrow. Mini-skirts have
> been in and out of fashion. Personally, I like jeens. Hairstyles are
> "in" one year and "out" the next. Their are also fads in recrea-
> tion. Like skateboards hula hoops and certain games. I remem-
> ber when everyone wore deely-boppers. You can go broke
> keeping up with all the latest fads. Save your money.

Keep This in Mind

- Revise the ideas, organization, and word choice of
  your paragraph. Proofread your paragraph.

Now Write   Use the guidelines in this lesson to revise the
first draft of your paragraph. When you are satisfied with your
paragraph, make a final copy. Save your paragraph.

The Process of Writing

The Process of Writing

As you work your way through the composition chapters in this book, you will do many kinds of writing. You will write stories and describe people and places. You will state your opinions, explain processes, and define words and ideas. Although the type of writing you do will change, the way you approach your writing will not. You will always use the process of writing to plan, write, and revise your paragraphs and compositions.

The three main stages in the process of writing are **Pre-Writing, Writing the First Draft,** and **Revising.** If you complete these three stages carefully, your writing will be clear and well organized. It will also have unity. When you have mastered the process, writing will be much easier for you.

In this chapter you can review the process of writing. First, read about each stage of the process. Then look at the example that shows what one student wrote during each stage.

Pre-Writing Success is usually the result of careful planning. That is why an actor rehearses before opening night. That is why an artist draws many sketches before beginning a painting. That is also why the pre-writing, or planning, stage of the process of writing is so important. What you do *before* you write will determine how successful you will be *when* you write.

Before you write, you must choose a good subject. You can discover interesting things to write about in a variety of ways. You can brainstorm, look through your journal, and do some reading in books, newspapers, and magazines. When you have chosen a subject, narrow it so that you can cover it well in a given length.

Make a list of interesting details about your subject. You will use these details to develop your subject. These might include sensory details, specific examples, facts and statistics, or incidents or anecdotes. You can gather these kinds of details through observation, brainstorming, and research.

When you have enough details, you must organize them. Organizing is a very important pre-writing step. If your details are not well organized, your writing will not be clear. First, look carefully at your list. Cross out any details that do not develop your topic. Then arrange the remaining details in a logical order. You might use chronological order, spatial order, the order of importance, or general to specific order. Be sure to choose an order that suits the type of writing you are doing.

Pre-Writing

<table>
<tr><td>u list
sible
opics
elect
one.

u list
tails,
oose
hose
that
velop
opic,
and
anize
hem.</td><td>

topics
Julie's new job   (Grandpa's workshop)
storm at the beach   the band room
details   scratchy
(5) floor covered with sawdust (7) oak candlesticks
~~Gramps is 65 years old~~ (1) smell of wood
(4) boards against the wall   sweet?
(2) workbench   (6) blueprints —
     planes, T-square   rolled up
~~We live on Taylor Avenue~~ (3) lathe and jig saw
                hum   buzz

</td></tr>
</table>

Writing the First Draft   At this point in the process of writing, you are ready to write your first draft. This is perhaps the most exciting stage of the process. Now you will turn your ideas into sentences and paragraphs. Simply put your pencil to paper and write. Let your ideas flow freely. Don't fuss with the writing. Don't be concerned about grammar or mechanics. Don't get slowed down by trying to make your writing perfect at this stage. This is a time to experiment, to discover what you want to say about your subject and how you want to say it. You will have time later to revise what you have written. Skip lines as you write. Then you will have plenty of space to add details, make corrections, and improve what you have written.

Writing the First Draft

You write a paragraph about your topic.

> Gramp's favorite spot is his workshop. Its neat. It smells great. His work bench has a hammer, a T-square, planes, jars of nails, and other stuff. Wood is against the walls. On the floor is sawdust and wood shavings. He's got a lathe and a jig-saw. Theres other things like blueprints. And candlesticks. He made them on the lathe. Like I said, Gramp's workshop is neat.

Revising When you have finished your first draft, you are ready for the third stage of the process of writing—revising. At this stage of the process you must work carefully and thoughtfully with what you have written. Did you include everything you wanted to? Do you like what you've written? Is it interesting? Your goal is to improve your writing. Here are some questions you should ask yourself as you revise your first draft.

1. Have I written a good topic sentence for each paragraph? Is it direct and informative? Is it interesting enough to capture the reader's attention?

2. Have I included enough details to develop my topic completely? Have I left out any details that do not relate to my main idea?

3. Have I arranged my details in a logical order? Does the order suit the type of writing I am doing?

4. Have I used lively, vivid language?

5. Have I written a strong ending? Does it bring my writing to a satisfactory conclusion?

Proofreading   The last step in revising is called proofreading. Read your first draft carefully. Find and correct any errors you made in grammar, capitalization, punctuation, and spelling. Check a dictionary and the Handbook sections of this book as you proofread.

As you revise your first draft, use the following proofreading marks to show your corrections and changes.

Proofreading Symbols

Symbol	Meaning	Example
∧	add	would gone ^have
≡	capitalize	United states
/	make lower case	our club President
∿	reverse	their
℘	take out	finished the the race
¶	make new paragraph	....be over. New ideas
⊙	period	....and stop Before we
∧	add comma	Red, blue and green are

Notice how the paragraph has been revised.

Revising

Gramps's favorite spot is his
workshop behind our house. The workshop is filled with the sweet smell
~~Its neat. It smells great~~ of pine
and cedar.
Gramps's work bench is cluttered with ~~His~~ ~~has~~ a hammer, a
several
T-square, planes, jars of nails,
tools.
and other ~~stuff.~~ Boards are stacked ~~Wood is~~ against
covered with
the walls. ~~On~~ the floor is sawdust
also has
and wood shavings. He's got a lathe
that hum and buzz as he works.
and a jig-saw. ~~Theres other things~~
Rolled-up are piled on a shelf above the bench.
~~like blueprints. And~~ candlesticks of solid oak
stand waiting for sanding and staining. Now that he's
~~He made them on the lathe. Like I~~
retired, Gramps spends hours in his workshop
~~said, Gramps workshop is neat.~~
every day. It has become his second home.

Making the Final Copy
When you are satisfied that your writing is clear and correct, write it in its final form. The final copy of your paragraph, composition, or report is important. This is the only copy of your work that your readers will see. Rewrite your work carefully. Include all of the changes that you made when you revised. Make your work as neat as possible.

When you have finished your final copy, proofread your work one last time. Neatly correct any errors you find. If you find that you've made more than three mistakes, you may want to redo your final copy. Remember, you want to make a good impression on your readers.

Gramps's favorite spot is his workshop behind our house. The workshop is filled with the sweet smell of pine and cedar. Gramps's workbench is cluttered with hammers, a T-square, several planes, jars of nails, and other tools. He also has a lathe and a jig-saw that hum and buzz as he works. Boards are stacked against the walls. The floor is covered with sawdust and wood shavings. Rolled-up blueprints are piled on a shelf above the bench. Candlesticks of solid oak stand waiting for sanding and staining. Now that he's retired, Gramps spends hours in his workshop every day. It has become his second home.

Now you are ready to begin your writing adventures. Whenever and whatever you write, complete all the stages of the process of writing. Each time you write, you will be learning something about writing and about yourself.

The Narrative Paragraph

Part 1 **The Big Event**
Pre-Writing: Developing a Narrative

Part 2 **Time Will Tell**
Pre-Writing: Using Chronological Order

Part 3 **Insiders and Outsiders**
Pre-Writing: Choosing a Point of View

Part 4 **Good Timing**
Writing the First Draft

Part 5 **Instant Replay**
Revising Your Narrative Paragraph

The Big Event

Pre-Writing: Developing a Narrative

Here's the Idea   You have learned what a paragraph is and how to write one. You have also learned how the process of writing can help you to write better paragraphs. Now you are going to learn how to write specific types of paragraphs.

There are several different types of paragraphs you can write. The kind of paragraph you write will depend on your purpose for writing. If your purpose is to tell a story, you will write a **narrative paragraph.** A narrative can be a true story, such as an account of your first dance class. Or a narrative can be an imaginary story, set in a different time or in another world.

As in any other kind of writing, the first pre-writing step is to choose and narrow a topic. Try to remember or to imagine an interesting or exciting event. Be sure the topic you choose is narrow enough to be covered well in one paragraph.

When you have chosen an event to write about, begin listing the details that will help you to tell your story. An event is made up of many smaller events, or incidents. For example, suppose the story you want to tell concerns your first ride on a New York City subway. This event includes such incidents as paying your fare and checking the subway map to figure out how to get to your destination. The event also includes such incidents as going down to the subway platform, boarding the train, and so on. Most of the pre-writing notes you make for your narrative paragraph will be the incidents that tell your story.

To make your narrative paragraph really interesting, however, you also need to include good sensory details. For example, how did the ticket agent *look*? How do subway trains *sound*? Add sensory details to each incident that you list. They will make your narrative come alive for your reader.

Check It Out   Read this narrative paragraph.

A faint, scratchy noise awakened me. In seconds I saw that someone was lifting the screen on my window. Just as I was about to cry out, I heard a loud thud. Then I heard hisses, snarls, and a scream. I jumped out of bed and switched on the light. Max, my cat, was sitting beside the open window, licking his paws. I peered into the darkness, then hugged Max, my protector.

- What incidents tell the story of Max and the burglar?
- What sensory details did the writer include?

Try Your Skill   Below are four situations. Choose one situation and make some pre-writing notes for it. First, list the incidents that would tell the story. Then add good sensory details to the incidents.

1. I had done my homework, but the teacher didn't know that, and I couldn't find my paper.
2. As Gwen shut the door, she suddenly realized that she had locked the key inside.
3. It took Tom a few minutes to realize that he was invisible.
4. Once in a while a strange thing happens to me.

Keep This in Mind

- A narrative paragraph tells a real or an imaginary story.
- A narrative is developed with incidents and sensory details.

Now Write   Choose an interesting story you would like to tell. Narrow your topic so that your story can be told in one paragraph. Then gather details to develop your narrative. List the incidents that will tell your story. Include good sensory details. Save your pre-writing notes in your folder.

Time Will Tell

Pre-Writing: Using Chronological Order

Here's the Idea To be a good storyteller, you need to plan your story before you write it. You began planning your story when you chose a topic and made pre-writing notes for it. Now you must organize your pre-writing notes. You must decide on a logical order in which to present your details.

The best order for a narrative paragraph is **chronological order.** Chronological order is the order of time. Your story should start with the first incident that happened and move along in time to the last incident.

Look at this narrative paragraph. Notice that the incidents are told in the order in which they happened.

> Outside, blinking against the sun, I left my bike in the rack and wandered down the street. Something was happening in front of the dime store. I could see a crowd of kids gathered at the doors while a policeman attempted to keep order. I slipped inside behind his back. The place was a madhouse. It was jammed with hundreds of shrieking children. They all pressed toward one of the aisles. Some kind of demonstration was going on.
>
> —FRANK CONROY

Check It Out Now read this narrative.

> His father's voice awakened him. Stretching his back against the mattress, he looked over at his parents' end of the sleeping porch. He saw that his mother was up too, though he could tell that it was still early. He lay on his back quietly. He watched a spider that dangled on a golden, shining thread from the rolled canvas of the blinds. The spider came down in tiny jerks, its legs wriggling, and went up again in the beam of sun. Then, from the other room, he heard his father's voice, loud and cheerful.
>
> —WALLACE STEGNER

- Are the events in this narrative in chronological order? Explain your answer.

Try Your Skill   Below are two lists of pre-writing notes for narratives. Read them. Then write the incidents in each list in chronological order.

1. (a) In the town square, we saw a statue of an insect—the boll weevil.
   (b) The farmers decided that the boll weevil had actually helped them, and they erected the statue.
   (c) Last fall, my family visited Enterprise, Alabama.
   (d) Then boll weevils came and destroyed the cotton crop.
   (e) We learned that many years ago, most of the people in Enterprise had grown cotton for a living.
   (f) When that happened, the farmers tried raising peanuts and made more money than before.

2. (a) A gorilla walked into a restaurant and ordered a sandwich.
   (b) When the waitress took the gorilla's money, she said that she did not often see gorillas in the restaurant.
   (c) The gorilla told her that at those prices she would not see many more, either.
   (d) The waitress was shocked to see a gorilla but brought the sandwich.
   (e) Because the waitress thought that a gorilla would be easily fooled, she charged it twenty dollars.

Keep This in Mind

- Use chronological order to organize the incidents in a narrative paragraph.

Now Write   Take out the pre-writing notes you made in the last lesson, **The Big Event.** Arrange the notes in chronological order. Save your organized pre-writing notes in your folder.

Insiders and Outsiders

Pre-Writing: Choosing a Point of View

Here's the Idea Who knows more about an avalanche? A person watching it from a distance or a person in its path? Actually, both know something about the avalanche, but they know different things. They have different **points of view.**

There are also different points of view in writing. "Point of view" means the eyes and mind through which something is written. In your narrative paragraph, you might use the first-person point of view or the third-person point of view.

When you use the **first-person point of view,** you use the pronoun *I*. *I* is the narrator, the one who tells the story. *I* tells only what he or she can see. This first-person narrator cannot tell what anyone else is thinking or feeling. You will probably use the first-person point of view when you write about something that happened to you. You can also write from the first-person point of view in a story that you make up.

Another point of view you can use is the **third-person point of view.** When you write from this point of view, you use the pronouns *he* and *she*. The narrator can see and hear everything that goes on, but the narrator is not a character in the story. You will probably use the third-person point of view to write about something that happened to other people.

Choosing a point of view is an important decision when you write a narrative. Once you have chosen an appropriate point of view, stick to it. Otherwise, your reader will be confused.

Check It Out Read the following two paragraphs.

1   At the base camp, the group of climbers was watching for the return of Andrew. He had not returned from what should have been an easy climb to check supplies on the ridge. Finally, Andrew's red parka was sighted. Far above him, however, a wall

of snow suddenly broke away from a rocky ledge. The massive cloud of snow roared down the mountain.

2   Near the top of the snowbound ridge the air was sharp and cold. I was exhausted. I was afraid I would not make it back to the camp. Just as I began my crawl to the tents, I heard an awesome rumbling. I felt my heart racing, but I was too weak to move.

- From which point of view is each paragraph written?
- Which words helped you identify each point of view?

Try Your Skill   Use these pre-writing notes to write two paragraphs. Write one paragraph from the first-person point of view. Write the other from the third-person point of view.

Waded across the river on a sandbar
Water got deeper and deeper
Up to knees, chest, chin
Halfway across, tripped on a hidden rock
Fell, was swept underwater
Was carried downstream

Keep This in Mind

- Point of view is the eyes and mind through which a story is told.
- The pronoun *I* signals the first-person point of view. *I* is the narrator.
- The pronouns *he* and *she* signal the third-person point of view. The narrator is not a part of the story.
- Choose a point of view and stick to it.

Now Write   Review your pre-writing notes and choose a point of view for your narrative paragraph. Write *third person* or *first person* at the end of your notes. Save your notes.

Good Timing

Writing the First Draft

Here's the Idea In the last three lessons you have been planning your narrative paragraph. Now you are ready to write the first draft. As you write, you want to make sure that the order of the incidents that tell your story is clear.

You can make the order of incidents clear by using transitions. These are words and phrases that carry a reader from one thought to the next. Here is a list of transitional words and phrases that are often used in narratives.

first	while	at the beginning	before
then	soon	in the middle	after
next	later	afterwards	by the time
finally	when	at the end	at the same time

This list shows some of the most common transitional words and phrases. However, there are many others. For example, you might use such phrases as *at that instant, before noon, two weeks later,* or *next year.* Whenever you write a narrative, use a variety of transitional words and phrases to show chronological order.

Check It Out Read the following narrative paragraph.

He sat motionless a minute longer. Then, his hand crept nervously onto the table and pushed a button. The room darkened. At that moment, a long section of wall became transparent, revealing a dozen silvery models of spaceships. He quickly touched another button. The models faded. At the same time the opposite wall showed the construction of a neutron-drive spaceship. A few seconds later, when he pushed a third button, another picture showed a section of Earth's surface. It also revealed in the far distance, the tiny reddish globe of Mars. Finally, a tiny rocket rose from the section of Earth and spread its silvery sails. —FRITZ LEIBER

- Find the transitional words and phrases in this paragraph. Do they help to make the order of the incidents clear?

Try Your Skill   Read the following paragraph. Then rewrite the paragraph, adding transitions to show the order of the incidents.

The taxi driver stomped on the gas pedal. The taxi sped up Grand Avenue. We reached a busy intersection. A bus pulled out in front of us. The driver slammed on the brakes. The taxi driver rolled down his window and hollered at the bus driver.

Keep This in Mind

- Transitional words and phrases make the order of events in a narrative clear.
- In a narrative, include transitions to show chronological order.

Now Write   Write the first draft of your narrative paragraph. Use transitional words and phrases to show your reader the order of events. Save your first draft in your folder.

Instant Replay

Revising Your Narrative Paragraph

Here's the Idea   You have completed the first draft of your narrative paragraph. Read it over carefully. How well does it tell your story? How might your first draft be improved? Now is the time to carefully revise what you have written. As you revise your first draft, keep these questions in mind.

1. Will the topic sentence capture the reader's interest?
2. Have I included good sensory details?
3. Are the incidents arranged in chronological order?
4. Did I stick to one point of view throughout my story?
5. Have I used transitional words and phrases to show time order?

As you revise your paragraph, you may see other ways to improve the narrative. A good way to make your writing interesting and lively is to use strong, specific verbs.

A verb is a word that tells what happens or what is. The strongest verbs show action, like *gallop, snarl,* and *climb.* Weak verbs just show state of being, like *is, become,* and *seems.* As you improve your narrative, change weak state-of-being verbs to strong action verbs whenever possible. For example, suppose you wrote "Jerry was in the pool." You could make this sentence more interesting by revising it to "Jerry swam across the pool," or "Jerry dove into the pool."

The verbs you use should be as specific as possible. Specific verbs give your reader a clear picture of the action you are describing. You might replace a general verb like *moved* with a more specific one like *raced, crawled, danced,* or *leaped.*

Remember to proofread your paragraph. Find and correct any errors in grammar, capitalization, punctuation, and spelling.

Check It Out Read the following paragraph.

> I tramped today through miles of open, snow-clad country. I slipped in the ruts of the road or ploughed through the drifts in the fields with such a sense of adventure as I cannot describe.
>
> —DAVID GRAYSON

- Pick out strong specific verbs in the paragraph. How do they make the paragraph come to life?

Try Your Skill Revise the following narrative paragraph. Improve it by adding transitions and by replacing the verbs in italics with stronger, more specific verbs.

> Katrina *was* on the diving board. She *looked* straight ahead. She *put* her arms out in front of her. She *put* her arms down and bounced on the board. She *put* her arms up. She *was* in the air, arching forward. She *went* toward the water. She entered the water. The crowd *was* loud.

Keep This in Mind

- Review your narrative paragraph to make it clear, lively, and interesting.
- Arrange the details in chronological order.
- Use transitions to show time order.
- Replace weak, general verbs with strong, specific ones.
- Keep the same point of view throughout the story.

Now Write Revise your narrative paragraph, following the guidelines in this lesson. Then make a final copy. Proofread your paragraph one last time. Save your narrative in your folder.

The Descriptive Paragraph

Part 1 **In a Sense**
Pre-Writing: Gathering Sensory Details

Part 2 **Words in Space**
Pre-Writing: Using Spatial Order

Part 3 **In the Mood**
Pre-Writing: Creating Mood

Part 4 **In Place**
Writing the First Draft

Part 5 **Share the Experience**
Revising Your Descriptive Paragraph

Part 1

In a Sense

Pre-Writing: Gathering Sensory Details

Here's the Idea   Have you ever experienced something that impressed you so much you wanted to share your experience with others? Maybe it was your first view of the Grand Canyon. It may have been a wonderful Mexican dinner you had at a friend's house. Perhaps it was a sleek imported sports car you saw at the auto show. One way you can share these kinds of experiences is by writing **descriptive paragraphs.**

The purpose of a descriptive paragraph is to describe a person, place, or thing as clearly and as vividly as possible. To accomplish this goal, you will want to develop your description with sensory details. Sensory details tell about things that can be seen, heard, touched, smelled, or tasted.

Sensory details can be gathered in two ways. The best way is through personal observation. Suppose you wanted to describe the lion house at the zoo. You would go to the lion house with a notebook and observe. You would write down everything you saw, heard, touched, smelled, or tasted.

Another way to gather sensory details is by searching your memory. Suppose you were at the Grand Canyon last summer and now you want to describe what you saw. You would think back to your experience and write down as many sensory details as you can remember. What did the colors look like? Was the air scented by the nearby pine forests? Could you hear any animals at night? If you have photos of the canyon, look them over carefully. They may jog your memory.

Check It Out   Read this descriptive paragraph.

> The brittle air stung Sonja's cheeks as her sleigh glided along the snow-packed road. As the horse clip-clopped homeward, his brass harness bells jingled. White steam puffed from his nostrils.

The sleigh whooshed past black, leafless trees silhouetted against the sunset. Through the blur of branches, Sonja watched the last light turn the sky rosy-pink. Woodsmoke drifted toward her, and the familiar scent told her they were almost home.

- Did the writer use sensory details? Which senses do the details appeal to? Give examples.

Try Your Skill   Choose one of the following places to describe. Make a list of sensory details related to the place you choose.

a neighborhood restaurant
the school library
inside a pet store
a subway on a hot day
your kitchen

Keep This in Mind

- In a description, use sensory details to describe your subject.
- Gather sensory details through observation or from memory.

Now Write   Think of a person, place, or thing that you would like to describe. Be sure you can describe your subject in one paragraph. Make a list of sensory details that tell about your subject. You can gather these details from personal observation or from your memory. Save your pre-writing notes in your folder.

Words in Space

Pre-Writing: Using Spatial Order

Here's the Idea   In a well-written description, the writer and the reader share an experience. If the writer is describing a forest, the reader should notice the details of the forest just as the writer noticed them. That is why it is so important that the details that develop a description be well organized.

One way to organize a description is to use **spatial order.** In other words, you arrange your details in the order that you want your reader to notice them. Begin with whatever detail you want your reader to notice first. This might be the most obvious detail or the detail that made the biggest impression on you. Then arrange the other details in an order that shows how they are related to the first detail. You might describe your subject from top to bottom, right to left, near to far, and so on.

Suppose that you want to describe a harbor scene. You might want to begin by focusing the reader's attention on a large oil tanker in the middle of the harbor. Then you might have your description move around this central subject. Mention the two tugboats near the ship. Then describe the darkening sky above it. Finally, describe the sun setting in the distance. You will have arranged your description in spatial order.

Check It Out   Read the following description of a mountain.

Our mountain has towered above the village since time began. Its base is densely wooded with birches and fir trees. Where trees had been cut down long ago, wild blackberries grow. A well-beaten path winds upwards through woods and berry patches, all the way to the tree line. Shrubs sparsely cover the middle of our mountain, and above that nothing grows. The top third of it is gray granite, deeply etched with crevasses, and a challenge for us young climbers.

- How does this description use spatial order?

Try Your Skill   Turn to your folder. Find the list of details that you gathered for **Try Your Skill** in Part 1 of this section. Arrange those details in spatial order, the order in which you want your reader to notice them.

Keep This in Mind

- Use spatial order to organize the pre-writing notes for your description.
- Arrange your details in the order that you want your reader to notice them.

Now Write   Use spatial order to organize the pre-writing notes for your descriptive paragraph. Arrange your sensory details in the order that you want your reader to notice them. Save your organized notes in your folder.

In the Mood

Pre-Writing: Creating Mood

Here's the Idea   People have many different moods. They express their moods by the way they talk, look, and act. Writing has mood, too. **Mood** is the feeling suggested by a piece of writing. A story might suggest a feeling of excitement or mystery. A description might suggest great beauty or great sadness. Writers express mood through the language they use.

Suppose two writers are describing a house. The first writer wants to suggest a feeling of sadness and despair. She might use words like these:

Nouns	Adjectives	Verbs	Adverbs
shack	dingy	litters	haphazardly
box	musty	tilts	dimly
shanty	drab	crumbles	loosely

A second writer wants to suggest a feeling of cheer and brightness. He might use words like these:

Nouns	Adjectives	Verbs	Adverbs
household	trim	nestles	snugly
homestead	sunny	protects	comfortably
cottage	cozy	surrounds	warmly

As you plan your description, think about the mood you want to create. Then make lists of nouns, adjectives, verbs, and adverbs you might use to help you suggest that feeling.

Check It Out   Read the following descriptive paragraph.

The kitchen, worn by our boots and lives, was scruffy, cluttered, and warm. The furniture seemed never the same but was shuffled around each day. A fireplace crackled with coal and beech twigs. The mantel was littered with fine old china, and oddly shaped potatoes. On the floor were strips of muddy matting. The windows were filled with plants. The walls were hung with several clocks and calendars. There were also six tables of different sizes, some stuffed armchairs, four boxes, books and papers on every chair, a sofa for cats, and a piano for dust and photographs.　　　　　　　　　　　　　　　　　—LAURIE LEE

- What feeling is suggested by this paragraph?
- What words help to create that mood?

Try Your Skill　Suppose you wanted to describe a park. Winter is over and spring is in bloom. There are children in the playground. A group of girls is playing softball on the diamond. People are walking along the pathways.

The feeling you want to suggest in your description is one of beauty and rebirth. Make a list of nouns, adjectives, verbs, and adverbs that will help you to create this mood. Compare your list with those of your classmates.

Keep This in Mind

- *Mood* is the feeling suggested by a piece of writing.
- Writers express mood through the language they use.

Now Write　Think about the descriptive paragraph you have been planning. What kind of feeling would you like the paragraph to suggest to your reader? Make a list of nouns, adjectives, verbs, and adverbs to help you create that mood. List as many words as you can think of. When you write your first draft, choose the best words from your list to help you create the mood you want in your paragraph. Save your list in your folder.

In Place

Writing the First Draft

Here's the Idea   Throughout this chapter, you have been planning your descriptive paragraph. After you gathered your sensory details, you arranged them in the order that you wanted the reader to notice them. Now you can write your first draft. How can you make the order of your details clear?

There are certain transitional words and phrases that can help you to make spatial order clear. These words and phrases help the reader to get a clear picture of the subject.

Here are some familiar transitional words and phrases.

above	beside	in the center	over
against	between	low	side by side
alongside	by	near	south
ahead of	down	next to	to the left
at the end of	east	north	to the right
at the top	facing	on	toward
around	high	on the bottom	throughout
behind	in	on the corner	under
below	in back of	on the edge	up
beneath	in front of	outside	west

Check It Out   Read the following paragraph.

The dashboard of my sister's sports car looks like the instrument panel of a jumbo jet. Directly in the middle of the dashboard is a large green radio dial. Below the dial are the knobs for volume and fine tuning. To the left of the radio are the levers and switches for the headlights, wipers, and air vents. In front of the driver are the speedometer and the gauges for gas, engine temperature, and oil. Below the dashboard is a stereo tape deck.

• Which words and phrases show spatial order?

Try Your Skill   Look at the illustration below. Decide how you would describe it to another person. Write a description of the illustration. Include each shape, and use specific transitional words and phrases. Make the spatial order clear.

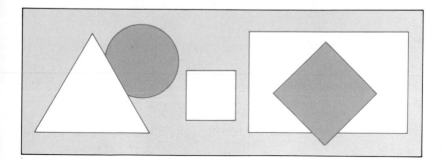

Now Write   Write the first draft of your descriptive paragraph. Follow your organized pre-writing notes as you write. Use transitional words and phrases to make the spatial order clear. Remember, you want the reader to share your experience, so make your description as clear as possible. As you write, use words from the list you developed in the last lesson to create a specific mood. Save your first draft in your folder.

Share the Experience

Revising Your Descriptive Paragraph

Here's the Idea When you have completed the first draft of your descriptive paragraph, revise it to make it clearer and more interesting. Try to make it come alive for the reader. Ask yourself these questions as you revise your work.

1. Have I written an interesting and informative topic sentence?

2. Have I developed my description with good sensory details?

3. Have I used spatial order to arrange the details?

4. Have I included transitional words and phrases to make the spatial order clear?

5. Have I used words to suggest a particular feeling or mood?

When you have revised the ideas, the language, and the organization of your description, proofread it. Find and correct any errors in grammar, capitalization, punctuation, and spelling.

Check It Out Read the following description of a Sunday breakfast.

> I love Sunday breakfasts in our family. Every one of them is the same. The family gathers around the kitchen table in the center of the room. The six of us sit there for hours, eating and talking. The old maple table is jammed with plates of chewy bagels, cream cheese, fried eggs, and smoked fish. From one corner of the table drifts the strong, rich aroma of coffee. Over the center of the table hangs a lamp with a stained glass shade. It is in the center that we spread out the Sunday newspapers that we all read at the end of our meal.

- Does the topic sentence introduce the subject of the paragraph?
- What sensory details has the writer included?
- Has the writer used transitional words and phrases? What are they?
- Does this paragraph suggest mood? Explain your answer.

Try Your Skill   Here is the first draft of a descriptive paragraph. As you read it, notice that it does not paint a very vivid word picture. It has strong verbs, but it also needs strong adjectives to bring the scene to life. Revise the paragraph, adding strong adjectives. Replace any weak, overused adjectives with more vivid ones.

It was a bad flood. A wall of water burst through the dam upstream. It tore down the valley and wiped out crops for miles. The water ripped out trees by their roots. It swept away cars and even houses with its force. The damage was unbelievable. A trail of destruction was left by the flood.

Keep This in Mind

- Include strong sensory details in your description.
- Organize your details in the order that you want your reader to notice them.
- Include transitions that show spatial order.
- Use language that helps you to create a particular mood.

Now Write   Use the guidelines in this lesson to revise the first draft of your descriptive paragraph. Include language to create a mood and to make your description more vivid. When your description is as clear and as interesting as you can make it, proofread it. Then make a final copy. Save your descriptive paragraph in your folder.

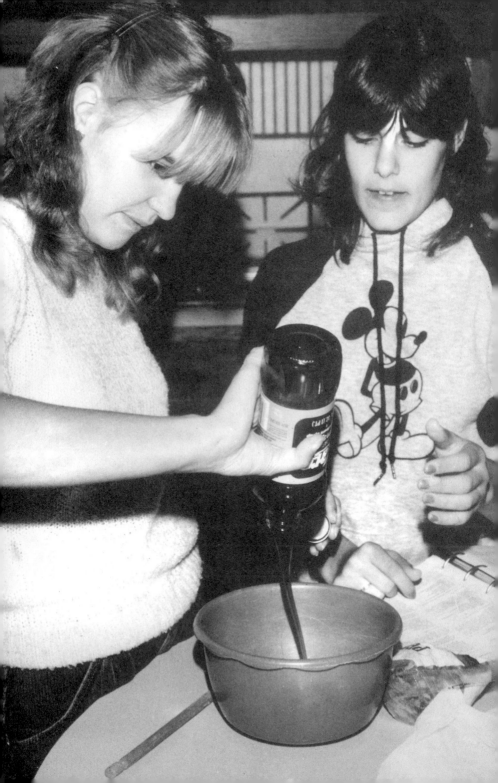

The Explanatory Paragraph

Telling *How*

Part 1 **Get into It**
Pre-Writing: Explaining a Process

Part 2 **One, Two, Three**
Pre-Writing: Using Step-by-Step Order

Part 3 **Follow the Plan**
Writing the First Draft

Part 4 **Clearing Things Up**
Revising Your Explanatory *How* Paragraph

Get into It

Pre-Writing: Explaining a Process

Here's the Idea An explanatory paragraph explains. It explains *why* something should be so or *what* something is. An explanatory paragraph can also explain *how* to do something or *how* something happens or works.

An explanatory *how* paragraph may explain how to do a science experiment or a type of math problem. An explanatory paragraph may also explain how a pacemaker works or how stars are formed. You can write an explanatory *how* paragraph to explain any process or skill that you know well. Be sure, though, that you choose a topic that can be developed well in one paragraph.

When you have chosen your topic, you need to list the details that will develop your paragraph. Because you are explaining a process, you must write down all the steps in that process. Suppose your topic was "How Paper Is Made." Your pre-writing notes would include each step in the process, from cutting down the trees to finishing the product.

As you write your pre-writing notes, make sure that you include all of the steps in the process. Write each step clearly and simply, so that your explanation is easy to understand.

Check It Out Read this explanatory *how* paragraph.

There is a technique to the difficult art of hitting a baseball. First, enter the batter's box. Place your feet to maintain your balance. Next, grip the bat firmly and hold it off your shoulder. After that, concentrate on watching the pitch. Swing the bat evenly to meet the ball. Be sure to follow through with your swing. Finally, as the ball sails deep into the outfield, head to first base.

- What process is explained? Is each step explained clearly and simply?

Try Your Skill   Take the first pre-writing step in writing an explanatory *how* paragraph. Brainstorm for some processes that you know well enough to explain, step-by-step. Your topics might be about how to do something, how something happens, or how something works. Make a list of at least five topics that you could write about. Be sure each topic is narrow enough to be covered well in one paragraph. Save your list of topics in your folder.

Keep This in Mind
- An explanatory *how* paragraph explains how to do something or how something happens or works.
- Make sure that all of the steps in the process are included.
- Explain each step clearly and simply.

Now Write   Look back at the topics you developed in **Try Your Skill.** Choose one topic that you could explain well in a paragraph. Write the topic at the top of a piece of paper. Then, list the steps that are involved in the process. Don't leave out any steps. Write each step clearly and simply. Save your pre-writing notes in your folder.

One, Two, Three

Pre-Writing: Using Step-by-Step Order

Here's the Idea   Imagine a cook trying to make a seafood gumbo from a recipe that is all mixed up. Think about a mechanic fixing the brakes on a car using instructions that have several missing steps. In both cases, the results might be disastrous. A written explanation of how to do something or how something happens or works must be complete. It must also be carefully organized. Then the reader will be able to follow the explanation easily.

The best way to organize your explanatory *how* paragraph is to use **step-by-step order.** This is the order in which a process happens or should be done. You begin with the first step in the process and then proceed, step by step, to the last step. Step-by-step order is similar to chronological order. In both cases, details are organized according to a natural time order.

As you organize your pre-writing notes, check again to make sure that no steps are missing.

Check It Out   Read this paragraph.

A bacon-lettuce-and-tomato sandwich is delicious and easy to make. First, slowly cook several pieces of bacon until crisp. Second, spread a thin layer of mayonnaise on two pieces of toast. Next, place lettuce on one piece of toast. After that, put tomato slices on the lettuce and bacon strips over the tomatoes. Finally, close and slice your sandwich. Enjoy your lunch!

- Does this explanatory *how* paragraph explain a process step by step?
- What transitions are used to show step-by-step order?

Try Your Skill Here are two sets of instructions that are confused. Organize the steps in each process into step-by-step order.

How To Take a Photograph

1. Focus on your subject, holding the camera steady.
2. Choose your subject.
3. Gently squeeze the shutter release button.
4. Stand so that the source of light is behind you.

How To Make Pancakes

1. When the edges bubble up, flip each pancake over.
2. Beat the batter until it's smooth.
3. Lightly grease a frying pan and preheat it.
4. Serve with butter, maple syrup, or powdered sugar.
5. First, combine two cups of pancake mix, one egg, and one and one-third cups of milk.
6. Cook pancakes until golden brown.
7. Pour small amounts of batter into the pan.

Keep This in Mind

- In an explanatory *how* paragraph, explain the process step by step.
- Arrange the steps in the order that they happen or should be done.

Now Write Organize your pre-writing notes into step-by-step order. Arrange the steps in the order that they happen or should be done. Make sure you haven't left out any important steps. Save your organized pre-writing notes in your folder.

Follow the Plan

Writing the First Draft

Here's the Idea   A builder follows a plan when he or she builds a house. The architect's blueprints are used as a guide. A writer needs a plan to follow, too. As you begin to write your explanatory *how* paragraph, follow your organized pre-writing notes.

To begin your first draft, write a good topic sentence. The topic sentence should tell the reader what process you will be explaining. It should also be interesting enough to capture your reader's attention.

Next, develop your topic sentence by explaining the steps in the process. Write each step clearly and simply. To help the reader follow the step-by-step order of your process, use transitions as you write. Study this list of transitional words and phrases. They are often used in explanatory *how* paragraphs.

first	when	the next step
second	afterwards	at the same time
third	later	while
as	after that	following that
next	at last	the last step
then	finally	

You needn't limit yourself to just these examples. Almost any word or phrase that refers to time order may be helpful to you when you are writing your explanatory *how* paragraph.

Check It Out   Read this paragraph.

You can make an old pair of leather shoes look new by dyeing them a different color. First, pick the new color you want. Second, be sure the leather is clean. Protect the surface you are working on with paper or plastic. Then, using a clean applicator, cover the whole surface of the shoes with leather dye. Make your strokes smooth and even. When the first coat is dry, see if a second coat is needed. After the second coat has completely dried, apply shoe polish and buff the shoes. The last step is to admire your new pair of shoes!

- What process does this explanatory *how* paragraph explain?
- What transitional words and phrases are used to show step-by-step order?

Try Your Skill   The following explanatory paragraph does not have a topic sentence. It also lacks transitions. Rewrite the paragraph, adding a topic sentence and good transitions.

In the bottom of the bag put the heavy items like canned soup, frozen foods, and bottles of ketchup. Wrap frozen foods separately in plastic. Use soft items, such as paper towels, to separate and protect breakable jars and bottles. Put non-crushable, lighter-weight foods like cereal boxes in the bag. Put fresh produce, such as broccoli and apples, in the bag. Place fragile foods, such as strawberries and potato chips, carefully on top.

Keep This in Mind

- In an explanatory *how* paragraph, begin with a good topic sentence. Then explain the process step by step.
- Use transitional words and phrases to show step-by-step order.

Now Write   Write the first draft of your explanatory *how* paragraph. Follow your organized pre-writing notes. Be sure your paragraph has a good topic sentence. Use transitions that show step-by-step order. Save your first draft in your folder.

Clearing Things Up

Revising Your Explanatory *How* Paragraph

Here's the Idea   To make an explanatory paragraph clear enough for your reader to follow easily, it is important that you revise it carefully. Read your first draft as if someone else had written it. Ask yourself these questions:

1. Does the topic sentence introduce the process?
2. Is every important step of the process included?
3. Are the steps arranged in the order that they happen or should be done?
4. Is each step explained clearly and simply?
5. Do the transitions help to lead the reader smoothly from one step of the process to the next?

When you are satisfied with your ideas and organization, proofread your paragraph. Correct any errors in grammar, capitalization, punctuation, and spelling. Then you are ready to write your final copy.

Check It Out   Read the following paragraph.

If you are patient, you can become an expert at photographing animals in their natural setting. First, decide what animal you want to photograph. Then dress in camouflage colors and go quietly to the area where the animal lives. The first time you go there, just sit quietly for half an hour so the animal can observe you. If you are still and make no sudden moves, it will see that you are not to be feared. On the second day, return to the area and move in a little closer. Have your camera around your neck, but don't use it. Just sit quietly again. Continue this procedure for several days, each day moving just a little closer. It may take a week or two to get really close to your subject. The final reward for your patience will be good close-up photographs.

- Does the topic sentence introduce the process?
- Are the steps arranged in the order they should be done?
- What transitions did the writer use?

Try Your Skill Read the following rough draft of an explanatory paragraph. Revise it, making sure to add a good topic sentence and clear transitions. Be sure to proofread the paragraph.

> You take a lump of wet clay. Roll the clay on the table until it is in long ropes. Before you roll the clay, knead it until all the bubbles are out of it. Second, coil the ropes round and round. Now press them together. Now smooth the coils. Now shape your vase or pot. Third, glaze it. Before you glaze it, let it dry for several days. You are ready to put it into a special oven called a kiln. You will have a piece of pottery that you made yourself.

Keep This in Mind

- Revise your explanatory paragraph so that each step is explained clearly and simply.
- Include all the steps in the process. Arrange them in step-by-step order.
- Use transitional words and phrases to show the order of each step.

Now Write Use the guidelines in this lesson to revise the first draft of your explanatory *how* paragraph. Don't forget to proofread your explanation. Correct any errors in grammar and mechanics. Then make a final copy of your paragraph. Save it in your folder.

The Explanatory Paragraph

Telling *Why*

Part 1 **A Matter of Opinion**
Pre-writing: Developing an Opinion

Part 2 **For What Reasons?**
Pre-Writing: Organizing an Opinion

Part 3 **Tryout**
Writing the First Draft

Part 4 **A Good Look**
Revising Your Explanatory *Why* Paragraph

A Matter of Opinion

Pre-Writing: Developing an Opinion

Here's the Idea   Not everyone thinks alike. People have different opinions about the world they live in, and they like to express those opinions. People write letters to newspapers and magazines. Newspapers and television stations print and broadcast editorials. People participate in debates. All of these activities have one purpose: the expression of opinions.

You have opinions, too. A good way for you to express your opinion is to write an explanatory *why* paragraph. This kind of paragraph presents an opinion, and then gives reasons to support the opinion. For example, an explanatory *why* paragraph might explain why the public library needs a new building.

The first pre-writing step in planning an explanatory paragraph is to choose an opinion that you want to express. Think about the world around you. Then think about your family, your school, your neighborhood, your after-school job. Look through newspapers and magazines. Ask yourself how you feel about the issues of the day. You will find that you have opinions about many topics. Choose one of them to write about.

When you have chosen an opinion, write a sentence that states your opinion clearly and directly. It can serve as the topic sentence of your paragraph, where it will make your opinion clear to the reader. Read these statements of opinion.

> Computer courses should be required of all high school students.

> The national speed limit should remain at fifty-five miles per hour.

Now you must gather information to back up your opinion. Make a list of accurate facts and logical reasons that support your view. To learn more about the importance of supporting your opinions, see pages 254–255.

Check It Out   Read the following statement of opinion and the list of reasons that support it.

Swimming is the best sport.
   –It can be enjoyed all year round.
   –It exercises every muscle in your body.
   –People of all ages can swim.
   –Physically handicapped people can enjoy the sport.
   –It can save your life.
   –It is one of the best ways to get in shape.

   • Do these reasons explain *why?* Are they clear and logical?

Try Your Skill   Here are five statements of opinion. Choose one. List five facts or reasons to support the opinion. Share your reasons with your classmates. Save your list.

A pet can benefit a person or family.
The holiday season is too commercial.
_____ is the best musical performer or group.
_____ is a great vacation spot.

Keep This in Mind

   • An explanatory *why* paragraph presents your opinion about something.
   • Support your opinion with logical reasons and accurate facts.

Now Write   Think of an issue that you feel strongly about. Write a clear, direct statement of your opinion. Then list facts or reasons to support your opinion. Be sure your reasons are logical and your facts accurate. Save your work.

For What Reasons?

Pre-Writing: Organizing an Opinion

Here's the Idea   At the end of a trial, the defense lawyer talks to the jury. The lawyer states his or her opinion—that the person on trial is innocent. Then the lawyer reminds the jury about all the reasons that have been presented during the trial to support that opinion. The lawyer saves the most important reasons for the end of the talk. That way, the jury goes to make its decision with the strongest points fresh in their minds.

When you write your explanatory *why* paragraph, the order in which you present your facts and reasons is important, too. The most effective order is to save your strongest reason for last. Arrange your facts and reasons from the least important idea to the most important. This type of organization is called the **order of importance.**

For example, in a paragraph about the need for a new recreation center, you might include the following reasons:

1. Recreation gives people pleasure.
2. Recreation strengthens you physically and mentally.
3. If people can gather together to enjoy recreation, life in the entire neighborhood will be improved.

You can see that these reasons have been listed in order, from the least important idea to the most important. You will leave your readers with the most powerful reason that supports your opinion.

Check It Out   Look at these notes for an explanatory *why* paragraph.

Opinion: Sunlight is the fuel of the future.
Reasons: costs less, does not pollute, is plentiful

Now read the completed paragraph:

> Sunlight can fuel our future. First, sunlight is free. Therefore, there will be only a few major expenses, such as the cost of solar converters. More importantly, the use of sunlight will not pollute the environment. In that way, sunlight is superior to oil and coal. Most importantly, the sun is a never-ending source of energy. Supplies of oil and coal, on the other hand, are being used up. The sun is an energy source on which we can always depend.

- Notice the order of the reasons in this paragraph. Did the writer organize them from the least important idea to the most important? Explain your answer.

Try Your Skill Reread the list of facts or reasons that you wrote for **Try Your Skill** in Part 1, **A Matter of Opinion.** Organize your list from the least important idea to the most important.

Keep This in Mind

- Organize the facts and reasons that support your opinion from the least important idea to the most important.

Now Write Look at the statement of opinion and list of reasons that you wrote in **A Matter of Opinion.** Organize your list from the least important idea to the most important. Save your organized pre-writing notes in your folder.

Tryout

Writing the First Draft

Here's the Idea Once you have made and organized your pre-writing notes, you can begin your first draft.

Begin your explanatory *why* paragraph by stating your opinion in the topic sentence. You may want to use the statement of opinion you wrote in your pre-writing notes. State your opinion clearly and directly. Do not say, "I think that . . . ," or, "In my opinion . . . ." The reader already knows it is your opinion.

After the topic sentence is written, turn your reasons and facts into sentences that support and develop it. Remember to present your reasons in the order of their importance.

Good transitions make your paragraph clear and interesting. There are two kinds of transitions. One kind helps you to state your reasons and facts. The second helps you to show their order of importance. Here are some examples.

To State Reasons or Facts:	because, so, since, if, therefore, as a result
To Put in Order of Importance:	the first reason, second, more important, most important, finally

After you have presented and supported your opinion, you should sum up your ideas with a strong ending sentence.

Check It Out Read the following paragraph.

Movie theaters are awful places to watch movies. In the first place, they have become very expensive. It can cost up to five dollars for one person to see a movie. Second, popular movies attract crowds. Consequently, moviegoers have to stand in long lines waiting to buy tickets. Also, many movie theaters are messy. Therefore, patrons have to put up with sticky floors and popcorn-filled aisles. Most important, though, is the fact that many moviegoers are rude. They talk and laugh throughout the movie. Why would anyone want to wait in line and pay good money to be treated rudely?

- Does the topic sentence state an opinion clearly?
- What transitional words and phrases help to show reasons? Which help to show the order of importance?
- Does the ending sentence sum up the writer's opinion and reasons?

Try Your Skill   Here is a set of pre-writing notes for an explanatory *why* paragraph. Write a good topic sentence. Organize the reasons in order of importance. Then write a good ending sentence.

Opinion: Fad diets are dangerous.

Reasons: permanent damage to health may result, good balance of foods is necessary for growth, weight usually returns after dieting

Keep This in Mind

- State your opinion clearly and directly in the topic sentence.
- Use good transitional words and phrases. These can help you to present your reasons and show the order of their importance.
- Sum up your opinion and reasons in your ending sentence.

Now Write   Write the first draft of your explanatory *why* paragraph. Include a good topic sentence. Use appropriate transitions. Write an ending sentence that sums up your opinion and reasons. Save your first draft in your folder.

A Good Look

Revising Your Explanatory *Why* Paragraph

Here's the Idea   Now that you have written your first draft, take a good look at it. Is your opinion as clear as you can make it? Are your reasons convincing? Ask yourself the following questions as you revise your first draft.

1. Does the topic sentence state my opinion clearly and directly?

2. Have I given enough logical reasons and accurate facts to support my opinion?

3. Are the reasons organized in the most effective order, from the least important idea to the most important?

4. Have I used transitions to present my reasons and make their order clear?

5. Have I ended the paragraph with a strong ending sentence that sums up my opinion and my reasons?

After you have revised your ideas and your organization, proofread your paragraph. Correct any errors in grammar, capitalization, punctuation, and spelling.

Check It Out   Read this first draft of an explanatory *why* paragraph.

In my opinion, the president of the U. S. should get just one six-year time in office. Four years isnt enough time to get programs through. Two more years would let the president help the country more. Another thing is how the president wouldnt have to spend the last year of his or her term campaigning. So the president could spend more time running the country. Most important, if the president didn't have to worry about getting reelected, they wouldn't have to do favors for anybody. The

146

president could just do the best job and then walk away. You wouldn't owe nobody nothing. That's my opinion.

- What specific things in this first draft would you improve? Use the guidelines in this lesson and the other revising skills you have learned to help you decide.

Try Your Skill · Use the guidelines in this lesson and your class discussion to revise the paragraph in **Check It Out.** Improve the topic sentence. Make the sentences clearer and more interesting. Add transitions. Write a better ending sentence. Remember to proofread the paragraph.

Keep This in Mind

- In an explanatory *why* paragraph, state your opinion clearly and directly in your topic sentence.
- Support your opinion with logical reasons and accurate facts.
- Use transitional words and phrases to state your reasons and facts and to show the order of their importance.
- Write an ending sentence that sums up your opinion and reasons.

Now Write Revise your own explanatory *why* paragraph. Follow the guidelines in this lesson. When you think your paragraph is the best it can be, make a final copy. Save your explanatory *why* paragraph in your folder.

The Explanatory Paragraph
Telling *What*

Part 1 **What's the Point?**
Pre-Writing: Learning About Definitions

Part 2 **What Do You Say?**
Pre-Writing: Developing a Definition

Part 3 **The Plain Truth**
Writing the First Draft

Part 4 **Checkpoint**
Revising Your Definition

What's the Point?

Pre-Writing: Learning About Definitions

Here's the Idea   Do you realize how often you are asked to define things? In class, you may be asked to explain *decimal, adverb, glacier,* or *monarchy.* At home, a grandparent may ask you to explain *break dancing.* A younger brother or sister might want to know what *geography* is.

An explanatory *what* paragraph is a definition of something. The subject might be a real thing, such as a *kiln* or a *laser.* The subject might also be a term or an idea, such as *recession* or *courage.*

A good definition does three things.

1. It presents the subject to be defined.
2. It puts the subject in the general class to which it belongs.
3. It shows the particular characteristics of the subject.

Imagine that you want to define *canary.* First, you would write that a canary is a bird. That puts canary in its general class. Now you have to show how a canary is different from other birds. You could write that a canary is a small bird. That's a start. That shows how canaries are different from large birds, such as pigeons, ravens, and parrots. However, there are many other small birds besides canaries. So you might add that a canary is a songbird. Because there are many small songbirds, you could add that canaries are greenish-yellow in color. Because there are other small, greenish-yellow songbirds, you also add that they are often kept as pets. Now you have a good definition.

> A canary is a small songbird, greenish-yellow in color, that is often kept as a pet.

Read the following explanation.

A shark is a large ocean fish covered with small, toothlike scales. Sharks have been on earth more than 350 million years. There are about 250 kinds of sharks, but only thirty kinds are dangerous to people. Sharks eat other fish, but they will gobble anything they can. That is an easy task because sharks have more than four rows of teeth, and they grow a new set every two weeks. Sharks have few enemies in the sea.

- Is the topic sentence a definition?
- Does the paragraph define the general class and the particular characteristics of the subject?

Try Your Skill Read these two explanatory *what* paragraphs. Explain which paragraph is a good definition.

1   A peacock has a huge tail. The tail has very long, beautiful feathers. They are different colors, like green and blue. It looks like a big fan. The bird's neck is long, and it walks strangely. You can see one at the zoo.

2   A mobile is a piece of sculpture that moves. It can be made of almost any materials. Most are made from metal, wood, or paper. The sculpture is designed to balance on slender threads or wires. With even a little breeze the mobile turns in the air.

Keep This in Mind

- An explanatory *what* paragraph explains what something is.
- A good definition puts a subject in its general class. Then it shows the particular characteristics of the subject.

Now Write Brainstorm a list of objects, terms, and ideas that you could define in an explanatory *what* paragraph. Try to list at least ten possible subjects. Save your list in your folder.

What Do You Say?

Pre-Writing: Developing a Definition

Here's the Idea   You have learned that there are many different subjects you can define in an explanatory *what* paragraph. You can define an object, such as a *banjo,* a *silo,* an *evergreen,* or a *zircon.* You can also define terms or ideas, such as *checkmate, fear, offside,* or *success.*

In an explanatory *what* paragraph, the subject is defined in the topic sentence. The rest of the paragraph develops that definition as completely as possible. To write a good definition, you must make some pre-writing notes about your subject. You may want to do some research. You may also want to use your own experience.

Some definitions are best developed in a detailed, factual way. For instance, if you define *evergreen,* you will probably use facts and statistics to develop your definition. You may want to use an encyclopedia or a dictionary in order to develop a complete and accurate definition.

Other definitions can best be developed in a detailed, but more personal way. For instance, if you define *courage,* you will probably use specific details from your own experience.

After you have completed your pre-writing notes, organize them. Explanatory *what* paragraphs are usually organized from the general to the specific. In other words, begin with a general statement like, "An artichoke is an odd-looking vegetable that resembles a thistle." Then continue with specific details that help the reader to understand just what an artichoke is.

Check It Out   Read the following definition of a leader.

> A leader is a person who directs or guides a group. A leader takes control of a situation and sets a good example for his or her

followers. My scoutmaster is a leader who shows me how to survive in the woods and how to depend on my own skills. The captain of my basketball team is a leader who sets up the game plan and directs our play. My parents are leaders who show me how to live as a useful family member and a good citizen. I am able to follow the valuable example of these leaders in my life.

- Does this paragraph develop the definition given in the topic sentence?
- Is the paragraph developed by personal details or by facts and statistics?

Try Your Skill Choose two topics from the columns below. For each of your choices, develop a short list of pre-writing notes. You may need to use a dictionary or encyclopedia to help you. You may also want to use personal experiences. Save your notes.

friendship	free throw	jazz
loneliness	arcade	socialism
hero	Middle Ages	word processor
family	haiku	balance beam

Keep This in Mind

- The topic sentence of an explanatory *what* paragraph gives a definition of the subject.
- An explanatory *what* paragraph is developed with personal details or facts and statistics.

Now Write Refer to the list of topics you brainstormed in Part 1. Choose one of those topics to be the subject of your explanatory *what* paragraph. Develop some pre-writing notes about your topic. Use research or your own personal experience. Save your pre-writing notes in your folder.

The Plain Truth

Writing the First Draft

Here's the Idea The topic sentence of a paragraph tells what the paragraph is all about. In an explanatory *what* paragraph, the topic sentence has other work to do as well. First, it gives the word to be defined. Then, it puts that word into its general class. Finally, the topic sentence tells a little about the particular characteristics of the subject. Here is an example of a good topic sentence for a definition.

> An orthodontist is a dentist who straightens teeth.

When you have a clear statement of definition as your topic sentence, expand the definition. Remember, your topic sentence is a general statement. Now you must develop that statement by adding specific details. Use the personal details or facts and statistics that you gathered and organized during prewriting.

Finish your explanatory *what* paragraph with a strong ending sentence. Leave your reader with an interesting thought or detail about your subject. Here is an example of a strong ending sentence.

> Thanks to my orthodontist, I've rediscovered how nice it is to smile.

Check It Out Read this explanatory *what* paragraph.

> Pride is a feeling of respect for yourself. A person may feel pride for doing a job well. He or she may be proud of overcoming some difficult problems, or of scoring well in a game or on a test. Someone may feel pride after helping another person or after refusing to get involved in something wrong. Being proud of yourself is another way of showing you believe in yourself.

- Does this paragraph have a good topic sentence that does three things? What are they?
- What details has the writer included to develop the definition?
- Is there a strong ending sentence? Explain your answer.

Try Your Skill   Look at the two lists of pre-writing notes that you developed for **Try Your Skill** in Part 2. Write a topic sentence for each group of notes. Be sure each topic sentence gives the word to be defined, the general class of the word, and some of its particular characteristics.

Keep This in Mind

- In an explanatory *what* paragraph, define the subject clearly and completely in the topic sentence.
- Develop the definition in the body of the paragraph.
- Write a strong ending sentence to conclude the paragraph.

Now Write   Write the first draft of your explanatory *what* paragraph. Be sure the topic sentence defines your subject. Include details from your pre-writing notes to develop your definition. Write a strong ending sentence. Save your first draft in your folder.

Checkpoint

Revising Your Definition

Here's the Idea   If you want your definition to be helpful to your reader, it must be as clear and complete as possible. Careful revision will help you to improve your paragraph. As you revise your paragraph, ask yourself these questions:

1. Does my topic sentence present and define my subject?
2. Have I included enough information to develop my definition completely?
3. Is the information organized from the general to the specific?
4. Does my ending sentence leave the reader with an interesting thought or detail about my subject?

After you have revised your definition, proofread your paragraph. Correct any errors in grammar, capitalization, punctuation, and spelling.

Check It Out   Read this revised explanatory *what* paragraph.

The lantern festival is *part of the New Year* a celebration. *in Malaysia. The celebration lasts* It goes for *15* *fifteen* days. The *Festival* lantern part comes at the end. Children *parade* go through the streets with *lighted* lanterns. *The children* They are led by a *colorful, papier-maché* dragon. Inside the dragon are men who make it dance and wriggle. *The Malaysian people believe that* The lanterns help people to find the *heavenly* spirits that fly by the light of the first full moon, *of the new year.* *them*

- How has the writer improved the topic sentence?
- Is the paragraph organized from the general to the specific? Explain.
- How else has the writer improved this paragraph?

Try Your Skill   Revise this rough draft of an explanatory *why* paragraph.

Ice hockey is where you have a hockey stick and a puck. Each team has six players. One is the goalie. He or she wears a mask and lots of protective clothing. The players skate back and forth, between the two goals. Sometimes they get in fights. The team who hits the puck inside the goal the most times wins.

Keep This in Mind

- In an explanatory *what* paragraph, define the subject in the topic sentence.
- Organize your details from the general to the specific.
- Include a strong ending sentence.

Now Write   Revise your explanatory *what* paragraph. Follow the guidelines in this lesson. Be sure to proofread your paragraph. Then make a final copy. Save your paragraph in your folder.

A Look at Compositions

Part 1 **Compose Yourself**
Learning About Compositions

Part 2 **First Steps**
Pre-Writing: Developing a Composition

Part 3 **Group Effort**
Pre-Writing: Organizing a Composition

Part 4 **Experiment!**
Writing the First Draft

Part 5 **Fine-Tuning**
Revising Your Composition

Part 6 **Name Game**
Writing a Title

Part 7 **Home Free**
The Final Copy

Part 8 **Don't Forget**
Guidelines for Writing a Composition

Compose Yourself

Learning About Compositions

Here's the Idea   You have learned that a paragraph is a group of sentences that develops one main idea. Sometimes, you may have a long story to tell or a detailed description to present. When you want to write about an idea that is too long for one paragraph, you can write a composition.

A **composition** is a group of paragraphs that develops one main idea. Like a paragraph, a composition can be narrative, descriptive, or explanatory.

There are three parts to a composition: an introduction, a body, and a conclusion. The **introduction** is the part that tells what the composition will be about. In this way the introduction is similar to the topic sentence of a paragraph.

The **body** of the composition is the part that develops the main idea. In a narrative, the body contains the events that tell the story. In a description, the body contains the sensory details that help the reader to share an experience. In an explanation, the body contains steps in a process, reasons, or details that define.

The **conclusion** brings the composition to a close. The conclusion may sum up the important ideas in the composition.

Check It Out   Read the following composition.

Grandpa's Pond

My grandfather lived in a small house in New Orleans. The house itself was ordinary, but the yard held a surprise. Grandpa had planted and cultivated the entire yard. It resembled a miniature wilderness. The highlight of this scene was a goldfish pond.

The pond was nestled in a shady corner of the yard, beneath a rock mountain that my grandfather made. The water was clear and cool. Beneath the surface the fish swam lazily. Some of them were scarlet, and some were silver-white. Only a few were actually gold.

The lovely green yard and the fish pond were special to Grandpa. His natural creations gave him pleasure and something to care for. He would take his chair into the yard and sit for hours, reading and resting.

Grandpa died six years ago, and his house was sold. The people who bought his house have continued to keep the pond alive. Their children play around the edge of the pond just as my cousins and I did. The pond still brings pleasure. I cannot imagine a better mark for Grandfather to have left on the world.

- What is the main idea of this composition?
- Which part of the composition is the introduction?
- Which is the body? Which is the conclusion?

Try Your Skill Which part of a composition is this?

The ancient Persians gave New Year's gifts of eggs, symbols of productiveness. The Celtic priests of what is now England gave the people mistletoe, which was considered sacred.

Keep This in Mind

- A composition develops one main idea in several paragraphs.
- A composition should have three parts: an introduction, a body, and a conclusion.

Now Write Answer these questions in complete sentences.

1. What is a composition?
2. When would you write a composition?
3. What are the three parts of a composition?

First Steps

Pre-Writing: Developing a Composition

Here's the Idea   When you write a composition, you will use many of the same skills you learned for writing paragraphs. You will choose a subject, gather details, organize your information, write a first draft, and revise.

Choosing a subject is the first step. Look in your journal. Do some reading. Page through a book of photographs. Try brainstorming. Choose a subject that is interesting to you and that you know something about. Work with ideas that are too broad to be covered well in a single paragraph. However, don't choose a subject that is too general.

For example, an explanation of how to eat with chopsticks is just right for a single paragraph. A description of a Japanese dinner, however, is much too broad to be covered well in only a few sentences. At the same time, the topics *Japan* or *Japanese Customs* are too general even for a composition.

When you have chosen a good subject, look for ideas to develop it. These ideas might include sensory details, specific examples, facts and statistics, or incidents or anecdotes. You can discover these ideas by brainstorming, through research, or from your own experiences. To learn more about gathering ideas, see pages 78–79.

Check It Out   Read the following composition.

A Japanese Dinner

When I lived in Baltimore, I had a Japanese friend named Takao Matsudo. One day I had a chance to learn about some of the differences in our ways of life. Takao had invited me to have dinner with his family.

Mr. and Mrs. Matsudo greeted me at the door. They invited me into the kitchen to show me how they cooked each dish we would eat. They showed me the preparation of the stir-fried beef and vegetables, of the rice, and of the green tea.

When we sat down to eat, the Matsudos asked if I wanted to use a fork or chopsticks. I saw that the Matsudos all had chopsticks. Foolishly, I asked for chopsticks, too. I was sure that I could master them. Takao showed me how to hold them. I awkwardly practiced wiggling the chopsticks in the air.

The meal began, but I was struggling. I kept trying to pick up a small morsel of beef. I could not get hold of it. Finally, I grasped my chopsticks more firmly. My tight grasp on the chopsticks made them snap past each other. The food shot across the table.

I stammered an apology over and over again. I was totally flustered, but the Matsudos were not. Mr. Matsudo told me that such problems were common when people first tried chopsticks. After that night, I was invited to many other dinners at the Matsudos' house. Happily, I learned to master chopsticks.

- Was the writer able to cover the topic well?

Try Your Skill   Suppose you were going to write a composition about a dinner at your house. What kinds of details would you choose? Think about the subject. Then make pre-writing notes. Write as many details as you can think of.

Keep This in Mind

- Choose a topic that can be handled well in several paragraphs.
- Develop your composition with sensory details, specific examples, facts and statistics, or incidents or anecdotes.

Now Write   Choose a topic you can write about in a composition. Use the information in this lesson to guide your choice. Be sure to choose a topic that interests you. Make some pre-writing notes. Save your notes in your folder.

Group Effort

Pre-Writing: Organizing a Composition

Here's the Idea   When you learned to write a paragraph, you discovered how important it was to organize your ideas. It is important to organize the ideas for a composition, too. However, because a composition is made up of several paragraphs, you have to organize your ideas a little differently.

Look over your pre-writing notes. Try to find two or three main ideas that run through the notes. For example, suppose your composition is a narrative about going to your first high-school dance. As you read through your pre-writing notes, you might discover that your ideas seem to be about three things: getting a date, getting ready for the dance, and the dance itself. These are your main ideas.

Next, group the details in your notes around the main idea that they tell about. For instance, asking Rob to go to the dance would fall under the main idea "getting a date." Details about the way the gym was decorated, the music the band played, and the refreshments served would be grouped around "the dance itself." Each main idea, along with the details grouped around it, will become a paragraph in the body of your composition.

When all of your details are grouped around main ideas, you are ready to choose an order in which to present them. Choose a method of organization that suits the type of composition you are writing. Because the composition about the school dance is a narrative, you will want to present your ideas in chronological order. First, arrange the main ideas in chronological order. Then do the same for the details grouped around each main idea. You will then have a clearly organized set of notes.

To learn more about the different ways to organize your pre-writing notes, see pages 88–89.

Check It Out   Here are some pre-writing notes for a descriptive composition about a supermarket.

shiny purple eggplants	10 kinds of cheese
"Fisherman's Wharf"	bok choy cabbage
creamy pasta salad	silvery rainbow trout
heaping tub of clams	"the Garden Spot"
black, green, and stuffed olives	cole slaw
ripe, red tomatoes	red emperor grapes
"Deli Delites"	huge Mexican shrimp
live lobsters in a tank	sliced baked ham

- What three main ideas do you find in these notes?
- What details would you group around each main idea?
- Do you see how each group of notes could be developed into a paragraph?

Try Your Skill   Make a list of ten or twelve details that come to your mind about one of these topics:

a shopping mall   our school   winter sports

Try to group the details around two or three main ideas.

Now Write   Organize the pre-writing notes you have made for your composition. Group your details around two or three main ideas. Then organize the main ideas and the details grouped around them. Save your organized notes in your folder.

Experiment!

Writing the First Draft

Here's the Idea   You have already planned and organized your composition. Now you are ready to write the first draft.

As you write your first draft, keep your purpose for writing in mind. Are you telling a story, describing a person, or explaining an opinion? If you know what you are trying to accomplish, you stand a better chance of reaching your goal.

Don't forget your audience as you write. Be sure you include the kind of information your audience needs in order to understand and enjoy your composition. Also, remember to choose language that suits your readers.

Make sure that each part of your composition fulfills its purpose. Write an interesting introductory paragraph that tells the reader what you are writing about. In the body paragraphs, develop your composition clearly and completely with good details. Conclude your composition with a strong ending paragraph that brings your composition to a close.

Finally, keep in mind that a first draft is really a discovery draft. Feel free to experiment with your ideas, your organization, and your language. Add new details. Leave out details that do not help you to develop your main idea. Move sentences and paragraphs around if that helps you to express your ideas more clearly. You will have time during the third step of the writing process to correct any mistakes.

Check It Out   Read this first draft.

Stanley Park

My family went to Canada last summer. Our favorite day was spent in Stanley Park. In Vancouver, B.C. It has 1,000 acres of forests, trails, beautiful views, restaurants. And even a zoo and a aquarum.

Stanley Park is a peninsula. Surrounded by water. A lot of it is a dense forest. There is a large pond called Lost Lagoon. Trails wind through the forest and a path goes around the lagoon. Dad liked the rose garden the best. Mom and I watched a cricket match. We all enjoyed walking along the seawall that surrounds the park. Its seven miles long we didn't walk the whole thing. You can get beautiful views of the city the ocean and the mountains. Dad took my picture by the totem poles.

We spent the afternoon at the zoo and the Aquarum. We watched the monkeys and polar bears. Peacocks were walking around. A lot of people had British accents. In the Aquarum we saw amazing sea creatures. The best part was the killer whale show.

That night we ate at a beautiful restaurant in the park. We had a view of the Pacific Ocean. All of us ate fresh samon it is a local specialty. After dinner we went to a concert by the Nylons. Their a fantastic group from Toronto.

Stanley Park is the greatest park. At least that I've been to. I hope I can go back sometime. Youd love it to.

- Does each part of the composition fulfill its purpose?
- Did the writer include enough details?

Try Your Skill   Look again at the first draft in **Check It Out.** Write five things about it that make it a good composition. Then write five things you think need to be improved.

Keep This in Mind

- Your first draft is a discovery draft. Experiment with your ideas, organization, and language.

Now Write   Use your organized pre-writing notes to write the first draft of your composition. Keep your purpose and audience in mind as you write. Be sure your composition has an introduction, a body, and a conclusion. Save your first draft.

Fine-Tuning

Revising Your Composition

Here's the Idea When your first draft is complete, put it away for a day or two. Then reread it. As you do, you will most likely see ways to improve what you have written. You will probably move some words around. You will add words, take out some, and look for errors in grammar and mechanics.

As you revise your first draft, ask yourself these questions.

1. Have I included enough details to develop my topic?
2. Are there any unrelated details that should be taken out?
3. Have I organized my details around two or three main ideas?
4. Will my introductory paragraph capture the reader's attention? Does it tell the reader what my composition is about?
5. Does each paragraph in the body tell about one main idea?
6. Have I arranged my paragraphs and the ideas within them logically?
7. Have I used transitional words and phrases to lead the reader from one idea to the next?
8. Have I used strong and specific verbs? Have I used vivid adjectives?
9. Have I written a good conclusion that sums up my ideas?

Check It Out Here is part of the first draft of a composition that is in the process of revision.

- In what specific ways have these paragraphs been improved?

My family went to ^Western^ Canada last summer. Our favorite day was spent ^at^ ~~in~~ Stanley Park. ~~In Vancouver, B.C.~~ ^British Columbia.^ It has 1,000 acres of forests, trails, beautiful views, restaurants, ^Stanley Park^ And even a zoo and a~~n~~ aquar^i^um. ^The park is a great tourist attraction.^

Stanley Park is a peninsula, Surrounded by water. ~~A lot of~~ ^much^ it is a dense ^evergreen^ forest. There is a large pond called Lost Lagoon. ^the park^ ^Near^ Trails wind through the forest and a path goes around the lagoon. ^Dad enjoyed the roses while^ ~~Dad~~ ~~liked the~~ ^the lagoon is a^ rose garden. ~~the best.~~ Mom and I watched a cricket match. ^Then^ We all enjoyed walking ~~around~~ ^along^ the seawall that surrounds the park. Its seven miles long ^but^ we didn't walk the ^entire length of it.^ ~~whole thing.~~ ^The^ ^park has^ You ~~can get~~ beautiful views of the city, the ocean, and the mountains.

Dad took my picture by the totem poles. ^Before we ate our picnic lunch,^

Try Your Skill   Use the guidelines in this lesson to revise the last three paragraphs of the composition about Stanley Park. Compare your revision with those of your classmates.

Keep This in Mind

- Revise your composition to improve your ideas, your organization, and your word choice.
- Proofread your composition to correct any errors in grammar and mechanics.

Now Write   Revise the first draft of your composition. Ask yourself the questions in **Here's the Idea** as you revise. Save your revised composition in your folder.

Name Game

Writing a Title

Here's the Idea You have to make many decisions when you write. You decide whether to write a narrative, a description, or an explanation. You choose a topic. You choose the right kind of details to develop your topic. You select specific words that express your ideas exactly. Writing is a series of such decisions.

For some of your writing, you will also need to write a title that expresses your idea. Most short pieces of writing, such as paragraphs, do not usually have a title. However, most longer pieces of writing, such as compositions and reports, need a title.

A title will probably be the last thing you write. However, a title is the first thing your reader will notice. That is why a good title should attract your reader's interest and attention. A good title should also suggest the main idea of your writing. A good title may be simple and clear, like "To Build a Fire." A good title may sometimes be surprising, like "The Night the Ghost Got In."

Check It Out Look at the following titles of stories you may have read.

"The Rocking Donkey"   "The Lady, or the Tiger?"
"Father's Day"   "After Twenty Years"
"The Colt"   "A Man Who Had No Eyes"
"The Possibility of Evil" "How John Boscoe Outsung the
                           Devil"

- Are these good titles? Why?

Try Your Skill   Choose four of the following composition topics. Write two possible titles for each topic. Write titles that express the idea of the topic in a simple or surprising way.

1. a story about a family that suddenly becomes wealthy
2. a report on famous zoos
3. a description of your favorite city
4. an explanation of how to make chicken soup
5. a report on solar energy
6. a story about two friends who quarrel
7. an explanation of what thunder is
8. an explanation of why _____ is a good movie

Keep This in Mind

- Write a title for compositions and reports.
- A good title should attract a reader's interest.
- A good title should suggest the main idea of your writing.

Now Write   Write four or five titles that would suit your composition. Be sure each title is interesting and suggests your main idea. Think about the titles you have written. Then, choose one. Write it at the top of your revised composition. Save your composition in your folder.

Home Free

The Final Copy

Here's the Idea   After the first draft of your composition has been completely revised, it is time to write the final copy. This copy should be neat, clean, and as free of errors as you can make it.

Write your final copy on clean, white, lined paper. Always use a pen, and not a pencil. If you want to, you may type your paper. In the upper right-hand corner of your paper, put your name, the subject, and the date. On the second line of your paper, write the title of your composition. Remember to center the title.

Copy each line of your composition carefully. Leave at least one inch on the right and left sides of your paper. Leave at least one line blank at the bottom of your paper. Write on only one side of a sheet of paper. If you need more than one sheet, number every sheet after the first one. Write the number of each page at the very top in the center.

When you are done, proofread your final copy one last time. Neatly correct any errors that you find. If you have to cross out more than three or four errors on a page, you should write that page again.

Check It Out   On the following page is the beginning of the final copy of the composition about Stanley Park.

- Does this final copy follow the form given in this lesson?

Jorge Diaz
English
December 9, 1985

Stanley Park
My family went to western Canada last summer. Our favorite day was spent at Stanley Park in Vancouver, British Columbia. Stanley Park has 1,000 acres of forests, trails, beautiful views, restaurants, and even a zoo and an aquarium. The park is a great tourist attraction.

Try Your Skill   Make a chart that lists all of the guidelines for writing a final copy. Tape this chart somewhere in your folder or notebook where you can refer to it easily.

Keep This in Mind
- The final copy of your composition should be neat and free of errors.

Now Write   Write the final copy of your composition. Proofread it carefully. Be sure it is neat and free of errors. Save your final copy in your folder.

Don't Forget

Guidelines for Writing a Composition

In the next few sections of this book, you will be writing many different kinds of compositions. Whatever type of composition you write, however, the process of writing will remain the same. Here is a checklist of the steps to follow when you write a composition. Refer to these guidelines often as you write your compositions.

Guidelines for Writing a Composition

Pre-Writing

- Choose a topic that interests you and that you know something about.
- Narrow the topic so that you can cover it well in the length of your composition.
- Gather details to develop your topic.
- Group similar details around two or three main ideas.
- Organize your details into an order that suits the type of composition you are writing.

Writing the First Draft

- Begin your composition with an interesting introductory paragraph. It should tell your reader what your composition is about.
- After your introduction, present the body of your composition. Use your organized details to develop your topic. Each group of details will become a paragraph in the body of your composition.
- Use transitional words and phrases to lead your readers from one idea to the next.

- Add, take out, and reorganize your ideas if you need to.
- Finish your composition with a concluding paragraph that sums up your ideas.
- Add an interesting title to your composition.

Revising

- Be sure your composition has an introduction, a body, and a conclusion.
- Check to see that you have included enough details to develop your topic.
- Organize the paragraphs and the ideas within them logically.
- Be sure the topic sentence of each paragraph presents the main idea of that paragraph.
- Use transitional words to make your ideas flow smoothly.
- Make sure you have used vivid language.
- Proofread to find and correct errors in grammar, capitalization, punctuation, and spelling.

Final Copy

- Rewrite your composition neatly in ink on white, lined paper.
- Write your name, subject, and the date in the upper right-hand corner of your paper.
- Proofread your final copy one last time. Neatly correct any errors you find.

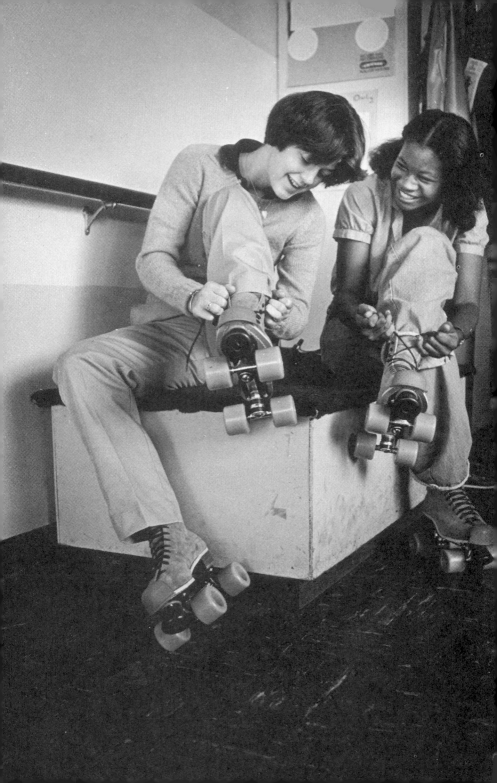

The Narrative Composition

Part 1 **Have You Heard?**
Pre-Writing: Planning a Story

Part 2 **I Can See It Now!**
Pre-Writing: Plotting a Story

Part 3 **What a View!**
Pre-Writing: Choosing a Point of View

Part 4 **It Goes Like This**
Writing the First Draft

Part 5 **Speak Up**
The First Draft: Dialogue

Part 6 **The Time Is Right**
The First Draft: Transitions

Part 7 **The Grand Finale**
Revising Your Narrative Composition

Have You Heard?

Pre-Writing: Planning a Story

Here's the Idea Have you ever greeted a friend with, "Have you heard about . . . ?" After catching your friend's attention, you probably went on to tell about something important that had just happened.

When you tell your story on paper rather than in person, you are writing a **narrative composition.** Many narratives are based on real life experiences. Others may be entirely made-up, written from the writer's imagination.

Whether a story is true or imaginary, it does more than just relate a series of events. It also makes a point. It tells how people think, feel, act, or react in a specific situation.

Every narrative contains certain basic elements. These elements are the setting, the characters, the plot, and the conflict.

The **setting** tells the reader when and where the story takes place. The time can be in the past, the present, or the future. The place can be a deserted beach, a crowded city street, or a classroom in the year 2000.

The **characters** are those directly involved in the action of the story. Characters may be people or animals.

The **plot** includes all the events that happen within a story. At the heart of the plot is the **conflict.** The conflict is the major difficulty that a character faces. It can be a struggle that one character has with another character. It can also be a struggle with a personal problem or with the forces of nature. The conflict creates interest and involves the reader in your story.

Check It Out Look at these pre-writing notes.

Setting: at home, last year
Characters: my little sister Tracy and me

> Plot: Tracy enters a radio contest to win circus tickets, she asks for my help in painting her entry
>
> Conflict: me with myself (personal problem)—should I help her?

- Does this writing plan contain all the elements necessary for a narrative composition?

Try Your Skill   Alone, or with a writing partner, develop pre-writing notes for a narrative about "the first day of high school." Make decisions about each basic element of the narrative. What is the setting? Who are your characters? What is the plot? What will the conflict be?

Keep This in Mind

- A narrative composition tells a story that makes a point.
- The elements of a narrative include setting, characters, plot, and conflict.

Now Write   Think of ideas for some stories you would like to tell. Is there something you remember from your childhood that you could turn into a story? Is there a hard choice you have had to make or some obstacle you have overcome? Think of conflicts that you have had with other people. Is there a story idea in your struggles? Is there a distant time or a foreign setting that sparks your imagination?

Write your answers to these questions and other ideas you have for real and imaginary stories on a piece of paper. Label the page "Story File." Save your story file in your folder.

I Can See It Now!

Pre-Writing: Plotting a Story

Here's the Idea   Every story, real or imaginary, is made up of many small incidents or events called the **plot.** After you decide on an idea for your narrative composition, you are ready to write down all of the events that will tell your story.

As you list these events, try to add some specific details that will make your story more interesting. Jot down names, dates, places, and times. You will also want to add sensory details to your list. Be sure all of your details are accurate.

The events in a story should be arranged in the order in which they occurred. This is called **chronological order.** First organize your notes. Then decide which events are important enough to be covered in separate paragraphs. Also decide which events can be combined into one paragraph.

You may want to interrupt the natural, chronological flow of events to tell the reader about an event that took place before the events in your story. Then you will use a **flashback.**

A flashback tells about an earlier event that says something about the present conflict. Suppose you were writing about an important race between you and an opponent. You might want to insert a scene from an earlier contest when your opponent had beaten you. This flashback could help explain to your reader why you want to win so badly.

Check It Out   Here are the plot details for the story about Tracy.

1. WRKT contest for Super Circus tickets
2. Tracy decides to enter and to win
3. Tracy made dozens of paintings—some pretty bad
4. wanted me to paint so she could win
5. wanted to help her but decided I shouldn't

6. remembered my soapbox derby contest when Dad wouldn't help me
7. learned that doing my best by myself was what mattered
8. Tracy's drawing won!

- Are these events arranged in chronological order?
- Do the notes contain a flashback? What is it?
- Do you see how these notes have been divided into paragraphs?

Try Your Skill   Here is part of a narrative composition. Create a flashback that would help to explain why Ann is so angry now. Rewrite this situation and insert your flashback.

Ann was so upset that she could hardly see the numbers on the combination lock of her gym locker. She couldn't believe what her best friend Carla had done to her! Ann jerked open her locker and pulled out her jacket and Spanish notebook. It looked like she'd be doing homework Saturday night, after all.

Keep This in Mind

- The events and details in a narrative composition are usually arranged in chronological order.
- You may interrupt the chronological flow of events to insert a flashback. A flashback is a scene from the past that helps to explain something in the present.

Now Write   Choose a topic from the story file you started in the last lesson, **Have You Heard?** Write down the story element, setting, characters, plot, and conflict. Make specific notes about each one. Then list the events that make up your story. Arrange these events in chronological order. If a flashback could add meaning to an event in your story, add it to your list. Save your notes in your folder.

What a View!

Pre-Writing: Choosing a Point of View

Here's the Idea Who will tell your narrative for you? Before you write, you must select a narrator. The narrator is the person who tells the story. In order to choose a narrator, you must decide on a point of view.

When you use the **first-person point of view,** your story is told by a character involved in the action. This character is identified by the pronoun *I.* When *I* tells the story, the reader knows only what this character knows. If you are telling a story in which you are one of the characters, the first-person point of view is a natural choice.

When you use the **third-person point of view,** your story is told by a narrator who is not a character in the story. The pronouns *he* and *she* are used. There are two types of third-person point of view. The first type is third-person limited.

In the **third-person limited** point of view, the narrator acts as a reporter who tells only what he or she sees and hears. The reader knows what the characters are thinking or feeling only if they say so themselves.

The second third-person point of view is not limited. It is called **omniscient** (om·ni′·shunt), which means "knowing all things." From this point of view, the narrator not only sees and hears everything, but also knows what every character thinks and feels.

Check It Out Read the following paragraphs. They continue the narrative about Tracy.

> When we reached home, Tracy headed straight for the desk where the paints and paper were stored. She took her supplies to the kitchen table and began painting. All afternoon she kept at it. I had never seen anyone concentrate so hard.

Just before supper, Tracy stopped working. She stared at the papers in front of her and then pushed them aside. She propped her elbows on the table, dropped her chin onto her hands, and started to cry. Tracy moaned that her pictures were no good. I tried to tell her that she was wrong, but Tracy would not believe me. At last she calmed down, but she ate hardly any supper. Afterwards, she came to my room to talk.

- Who is the narrator of this story? How is the narrator identified?
- From what point of view is this narrative composition written? How do you know?

Try Your Skill   Rewrite the paragraphs in **Check It Out,** from another point of view.

Keep This in Mind

- In the first-person point of view, the reader knows only what the narrator, *I,* knows.
- In the third-person limited point of view, the reader knows only what the narrator can see and hear. The narrator does not report thoughts or feelings.
- In the third-person omniscient point of view, the reader learns about the thoughts, feelings, and actions of the characters from the "all-knowing" narrator.

Now Write   Reread your pre-writing notes. Decide on a point of view from which to write your narrative. Write *first-person, third-person limited,* or *third-person omniscient* at the side of your notes. Save your notes in your folder.

It Goes Like This

Writing the First Draft

Here's the Idea   Different types of compositions have different purposes. Some describe, some explain, and some tell stories. All compositions, however, have the same three parts: introduction, body, and conclusion.

In a narrative, the **introduction** presents the characters and sets the scene. As you write your introduction, give specific details about the time and place of the setting. Present the situation that will lead to the conflict. Use the introduction to capture the reader's interest.

The plot is developed in the **body** of the composition. The body includes all the events that tell your story. The body also introduces the story's conflict. The conflict should develop naturally from the story's events. Show the conflict developing through the actions of the characters.

The **conclusion** draws the events of the story to a close. It also settles the conflict. The conclusion should not leave the reader in suspense or with questions in mind. The ending of your story should follow naturally from the events that have come before it. For instance, if your imaginary story is very true-to-life, do not introduce super heroes to "save the day" in the end.

As you write the first draft, follow through with your prewriting decisions. Don't change the point of view. Don't have a character suddenly change his or her personality or attitude unless the change comes from the solution of the conflict.

Check It Out   Read this introduction.

> My favorite family snapshot shows my six-year-old sister Tracy riding an elephant. Tracy's adventure began one day last summer when she and I were shopping at Bernsten's Market. Near the

check-out counter Tracy spotted a poster that showed elephants, lions, and clowns. Radio station WRKT was inviting children to paint pictures that captured the excitement of the circus. The winning artists and their families would receive free tickets when Super Circus came to Dallas. Tracy told me that she was going to be the winner.

- Does the introduction present the main characters?
- Does the introduction include specific details about the setting? What are they?
- Does the introduction set up a situation that will lead to a conflict?

Try Your Skill The following introduction to a narrative composition is incomplete. Although the narrator introduces the main characters, there is little to catch the reader's attention. Rewrite the paragraph. Use your imagination. Include specific details about the characters and a setting. Introduce a situation that could lead to a conflict.

Everyone thinks my older brother is great. As for me, I'm just Jack's younger brother.

Keep This in Mind

- The introduction of a narrative presents the characters, the setting, and the situation that will lead to conflict.
- The body of a narrative develops the plot and conflict of the story.
- The conclusion of a narrative brings the plot to a close and solves the conflict.

Now Write Using your pre-writing notes, write the introduction for your first draft. Include details about characters and setting. Add a situation that will lead to conflict.

Speak Up

The First Draft: Dialogue

Here's the Idea   A **dialogue** is a conversation between two or more characters. Using dialogue is a way to bring characters to life. It is also a way to show what they are like. A polite character might ask, "Excuse me, sir. Could I pass through?" A bully, however, might snap, "Get out of my way, you."

Dialogue can also move your story along. It is a good way to *show* your readers the developing action. Don't have the narrator say "Jenny got into her car and turned the key. The car wouldn't start." Instead, let dialogue reveal the action.

> "There's Jenny getting into her car now," Tom said. He heard the engine sputter and die. "Sounds like her car won't start," he said.

Dialogue always includes **dialogue tags.** A dialogue tag is a short phrase such as *Tina said* or *Rob asked.* Dialogue tags identify the character who is speaking. They also tell how the words are spoken.

Dialogue tags are another way for you to show a character's personality or feelings. Don't always use tags like "he said." Sometimes you can be more precise by writing "she mumbled" or "he insisted" or "Chris snarled."

Always put quotation marks around the speaker's exact words. Begin a new paragraph every time a different speaker talks. For more information about writing dialogue correctly, look at Handbook Section 19 on pages 679–680.

Check It Out   Read the following dialogue. It continues the narrative about Tracy.

> "Will you help me, Greg? I can't do it all by myself," Tracy pleaded.

"Sure you can," I insisted. "The paintings you did this afternoon are really good."

"You're just saying that because you don't want to help me," she cried. "My pictures are terrible. I'm going to tear them up."

I tried to tell Tracy that she shouldn't tear her pictures, that she would feel better about them in the morning.

Tracy screamed, "You don't care if I win or not!"

"I do care," I said softly, "but this is something you have to do by yourself."

- Does this dialogue reveal anything about Tracy and Greg? Does it move the story forward?
- Does the writer use good dialogue tags?

Try Your Skill Rewrite the following dialogue correctly. Substitute better dialogue tags.

Am I tired said Janet I didn't get to bed until midnight. Why were you up so late asked Ron. Janet said I was studying for the big test today. What test said Ron. Don't you remember the history test scheduled for today. Ron said that he had forgotten to study.

Keep This in Mind

- Dialogue can reveal the feelings and the personalities of the characters in a narrative. It can also move the story forward.
- Dialogue tags identify who is speaking and how the words are spoken.

Now Write Continue writing the first draft of your narrative composition. Include some dialogue as your story develops. The dialogue should reveal the personality or feelings of the characters. It should also help to move your story along. Save your writing in your folder.

The Time Is Right

The First Draft: Transitions

Here's the Idea   In narrative compositions, transitions are used for the same reason that they are used in narrative paragraphs. They help to make the order of events clear.

Within a paragraph, transitions form a bridge between sentences. In a composition, transitions also form bridges between paragraphs. They connect the events of one paragraph with those of the next. Transitions also place the events of each paragraph in time. For example, suppose that you wanted to write a composition about an eventful day. If you wrote four paragraphs, they might begin with these transitional phrases: *At breakfast, After lunch, Later that day,* and *Early in the evening.*

Transitions are especially important when you add a flashback. They help to prevent confusion. For example, you could signal the beginning of a flashback with transitional phrases such as *each year, only last week,* or *in the past.* To show your reader that the flashback has ended, you could use a transition such as *now* or *at this moment.*

Check It Out   Read the following paragraphs that continue the narrative about Tracy.

> For the next few days I thought maybe I was being too tough on Tracy. Who would ever find out if I helped her a little? After all, she was only six years old. Besides that, she had been working so hard. Didn't she deserve a little help? Yet, as the contest deadline drew nearer, I still could not convince myself. Finally, I knew that I had to stay out of it, and I knew why. I decided to tell Tracy a story.
>
> Five years ago, I had entered a race. I had been building a racer for a soapbox derby, and I had asked Dad to help me. I was

sure there was no way I could win without his help. When Dad refused to help me, I felt angry at first. Later, however, Dad talked about the faith he had in me. He believed that I should try to do my best. Then I, too, started to believe that I should. Finally, I understood that I had to win or lose all on my own. Doing my best was what really mattered.

- What transitional words and phrases within each paragraph help to carry the reader from one time to another?
- What transition words and phrases between paragraphs help make the time sequence clear?

Try Your Skill   Add a flashback to the following narrative. Use transitional words or phrases that will help your reader to follow the action into and out of the flashback.

I got up and ate my breakfast as usual, but I could not get the basketball game off my mind. I slowly drank my orange juice and wondered what the guys at school would say.

Keep This in Mind

- Use transitional words and phrases to make the order of events clear. Use them within paragraphs and between paragraphs.
- Use transitional words and phrases to signal the beginning and ending of a flashback.

Now Write   Finish writing the first draft of your narrative. Use transitional words and phrases to help you show the order of events. Be sure that your conclusion brings your story to a close and successfully settles the conflict. Save this draft in your folder.

The Grand Finale

Revising Your Narrative Composition

Here's the Idea   The revision stage of the process of writing is your chance to improve your writing. Now you can work to make your narrative as good as it can be.

Read over your first draft several times. As you do, ask yourself the following questions.

1. Does my narrative have a point?
2. Have I introduced the characters and set the scene in my introduction?
3. Is there a conflict at the heart of my story? Is it well developed in the body of my composition?
4. Have I used sensory and specific details to give my readers a clear picture of the action?
5. Have I used a clear time order to present the events?
6. Are flashbacks used effectively?
7. Have I kept the same point of view throughout my story?
8. Does dialogue help move the story along and reveal character traits? Have I used the correct form for writing dialogue?
9. Have I used transitional words and phrases where necessary?
10. Does the conclusion offer a solution for the conflict and bring the events to a close?

After you have finished making improvements in the content and the organization of your story, proofread it. Correct any errors you find in grammar, capitalization, punctuation, and spelling.

Check It Out   Here is the conclusion of the narrative composition about Tracy. The writer has just finished revising it.

A When
∧ Super circus came to Dallas. We were there. Tracy's own
WRONG
drawing of a parade of elephents had been a winner in the
                                              my sister.
contest. I had never been prouder of Tracy. Tracy herself was
                                                    a
alowed to join the parade of circus performers. Tracy set on top
       a   colorful
of the leed elephent and smiled and waved to everyone. I
cheered wildly waving to Tracy all the while. Tracy had done her
                                   special
best, and she would remember her reward for a long time.

- What are some of the improvements that the writer has
  made in this revision?

Try Your Skill   Write a final copy of the paragraph in **Check
It Out.** The writer overlooked two errors when he revised. Be
sure to find and correct them before you write the final copy.

Keep This in Mind

- Revision is an opportunity to review your first
  draft and to make changes in it. Your goal is to
  make your story the best it can be.

Now Write   Revise your narrative composition. Refer to the
guidelines in this lesson. When you are satisfied with the
results, make a final copy. Save your narrative composition in
your folder.

The Descriptive Composition

Part 1 **Show and Tell**
Pre-Writing: Using Sensory Details

Part 2 **Paint a Picture**
Writing the First Draft

Part 3 **See It Through**
The First Draft: Ending a Description

Part 4 **The Final Picture**
Revising Your Descriptive Composition

Show and Tell

Pre-Writing: Using Sensory Details

Here's the Idea   Your senses of smell, hearing, taste, and touch tell you about the world around you. If you use your senses when you write a descriptive composition, your reader will experience through words what you have experienced in real life.

Begin planning your composition by choosing and narrowing a subject. First, select an interesting subject that you would enjoy describing in detail. Make certain you can describe your subject completely in the assigned length of your composition. The subject *Yosemite National Park* is too broad even for a composition. But you could describe a campground or a mountain that you explored in the park.

After you choose your topic, make a list of specific sensory details that describe your subject. Find details that appeal to as many senses as possible. Remember, a good description helps your reader to see, hear, smell, taste, or touch your subject. You can gather your details by observing your subject. You can also work from memory. You might find it helpful to look at a picture of your subject as you list your details.

Now organize your sensory details. First, group your details around a few main ideas. For example, if you are describing a person, you might group your details around looks, clothing, and mannerisms. As your idea groups develop, add other details that occur to you. Each of these idea groups will become a paragraph in your composition.

Next, arrange your main ideas and the details grouped around them in a logical order. The best method for organizing the details in a description is spatial order. Arrange your ideas and details in the order that you want your reader to notice them.

Check It Out   Look at these pre-writing notes.

Topic   The Delicatessen at Saveway Supermarket

red and green striped canopy—colorful display of
tempting foods—aroma makes my mouth water

center and left side of display case
roast beef and hams—spicy sausage smell
cheese (far left)—mild and sharp

right side of display case
vegetable and macaroni salads (bottom row)
fruit, gelatin salads (middle row)—like a rainbow
desserts—pies, puddings, cheesecakes (top row)

shelf above display case
pickle jars (far right)—smell of garlic
Greek olives, clams and egg rolls (middle)
meat slicer (far left)—humming sound

- Notice how spatial order was used to organize details.

Try Your Skill   Choose one of the following topics. Narrow
the topic to a *specific* person, place, or thing. Then make a list
of interesting sensory details. Group your details around a few
main ideas, arranged in spatial order.

a large machine   an unusual animal   an exciting place

Keep This in Mind

- Use sensory details to develop your description.
- Group your details around a few main ideas.
- Use spatial order to organize ideas and details.

Now Write   First, choose and narrow a topic for a descriptive composition. Then, make a list of sensory details to develop your description. Group these details around several
main ideas. Organize your notes in spatial order. Save your
notes.

Paint a Picture

Writing the First Draft

Here's the Idea After you have gathered and organized your sensory details, you are ready to write your first draft. Remember, writing is an ongoing process. You can change your pre-writing plans whenever you need to.

Begin your descriptive composition with an **introduction.** Keep in mind that the introduction in a descriptive composition is like the topic sentence of a descriptive paragraph. The introduction presents the person, place, or thing you are describing. Often, the introduction will also describe the setting.

The **body** of the composition describes your subject. It includes the sensory details you collected. Each paragraph develops one of the idea groups from your organized pre-writing notes.

The **conclusion** is the last paragraph of your descriptive composition. It draws your ideas together and brings the composition to a close.

To lead your reader smoothly from sentence to sentence and from paragraph to paragraph, use transitional words and phrases. Words and phrases such as *on the bottom, around, through, to the left, to the right,* and *next to* help to make the order of your details clear.

Check It Out Here are the introduction and first body paragraph from the description of the delicatessen.

> When it is my turn to plan and prepare a family supper, I head for the delicatessen at the rear of Saveway Supermarket. A red-and-green-striped canopy marks the deli counter. Below the canopy is a long display case. Behind its shiny glass, spread out temptingly, lie the wonders of the deli world. The combined aromas of the wide variety of foods make my mouth water.

Filling center stage are the meats and cheeses. There is a huge slab of nearly-rare roast beef and several large pink, glazed hams. To the left of these are strings of fragrant sausage and speckled salamis. Beside these meats are blocks of cheese, from mild-flavored Gouda to pungent Limburger.

- Does the introduction describe the setting?
- Point out the sensory details. Which senses are included?
- What transitional words and phrases has the writer used to make the order of the details clear?

Try Your Skill   Write the second and third paragraphs for the body of the description of the delicatessen. Use the pre-writing notes on page 195. You may add to them. Be sure your paragraph has a good topic sentence and strong sensory details. Use transitional words and phrases to make the order of your details clear. Share your paragraphs with your class.

Keep This in Mind

- The introduction of a descriptive composition presents the person, place or thing described.
- The body describes the subject. Each paragraph in the body has its own topic sentence and is developed with sensory details.
- The conclusion sums up the description.
- Use transitions between sentences and paragraphs to make spatial order clear.

Now Write   Review the pre-writing notes for the description you planned in the last lesson. Use the sensory details that you gathered and organized to write a first draft of your descriptive composition. Write the introduction and the body. Include good transitions as you write. Save your first draft.

See It Through

The First Draft: Ending a Description

Here's the Idea   A well-written composition needs a strong ending paragraph. This paragraph should sum up the important ideas in the composition.

To write a strong ending, first look back at the topic sentence of each paragraph you have written. Identify the main idea in each sentence. Think about these main ideas as you summarize your description. However, remember that a conclusion should not just repeat what you have already said. Try to express your ideas in a slightly different way.

As you plan your ending paragraph, keep in mind that a good description is not just a list of sensory details. It also should leave your reader with a general feeling or impression about the subject. Is the place you are describing busy and confusing? Is the person kind and sympathetic? Is the object sleek and expensive? In your conclusion, share these feelings and impressions with your reader. They will help you to explain why you found your subject interesting and important.

A good conclusion follows naturally from what has come before it. If you have praised an object throughout your description, don't criticize it in your conclusion. If you have created a feeling of suspense, end on a note of mystery.

Check It Out   Here is the topic sentence of the conclusion of the paragraph about the delicatessen.

> As I wait for my order, my eyes feast on the banquet under glass.

- Does the topic sentence of the conclusion tell you that this paragraph will summarize the main ideas of the composition?

Try Your Skill   Reread the descriptive composition about the delicatessen, including the two paragraphs that you wrote. Write an ending paragraph for this composition. Be sure your ending sums up the important ideas in the description. Give the reader your feelings and impressions about the deli. Remember that an ending paragraph should follow naturally from what has come before. Save your conclusion in your folder.

Keep This in Mind

- In your conclusion, summarize the main ideas in your description.
- Include your feelings about and impressions of the subject.
- Your conclusion should follow naturally from what has come before.

Now Write   Write a conclusion for the composition that you have been writing. Summarize the main ideas in your description. Share with the reader your feelings and impressions about the subject. Save your work in your folder.

The Final Picture

Revising Your Descriptive Composition

Here's the Idea   When you revise your descriptive composition, your goal is to create a vivid word picture There should be enough sensory details to bring your subject to life.

As you reread your first draft, ask yourself these questions.

1. Have I included good sensory details?
2. Are the details arranged in clear spatial order?
3. Have I used transitional words and phrases between and within paragraphs to make the order of my details clear?
4. Does the introduction present the subject of my composition? Will it make the reader want to continue?
5. Does each paragraph have a good topic sentence?
6. Does my conclusion summarize the main ideas in my composition? Does it show how I feel about my subject?

When you are pleased with your ideas and organization, proofread your composition. Correct any errors in grammar, capitalization, punctuation, and spelling.

Check It Out   Here is a paragraph from a descriptive composition. Note the changes the writer made.

> The gymnast stood~~ready. He waited~~ for ~~the~~ signal. His hands~~,~~ *at attention,* ~~ing~~ *a* *from the judges.*
> ~~covered in chalk,~~
> hung~~,~~ at his sides~~,~~ (His uniform was white.) His feet pointed *loosely* *and*
> straight ahead. ~~He stood at attention.~~ His arms and neck were~~,~~ *thick and*
> muscular. ~~He must have worked out with weights.~~ He smiled~~,~~ but
> he looked nervous. A~~,~~ buzzer ~~went off.~~ *Suddenly,* *shattered the silence.*
> *loud*

- In what ways has the writer revised this paragraph? How have these changes improved the paragraph?

Try Your Skill   Below is more of the first draft of the descriptive composition about a gymnast. Continue to revise the composition, following the guidelines in this lesson.

The gymnast got on the trampoline. He jumped up and down he bounced higher and higher. He almost touched the cieling. He did flips, somersaults. He didn't look nervous anymore.

His routine was over. He jumped off the trampoline, he looked over at the judges. His score was posted. It was 9.6. The gymnast smiled and walked to the bench.

Keep This in Mind

- Revise your description to help your reader share your experience. Include details that allow your reader to see, hear, touch, taste, and smell what you did.
- Use spatial order to organize your details. Add transitional words and phrases to make the order of the details clear.
- Be sure your introduction catches your reader's interest. It should also introduce the subject of your composition.
- Write a conclusion that sums up your ideas and leaves your reader with a definite feeling or impression about your subject.

Now Write   Use the guidelines in this lesson to revise the first draft of your descriptive composition. When you have completed your revisions, make a final copy. Proofread your composition one last time. Correct any errors neatly. Save your completed composition in your folder.

The Explanatory Composition

Telling *How*

Part 1 **Talent Show**
Pre-Writing: Planning an Explanation

Part 2 **Follow Me**
Pre-Writing: Using Step-by-Step Order

Part 3 **Marking Time**
Writing the First Draft

Part 4 **Getting It Right**
Revising Your Explanation

Talent Show

Pre-Writing: Planning an Explanation

Here's the Idea   What is your special talent? Do you make the best chocolate-chip cookies in town? Do your friends ask you to show them the latest dance step? Do people seek your help in repairing their stereos or ten-speed bikes?

One way to share your talent or to show your knowledge is by writing an explanatory *how* composition. In this kind of composition, the writer tells the reader how to do something or how something happens or works. In other words, an explanatory *how* composition explains a process.

To write an explanatory *how* composition, you must first select a topic. The process you explain should be one that interests you. Is your hobby computers? You might explain how to design a simple computer game. Do you play baseball? You might write about how to steal second base.

Make sure that your topic can be explained well in the assigned length of your composition. For instance, the subject "how to play football" is too broad. However, a topic limited to a single football skill, such as "the way to make a tackle" is specific. It could be explained well in several paragraphs.

The pre-writing notes you develop for your topic should list all the steps in the process. The list should also include any materials, tools, or ingredients required. Take the time to think carefully about the process you are going to explain. Don't overlook any steps. Write each step simply and clearly.

Check It Out   Read these pre-writing notes.

How To Make a Mobile

1. Collect materials.
   wire, cardboard, tape, paper clips, string, pliers, scissors, wire clippers

2. Prepare mobile.
    cut wire, form loops, and bend wire
    cut cardboard, attach to wire
    find point of balance, bend with pliers
    repeat the process
3. Hang mobile.
    put two sections together—hang mobile from ceiling

- Do these notes list all the necessary steps in the process? Do the notes include materials needed?

Try Your Skill   Choose one of the following topics for an explanatory *how* composition. Decide how you would develop an explanation. Make a set of pre-writing notes. List the steps in the process. Be sure to include any necessary materials.

how to make brownies	how to wrap a present
how hail is formed	how a jet engine works
how to take good notes	how to make new friends

Keep This in Mind

- An explanatory *how* composition explains a process. It may explain how to do something or how something happens or works.
- To develop the details for your pre-writing notes, list the steps in the process. Also list any materials, tools, or ingredients required.
- State each step clearly and simply.

Now Write   Think about some processes that you know well and that you would like to explain. Then, choose a topic for your explanatory *how* composition. Narrow your topic so that it can be explained well in the assigned length of your composition. Make a list of pre-writing details. These will include all the important steps in the process and all the necessary materials. Save your pre-writing notes in your folder.

Follow Me

Pre-Writing: Using Step-by-Step Order

Here's the Idea   Do you know how many steps it takes to program a robot to make toast with jelly? About forty steps are required to direct the robot just to find the jelly and the bread! If a step is missing or in the wrong order, the robot will just stop, and you'll never get your toast.

People, of course, are smarter than robots. However, people still get confused by explanations that are incomplete or jumbled. That is why it is important for you to organize the details in your explanatory *how* composition. You must arrange the steps of the process you are explaining in the order they happen or should be performed. This is called **step-by-step order.**

The first step in organizing your pre-writing notes is to find the two or three most important steps in the process you are explaining. Then group the rest of your pre-writing notes around the major step they help to explain. Each of these idea groups will become a paragraph in your composition. When you have grouped all of your pre-writing notes, arrange the group and the details within them into step-by-step order.

Check It Out   Read the body of the explanatory *how* composition about making a mobile.

> To make a mobile you need wire, cardboard, Scotch tape, paper clips, string, pliers, scissors, and wire clippers. For the wire, you can straighten two coat hangers and cut them with clippers. The cardboard from a plain box will do. If you can find a brightly colored cardboard box, all the better.
>
> To begin, cut an eighteen-inch length of wire. Then form little loops at each end of the wire. Use the pliers to do this. Next,

bend the wire into a graceful arc. Now cut out two shapes about the same size from the cardboard. Firmly tape a paper clip to the center of each shape. Then place the loops of wire through these clips. To find the place on the wire at which the cardboard shapes will balance, tie a string around the wire and move it until the point of balance is found. Form a third loop in the wire at this point, using the pliers. Repeat the entire process with another eighteen-inch wire and two cardboard shapes.

When you have made a loop at the point of balance in the second wire, tie a string to this loop and attach the string to the third loop in the first wire. Then hang the completed mobile from the ceiling. If your mobile doesn't swing in the air currents of your room, you must have missed the point of balance of one of the wires. Try again.

- What steps are explained in the body of this composition?
- Are the steps presented in the right order?

Try Your Skill   Here are some jumbled notes for the body of a composition about making lemonade. List the steps below in the correct step-by-step order. Add any other details that seem necessary to you. Keep your work in your folder.

Add sugar.	Pour lemon juice into pitcher.
Squeeze three lemons.	Fill pitcher two-thirds full with water.
Stir vigorously.	Add ice and allow to chill.

Keep This in Mind

- Use step-by-step order to organize the details of an explanatory *how* composition.

Now Write   Look at the pre-writing notes you made in the last section, **Talent Show.** Use step-by-step order to organize your notes. Check them carefully. Add any steps that you may have left out. Save your organized notes in your folder.

Marking Time

Writing the First Draft

Here's the Idea Early American explorers marked their trails in a forest by making notches on tree trunks with a hatchet. The notches were a guide for those who followed so they would not get lost. As you write your first draft, remember that you are leading your reader from the beginning to the end of a process. To insure that the reader does not get lost, you have to provide clear transitions. These transitions are like the explorers' notches on the trees. They help to guide your reader through the steps of the process you are explaining.

Transitions can help make clear the order of details within a paragraph. Transitions can also help to link the ideas in one paragraph with those in another.

The transitions used in an explanatory *how* composition should show the natural time order of the process. They should tell the reader *when* to do something or *when* something happens. Transitions words like *first, then, next,* and *finally* are helpful. Transitional phrases such as *to begin, after that, at the same time,* and *the last step* are also useful.

Check It Out Here are the introduction and conclusion of the composition on making a mobile.

Introduction

A mobile is a special kind of room decoration with a spirit all its own. When properly balanced and hung from the ceiling, it will swing gently with the air currents of any room. A simple mobile is not hard to make, and you might like to try making one yourself.

Conclusion

As soon as your mobile is working properly, you may want to experiment with more complicated models. Instead of using cardboard, you might use Christmas tree ornaments. You might also make your own special figures. You could add a third or fourth section to your mobile. Once you have mastered the art of balancing, your mobile can become as exciting as your imagination.

- What transitions are used within the introduction? within the conclusion?

Try Your Skill   List the transitions used in the body of the composition on mobiles, pages 206–207. Which are used to link ideas within paragraphs? Which are used to link one paragraph to another?

> ### Keep This in Mind
>
> - In an explanatory *how* composition, use transitions to guide your readers through step-by-step order.
> - Use transitional words and phrases to link ideas within paragraphs and between paragraphs.

Now Write   Use your organized pre-writing notes to write the first draft of your explanatory *how* composition.

In the introduction, present your topic in a way that will capture your reader's attention.

In the body, give your step-by-step explanation of the process. Don't leave out any steps. Write each step simply and clearly.

In the conclusion, develop the final step of the process.

Use transitions to help your reader move smoothly through the process you are exploring.

Save your first draft in your folder.

Getting It Right

Revising Your Explanation

Here's the Idea   Your goal in writing an explanatory *how* composition is to explain a process simply and clearly. You want your reader to be able to successfully follow or understand the process you are explaining. To accomplish your goal, you need to revise your composition so that it is clear, complete, and correct.

Read over your first draft carefully. Ask yourself the following questions.

1. Does the introduction present my topic and capture the reader's interest?

2. Does each paragraph in the body of my composition have an informative topic sentence?

3. Have I included all of the important steps in the process I am explaining?

4. Have I arranged my details in step-by-step order?

5. Have I explained each step simply and clearly?

6. Have I used transitional words and phrases within paragraphs and between paragraphs? Do these transitions lead the reader smoothly from one step to another?

7. Does my conclusion either summarize the process or explain the final step in the process?

When you are sure your explanation is as clear, complete, and correct as it can be, proofread it. Correct any errors in grammar and mechanics.

Check It Out   Here is the first draft of the first body paragraph from the composition about mobiles. After reading it, reread the final version of the same paragraph, on page 206.

You need wire, cardboard, scotch tape, paper clips, string, pliers. Straighten two coat hangers. Get cardboard from a plain box. Or a colored box. Cut it into shapes.

- What specific details were added to the final copy?
- What corrections were made during proofreading?

Try Your Skill   Revise this paragraph from an explanatory *how* composition. Refer to the guidelines for revision in this lesson. Remember to proofread the paragraph.

Pearls are formed in oysters. And in other shellfish. A grain of sand gets inside. The grain of sand is covered with nacre. Which is a pearly substance. My sister has a pearl ring. This happens very slowly. A pearl is their in too or three years. Then you can get the pearl out and if its shiny it could be valuable but if its dull its worthless.

Keep This in Mind

- Make sure your explanatory *how* composition is clear, complete, and easy to follow.
- Use step-by-step order to arrange your details.
- Use transitional words and phrases to make the order of your details clear.

Now Write   Use the guidelines in this lesson to revise your explanatory *how* composition. Try to make your explanation as clear as possible. Proofread your composition for errors in grammar and mechanics. When your composition is completely revised, make a final copy. Save your work.

The Explanatory Composition

Telling *Why*

Part 1 **Why, Oh Why?**
Pre-Writing: Developing an Opinion

Part 2 **Saving the Best**
Pre-Writing: Organizing Your Details

Part 3 **It Stands to Reason**
Writing the First Draft

Part 4 **The Final Lap**
Revising Your *Why* Composition

Why, Oh Why?

Pre-Writing: Developing an Opinion

Here's the Idea One of the most precious freedoms anyone can have is the right to free speech. The United States was
founded with the idea that people have different opinions and
they have the right to express them. Because you have this
right, it is important for you to learn to use it well.

An explanatory *why* composition is one way for you to
present an opinion. In this type of composition you explain
clearly and directly why you believe something. You also offer
reasons to support your belief.

To find a topic for your explanatory *why* composition, think
about your own life. What issues do you feel strongly about?
How do you feel about your school, your neighborhood, or your
town? How do you feel about TV, the space program, industrial pollution, or the draft? Think about the world around you.
It is important to choose a topic that has meaning for you.

Once you have selected a topic, write a clear sentence that
expresses your opinion. When you write your first draft, this
sentence can become the basis for your first paragraph.

Next, gather details to support your opinion. Although
everyone has a right to his or her own opinion, opinions should
have some evidence to back them up. It is important, therefore, to collect strong, specific facts, reasons, and examples to
support your opinion. Make sure that your facts are accurate
and your reasons clear and logical.

You may gather your details from direct experience. For
instance, if you believe that Lake Crystal is polluted, you could
go there and count the number of dead fish on the shore. You
may also want to gather details from encyclopedias or other
reference books at the library.

Check It Out   Read these pre-writing notes for an explanatory *why* composition.

Opinion: The city should install a traffic light at the busy intersection of Third Avenue and Jackson Street.

Support: traffic light would bring order
60% of serious accidents not on highways
improve rush hour flow of traffic
traffic light would protect children
impossible to make left turn
police not always there to direct traffic
traffic light would prevent accidents
children sometimes run into street
accidents include serious injuries, even death
two children hit by cars in last month

· Is the opinion stated clearly and directly?
· Do these notes support the opinion well?

Try Your Skill   Write one sentence about each of the following topics. The sentence should clearly and directly state your opinion on the subject.

violence on TV   a woman for President   salaries of doctors

Keep This in Mind

· An explanatory *why* composition presents an opinion.
· State your opinion clearly and directly.
· In your pre-writing notes, gather reasons, facts, and examples to support your opinion.

Now Write   List several strong opinions that you have. Choose one that you would like to write about. State your opinion clearly in your pre-writing notes. List the reasons, facts, and examples you will use as support. Save your notes.

Saving the Best

Pre-Writing: Organizing Your Details

Here's the Idea   Have you ever heard someone say, "We're saving the best until last"? The *best* might refer to the best news, the best present, or the best entertainer.

In explaining an opinion, saving the best until last means that you arrange your details so that the most important reason is presented last. When you organize your notes from the least important idea to the most important, you are using **order of importance.**

Order of importance is a powerful way to organize your supporting ideas. It helps you to hold your reader's attention and interest. More important, your reader will be left with your most convincing reason clearly in mind.

Once you have gathered a list of supporting details for your opinion, look them over carefully. Try to identify two or three major ideas. Make these major ideas the main reasons that you use to explain your opinion. Group each of your remaining details around the main reason they help to explain. Each of these idea groups will become a paragraph of support for your opinion.

As a final step, look at your idea groups. Organize them in the order of their importance. Make sure that the best reason is mentioned last.

Check It Out   Read these organized pre-writing notes.

1. traffic light would bring order
    –improve rush hour flow of traffic
    –impossible to make left turn
    –police not always there to direct traffic

2. traffic light would prevent accidents
   –60% of serious accidents not on highways
   –accidents include serious injuries, even death
3. traffic light would protect children
   –children sometimes run into street
   –two children hit by cars in last month

- Do you see how these details have been grouped around three main ideas?
- Do you see how each of these idea groups could become a paragraph in an explanatory *why* composition?
- Have these notes been arranged in the order of their importance? Explain your answer.

Try Your Skill   Review the opinions you stated in **Try Your Skill** in the last lesson. Choose one of them. List three specific reasons or facts to support that opinion. Then organize your evidence in order of importance, from the least important idea to the most important.

Keep This in Mind

- In an explanatory *why* composition, organize your details from the least important idea to the most important.

Now Write   Look at your pre-writing notes from the last lesson, **Why, Oh Why?** What are the main ideas that support your opinion? Write these down. Under them, list the facts and examples that further help to develop each reason. Organize these idea groups in the order of their importance. Save your organized pre-writing notes in your folder.

It Stands to Reason

Writing the First Draft

Here's the Idea   Your first draft gives you a chance to fit your ideas together in the form you will present to your reader. Keep in mind that each part of the explanatory *why* composition has a special role.

It is most important to state your opinion clearly in the **introduction.** Use the sentence from your pre-writing notes or write a slightly different version of that sentence.

In the **body** of your composition, you present the reasons that support your opinion. The idea groups that you organized in your pre-writing notes will become paragraphs in the body.

Make sure that you restate your opinion in the **conclusion.** Sum up your reasons in an effective way.

To link the points of your argument, you will need to use transitions. There are two kinds of transitional words and phrases that are useful in an explanatory *why* composition. One kind helps you to present your reasons in the order of their importance. This kind includes such words and phrases as *the first reason, second, most important,* and *finally.* You may want to use such transitions at the beginning of a new paragraph.

The second kind of transition helps you to state reasons. Some examples are *because, since, if,* and *as a result.*

Check It Out   Read this introduction and conclusion.

Introduction

Traffic is a problem in our neighborhood. It is a source of noise and pollution. Also, the heavy traffic is dangerous. The most serious danger exists at the busy intersection of Third Avenue and Jackson Street. We probably cannot have cars eliminated from this busy intersection. However, we need to make the neighborhood a safer place. Therefore, we should urge the city to install a traffic light at this intersection.

Conclusion

If a traffic light were installed at the intersection of Third Avenue and Jackson Street, drivers would be more cautious. As a result of drivers' caution, there would be fewer traffic jams, fewer accidents, and fewer injuries to children. If these traffic problems are eliminated, we will have a safer neighborhood.

· Does the introduction clearly state an opinion?
· Does the conclusion sum up the argument? How?

Try Your Skill   List the transitions in this paragraph.

The most important reason for putting a traffic light at the intersection is to protect children. The neighborhood around Third Avenue and Jackson Street is heavily populated. Because there is no room anywhere else, children play on the sidewalks. Sometimes they run out into the streets. As a result, two children were hit by cars in the past month.

Keep This in Mind

· In the introduction, state your opinion clearly.
· Use transitions to help state the reasons and to show the order of their importance.
· In the body, give reasons to support your opinion.
· In the conclusion, sum up your opinion.

Now Write   Using your pre-writing notes, write the first draft of your explanatory *why* composition. State your opinion in the introduction. Develop each major reason from your notes into a separate body paragraph. Use transitions to present your reasons and show their order of importance. Sum up your reasons and opinion in the conclusion. Save your first draft.

The Final Lap

Revising Your Explanatory *Why* Composition

Here's the Idea All good runners save a little energy for the final stretch of a race. They know they cannot let up until *after* the finish. They know it is important to end well.

The same thing is true in writing. You have put a lot of effort into the first two stages of writing. Do not "let up" during the final stage—revision. With careful revision, you will finish with a composition to be proud of.

As you read your first draft, ask these questions.

Will my reader be convinced that I have good reasons for holding my opinion?

How can I make my opinion even more convincing?

Here are some other questions to ask when revising.

1. Is my opinion stated clearly and directly in the introductory paragraph?
2. Have I given convincing reasons, facts, and examples?
3. Are my reasons clear and logical? Are my facts accurate?
4. Have I organized my reasons from the least important idea to the most important?
5. Have I used transitional words and phrases to show the order of my ideas?
6. Have I used transitions to state my argument clearly?
7. Have I summed up my opinion and reasons in my conclusion?

When you are satisfied that the explanation of your opinion is clearly organized, proofread your composition. Check for errors in grammar, capitalization, punctuation, and spelling.

Check It Out   Notice how this paragraph has been revised.

> *More important,*
> A traffic light would help to ~~stop~~ *prevent* accidents. According to
> *Safety Commission   serious traffic*
> statistics, over 60% of all accidents did not happen on highways.
> *Sixty percent   in the last year*
> They happened at intersections, like Third and Jackson. These
> *city   even*
> accidents caused injuries and deaths. Most of the people injured
> *severe   one-fourth*
> were drivers and passengers. However, more than 1/4 of those
> *pedestrians.*
> hurt were ~~people on the street.~~

- How has this paragraph been improved?

Try Your Skill   Here is another first-draft paragraph. Use the guidelines in this lesson and your other revising skills to help you revise it.

   A traffic light would bring order to the corner. The intersection is crowded during rush hour. Traffic gets backed up. Drivers get mad and blow there horns. You cant make a left turn. It gets good when the cops are there. To direct traffic. Lots of times their not there.

Keep This in Mind

- State your opinion clearly in your introduction.
- Present your reasons in order of importance.
- Use transitional words and phrases to highlight the order of your reasons and to present them clearly.
- Sum up your argument in your conclusion.

Now Write   Using the guidelines in this lesson, revise your explanatory *why* composition. When you have done the best job you can do, write your final copy. Proofread this copy one last time. Correct any errors you find. Save your composition.

The Explanatory Composition
Telling *What*

Part 1 **A Chance To Explain**
Pre-Writing: Developing a Definition

Part 2 **Exactly So**
Pre-Writing: Organizing a Definition

Part 3 **Which Way Is Best?**
Writing the First Draft

Part 4 **Clean-Up**
Revising Your Definition

A Chance To Explain

Pre-Writing: Developing a Definition

Here's the Idea   Defining things is a part of everyday life. Your teacher may ask you to define a *cloud,* or an *equation.* When you tell your friends about your vacation, they may ask you to define *para-sail, trolley car,* or *silo.* Your brother may ask the mechanic to define *crankshaft* or *idle.*

An explanatory *what* composition is a written definition of something. What is defined may be a real thing, such as a *space station* or a *tropical rain forest.* What is defined may also be an idea, such as *loyalty,* or a term, like *hypnotism.*

When you have decided on a thing, an idea, or a term to define, write a one sentence definition of it. This definition should do three things. First, it should give the name of the thing being defined. Second, it should place the thing being defined into a general class. Third, it should tell how the thing being defined is different from other members of its class. Here is an example of such a definition.

> A space station is a special kind of earth satellite where people live and work on scientific projects.

To gather the details you will use to expand your definition, take some time to think about your topic. If you are defining a real thing, you will want to use facts and figures to develop your definition. A dictionary or an encyclopedia can help you to find accurate information. An idea may be defined in a more personal way. You might use incidents or anecdotes from your own experience to develop this kind of definition. A term is usually defined with specific details. These may come from your own experience or from research.

As you think and read about your topic, write down all of the information you will need to develop your definition.

224

Check It Out Read these pre-writing notes.

Topic: Grandmother
Notes: "the mother of one's father or mother"
comforts Dad when he worries
tells me stories of when Dad was a boy
knew what to say when I broke my leg
come to all my basketball games
shares her time, gives a calm influence
tells stories of 1930's and 1940's
tells stories of Great-Uncle George
sews on my scout badges
knew what to do when Susan got burned
tells stories of great-grandfather
gives me a sense of history

- What is the writer going to define?
- Do these pre-writing notes come from research or from personal experience?
- Do these notes include information that will give a good definition of the topic? Explain your answer.

Try Your Skill Imagine that you are going to define an animal. Choose an animal you know about. Make pre-writing notes for an explanatory *what* composition.

> **Keep This in Mind**
> - An explanatory *what* composition defines a real thing, an idea, or a term.
> - Use facts and figures, personal experiences, or specific details to develop your definition.

Now Write Choose a topic for an explanatory *what* composition. You may define a real thing, an idea, or a term. First, write a short definition. Then list pre-writing notes that expand that definition. Save your pre-writing notes.

Exactly So

Pre-Writing: Organizing a Definition

Here's the Idea If someone asked you to explain what a space station is, you would probably start out with a very general statement. You might say, "A space station is a place in outer space where astronauts can stay and do scientific experiments." That's actually a pretty good definition. However, if you gave the subject more thought, you could probably say much more about what a space station is. You would add all sorts of specific details that would expand and develop your general statement. In other words, your definition of a space station would go from the **general to the specific.**

Your explanatory *what* composition should be organized in the same way. The introductory paragraph should present a general definition of your topic. The rest of the paragraphs should add specific details to make the definition more exact.

You can start organizing your pre-writing notes by looking them over carefully. Try to find several main ideas that help to define your subject. Then group your remaining details around these main ideas. Each of these idea groups will become a paragraph in your composition.

Check It Out Here are the pre-writing notes for the explanatory composition defining *grandmother.* Notice how they have been organized.

> **Topic:** Grandmother
>
> Gives a Sense of History
>   stories of when Dad was a boy
>   stories of 1930's and 1940's
>   stories of great-grandfather
>   stories of Great-Uncle George

Shares Her Time
   comes to all my basketball games
   sews on my scout badges

Provides a Calming Influence
   comforts Dad when he worries about paying the bills
   knows what to do in an emergency (when Susan got burned)
   knew what to say when I was upset about breaking my leg

- What three main ideas have these pre-writing notes
  been grouped around?
- Do you see how each of these main ideas could become
  a paragraph in a composition?

Try Your Skill   These pre-writing notes about a space station contain three main ideas. Find them, and group the remaining details around them.

   space station provides living quarters
   can study the earth, moon, sun, stars
   space station can be a laboratory
   enough food, oxygen, water for weeks/months
   space station can be launch base for interplanetary flights
   check laws of nature and test scientific theories
   size of crew limited to size of station
   flights to Venus/Mars might refuel there
   entire families could stay
   send robot probes into deep space

Keep This in Mind

- Organize an explanatory *what* composition from
  the general to the specific.
- Group pre-writing notes around two or three
  main ideas.

Now Write   Look at your pre-writing notes. Find two or
three main ideas that define your topic. Group the rest of your
details around these main ideas. Save your notes.

Which Way Is Best?

Writing the First Draft

Here's the Idea   When you have organized your notes, begin the first draft of your composition. Remember that your definition should move from the general to the specific.

The **introduction** should include a sentence that gives a clear, general definition of your subject. This definition serves as a starting point for the entire composition.

The **body** should develop the main ideas that define your subject. Each paragraph should explain a different main idea.

The **conclusion** sums up the main ideas. Try to express your ideas in a slightly different way in the conclusion.

Check It Out   Read this explanatory *what* composition.

Have you ever looked up a word in the dictionary and thought, "Technically, that's right, but it doesn't really cover *my* experience"? The dictionary defines *grandmother* as "the mother of one's father or mother." To me a grandmother is this and much more. My grandmother is someone who gives me a sense of history, who shares her time, and who provides calm support.

Talking with my grandmother gives me a personal feeling for history and a sense of my family roots. She tells me what life was like when Dad was young, and what life was like for her during the Great Depression and the second World War. Grandmother is also my link to family history. She remembers her own grandfather, who came from Ireland and worked in the Wisconsin lumber mills. Great-Uncle George becomes more to me than just a photograph in an album.

Not only does Grandmother give me a sense of past times, she also shares her present time. Grandmother is often busy with her computer class and working part-time at the bank. Yet she still finds the time to attend my home basketball games. She also finds the time to sew on the merit badges on my Scout uniform.

Finally, *grandmother* also means a calming influence in troubled times. When Dad wonders how he will pay all of the bills, Grandmother reminds him of how the family managed when Grandpa lost his job. When my cousin Susan was burned, Grandmother gave Susan first aid. When I broke my leg and worried that I would never play ball again, Grandmother knew how to make me feel better.

Grandmother is my father's mother, but that is only the beginning. She is a family historian, a counselor, and a special friend. She is a part of my past, my present, and my future.

- Does the introduction contain a general definition?
- Does the body expand the definition with details?
- Does the conclusion sum up the ideas in the composition? How?

Try Your Skill   Practice writing the kind of one-sentence definition you must include in the first paragraph of your explanatory *what* composition. Write a one-sentence definition for two of the following topics.

dance   diesel   bicycle   winning   credit card

Keep This in Mind

- In an explanatory *what* composition, include a clear, general, one-sentence definition of your subject in the introduction.
- Develop the body with specific details that expand the definition.
- Summarize your definition in the conclusion.

Now Write   Use your pre-writing notes to write a first draft of your explanatory *what* composition. Include a general definition in the introduction. Use the idea groups you organized in your pre-writing notes to develop the body. Sum up your ideas in a slightly different way in the conclusion. Save your work.

Clean-Up

Revising Your Definition

Here's the Idea   When you have completed your first draft, take a break before you begin revising. The break might be as short as half an hour. It might be several days. The length of time is not important. What is important, is that you look over your work with a fresh eye. Then you will be able to check your definition more carefully. To be sure that your subject is clearly defined, ask yourself these questions.

1. Does my introduction contain a general defintion of my subject?
2. Does my general definition have three parts?
3. Have I expanded my general definition with specific details?
4. Does my conclusion sum up the main ideas?
5. Is my composition organized from the general to the specific?

After you are satisfied that you have written a good definition, proofread and correct your composition.

Check It Out   Notice how this introduction from an explanatory *what* paragraph has been revised.

¶ The object floats one thousand resembles the earth. shiny, silver
~~It is 1,000~~ miles above ~~us.~~ It is covered with insulation. It looks On the other end like a long pipe. ~~On~~ one end ~~there are~~ antennas. There are ~~also~~ solar is loaded with communication panels ~~for the sunlight to run it.~~ A space shuttle ~~comes~~ to dock that provide power. edges closer and closer, preparing with it. ~~It is~~ a space station, a special kind of satellit where people The object earth live and work on scientific projects.

230

- In what ways has this paragraph been improved?
- Is this an interesting introduction for an explanatory *what* composition? Explain your answer.

Try Your Skill   Using the guidelines in this lesson and your other revising skills, revise this paragraph from an explanatory *what* composition. Compare your revision with those of your classmates.

> After the cocoa beans are roasted they are ground up. The shells are used as fertilizer. Cocoa beans come from trees. In central and south america. The ground beans are processed. Cocoa powder is one product. Its used for making my favorite drink hot chocolate. Other ground cocoa beans are mixed. With cocoa butter. Also sugar and sometimes milk. This becomes candy. Which is the best use of cocoa in my opinion.

Keep This in Mind

- In an explanatory *what* composition, define your subject clearly and directly in the introduction.
- Expand the definition with specific details in the body.
- Sum up the main ideas in the conclusion.
- Organize your definition from the general to the specific.

Now Write   Use the guidelines in this lesson to revise your explanatory *what* composition. Remember to proofread your definition. When you are satisfied that your definition is as good as it can be, make a final copy. Proofread this copy one last time. Save your completed composition in your folder.

Writing a Report

Part 1 **Get the Facts**
Learning About Reports

Part 2 **Take Note**
Gathering Information

Part 3 **Sorting It Out**
Organizing Your Notes

Part 4 **Get It on Paper**
Writing the First Draft

Part 5 **The Last Detail**
Revising Your Report

Part 6 **Where Credit Is Due**
Preparing a Bibliography

Get the Facts

Learning About Reports

Here's the Idea Now you are going to learn to write a special type of composition called a **report.** In some ways, a report is very much like the compositions you have been writing. A report presents information about a single topic. A report also has an introduction, a body, and a conclusion.

In other ways, a report is very different from a composition. For example, a report is never written from the first-person point of view, as some narratives are. A report also never includes the opinions of the writer.

A report is written entirely from **facts.** A fact is a statement that can be proven true. Facts for a report are gathered from **outside sources.** These sources usually include books, magazines, newspapers, and encyclopedias.

Sometimes a teacher will give you a specific topic for a report. At other times, a teacher will tell you to choose a topic. Then you must first find a subject that interests you. Next you must narrow your subject so that you can cover it properly.

For example, if your teacher has limited you to five paragraphs, you know that you can't handle a subject as general as "Canada," or "Rock Music." One way to narrow a topic is to start reading about it. For instance, suppose you wanted to write about Canada. You could do some reading about Canada in books, magazines, and encyclopedias. As you read, you might discover that you want to write something about the Klondike Gold Rush, or French customs in Quebec.

When you have decided on a topic, you may wish to write a sentence or two that states your topic and your purpose for writing about it. This is called a **thesis statement.**

Check It Out   Read this paragraph from a report on the wildlife of Antarctica.

> Antarctica is also home to many species of birds. The best known are the penguins. Penguins cannot fly. They use their wings to help them swim through the water in search of food. Other birds that inhabit Antarctica include cape pigeons, giant fulmars, and skuas. Skuas are hawklike birds. They feed on penguin chicks and eggs. Probably the most amazing birds in Antarctica are the arctic terns. Each year these birds migrate from their breeding grounds in the Arctic to the coast of Antarctica and back again—a journey of 22,000 miles!

- Is this paragraph written from facts?
- Where do you suppose the writer got the facts?

Try Your Skill   Here is a list of possible topics for a five-paragraph report. Some of these topics are too general for a report. Some of the topics state personal opinions. Which topics would be just right for a report of this length?

volcanoes	the Tower of London
my personal heroes	music
the destruction of Pompeii	why I don't like science fiction
computers	inventions of Leonardo da Vinci

Keep This in Mind

- A report is written from facts gathered from outside sources.
- A report doesn't include the writer's feelings or opinions.

Now Write   Choose a subject that appeals to you and do some reading about it. As you read, try to discover some specific aspect of your subject that would make a good topic for a report. Save your topic.

Take Note

Gathering Information

Here's the Idea Now that you have chosen your topic, you need to find facts to develop it. The library has two general areas where you can start your research. The first area is the reference section. There you will find the encyclopedias and the *Readers' Guide to Periodical Literature*. The *Readers' Guide* will help you to find magazine articles about your topic.

The other area is the card catalog, where you can locate the titles of books on your chosen topic. To find out more about how to use the library, see pages 261–273.

As you read about your topic, write the important facts on note cards. Follow these guidelines.

1. Use a separate 3″ × 5″ note card for each fact or idea.

2. Write down exactly where the fact or idea came from. Include the name of the source, the date if the source is a newspaper or magazine, and the page number where you found the information.

3. Take notes in your own words. It is not acceptable to use another writer's work word for word.

4. Make a bibliography card for each source you use. Write the following information for each type of source. You will need this information when you list your sources.

Book:	author, title, publisher, date published
Magazine:	author of article (if there is one), title of article, name of magazine, date published, page
Encyclopedia:	author of article (if there is one), name of encyclopedia, volume and page, date published
Newspaper:	author of article (if there is one); title of article; name of newspaper; date published; section, page, and column number

Check It Out Read this note card.

> *There are more than 800 languages*
> *spoken in Africa.*
>   *World Book*
>   *Vol. 1, page 95*

- Does this note card include just one fact?
- Does the card contain the source of the information?

Try Your Skill A student found this information for a report on stars. Make some note cards using the information.

> Stars are glowing balls of gas. They are the basic objects of the universe and exist throughout space. Except for the sun, all stars are too far from the earth for their distance to be conveniently measured in miles or kilometers. For this reason, astronomers measure distances to and between stars in *light-years.*
>   —*World Book,* Vol. 1, page 802

Keep This in Mind

- As you read about your topic, write the important information, in your own words, on note cards.
- Put one fact on each note card.
- Label each card with the name of the source and the number of the page where the fact is.
- Make a bibliography card for each source you use.

Now Write Find several outside sources of information for your report. Make note cards as you read about your topic. Make bibliography cards, too. Be sure to follow the guidelines in this lesson. Save your note cards and bibliography cards.

Sorting It Out

Organizing Your Notes

Here's the Idea You have finished taking notes on your report topic. Now you must organize your notes. When you arrange your facts in a clear, logical order, you create a plan you can follow as you write your first draft.

The best way to organize your notes is to first spread out your notecards. That way, you have all of your facts in front of you. If you did a good job of gathering information about your topic, you may have twenty or more notecards.

Read your notecards carefully. Try to find two or three main ideas among them. Then arrange your cards into piles. Make a separate pile for each main idea. Each pile of cards will supply the information for one paragraph in your report.

When you have grouped your cards into piles, reread the notes in each pile. Then write a sentence that describes the main idea of each pile. These sentences can become topic sentences when you write your report.

Finally, arrange your notes in the order that you want to present them. First, arrange the piles of cards in the order you will write about them. Then, do the same with facts in each pile.

Take time to arrange your cards in an order that makes sense. You may have to rearrange the cards several times until you are satisfied. Then write an outline from your organized notes. Write down the sentences you wrote to describe each pile of notecards. Then list your facts under each sentence. After you make your outline, you are ready to write your first draft.

Check It Out Read these organized notes for a report about penguins.

Where Penguins Live
penguins live south of the Equator
they live on the coast of Argentina, New Zealand, Australia,
  and South America

How Penguins Get Around
on land, they walk awkwardly upright
toboggan down icy hills on their bellies
"fly" through the water with their flippers

Nesting Habits
nests are often piles of pebbles
lay 1 to 3 eggs
both parents incubate eggs

• Do you see how each group of details develops just one
main idea?

Try Your Skill Read each group of details in **Check It Out.**
Write a sentence that tells about the main idea of each group.
Write sentences that could serve as topic sentences in a report.

Keep This in Mind

• Group your note cards in piles. Each pile of
cards should develop one main idea.
• Arrange the main ideas and the facts grouped
around them in the order you wish to present
them.

Now Write Spread your note cards out in front of you.
Group the cards into piles. Each pile of cards should develop
one main idea. Write a sentence that describes the main idea of
each pile. Then arrange your notes in the order that you wish to
present them. Use your organized notes to write a simple
outline. Save your notes and outline in your folder.

Get It on Paper

Writing the First Draft

Here's the Idea   Writing the first draft of a report is like writing the first draft of any composition. You follow your organized pre-writing notes as you write the introduction, the body, and the conclusion.

The **introduction** is the first paragraph of your report. This paragraph should tell the reader what your report is about. The introduction should also be interesting enough to capture and hold the reader's attention.

The **body** of your report is made up of several paragraphs. Each paragraph should have a strong topic sentence and should tell about one main idea. Use your grouped notecards to help you to develop these paragraphs.

The **conclusion** is a paragraph that brings your report to a close. The conclusion sums up and ties together everything you have written about your topic.

Check It Out   Read this introduction.

> Antarctica is a cold, forbidding land. The entire continent is a mass of ice surrounding the South Pole. Winter temperatures as low as 127 degrees below zero have been recorded. Even in midsummer, inland temperatures remain below zero. Surprisingly, this bleak landscape is home to an astonishing variety of birds, land animals, and marine life.

- Does this introductory paragraph tell the reader what the report is about?
- Is this introduction informative and interesting? Explain your answer.

Try Your Skill Read these pre-writing notes. Then write a paragraph for the body of a report on animal behavior. Include a good topic sentence in your paragraph.

Animal Defenses

Armadillo
   covered with bony armor
   curls up into ball when attached

Porcupine
   quills (sharp, barbed) cause painful wounds
   come off when touched
   can also be shot off

Snakes
   poisonous fangs

Impala
   speed—can outrun attackers

Big Cats
   sharp claws for slashing
   strong, sharp teeth

Keep This in Mind

- In a report, the introduction presents the topic in an informative and interesting way.
- The body develops the topic with facts gathered from outside sources.
- The conclusion sums up and ties together the important information in the report.

Now Write Using your organized pre-writing notes as a guide, write the first draft of your report. Be sure your report has a good introduction, body, and conclusion. Save your first draft in your folder.

The Last Detail

Revising Your Report

Here's the Idea Throughout this chapter, you have been carefully and thoughtfully developing your report. Now is the time to see how well you've done.

Read your first draft all the way through. What impression does it make on you? You may want to express your ideas more clearly. You may find a paragraph that needs a few more details to develop its main idea. Perhaps you will want to make the language you have used livelier and more interesting. Don't feel discouraged if your report seems to need more work than you thought. Remember, a first draft is just a start.

Use the guidelines on pages 174–175 to help to improve your report. Here are some questions to guide your revision.

1. Is my introduction informative and interesting?
2. Does my report include enough facts to develop my topic?
3. Are my facts accurate? Have I stated them clearly?
4. Does each paragraph in the body tell about one main idea?
5. Do all the facts in each paragraph develop the main idea of that paragraph?
6. Does my conclusion sum up the information in my report?

As you revise your report, make sure that all of your facts are correct. Check the accuracy of dates and figures. Do the same for the spelling of names and special words. Go back to your sources if you are unsure about any of your information.

When you have finished revising the content, language, and organization of your report, proofread it. Correct any errors in grammar, capitalization, punctuation, and spelling.

Check It Out Read this paragraph on a winner of the Nobel Peace Prize. Notice how it has been revised.

In 1960, the *nobel* commitee gave the *peace* prize to Albert John Luthuli. He was an ~~a South~~ african. He was a zulu chief, *who* He led the African National Congress. *Luthuli* He tried to get *encouraged* the South African government to end racial discrimination. Like Dr. *Martin Luther* King he did peaceful *believed in using* things to ~~meet~~ *achieve means* his goals. He thought *believed that* everyone *in africa* sheould be *treated* equal*ly*.

- How has this paragraph been improved?

Try Your Skill   Here is another paragraph from the report on Nobel Peace Prize winners. Use the guidelines in this lesson as well as your other revising skills to improve this paragraph.

Mother Teresa won the prize in 1979. She was born in Yugoslavia. Mother Teresa is a nun. She works with poor people in India. She is a roman catholic nun. She founded an order of nuns in calcutta. Which is in India. She has won other awards. The Pope John XXIII peace prize and the Jawaharlal Nehru award. The order operates hospitals, schools, orphanages, shelters for lepers. She is known as the *saint of the gutters*.

Keep This in Mind

- When you revise a report, try to improve the ideas, the language, and the organization.
- Proofread the report to correct errors in grammar, capitalization, punctuation, and spelling.

Now Write   Use the guidelines in this lesson as well as the other revising skills you have learned to revise the first draft of your report. After revising and proofreading your report, make a final copy. Proofread this copy once more. Save your work.

Where Credit Is Due

Preparing a Bibliography

Here's the Idea   When you write a descriptive composition, the information in the composition comes directly from you. It comes from your observations or memories. The same is true in most compositions. You, the writer, supply the details that develop the main idea of the composition.

In a report, however, the information that develops the topic comes from outside sources such as books, magazines, and newspapers. When you use information that is not your own, you must tell the reader where the information came from. You must prepare a list of sources. This list is called a **bibliography.**

When you prepare the bibliography for your report, use the bibliography cards that you made as part of your pre-writing notes. First arrange these cards in alphabetical order, according to the author's last name. If no author is mentioned, use the first main word of the title.

When you have arranged your cards in alphabetical order, you are ready to write your bibliography. Each type of source has its own special form. Here are the correct forms. Note the correct punctuation, capitalization, and abbreviations.

Book: Gilbert, Bil. *Westering Man.* Atheneum Publishers, 1983.

Encyclopedia: "Cave Life." *Encyclopedia Americana.* Volume 6, p. 105, 1980.

Magazine: Begley, Sharon. "Jobs." *Newsweek.* 18 October 1982, pp. 87–88.

Newspaper: Kelly, Nash. "Living with Cancer." *Wanakee Tribune,* 20 May 1984, Sec.1, p. 2, Cols. 1–5.

Check It Out   Look at the bibliography on the next page.

Bibliography

Cunningham, Christy. "The Sun Did It!" *The Altoona Herald Sun,* 12 October 1983, Sec. 2, p. 1, Cols. 1–2.

Marbach, William D. "Steam from the Sunshine." *Newsweek,* 13 December 1982, pp. 92–93.

"Solar Energy." *Colliers Encyclopedia.* Volume 21, p. 167, 1980.

- Are these entries arranged in alphabetical order?
- Does each entry contain the required information?
- Is the information in each entry arranged in order?

Try Your Skill   Make a sample bibliography using these sources. Use the correct form for each type of source.

a book titled *Photography in America,* by Robert Doty, published by Random House in 1974.

an article titled "Photography," in *The World Book Encyclopedia,* pages 370–381, Volume 15, 1984.

an article titled "New Photography Draws Critical Fire," in *Photography Review Magazine,* June 6, 1984, pages 45–50.

Keep This in Mind

- If you use outside information in your writing, you must state where it came from.
- The last page of your report should be a bibliography.
- In a bibliography, each type of source has its own special form.

Now Write   Use the guidelines in this lesson to prepare a bibliography for your report. Use your bibliography cards to help you. Write your bibliography on a separate sheet of paper and place it at the end of your report. Save your report.

Clear Thinking

Part 1 **Nothing but the Facts**
Identifying Facts

Part 2 **Says Who?**
Using Good Sources

Part 3 **Prove It!**
Distinguishing Fact and Opinion

Part 4 **The Reasons Why**
Supporting Opinions

Part 5 **Spinning Wheels**
Circular Reasoning

Part 6 **Snarl and Purr**
Recognizing Loaded Language

Nothing but the Facts

Identifying Facts

Here's the Idea   Every day you receive hundreds of pieces of information. Information comes from many sources:

Other people	Movies	Newspapers
Books	Television shows	Signs and posters
Magazines	Advertisements	

You want to be able to use this information well when you write, speak, or make decisions. To do this you have to be able to tell what is fact and what is not.

A **fact** is a statement that can be proven. There are two kinds of facts: definitions and observations. A **definition** simply tells the meaning of a word. An **observation** tells about something that can be seen, tasted, touched, heard, or smelled.

> Definition: A *judoka* is an expert in judo.
> Observation: Male Siberian tigers average over ten feet in length.

Definitions can be proven by checking a dictionary. Observations can be proven in three different ways:

Proving Observations

1. Make the observation yourself. Use your senses of sight, touch, taste, hearing, and smell.
2. Ask an expert or authority.
3. Check a reliable written source. Such sources include encyclopedias, atlases, almanacs, and dictionaries.

To prove the observation about Siberian tigers, for example, you can visit a zoo. You can ask an expert on big cats. You can also read about these tigers in a book or encyclopedia.

Check It Out   Carlotta was asked to do a report on India for her social studies class. She was having a hard time narrowing her topic, so she spoke with Sashir. Sashir told her that there are many beautiful temples in India.

- What kind of fact is Sashir's comment? Is it a definition or an observation?
- How can Carlotta check this fact? What sources of information can she use?

Try Your Skill   The following statements are facts. Tell whether each is a definition or an observation.

1. A foal is a young horse, mule, or donkey.
2. *Wraith* is a Scottish word for "ghost."
3. Angel Falls, in Venezuela, is over three thousand feet high.
4. Jupiter has rings like those around Saturn.

Keep This in Mind

- A fact is a statement that can be proven true.
- Facts may be definitions or observations.
- Definitions can be checked in a dictionary.
- Observations can be checked personally. They can also be checked by asking an authority or by looking in a written source.

Now Write   Go to the library. Look in encyclopedias, atlases, dictionaries, almanacs, books, and magazines. Make a list of five interesting or unusual facts. On your list, tell the source of each fact. Do not use any source more than once. Label your paper **Nothing but the Facts.** Save it in your folder.

Says Who?

Using Good Sources

Here's the Idea   Whenever you write, it is important that your facts be accurate. This is especially important when you write a report or an informative talk. To make sure that your facts are correct, check them by using good sources. The following guidelines will help you:

Guidelines for Checking Facts

1. Make sure that your source is reliable. A reliable source is one you can count on to give you the right information. One reliable source is people who have special training, experience, or knowledge. Consider the fact "Jogging on hard surfaces can cause sprains." This fact can be checked by talking to a doctor or to an experienced jogger. Other good sources include the following:

   a. Reference books such as dictionaries, encyclopedias, almanacs, and atlases.

   b. Books, magazines, and newspaper articles written by people with special training, experience, or knowledge.

2. Make sure that your source is up-to-date. A book written in the 1950's will tell you that no one has been to the moon. Of course, this is no longer true. Always use the most recent sources available.

3. Make sure that your source is fair. A fair source is one that doesn't take sides. For example, the son of a political candidate would not be a good source of information on the candidate's abilities. The son couldn't be fair because of the close family connection.

Check It Out   Carlos read an interesting article about building houses. Carlos started thinking about becoming a carpenter someday. He decided to check the facts in the article. He looked under "Carpentry" in an encyclopedia. He talked to the wood-shop teacher at school. He also called the headquarters of the carpenter's union in his town.

- How good are Carlos's sources?
- What other sources of information could Carlos use?

Try Your Skill   Study the following situations. Then explain what is wrong with the sources mentioned.

1. In English class, Phil read a story by Ray Bradbury from *The Martian Chronicles.* He wondered if the story was based on actual facts. He decided to find out everything he could about Mars. At home he found a book called *Our Solar System.* The copyright page had the date 1962.

2. Marsha read an ad for CURES-ALL brand cold remedy. The ad said, "This is the most effective cold remedy on the market today." Therefore, Marsha later bought some CURES-ALL when she became sick.

3. Charmagne did a report on Carrie Fisher. One of her sources was a newspaper that is known for its gossip columns.

Keep This in Mind

- Whenever you write, make sure that your facts are accurate.
- Use sources that are reliable, up-to-date, and fair.

Now Write   Look through some magazines and newspapers. Choose two articles that contain facts. One article should be a good source. The other one should be a poor source. If you have trouble finding a poor source, ask your teacher for suggestions. Write a brief paragraph about each article. Tell why you think it is a good or bad source. Save your paragraphs.

Prove It!

Distinguishing Fact and Opinion

Here's the Idea In Part 1 you learned that a fact is a statement that can be proved. A statement that cannot be proved is an **opinion**. Look at the following examples:

    Fact: The guitar was invented in Spain.

    Opinion: The guitar is the best of all instruments.

The first statement is a fact because it can be proved. You can check the truth of the statement by looking at an encyclopedia article. The second statement is very different. There is no way to prove it. It just expresses how some people feel. Because there is no way to prove this statement, it is an opinion.

To tell whether a statement is a fact, ask yourself whether it can be proved. If it can be proved, it is a fact. If it can't be proved, it is an opinion.

Opinions often contain **judgment words.** These are words that express personal feelings.

Judgment Words	
good, better, best	excellent, wonderful
bad, worse, worst	terrible, awful
ugly, beautiful	clever, intelligent
valuable, worthless	boring, interesting

Other opinions contain **command words.** These are words that tell what should be done.

Command Words		
should	ought to	must

Check It Out   Study the following dialogue:

Gwen: Michael Jackson is wonderful!
Miguel: You've got to be kidding!
Gwen: I certainly am not! He's got the best voice in popular music, and he does some excellent songs, too.
Miguel: I don't know how you can listen to his terrible music.
Gwen: Terrible? He's fantastic!

- What opinions are given in this dialogue?
- What judgment words can you find?
- Can any of the arguments in the dialogue be proved true? Explain your answer.

Try Your Skill   Tell whether the following statements are facts or opinions. If it is a fact, tell how you could prove it. If it is an opinion, identify any judgment words it contains.

1. Hank Aaron hit more home runs than any professional baseball player in history.
2. Everyone should learn how to swim.
3. Susan Sarandon is a marvelous actress.
4. One painting by Turner was sold for over six million dollars.
5. Barbara Krause won three gold medals in Olympic swimming competition.

Keep This in Mind

- A statement that cannot be proved is an opinion.
- Opinions often contain judgment words or command words.

Now Write   Using the lists of judgment and command words on page 252, write one fact and one opinion about each of these subjects:

arcade games   homework   football   pets

Label your paper **Prove It!** Save it in your folder.

The Reasons Why

Supporting Opinions

Here's the Idea All opinions are not created equal. Some opinions are sound. Some are not. A sound opinion is one that can be supported by facts. Such an opinion can be believed. An unsound opinion is one that cannot be supported by facts. Unsound opinions should not be believed. Read these opinions:

> Regular exercise is important to a person's health.
> Regular exercise is not important to a person's health.

The first opinion is sound. It can be supported by facts such as these:

> People who exercise regularly live longer.
> Regular exercise strengthens muscles, including the heart.
> Regular exercise increases alertness.

The second opinion has no facts to support it.

Whenever you read or hear an opinion, see if it is supported by facts. Whenever you give an opinion of your own, support it with facts that tell why the opinion should be believed.

Check It Out Read about this situation.

> The seniors at Morton High wanted to hold a party to welcome the incoming freshmen. Marsha and Alec were chosen to organize the activities. They decided to show a movie. Marsha said, "I know what we ought to show—*Raiders of the Lost Ark.* It's wonderful! It was also a big hit at the box office."
>
> "No," said Alec. "I think we ought to show *A Night at the Opera,* by the Marx brothers."
>
> "But Alec," replied Marsha, "very few students today have even heard of the Marx brothers."
>
> "I don't care," said Alec. "*A Night at the Opera* is great."

- What opinions are expressed by Marsha and Alec?
- Which opinion is supported with facts? Which is not?

Try Your Skill Write two facts to support each of the following opinions:

1. More people should participate in sports.
2. Many television programs are too violent.
3. Students in shop classes should obey safety rules.
4. Cigarette smoking is harmful.
5. Zoos are fascinating places to visit.

Keep This in Mind

- A sound opinion is one that can be supported by facts.
- An unsound opinion is one that cannot be supported by facts.
- Always support the opinions you give with facts.

Now Write Write an opinion about one of the following subjects:

automobiles
club or class
  elections
a career you
  would like
  to have someday

game shows
a favorite book
  or short story
a hobby or other
  activity that
  you enjoy

Use this opinion as the topic sentence of a paragraph. In the rest of the paragraph, support your opinion with facts. Label your paper **The Reasons Why.** Save it in your folder.

Spinning Wheels

Circular Reasoning

Here's the Idea   Sometimes an unsound opinion comes from an error in reasoning. One common error is circular reasoning. **Circular reasoning** occurs when someone tries to support a statement by repeating it in different words. Read the following example:

> Paul's drum set is better than Lisa's because Paul's is of higher quality.

The opinion given here is that "Paul's drum set is better than Lisa's." Notice that no facts are offered to support this opinion. Instead, the opinion is simply restated in the words "Paul's set is of higher quality." The reasoning is going in circles. It ends up where it began. Therefore, the opinion is unsound.

The error of circular reasoning occurs whenever someone says that something is so simply because it is so. Learn to recognize this error in the speaking and writing of others. Avoid the error yourself by supporting your opinions with facts.

Check It Out   Read the following statements:

1. Juanita is the most valuable player on our team. This is because she is the one who is worth the most to us.
2. Unemployment is a terrible thing because being out of work is awful.

- What is wrong with the reasoning in these statements?
- How could this reasoning be improved?

Try Your Skill   Read the following statements. Tell which ones are examples of circular reasoning. Explain your answers.

1. Literature is an important part of every person's education. This is because everybody needs to be familiar with literature.

2. The United States should develop solar energy resources because there is a limited amount of oil and natural gas.

3. The Cardinals are the most interesting baseball team because they are so fascinating.

4. Martin guitars are the best guitars made because they are constructed better than other guitars.

Keep This in Mind

- Circular reasoning is the error of supporting an opinion by restating it in different words.
- Avoid circular reasoning by supporting your opinions with facts.

Now Write   The following opinions show circular reasoning. Choose one of these opinions. Use the opinion as the topic sentence of a paragraph. In your paragraph, avoid circular reasoning by supporting the opinion with facts. Label your paper **Spinning Wheels.** Save it in your folder.

Students should do their homework regularly because this is what students are supposed to do.

Video games are a lot of fun because they are so enjoyable.

Some television shows are not fit for young children because they are not the sort of programs young children should watch.

Snarl and Purr

Recognizing Loaded Language

Here's the Idea In Part 5 you learned that unsound opinions can result from circular reasoning. Another common cause of unsound opinions is loaded language.

Loaded language is made up of words and phrases that create strong feelings in the reader or listener. Such words and phrases are sometimes used in place of facts. This is done to sway the opinions of an audience. Read the following selection from a political speech:

> The voters of America are *fed up* with *dishonest* politicians. They are tired of *crooks* like my opponent. Instead, they want *leaders* they can count on, people who will keep their word. They are looking for *honesty* and *integrity*.

In this example the speaker is trying to get the audience to view his or her opponent as someone who can't be trusted. However, notice that the speaker gives no facts to support this opinion. Instead, the speaker uses loaded language to stir up emotion in the listeners. This loaded language is made up of snarl words and purr words.

Snarl words are words that create negative feelings in the audience. Examples from the selection include *fed up*, *dishonest*, and *crooks*. **Purr words** are words that create positive feelings. Examples from the selection include *leaders*, *honesty*, and *integrity*.

Whenever a person uses name-calling to make a point, he or she is using loaded language. Such language should be avoided at all times. It is usually used to hide the fact that the speaker or writer has no real facts to support his or her opinions.

Check It Out Read the following selection from an editorial:

The bleeding-heart liberals in Washington are at it again. This time they want to limit even further the rights of businesses to drill for oil on government land. No decent citizen will allow this. Limiting the activities of business is both un-democratic and un-American. I urge all real patriots to write to Washington. Let's stop this nonsense once and for all.

- What opinions are expressed in this editorial?
- Are any facts offered to support these opinions?
- What loaded words are used to sway emotions? Are these purr words or snarl words?

Try Your Skill Identify the snarl words and purr words in the following sentences:

1. I wouldn't vote for him. He has shifty eyes.
2. Only respectable books should be allowed in libraries.
3. People with real class will not wear such rags.
4. Ms. Jones is fabulously wealthy. Ms. Smith is filthy rich.

Keep This in Mind

- Unsound opinions can result from loaded language.
- Loaded language is made up of snarl words and purr words.
- Snarl words cause negative feelings.
- Purr words cause positive feelings.

Now Write Pick a subject that you feel strongly about. Write an opinion on this subject. Then, support your opinion in a paragraph. Avoid using snarl words and purr words. Instead, support your opinion with facts. Label your paper **Snarl and Purr.** Save it in your folder.

Using the Library

Part 1 **One for the Books**
How To Use the Library

Part 2 **It's in the Cards**
How To Use the Card Catalog

Part 3 **First Stop**
How To Use an Encyclopedia

Part 4 **Fact Finding**
How To Use Reference Works

One for the Books

How To Use the Library

Here's the Idea   When you want something to read, go to the library. There you will find books to read for pleasure or for research. Become familiar with how and where the materials are arranged in the libraries you use.

You will find that library books are classified into two general groups, **fiction** and **nonfiction.** Fiction books have their own section of shelves. The books are arranged alphabetically according to the author's last name. For instance, *No Promises in the Wind,* written by Irene Hunt, would be filed under **H.**

Nonfiction books are arranged on the shelves according to their subjects. Many libraries use a system called the **Dewey Decimal System.** This system groups nonfiction books into ten major, numbered categories. These are the ten categories.

000–099	**General Works**	(encyclopedias, almanacs)
100–199	**Philosophy**	(ethics, psychology, occult)
200–299	**Religion**	(the Bible, mythology)
300–399	**Social Science**	(economics, law, education, government)
400–499	**Language**	(languages, grammars, dictionaries)
500–599	**Science**	(math, biology, astronomy)
600–699	**Useful Arts**	(cooking, farming, carpentry, television, business)
700–799	**Fine Arts**	(music, sports, painting, dance)
800–899	**Literature**	(poetry, plays)
900–999	**History**	(biography, travel, geography)

On the spine of each nonfiction book is its **call number.** This number includes the Dewey Decimal number and other useful information. Some libraries may also add the letter *B* to the spine of a biography or the letter *R* to the spine of a general reference work like an encyclopedia.

Look at this nonfiction book:

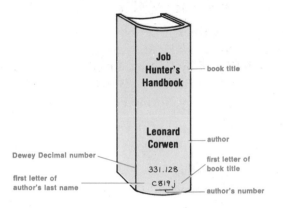

Job Hunter's Handbook — book title

Leonard Corwen — author

Dewey Decimal number — 331.128

first letter of author's last name — C819.j — first letter of book title

author's number

Check It Out   Look at the books represented below.

Viva Chicano	Zoo Cavalcade	The Old Man and the Sea	Fog	The Pearl	The Nurse's Alamanc	Faces of Japan	The Simple Story of Music
Frank Bonham	E. G. Boulenger	Ernest Hemingway	Mildred Lee	John Steinbeck	Howard S. Rowland	Bob Davis	Charles David Isaacson
	590 B661				R 610.73 R796n	915.2044 DAV	C70 IS1

- How can you tell which books are fiction and which are nonfiction?
- How can you tell what the general category of each nonfiction book is?

Try Your Skill   Write the answers to the following questions.

1. Under what letter on the library shelves would you find the following books of fiction?

Animal Farm by George Orwell
Leap Before You Look by Mary Stolz
The Upstairs Room by Johanna Reiss
Z for Zachariah by Robert C. O'Brien
A Figure of Speech by Norma Fox Mazer

2. In which categories of the Dewey Decimal System would you find information on the following subjects?

how to grow vegetables
what to see in Washington, D.C.
the Greek myths
the plays of William Shakespeare

Keep This in Mind

- In the library, fiction books are filed alphabetically by the author's last name.
- Nonfiction books may be classified in ten major categories of the Dewey Decimal System. Each nonfiction book has its own call number.

Now Write   As your teacher directs, become familiar with your school or public library. Find out where the fiction and nonfiction books are shelved. Find out where reference books and any special collections are kept.

On your visit to the library, find three fiction and three nonfiction books that you might like to read. Write the titles and authors of these books. Copy the call number or special marking that is written on the spine of any of the books. Label your paper **One for the Books,** and put it into your folder.

It's in the Cards

How To Use the Card Catalog

Here's the Idea   To find out if the library has a book you want, use the **card catalog.** This file lists every book in the library at least three times.

Every library book is recorded on an author card, a title card, and at least one subject card. For a nonfiction book, all three kinds of cards include the call number in the upper left corner. The same number appears on the spine of the book and determines where in the library the book is shelved.

All three cards give the author, title, publisher, date of publication, and number of pages in the book. A notation tells whether the book has illustrations or maps. There may also be a description of the book or a list of other related books. Although all three cards contain the same information, the information is arranged differently on each one.

On an **author card,** the author's name is given at the top, last name first. Author cards are filed alphabetically by the author's last name.

Author
Card

650.14 STA	Stanat, Kirby
	Job hunting secrets and tactics / by Kirby Stanat, with Patrick Reardon. —Milwaukee: Westwind Press; Chicago: distributed by Follett Pub. Co., c1977.
	iv, 220 p. : ill.; 24 cm.
	O

On a **title card,** the title appears on the top line. Only the first word of the title is capitalized. Title cards are filed alphabetically by the first word of the title. However, if *A, An,* or *The* appears as the first word in a title, look for the card under the first letter of the second word in the title.

Title Card

650.14   Job hunting secrets and tactics
STA
                    Job hunting secrets and tactics /
                    by Kirby Stanat, with Patrick
                    Reardon. —Milwaukee: Westwind
                    Press; Chicago: distributed by
                    Follett Pub. Co., c1977.

                    iv, 220 p. : ill.; 24 cm.

                              O

On a **subject card,** the subject appears on the top line. The subject may be written in capital letters or in red. Subject cards are filed alphabetically by the first word of the subject.

Subject Card

650.14   **JOBS**
STA
                    Job hunting secrets and tactics /
                    by Kirby Stanat, with Patrick
                    Reardon. —Milwaukee: Westwind
                    Press; Chicago: distributed by
                    Follett Pub. Co., c1977.

                    iv, 220 p. : ill.; 24 cm.

                              O

Sometimes you will find a card that states *See* or *See also.* This **cross reference card** refers you to another subject heading closely related to the one you want.

Your search for cards in the card catalog will be easier because of **guide cards.** These blank cards have tabs on which are written general subject headings. These headings show you the alphabetical arrangement of the card catalog.

Check It Out   Look at the three sample cards shown, and answer the following questions.

- Under what letter would each card be filed?
- Where would you look for more books by Kirby Stanat?
- Where would you find more books about jobs?

Try Your Skill   Here are the title, author, and call number for a book about astronomy. Draw three rectangles to represent file cards. Use the information below to make an author card, a title card, and a subject card. Make up other details for the cards.

Beyond the Milky Way, by Thornton Page, 523 P145B

Keep This in Mind

- In a library, every book is listed in the card catalog on at least three cards—author, title, and subject.
- Each card gives the author, title, publisher, date of publication, number of pages, and other important information. The card includes the call number of a nonfiction book.

Now Write   Think of a job that interests you. It might be related to music, sports, or medicine. Go to the library. Using the card catalog, find a subject card, title card, and author card related to your possible job. Draw three rectangles to represent the file cards and copy the information from the actual cards. Label your paper **It's in the Cards** and keep it in your folder.

First Stop

How To Use an Encyclopedia

Here's the Idea An encyclopedia is the first source you might want to check for general information. An encyclopedia is a reference work that contains articles on a great many different subjects. The subjects of the articles are arranged in alphabetical order from the first volume through the last. On the spine of each volume is a single letter or guide letters that tell you what subjects are included. Look at the set of encyclopedias arranged below.

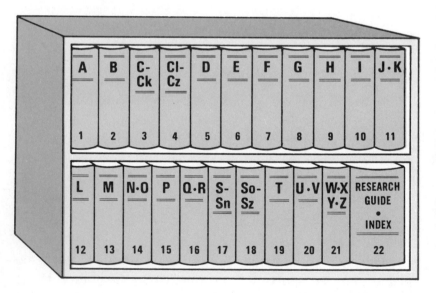

Suppose that you were writing a report on what to see in Washington, D.C. You might use the *World Book Encyclopedia, Collier's Encyclopedia,* or the *Britannica Junior Encyclopaedia.* Find the appropriate volume and look up "Washington,

D.C." Notice that there are guide words at the top of each page, just as there are in a dictionary. These guide words help you to find your subject quickly.

An encyclopedia article on a major subject is usually presented in various parts with subtitles. An article on Washington, D.C. may include such parts as "The City," "People," "History," "Local Government," "Economy," and "A Visitor's Guide." Sometimes you may want to read only the parts related to your specific topic. At other times you may need to read the entire article.

It is always a good idea to check the end of the article for a list of related articles in the encyclopedia or for a list of books for further reading. In addition, some encyclopedias present a guide to help you organize your study of a particular subject.

Many encyclopedias include an index. It may be the first or last volume of the set. You may need the index to find information that is presented under different related subjects in different volumes. Some encyclopedias also publish yearbooks, which contain up-to-date information on certain subjects.

Besides general encyclopedias, there are others that deal with specific subjects. Some of the special encyclopedias may deal with careers, art, sports, or cooking, for example. Others may cover music, animals, or health. These encyclopedias will probably be located in the reference area of the library.

Any large library will have several sets of encyclopedias. Different encyclopedias will have different reading levels. To find the one that will help you, skim through several or ask a librarian for help.

Try to use more than one encyclopedia as a source of information. Check other encyclopedias or kinds of reference books. If different sources give different information, try to use the most recent or most reliable source. Remember that if you use the exact words from any encyclopedia or source, you must use quotation marks. Quotation marks show that you have copied material exactly from an original source.

Check It Out Look at an encyclopedia in your school or public library. Answer the following questions.

- In what volume will you find information about dancing? spiders? sculpture? the Allegheny Mountains? ancient Egypt? the United Nations?

Try Your Skill Number your paper from 1 to 8. Write the key word in each question below that tells you what to look up in an encyclopedia.

1. When did the game of basketball begin?
2. What planet is farthest from the sun?
3. Name five animals that are mammals.
4. How many pounds of coffee a year does Brazil export?
5. What common foods are made from flour?
6. What was the total number of home runs that Babe Ruth hit?
7. What is the name of the largest natural lake in the world?
8. What was daily life like in the ancient Roman Empire?

Keep This in Mind

- An encyclopedia is a general reference work that contains information on many different subjects.
- Articles are arranged alphabetically in numbered volumes. Examine a variety of encyclopedias. Choose one that you can read easily.

Now Write Write the name of the job that you chose in the last lesson. Look up the job or related field in at least two encyclopedias. Jot down a few of the most interesting facts. Compare the information you find in the two encyclopedias. Be sure to list the name of each encyclopedia that you used, the number and guide letters of the volume, the guide words on the page, and the title of any other articles or books on the subject. Label your paper **First Stop** and put it into your folder.

Fact Finding

How To Use Reference Works

Here's the Idea In addition to encyclopedias, you will find several other kinds of books in the reference section of your library. Each kind of reference work deals with one particular area of information. Most of these specialized books explain the symbols and abbreviations used, how the information is arranged, and show sample entries. When you use any reference work for the first time, examine this introductory explanation so that you can use the book most effectively. There are several major kinds of reference works you will find helpful.

An **atlas** is a book of maps. However, atlases may also contain information about population, weather, and particular places in every part of the world. Some widely used atlases include the *National Geographic Atlas of the World, The International Atlas from Rand McNally,* and the *Atlas of World History.*

Almanacs and yearbooks are published each year. They are the most useful source of up-to-date facts and statistics. These reference works contain current information about world events, governments, population, sports, and annual awards. You may want to use the *Guinness Book of World Records,* the *World Almanac and Book of Facts,* the *Information Please Almanac, Atlas, and Yearbook,* or the *Statesman's Yearbook.*

Biographical references are books that contain information about the lives of important people. Usually, these reference works deal with people who are grouped together into one classification, such as presidents or authors. Among the most useful biographical references are *The Book of Presidents, Current Biography, Who's Who, Twentieth Century Authors,* and the *Dictionary of American Biography.*

A **vertical file** is the name of a collection of assorted pamphlets, handbooks, catalogs, and clippings that are kept in a file cabinet. This collection will vary from library to library. However, it may include special information about careers, travel, and local events, and catalogs of schools and colleges.

Magazines are valuable sources of information about a wide range of subjects. A library may subscribe to any number of the leading magazines published in the U.S. In order to find specific information in magazine articles, you need to become familiar with the *Readers' Guide to Periodical Literature.* The *Readers' Guide* lists the titles of articles, stories, and poems published in more than 100 leading magazines. One hardcover volume of the *Readers' Guide* covers material for an entire year. Several smaller, paperback volumes cover shorter time periods. The *Readers' Guide* is a useful tool to help you research any subject. It is important to learn to use this specially abbreviated source book.

Check It Out   Here is a portion of a page from the *Readers' Guide to Periodical Literature.*

Juniper
Don't overlook the low-growing junipers. N. B. Simpson.
name of magazine ——————— il| *South Living*|18:114-17 N '83
Junk
The Age of Junk [symposium] il *Roll Stone* p95+ D 22
'83-Ja 5 '84
Junk food
author ——————— Life is a hamburger| A. Latham.|il *Roll Stone* p103-9 D
22 '83-Ja 5 '84
Junor, Penny
title of article ——————— |Christmas with the royal family| il *McCalls* 111:90-1+ D
'83
Jupiter (Planet)
cross reference ——————— | *See also*|
Space flight—Voyager flights
Space flight to Jupiter

Atmosphere
volume number ——————— X-rays from Jupiter. il *Sky Telesc*|66| 398-9 N '83

Magnetic properties
Jupiter's tail at Saturn: the clincher [Voyager data] J.
page reference ——————— Eberhart. *Sci News* 124:|215|O 1 '83

Ring system
Around and around with planetary rings [Voyager data]
date of magazine ——————— J. Eberhart. il *Sci News* 124:295|N 5 '83|

- Read through one listing for an article in this sample and explain completely the information given. Where is the *Readers' Guide* kept in your school or public library? What other kinds of reference works are in the reference section of your library?

Try Your Skill   What reference works would you probably use to answer each of the following questions? Write your answers. Mention a specific reference if possible. If you think magazines might be the best reference, write *Readers' Guide* as the place you would look.

1. How many states in the United States have a city or town named Paris?
2. Who is the current head of state in China?
3. Name two guidelines for jogging safely.
4. What is the area of Texas?
5. Name two books by Pearl S. Buck.
6. Name five current leaders in major United States businesses.
7. What is the most efficient way to insulate a home?
8. What jobs might be listed in a pamphlet called "Careers in the Food Industry"?

Keep This in Mind

- There are several major kinds of specific reference works. Learn to use the ones in your library.

Now Write   Choose a person you admire or a place you'd like to visit. Look up information on your topic in several specific reference works. Jot down at least four interesting facts that you learn. List the references that contain the information. Give their titles, call numbers, and the volumes and page numbers where you find the information. Label your paper **Fact Finding.** Keep your work in your folder.

Study and Research Skills

Part 1 **Note Well**
Understanding the Assignment

Part 2 **This Way, Please**
Following Directions

Part 3 **A Quiet Place**
A Time and a Place for Studying

Part 4 **Making the Most of It**
The SQ3R Study Method

Part 5 **Remember This**
Taking Notes

Part 6 **One Way or Another**
Adjusting Your Reading Rate

Part 7 **Seeing Is Believing**
Using Graphic Aids

Part 8 **Graphic Descriptions**
Reading Graphs

Part 9 **Testing, Testing**
Preparing for and Taking Tests

Part 10 **The Answer Key**
Answering Objective Test Questions

Part 11 **Get It in Writing**
Answering Written Test Questions

Note Well

Understanding the Assignment

Here's the Idea   One of the most important study skills is understanding your assignments. Whenever your teachers give you an assignment, you must listen closely. Then, you must record the assignment carefully in an assignment notebook. Make sure that you record both the subject of the assignment and all specific instructions. You should also record the date the assignment is given and the date it is due. Here is a sample page from an assignment notebook:

Subject	Assignment	Date Given	Date Due
Soc. Studies	Read Chapter 8. Answer questions 1 and 3 on p. 148.	Jan. 9	Jan. 11
Spanish	Memorize dialogue on p. 218.	Jan. 9	Jan. 12

Before you begin an assignment, ask these questions.

1. Will I have to read, study, or memorize? Will I have to write, answer questions, or make something?
2. Will I hand in a composition, a report, a list of answers, or a written copy of a speech? Will I present a demonstration?
3. Do I need any special supplies? Do I need materials from the library?
4. When is the assignment due? How much time do I have?

Check It Out   Read the following sample science assignment.

Make a chart showing the daily weather forecast and the actual weather for an entire week. Write the forecast in blue ink and the actual weather in red ink. The chart will be due on Friday.

- What does this assignment ask you to do?
- What will the final product be?
- What supplies or resources will you need?
- When is the assignment due?

Try Your Skill   Read the sample English assignment below. What kind of assignment is it? What will your final product be? What materials will you need to complete the assignment? When is it due?

By Wednesday, find two advertisements that use characters or events from ancient myths. The best places to look for these ads are in newspapers, magazines, and the telephone book. Bring the ads to class.

Keep This in Mind

- Write all information about assignments in an assignment notebook.
- Know what to do to complete the assignment.
- Know what your final product will be.
- Know what materials you will need.
- Know the due date of the assignment.

Now Write   Start an assignment notebook. Make four columns on a sheet of paper. Label the columns as shown in **Here's the Idea.** Use these columns to record information about your assignments.

This Way, Please

Following Directions

Here's the Idea Whenever you play a game, you follow a set of directions. These directions tell you what to do, how to do it, and when it must be done. If you do not follow the directions, the game will not make sense.

The same is true of the directions you are given for completing assignments. You must follow these directions carefully if you want to complete your work correctly. Directions may be either spoken or written.

These guidelines will help you to follow spoken directions:

Following Spoken Directions

1. Listen carefully. Write down the directions as you hear them.
2. Notice what steps are involved in the assignment. Also notice the order of these steps.
3. Listen for the key word in each step. These are words that tell you what to do. Examples are *read, write, organize,* and *memorize.*
4. If you do not understand, ask your teacher to explain the directions.

These guidelines will help you to follow written directions:

Following Written Directions

1. Read all the directions before you begin the assignment.
2. Divide the assignment into steps. Put these steps in a logical order.
3. Ask your teacher to explain any steps that you don't understand.
4. Before you begin work, gather all books and other materials you need to complete the assignment.

Check It Out Read the following sample assignment.

Make a list of six words that sound like what they describe. Examples include words like *meow* and *buzz*. Make sure that the words you choose can be found in a dictionary. Then, on a separate piece of paper, write three sentences. In each sentence, use at least two words from your list.

- What steps are included in this assignment?
- What materials will you need?
- What questions could you ask to make the assignment clearer?
- Do you know when the assignment is due?

Try Your Skill Read and follow this set of directions.

1. On a piece of paper, write two last names that are also names of places. (Example: *York*)
2. Write two last names that are also names of colors.
3. If your last name begins with a letter between *A* and *P*, do only number 1, above.
4. If your last name begins with a letter between *Q* and Z, do only number 2, above.

Keep This in Mind

- Carefully listen to or read all directions before you begin an assignment.
- Divide your assignments into steps. Place these steps in logical order.
- Ask your teacher to explain if you don't understand.

Now Write Imagine that you are writing a student handbook to be used by next year's new students. Write directions for checking out a book from your school library. Include all the necessary steps. Place these steps in a logical order. Label your paper **This Way, Please.** Save it in your folder.

A Quiet Place

A Time and a Place for Studying

Here's the Idea Studying should be done in a special place. This place may be at home, at school, or in a library. Make sure that your study area meets the following requirements:

The Study Area

1. **A study area should be quiet.** Distractions such as conversation, television, or loud music can hurt your concentration.
2. **A study area should be well lit.** Studying in poorly lighted areas can cause eyestrain and headaches.
3. **A study area should be neat and organized.** Working in a messy study area can cause you to waste time searching for materials.
4. **A study area should be properly equipped.** Keep paper, pens, pencils, a dictionary, and other materials close at hand.
5. **A study area should be available at a regular time.** Set aside a specific time for study each day. Make sure that your study area is available at this time.

In addition to organizing your study area, you must also organize your study time. After school each day, look over your assignments. Think of each assignment as a goal. An assignment that is due the next day is a short-term goal. An assignment that is due after several days or weeks is a long-term goal.

To complete each type of assignment, work out a schedule for yourself. If an assignment is short-term, set a time to complete it before the next day. If an assignment is long-term, divide it into steps. Set a time for completing each step.

To help you to schedule your short- and long-term goals, make a study plan each week. Record the time when you will complete each of your assignments.

Check It Out Bill was asked to memorize a poem to recite in speech class. He broke this long-term assignment into steps. He included these steps on his study plan, as follows:

Monday	Tuesday	Wednesday	Thursday	Friday	Saturday
Go to library Get book of poems .... Study for history test	Track practice (4:00) .... Study for history test .... Read poems and choose one	Guitar lesson (5:00) .... Study for history test	Finish memoriz- ing poem	Practice poem .... Danny's birthday party	Dinner at the Smith's ....

- How did Bill divide up his long-term assignment?
- Do you see how this study plan made it easier for Bill to complete his assignment?

Try Your Skill Break up the following sample long-term assignment into several steps. Arrange the steps in order.

Do some research on a famous artist, explorer, or inventor. Write a one-paragraph biography of this person. Tell when and where this person was born. Describe his or her major accomplishments. Today is Monday. The report is due on Friday.

Keep This in Mind

- Choose a study area that is quiet and organized.
- Break all long-term assignments into smaller steps.
- Make a study plan every week.

Now Write Make a study plan like the one shown in **Check It Out**. Include on this plan all your assignments and major activities for one week. Make a study plan every week.

Making the Most of It

The SQ3R Study Method

Here's the Idea Have you ever read an assignment and then forgotten most of what you read? This can be frustrating. It can also lead to poor scores on tests. To avoid this, you should follow a study method. Following a study method can help you to make the most of your reading. One such method is called SQ3R. SQ3R stands for *Survey, Question, Read, Recite,* and *Review.* The following chart describes the SQ3R study method.

Using SQ3R	
Survey.	Look over the material to get a general idea of what you will be reading. Read the introduction and, if there is one, the summary. Check the titles and headings. Look at any illustrations.
Question.	Prepare a set of questions. Decide what questions you should be able to answer at the end of your reading. Use any study questions presented in the book or provided by your teacher. Make up your own study questions by turning each title and heading into a question. Pictures, maps, or charts can also be used to make up questions.
Read.	Look for the answers to your questions as you read. Also identify the main ideas in each section.
Recite.	After you finish your careful reading, recite in your own words the answers to your questions. Make notes on the answers. In addition, make sure you understand any other important points of the selection. Record these too.
Review.	Quickly read over your notes. Look over the main ideas in the book so you will remember them. Look up the answers to any questions you could not answer in the previous step.

Check It Out   Rolanda had to study for a test on Chapter 3 in her biology book. She read the introduction and summary. She glanced at the titles and headings. She made up a list of study questions. Then she read the chapter closely, looking for answers to her questions.

 • What else should Rolanda do?

Try Your Skill   Study this passage, using the SQ3R method.

The **alligator** is a large reptile related to the crocodile. It is found in the southeastern United States and in the lower Chang Jiang river valley in China.

Body. Alligators look like enormous lizards. They have short, stocky legs used for walking and long, powerful tails used for swimming. The jaws of an alligator are filled with many sharp teeth. The muscles that close these jaws are very strong. However, once an alligator's jaws are closed, they can easily be held shut by a human being.

Size. Alligators may grow to twelve feet or more in length. An adult male may weigh from 450 to 550 pounds. An adult female usually weighs much less.

Diet. Alligators eat small animals of all kinds. Their diet includes fish, snakes, frogs, turtles, and various small mammals. Large alligators occasionally attack dogs, pigs, or even cattle. However, alligators rarely attack people.

Keep This in Mind

 • The SQ3R study method consists of five steps: *Survey, Question, Read, Recite,* and *Review.*
 • Use the SQ3R method to study for all your classes.

Now Write   Choose any reading assignment you receive in school today. Using the SQ3R method, study this assignment. First, survey the material. Then, write a list of questions you should be able to answer after you finish reading. Save the list.

Remember This

Taking Notes

Here's the Idea Every day in school you read and hear a great deal of information. Remembering all this information can be difficult. If you take good notes, however, you can review the information at a later time. That's why it is important for you to learn how to take good notes.

Always keep your notes in a notebook. Divide your notebook into sections for each class. Write the date and the subject at the top of each page of notes. Take notes on ideas presented in class and in your reading. Include in your notes any questions that arise when you are studying.

In class, listen for clues that tell what information is important. These clues include phrases such as *most importantly, for these reasons, to conclude, for example, the cause was,* and *to review.* Also listen for vocal clues. Your teacher might slow down, repeat a key word or definition, or pause for emphasis.

As you read, take notes on key words, definitions, and main ideas. Also write the answers to any questions that you develop when using the SQ3R study method.

One way to take good notes is to make a rough outline. As you listen or read, jot down main ideas. Under these main ideas, jot down any supporting examples or details.

When taking notes, write neatly. Make sure that you will be able to read your notes later. Do not waste time writing complete sentences. Instead, use phrases, abbreviations, and symbols.

If you wish to do so, make up your own abbreviations. However, make sure that you will be able to understand these abbreviations when you come back to your notes. The following abbreviations and symbols are often used in note-taking.

Abbreviations and Symbols for Note-Taking

w/	with	info.	information
w/o	without	def.	definition
+	and	Amer.	American
bef.	before	hist.	history
*	important information	tho.	though
		=	is, are, equals

Check It Out Read these notes in rough outline form.

> Science
> Nov. 1
>
> Amphibians
>   -def: animal that lives part of
>   life in water, part on land
> Types of amphibians
>   -Frogs and toads (4 legs, w/o tails)
>   -Salamanders (2 or 4 legs + tails)
>   -Caecilians (look like earthworms)

- What abbreviations and symbols has this student used?

Try Your Skill Using the guidelines in this lesson, take notes on the selection on alligators in Part 4.

Keep This in Mind

- Use a rough outline form when taking notes.
- As you take notes, use phrases, abbreviations, and symbols. Do not use complete sentences.

Now Write Reread Part 2, **This Way, Please.** Take notes on this material, using a rough outline form. Save your notes.

Part 6

One Way or Another

Adjusting Your Reading Rate

Here's the Idea   When you are in a hurry, you run or walk quickly. When you are not in a hurry, you walk more slowly. In other words, you change your speed depending on your purpose. Similarly, you can change the way you read depending on what you are reading and why you are reading it.

In-Depth Reading   When you need to learn new or difficult material, read slowly and carefully. Follow the SQ3R method. Read every word. Pay particular attention to definitions, key words, topic sentences, and headings. These will help you to find the main ideas. Once you have identified the main ideas, look for any supporting details.

Fast Reading   Sometimes you may need to use a faster type of reading. Two useful types of fast reading are skimming and scanning.

   1. **Skimming** involves moving your eyes quickly over a whole page or selection. When skimming, do not read every word. Instead, note titles, subtitles, headings, pictures, and graphic aids. Use skimming to get a general idea of the content of a selection. You can also use it to survey material as the first step in the SQ3R study method.

   2. **Scanning** involves moving your eyes quickly across a line or down a page. It is used to locate specific information. Again, do not read every word. Instead, look for a key word or phrase that shows that you are close to the information you need. When you locate such a clue, read more slowly.

Check It Out   Tim took a test in his science class. One of the questions asked for a definition of the word *Phylum*. Tim couldn't remember the definition. After the test, he checked the definition in his science book. He knew it was in Chapter 2.

- What kind of fast reading should Tim do, skimming or scanning? Explain your answer.

Try Your Skill Follow these directions one at a time. Do *not* read all of the directions first.

1. Read the passage in depth.
2. Scan to answer the following questions:
   a. How large is the Dismal Swamp?
   b. What plant life grows there?
   c. What animals live there?

One of the most interesting places in America is the Dismal Swamp. This is a wild marshland in northeastern North Carolina and southeastern Virginia. The swamp covers about 750 square miles. It is a tangle of vines and trees. Its trees include pines, junipers, and bald cypresses. Its wildlife includes bears, deer, opossums, raccoons, and snakes.

Keep This in Mind

- Choose a reading speed that suits the material you are reading and your reason for reading it.
- Use in-depth reading when you wish to learn new or difficult material.
- Use skimming to survey material.
- Use scanning to locate specific information.

Now Write Find a recent copy of a local newspaper. First, scan the front page. Make a list of people whose names are in the news. Second, skim the articles on the front page. Tell what each article is about. Finally, read one article in depth and summarize it. Write your answers on a piece of paper. Label this paper **One Way or Another.** Save it in your folder.

Seeing Is Believing

Using Graphic Aids

Here's the Idea Not all information is presented in words. Some information comes in the form of photographs, illustrations, diagrams, maps, tables, charts, and graphs. Such materials are called **graphic aids.** The following are the most common graphic aids:

Photographs and illustrations are used to show how things look. They are also used to create a mood or a feeling. Always read any captions or labels given with a picture.

Diagrams are drawings that show the parts of a thing. They allow you to identify each part and to see how the parts are related. Always read any captions or labels given with a diagram.

Maps show locations of cities, countries, oceans, mountains, rivers, and other parts of the Earth. They can also show such information as population or climate. Always look for the legend that is found on most maps. The **legend** will help you to figure out distances or directions on the map.

Tables and charts are used to list or compare information. Information is usually presented in labeled columns. Always read any captions or titles given with tables or charts.

Graphs show relationships between facts. Sometimes they show how facts change over time. (See Part 8 for more information on graphs.) Always read any captions, titles, or labels included with graphs.

Check It Out Study the graphic aids on the next page.

- Which graphic aid is a map? an illustration? a diagram? a graph? a table?

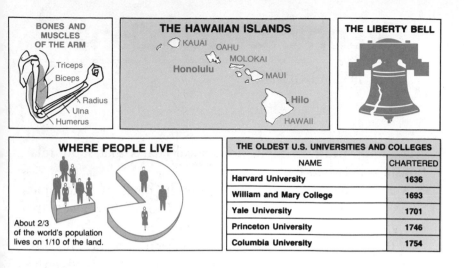

THE OLDEST U.S. UNIVERSITIES AND COLLEGES	
NAME	CHARTERED
Harvard University	1636
William and Mary College	1693
Yale University	1701
Princeton University	1746
Columbia University	1754

Try Your Skill   Look at the graphic aids in **Check It Out.** Answer these questions:

1. On which island is Hilo situated?
2. What proportion of the world's population lives on 9/10 of the land?
3. Name two muscles of the upper arm.
4. Which is the second oldest university in the United States?

Now Write   Make one of the following graphic aids.

1. **A Map.** Using a ruler, draw a map of the main floor of your school. Show where important areas, such as the library or gym, are located. Include a caption and a legend.
2. **A Diagram.** Trace a picture of a musical instrument or an automobile. Then, using information from an encyclopedia, label the parts of your drawing. Write a caption for your diagram.

Graphic Descriptions

Reading Graphs

Here's the Idea   Graphs are special charts that show relationships between facts.

A **circle graph** uses a circle to show the parts of something. The circle represents all of something. The sections inside the circle represent the parts of the thing.

A **bar graph** shows relationships between two sets of facts. One set of facts is given in numbers. The other is given in words. Bars are used to show how the facts are related.

A **picture graph** is similar to a bar graph. However, it uses pictures instead of bars.

A **line graph** uses a line to show how something has changed over a period of time.

Check It Out   Study these graphs.

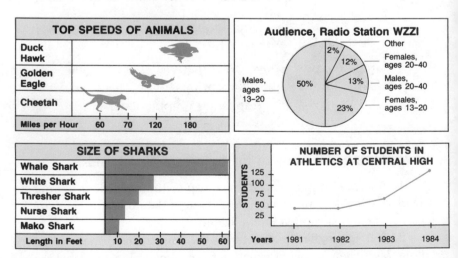

- Which is a circle graph? a bar graph? a picture graph? a line graph?

Try Your Skill Study the graphs given in **Check It Out.** Then answer these questions:

1. What percentage of the audience of Station WZZT is female?
2. What is the second largest shark?
3. What is the top speed for a land animal?
4. What happened to student athletics at Central High after 1983?

Keep This in Mind

- Graphs show relationships between facts.
- Always read any titles, captions, or labels given with a graph.

Now Write Find a graph in a newspaper, magazine, or textbook. Copy the graph onto your own paper. Under the graph, describe its purpose. In other words, tell what information it contains. Label your paper **Graphic Descriptions.** Save it in your folder.

Part 9

Testing, Testing

Preparing for and Taking Tests

Here's the Idea   Test-taking is a skill, just as playing football or riding a bicycle is. You can improve your performance in any skill by working at it. The way to improve test-taking skills is to learn how to prepare for and complete tests.

Before you take a test, make sure that you are properly prepared. The following guidelines will help you.

Preparing for Tests

1. **Know exactly what you will be tested on.** If you have questions, ask your teacher.

2. **Make a study plan.** Allow yourself plenty of time to review.

3. **When you review, reread your notes.** Skim any reading materials covered by the test. Answer any questions that you wrote while using the SQ3R study method. Also answer any study questions given by your teacher.

4. **Make lists of important names, dates, definitions, or events.** Ask a friend or family member to quiz you on these.

5. **Go over your materials more than once.**

6. **Eat well and get plenty of sleep before the test.**

Knowing what to do before a test is important. So is knowing what to do during a test. The following guidelines will help you to use your test-taking time wisely.

Taking a Test

1. **Survey the test.** Look at the test to see what types of questions are included.

2. **Plan your time.** Decide on the order in which you will answer the questions. Decide how much time you will need for each part of the test. Answer the easiest questions first. Be sure to allow extra time for long or complicated questions.

3. **Read all directions and test questions carefully.** Read all the directions before you answer any of the questions. Make sure that you understand the directions completely.

4. **Save time for review.** Once you have finished, look over the test. Make sure you have not left out any answers. Reread any answers you are unsure of. Try to answer any questions that you skipped.

Check It Out Larry's history teacher announced a test on Chapter 12, "The Civil War." Larry read the chapter twice.

- What else should Larry have done?

Try Your Skill Reread the guidelines on these pages. Write a few guidelines that you could add. Compare your list with those of your classmates.

Keep This in Mind

- Prepare carefully before taking tests.
- When taking tests, read all of the directions and plan your time well. Save time for review.

Now Write Think about a test that you took recently. What could you have done to prepare more fully for this test? Write a paragraph telling what you can do to improve your test-taking skills. Label your paper **Testing, Testing.** Save it in your folder.

The Answer Key

Answering Objective Test Questions

Here's the Idea One way to prepare for tests is to learn guidelines for answering the many types of test questions. This chart describes the kinds of questions found on objective tests. **Objective tests** require simple right or wrong answers.

Questions Found on Objective Tests	
Description	**Guidelines**
TRUE/FALSE You are given a statement and asked to tell whether the statement is true or false.	1. Remember that if any part of a statement is false, all of it is false. 2. Words like *all, always, only, never,* and *everyone* often appear in false statements. 3. Words like *some, a few, usually, often,* and *most* often appear in true statements.
MATCHING You are asked to match items in one column with items in another column.	1. Check the directions. See if each item is used only once. Also check to see if some are not used at all. 2. Read all items before starting. 3. Match those you know first. 4. Cross out items as you use them.
MULTIPLE CHOICE You are asked to choose the best answer from a group of answers given on the test.	1. Read *all* choices first. 2. Eliminate incorrect answers. 3. Choose the answer that is most complete or accurate. 4. Pay particular attention to choices such as *none of the above* or *all of the above*.

Check It Out Read the following test questions.

1. True or False: Norway is located in the northern hemisphere. ___T___

2. Which of the following is not part of Scandinavia?
   a. Denmark b. Sweden c. Scotland d. Norway e. Finland

3. Match the country in the first column with its capital in the second column.

Norway — Stockholm
Finland — Oslo
Sweden — Copenhagen
Denmark — Helsinki

- What kind of answer is called for by each of these questions?

Try Your Skill Tell what type of test each phrase below describes.

1. is often set up in columns
2. can be made false by words such as *all* or *never*
3. may contain answers such as "all of the above"

Keep This in Mind

- There are three types of objective test questions: true/false, multiple choice, and matching.
- Follow specific guidelines for answering different types of test questions.

Now Write Choose a popular television program or movie. Write an objective test about it. Include three true/false questions and three multiple choice questions. Also include a matching question with a list of five items to match with five other items. Exchange tests with a classmate. Answer the questions on your classmate's test. Return it to be graded.

Part 11

Get It in Writing

Answering Written Test Questions

Here's the Idea Completion, short answer, and essay questions all require written answers. This chart offers guidelines for answering three types of written test questions.

Types of Written Test Questions	
Description	**Strategies**
COMPLETION You are required to add a word or a phrase to an incomplete sentence given on the test.	1. If several words are required, give all of them. 2. Write neatly. Use good spelling, grammar, punctuation, and capitalization.
SHORT ANSWER You are required to write one or two sentences to answer the question.	1. Use complete sentences. 2. Answer the question completely. 3. Use correct spelling, grammar, punctuation, and capitalization.
ESSAY You are required to write one or more paragraphs to answer the question.	1. Follow pre-writing steps before answering the question. 2. Look for action words like *explain* or *compare*. These are words that tell you what to do. 3. Make a rough outline of your essay on a separate sheet of paper. 4. Make sure each paragraph contains a topic sentence. 5. Proofread your completed essay.

Check It Out   Read the following questions.

    1. _____ live longer than any other animals.

    2. In a paragraph or two, explain what a *barometer* is and how it works.

    3. In a couple of sentences, define "myth" and give an example.

    • Which of these is an essay question? Which is short answer? Which is completion?

Try Your Skill   Review Part 10, **The Answer Key.** Then, answer the following questions.

    1. A question that asks a student to pick the best answer from a list provided on the test is a _____ question.

    2. What is a *matching question?* (Answer in a complete sentence.)

    3. What strategies can be used to answer a true/false question? (Answer in a complete paragraph.)

Keep This in Mind

- Completion questions are answered with a word or a phrase.
- Short answer questions are answered with complete sentences.
- Essay questions are answered with one or more paragraphs.

Now Write   Choose a reading assignment from one of your classes. Write an essay question that you might be asked on a test covering this material. Then, write an answer to your essay question. Follow the guidelines for answering essay questions given on page 296. Label your completed essay **Get It in Writing.** Save it in your folder.

Letters, Forms, and Applications

Part 1 **Mail Call**
How To Write a Friendly Letter

Part 2 **A Proper Send-off**
How To Prepare Letters for the Mail

Part 3 **Thanks So Much**
How To Write Social Notes

Part 4 **Be Businesslike**
How To Write a Business Letter

Part 5 **Help!**
How To Write a Letter of Request

Part 6 **Letters That Work**
How To Write Letters of Application

Part 7 **Apply Yourself**
How To Complete a Job Application

Part 8 **Paperwork**
How To Complete Work-Related Forms

Mail Call

How To Write a Friendly Letter

Here's the Idea Writing a letter is one of the best ways of keeping in touch with someone. A letter to someone you know is called a **friendly letter**. A friendly letter should be detailed and lively. It should sound natural and be neat and easy to read.

The form of any friendly letter has five main parts: the *heading*, the *salutation* or greeting, the *body* or main part, the *closing*, and the *signature*.

The **heading** tells where you are. It consists of three lines: two for your address and one for the date. Do not use any abbreviations. The heading appears at the top right corner.

The **salutation** is your way of saying "hello" on paper. It can be simply "Dear Bob" or "Hi." The salutation is written on the next line below the heading. It starts at the left margin of the page and is followed by a comma.

In the **body,** the main part of the letter, you say what you want to say. Try to be interesting and specific. Imagine that you are in the same room with your friend. What would you talk about? The body begins on the line following the salutation. The first word of the body and of each new paragraph should be indented.

The **closing** is your way of saying "goodbye." Common closings are *Sincerely, Yours truly, Love,* or *Your friend.* The closing is written on the line below the last word of the body and is followed by a comma. The first word of the closing should line up with the first words of the heading.

Your **signature** is the last part of your letter. Skip a line after the closing, and sign your name in line with the first word of the closing. If you are writing to someone you know well, use your first name. Otherwise, sign your full name.

32 Fifth Street
Wheaton, Illinois 60187
February 18, 1985

Dear Dan,

I'm so glad to hear that you will be out of the hospital next week. I imagine you'll be glad to be back at home and school. The whole class has missed your corny jokes.

The school play almost went off smoothly yesterday. Jeff stole the show. He was supposed to fall down and act dead, and he did. Then, about five minutes later, when everyone had assumed he was dead, he gave one enormous shudder and kick. For the rest of the act, everyone kept watching to see if he'd do something else. It was really funny.

Your mom said you would be home on Thursday. See you then!

Your friend,
Jean

- What details make this letter interesting?
- Identify the five parts of the letter.

Try Your Skill Put the following information in the correct form.

> 11 Madison Street, Boston, Massachusetts 02109, July 21, 1985, Dear Greg, I'll be glad to meet your train. Let's plan to meet next to the information booth under the clock. I've had my hair cut, but you'll still recognize me. Your friend, Ben.

Keep This in Mind

- A friendly letter should be lively, natural, and neat.
- A friendly letter should follow the correct form. The heading, salutation, body, closing, and signature should each be written correctly.

Now Write Write a letter to a friend or relative. Tell about what you've been doing in school or at home. Use your home address and today's date in the heading. Be sure that the five main parts of your letter follow the correct form. Label your paper **Mail Call** and save it in your folder.

A Proper Send-off

How To Prepare Letters for the Mail

Here's the Idea   When you have finished writing a letter, fold it neatly. Choose an envelope that matches the width of the stationery. Insert the folded letter and seal the envelope.
Prepare the envelope carefully. Follow these steps:

1. Address the envelope. Add your return address.
2. Double-check all numbers to make sure they are correct.
3. Include the correct **ZIP** code.
4. Put a stamp on the envelope.

Always check envelopes and packages for accuracy. If you need information about mailing procedures, call your local post office.

Check It Out   Look at the envelope below.

Bonnie Calhoun
127 Las Olas Avenue
Orlando, FL 32802

Paul Berman
21 Holden Street
Minneapolis, MN 55401

- Who will receive the letter? Who sent the letter? What state abbreviations are used? How could you check that the ZIP codes are correct?

Try Your Skill   Write each of the jumbled addresses below as it should appear on an envelope. Also write a return address using your own name and address.

1. Madison, Wisconsin 53705, Chris Dombrowski, 26 Marshall Avenue

2. Dr. Linda S. Adams, 421 Woodfield Road, Gulfport, Mississippi 39503

3. 85 East 121st Street, New York, New York 10035, Peter Bucci

4. Barbara McKenna, Tulsa, Oklahoma 74101, 1728 Columbus Avenue

5. Mr. and Mrs. Luis Perez, 882 Fairfax Road, San Leandro, California 94577

Keep This in Mind

- Be careful when preparing letters for the mail. Fold your letters neatly. Check addresses for accuracy. Make sure all information is correct and clear.

Now Write   Take out the friendly letter you wrote in the last lesson, **Mail Call.** Address an envelope to your friend or relative. Fold your letter and put it into the envelope.

Save your letter in your folder.

3

Thanks So Much

How To Write Social Notes

Here's the Idea   A social note is written for a special occasion. Invitations and thank-you notes are social notes. Because they are forms of friendly letters, social notes also have five main parts. The heading, however, may be shortened to the date only.

If you send an **invitation,** you must include specific information about *what, when,* and *where.* When you receive an invitation, you should reply immediately. Tell whether or not you can attend.

You may also send **thank-you** notes. One kind of thank-you note is written after you have received a gift. You do not only thank the sender for the gift. You also thank that person for thinking of you. Maybe the sweater you received is not your favorite color. However, you should say thanks graciously for the time and effort that went into choosing the gift and sending it. If you received a gift that you really do enjoy, tell what makes it so special. Let the sender share your pleasure.

A second kind of thank-you note is a **bread-and-butter** note. It thanks someone for his or her hospitality. If you stayed overnight as a guest in someone's house, you would write this kind of social note.

Whenever you write either of these kinds of thank-you notes, be sure to express your appreciation to the other person. It is also important that you write your thank-you note as soon as possible.

Check It Out   Read the social note on page 306.

- What kind of social note is this? How is the form of this letter different from that of the friendly letter shown on page 301?

September 5, 1985

Dear Stan,

The box of candy you sent was one of the best birthday presents I've ever received. How did you know how much I like chocolates? What a luxury to have an entire box! I will enjoy every last piece. I only wish you were here to share the candy with me.

Again, thanks for the candy.

Your friend,
Jesse

Try Your Skill You have received a purple sweater as a birthday gift from your best friend. Write a thank-you note.

Keep This in Mind

- Social notes are short forms of friendly letters
- Invitations should include *what*, *when*, and *where*.
- Thank-you notes should express your appreciation. They should be sent immediately after you receive a gift.

Now Write Label your paper **Thanks So Much.** Write an invitation, a thank-you note, or a bread-and-butter note to someone you know. Use the correct form. Save your work in your folder.

Be Businesslike

How To Write a Business Letter

Here's the Idea   Sometimes you may want to order a product by mail, complain about something you ordered, or request certain information. In each of these situations, you would need to write or type a **business letter.**

A business letter has the five parts that a friendly letter has. These parts are the **heading,** the **salutation,** the **body,** the **closing,** and the **signature.** Business letters also have one additional part, the inside address. The **inside address** contains the name and address of the company to which you are writing. Whenever possible, the inside address should also include the name of a particular department or employee within the company. The inside address comes below the heading and above the salutation. It begins at the left margin.

The salutations and closings are more formal in a business letter than in a friendly letter. If you are writing to a specific person, use *Dear Mr., Mrs., Miss,* or *Ms.* before the person's name. Otherwise, use a general greeting like *Dear Sir or Madam.* The salutation appears two lines below the inside address and is followed by a colon (:).

For the closing, use the words *Sincerely, Very truly yours,* or *Yours truly,* followed by a comma. If your letter is typed, leave four lines of space between the closing and your typed signature. Then, write your signature in the space.

A business letter may use one of two forms. The easiest to remember is the *block* form. This should be used only if you type a letter. In a block form, every part begins at the left margin. Two lines of space are left between paragraphs, and the paragraphs are not indented. A *modified block* form may be used either for handwritten or typewritten letters. This form puts the heading, closing, and signature at the right side of the page. The paragraphs are indented, and no extra space is left between them.

Whether you write or type a business letter, it is important to make it neat and to use the correct form. Be direct and clear. Always make copies of business letters to keep for your records.

Check It Out   Read this business letter.

1132 Davis Boulevard
Arlington, Virginia 22209
June 3, 1985

Sweetsound Products
43 Chestnut Street
Durham, North Carolina 25710

Dear Sir or Madam:

On March 8, 1985, I sent you an order for the special record album that you advertised in Stereo magazine. The record was called Michael Jackson: The Early Years.

The album has not yet arrived and I have not heard from your company. However, my check for $10 has been cashed. Enclosed is a copy of the canceled check. Please let me know when I may expect to receive the record or a refund.

Sincerely,

Donna Lee

Donna Lee

- What is the purpose of this business letter?
- In what form is this letter typed? Identify the six parts of the letter.

Try Your Skill   Write a letter from the sales manager of Sweetsound Products to Donna Lee. Have the company respond to her letter. Make up any necessary details. For this exercise, you may use either the block form or the modified block form.

Keep This in Mind

- A business letter may be written to express a request, to order a product, or to send a complaint. A business letter may be typed or handwritten. Always keep a copy of a business letter.
- *Block* and *modified block* are two forms for writing a business letter. Both forms have six parts, including an inside address.

Now Write   Using any newspaper or magazine, find an advertisement for a free booklet or free information. Write a business letter asking for the advertised item. Write the letter in block or modified block form. Make a copy of the letter. Also, address an envelope. Fold your original letter properly and put it in a stamped envelope. Mail the letter. Save the copy of your letter in your folder. When you get the item you ordered, bring it to school to show to your class.

Help!

How To Write a Letter of Request

Here's the Idea Sometimes you will want to write a letter to request information. You may be planning a trip to another state and want information about its points of interest. Perhaps you would like a company to send you a brochure explaining its products. Maybe you would like a school or camp to send you a catalog describing its program. You can receive this valuable information by writing a **letter of request.**

A letter of request is a type of business letter. It should contain the six main parts of a business letter: *heading, inside address, salutation, body, closing,* and *signature.* You may follow either the *block* or *modified block* form when you write or type a letter of request.

Be specific when you make a request of any kind. Be sure you have included every bit of information necessary to get just what you want. If you are writing to get product information, be specific about the product you are interested in. Include important details about the product such as its size, color, cost, or identification number.

Besides being specific, you should be brief. A letter of request should be direct and to the point. If you want information about motels near Cooperstown, New York, you do not have to explain that you have always wanted to visit the Baseball Hall of Fame. Simply ask the Chamber of Commerce for a list of motels. However, if you want to know what you can see in Cooperstown besides the Baseball Hall of Fame, ask for sightseeing information.

Finally, remember that someone will have to take the time to send you what you have requested. Be sure you have asked for help in a polite way.

Check It Out Read the following letter of request.

11 Lakewood Drive
Lincoln, Nebraska 68501
January 15, 1985

Clowns of America
2715 East Fayette Street
Baltimore, Maryland, 21224

Dear Sir or Madam:

   I am writing a term paper on clowns. I would like to know what training or schooling is necessary to become a circus clown. Where can people receive such training? Please send me whatever information you have available.

Sincerely,

Lee Bowen

Lee Bowen

- Is this letter of request specific, brief, and polite?
- How does the modified block form of this letter differ from the block form of the letter on page 308?

Try Your Skill   Write a letter to the Society of American Magicians, 66 Marked Tree Road, Needham, Massachusetts 02192. Ask for information about joining the society. For this exercise you may use either the block form or the modified block form.

Keep This in Mind

- A letter of request should be specific, brief and polite. It may be either handwritten or typewritten.
- The *block* or *modified block* form may be used for this kind of business letter.

Now Write   Write a letter of request to a business or organization in your area. For example, you might want to write to the Chamber of Commerce to ask for a list of local restaurants. Use the phone book to find the address of the business. Address and stamp an envelope. Make a copy of your letter to save in your folder. Mail your letter of request. Bring any reply you receive to class.

Letters That Work

6

How To Write Letters of Application

Here's the Idea Writing a business letter can be useful when you decide to look for a job. By writing letters of application, you can find out which jobs are available.

When writing to an employer, be neat and careful. This letter will be the first example of your work that the employer sees. The following guidelines will help you.

Guidelines for Letters of Application

1. State the exact title of the job you are seeking. Do you want to be a *bagger?* Do you want to be a *cashier?*

2. Tell the employer whether you want to work part-time or full-time. Also let the employer know if you are seeking a temporary job. A job is **temporary** if it will only last for a short period of time.

3. Give some information about yourself. State your age and grade level in school. Tell the employer why you are qualified for the job. Mention any previous work experience or courses in school that have prepared you for the job. Also mention any special skills or personal qualities that you have. For example, if you are good at math, you could say so.

4. Be specific about when you can work. Let the employer know when you can start and what hours you are available.

5. Request an interview if the job is located near you. If you are writing to a large company, address the letter to the *personnel director.* If you are writing to a small business, address your letter to the *manager* or *owner.* If you are answering a newspaper advertisement, read the ad carefully to find out how you should reply. Send your letter to the address given.

111 Hampton Road
Springfield, IL 62708
April 3, 1985

Ms. Carol Wolf
Sunnyday Camp
29 Capitol Road
Springfield, IL 62708

Dear Ms. Wolf:

I am interested in working as a day camp counselor at your camp
this summer. I am 14 years old and a freshman at Liberty High
School. I am now taking a course in child development. Last
summer I worked as a junior counselor for the Park District. I
also babysit for several neighbors' children during the school
year. You will find that I am reliable and hardworking. I get
along well with children and know a great deal about arts,
crafts, games, and other camp activities.

I will be available for full-time work on June 12. I can work
until the end of the camp session, August 22.

Please contact me for an interview at your convenience. My
telephone number is (217) 555-0900.

Thank you,

Sheila Logan

Sheila Logan

- Does this letter follow all of the **Guidelines for Letters of Application?** Explain your answer.

Try Your Skill   Write a letter answering one of the following newspaper ads.

1. Wanted: Groundskeeper for Lakeshore Inn, Seaside Road, Greenlake, Wisconsin 54941. Temporary position: June 5–August 25.
2. Wanted: Dining room help for Redwood Inn. Part-time. Write Mr. Ed Kelly, PO Box 222, Portland, Oregon 97208.
3. Wanted: Cashier. Christmas vacation only. Contact Tiny Tots Toys, 40 Surrey Lane, Augusta, Georgia 30903.

Keep This in Mind

- Letters to employers should be neat, informative, and courteous.
- Include specific information about yourself and about the job you want.

Now Write   Choose a department store or restaurant near or in your town. Write a letter asking for a job. Follow the guidelines given on page 313. Include all the necessary information. Proofread your letter carefully. Title your paper **Letters That Work.** Save it in your folder.

Apply Yourself

How To Complete a Job Application

Here's the Idea When you write a letter requesting a job, you may get one of several responses. You may be told that there is no job available or that the job is not right for you. You may be asked to come in for an interview. You may receive an application form and be asked to complete and return it. Whatever the response, make sure you follow the employer's instructions exactly.

When it comes time for you to complete a job application form, follow these guidelines.

Completing Job Applications

1. **Read all directions carefully, especially those in fine print.** For example, you may be asked to give your last name first or your first name first. Only by reading the directions can you tell what to do. The ability to follow directions is an important job skill. Show the employer that you can follow directions well.

2. **Be neat.** Print your answers carefully. Use a good pen with blue or black ink. You will find that there is often very little space for the information requested. Therefore, plan your answers before you print them. If you do make an error, erase it. If you cannot erase it, draw a single line through the error and write in the correct information above the line.

3. **Be prepared to answer several basic questions.** Study the sample job application form on page 318. You can expect to have to answer similar questions on most job application forms. Have this information with you when you complete the form. In particular, make sure you have the names and addresses of two or three references. These are people not related to you who have known

you a long time and who would be willing to discuss your abilities. For example, a reference may be a former employer, a teacher, or a clergyman.

4. **Complete every item.** There may be questions that you cannot answer, such as a question about military service. However, you must never leave any space blank on an application. Leaving a blank space is confusing. If an item does not apply to you, write "Does Not Apply" in that space.

5. **Be honest.** You will be asked to sign your name to a statement declaring that all your information is accurate.

Check It Out   Examine the completed job application on the next page.

- Has the application form been filled in neatly and carefully? Have all the instructions been followed?
- Have all items on the application form been answered completely? How might an employer check that the answers are honest and accurate?

Try Your Skill   Suppose you were applying today for a summer job as an assistant at the public library. On a sheet of paper, copy the sample application form as it is shown on page 318. Fill out the application as you would actually complete it.

Keep This in Mind

- Fill in the items on an application by printing as neatly. Read all directions on the form.
- Answer all items honestly and accurately.

Now Write   Obtain a job application form from your teacher or from a local business. Complete the form neatly and honestly. Save it in your folder.

Application for Employment

Personal Information 9/1/85 869-28-0827
Date   Social Security Number

Name Block   Thomas   Carl
      Last   First   Middle

Present Address 1507 Kennedy Drive, Waltham, Mass. 02154
                 Street   City   State   Zip

Phone Number 555-1742 Date of Birth 3/8/70 U.S. Citizen (Yes) No

Employment Desired

Position part-time kitchen help (after school) Date You Monday Salary
                                                Can Start 9/10/85 Desired open

Are You Employed Now? No Where? Does not apply Duties Does not apply

Education	Name and Location of School	Years Attended	Date Graduated	Course of Study
Grammar School	Brookside School Merrick, New York	1975-1984	June, 1984	Does not apply
High School	North High School Waltham, Mass.	1984-present	Does not apply	Business Course

College or Trade School Does not apply

Military Service Does not apply

Former Employers *(List your last two employers, starting with the more recent one)*

Dates	Name and Address of Employer	Salary	Position	Reason for Leaving
From To Christmas 1984	Simpson's Department Store Arlington, Mass.	$2.90 per hour	Stock boy	Christmas only
From To	Does not apply			

References *Name two persons, not related to you, who have known you at least one year.*

Name	Address	Business
Ms. Emily Norcott	North High School Waltham, Mass. 02154	math teacher
Dr. John McGrath	173 Wesley Street Waltham Mass. 02154	family doctor

In Case of Emergency Notify Carl and Janet Block 1507 Kennedy Drive Waltham, Mass. 02154 555-1742
                             Name   Address   Phone No.

I authorize investigation of all statements contained in this application. I understand that misrepresentation or omission of facts called for is cause for dismissal.

September 1, 1985   Thomas Carl Block
Date   Signature of Applicant

318

Paperwork

How To Complete Work-Related Forms

Here's the Idea   Once you accept a job, you may be asked to complete several other job-related forms. When completing these forms, follow the guidelines for neatness, completeness, and accuracy that you learned in the last lesson.

The following job-related forms are common:

Social Security Card.   You need a social security number in order to get paid. To get a number, you must fill out a form. The form asks for information about when you were born. It also asks whether you are a citizen of the United States. You can get this form from your local Social Security office.

Work Permit.   In most states, if you are under 16 years old, you'll need a work permit to begin a job. The application for a work permit asks information about your birth date. It also asks about where your job is located, the kind of job you have, and how many hours a week you will work. The application asks about your health and school record. Forms for work permits are available from your school's guidance office.

W-4 Form.   Once you are working, you will have to pay taxes. The Federal Government requires every worker to fill out a W-4 form. This form asks you how many people you will support with your salary. There is also a place on the form where you can indicate that you are not self-supporting and earn a minimum amount of money. If your state has a state income tax, you may have to fill out a similar form for your state taxes. Your employer will give these forms to you.

Check It Out   Examine the sample W-4 form on the following page.

6-82

Form **W-4**
(Rev. January 1983)

Department of the Treasury—Internal Revenue Service

Employee's Withholding Allowance Certificate

W-4 1

OMB No. 1545-0010

Expires 8-31-87

1 Type or print your full name

Arletta Vaughn Davis

Home address (number and street or rural route)

800 W Argyle

City or town, State, and ZIP code

Chicago, IL 60640

2 Your social security number

427-58-9178

3 Marital
Status

☒ Single ☐ Married
☐ Married, but withhold at higher Single rate

Note: If married, but legally separated, or spouse is a nonresident alien, check the Single box.

4 Total number of allowances you are claiming (from line F of the worksheet on page 2) .... | 1

5 Additional amount, if any, you want deducted from each pay .... | $ | 0

6 I claim exemption from withholding because (see instructions and check boxes below that apply):

a ☒ Last year I did not owe any Federal income tax and had a right to a full refund of ALL income tax withheld, AND

b ☒ This year I do not expect to owe any Federal income tax and expect to have a right to a full refund of ALL income tax withheld. If both a and b apply, enter the year effective and "EXEMPT" here .... ▶ | Year | 1985 Exempt

c If you entered "EXEMPT" on line 6b, are you a full-time student? .... ☒ Yes ☐ No

Under the penalties of perjury, I certify that I am entitled to the number of withholding allowances claimed on this certificate, or if claiming exemption from withholding, that I am entitled to claim the exempt status.

Employee's signature ▶ Arletta Vaughn Davis   Date ▶ December 15   19 85

7 Employer's name and address (Employer: Complete 7, 8, and 9 only if sending to IRS)

8 Office code

9 Employer identification number

- Have all items been answered completely, neatly, and carefully?
- Have all instructions been followed?

Try Your Skill   Ask your school's guidance office for an application for a work permit. Using the guidelines in this lesson, complete the form neatly, completely, and accurately.

Keep This in Mind

- The three most common job-related forms are the social security application, the work permit application, and the W-4 form.
- These forms must be filled out neatly, completely, and accurately.

Now Write   Obtain a social security card form from your local Social Security office. If you don't know where the office is, look up the address in your phone directory. Fill out the form, using the skills you have learned. If you do not already have a card, return the finished form to the Social Security office.

ACTUAL RELIEF
MODEL OF THE
UNITED STATES
■ ABOVE 9843 FEET
■ 6562 TO 9842 FEET
■ 1640 TO 6561 FEET
■ SEA LEVEL TO 1639 FEET
■ SEA LEVEL TO 6562 FEET DEEP
■ BELOW 6561 FEET DEEP
HORIZONTAL SCALE 1:5,000,000
VERTICAL SCALE 1:2,00,000

Preparing a Talk

Part 1 **A Manner of Speaking**
Formal and Informal Talks

Part 2 **Look Before You Leap**
Preparing an Informal Talk

Part 3 **A Formal Engagement**
Preparing a Formal Talk

Part 4 **Source Sorcery**
Gathering and Organizing Information

Part 5 **Together at Last**
Writing a Formal Talk

Part 6 **Special Delivery**
Presenting Yourself to an Audience

Part 7 **Mirror, Mirror**
Practicing a Talk

Part 8 **Have You Heard?**
Listening to and Judging Talks

A Manner of Speaking

Formal and Informal Talks

Here's the Idea Do you know what tops the list of the most commonly reported fears? Fear of the dark? Fear of spiders? Fear of falling? No. The most commonly reported fear is stage fright—fear of speaking in front of people.

There are two ways to overcome stage fright. One way is to give lots of talks. Each talk you give increases your confidence. Another way is to be prepared when you give a talk. You can feel much more at ease if you know exactly what you want to say.

The amount of preparation required for a talk depends on the type of talk you give. **Informal talks** require little preparation. They are short and are used to present information quickly. The following are some types of informal talks:

1. Announcements tell about some past or future event. A talk about an upcoming art fair would be an announcement.

2. Directions tell other people how to do something or how to get somewhere. A talk explaining how to get from your school to a local amusement park would be an example of giving directions.

3. Introductions present people to audiences. A talk presenting a candidate for the student council would be an introduction.

4. Demonstrations show how something is done. A talk showing how to make a videotape would be a demonstration.

Formal talks require more preparation than informal talks. They are also usually longer. They present a specific subject in detail. An in-depth talk on the origins of football would be a formal talk.

Check It Out   Read the following selection from a talk.

Ladies and gentlemen of the jury, you have seen much evidence against Mr. Moriarity. This evidence may seem convincing. However, I will now prove that my client is innocent. Let me begin by reminding you that no one saw Mr. Moriarity at the scene of the crime. This is odd, indeed, for the crime took place in broad daylight. (The speaker continues to talk for two hours.)

- Is this an informal talk or a formal talk?

Try Your Skill   Read the following descriptions of talks. Which are informal talks? Which are formal talks?

1. The President of the United States giving the "State of the Union" address
2. A play director telling when and where tryouts will be held
3. A teacher explaining to a group of new students how to get to the school library
4. A student giving a report to her science class on differences between the planets in our solar system

Keep This in Mind

- Practice and preparation can reduce stage fright.
- Informal talks are short. They require little preparation. They are used to present information quickly.
- Formal talks are longer. They require much more preparation than informal talks. They cover a specific subject in detail.

Now Write   Think of a time when you delivered a talk. What was the subject of your talk? To whom did you give your talk? Was it a formal talk or an informal one? Did you feel stage fright? Why? Answer these questions in a paragraph. Label your paper **Speak Up.** Save it in your folder.

Look Before You Leap

Preparing an Informal Talk

Here's the Idea   Even informal talks require some preparation. Whenever you are asked to give a talk, first think it through. What do you want to say? What details must you include? The answers to these questions will depend upon the type of talk you are going to give.

1. Announcements should be short and clear. They should answer the questions *who? what? when? where?* and *why?*

> Tomorrow at 2:00 in the gymnasium, the marching band will meet to practice for the Labor Day Parade. Band members, please bring your uniforms and sheet music with you to the gym.

This short announcement answers all five questions.

2. Directions should be exact. They should include all necessary or helpful details. They should not leave out any steps.

> To get to the Lilly Library, walk two blocks north on Dunn Street. At the corner of Dunn and 7th Street, turn right. Walk east on 7th Street, past the Student Union, until you come to a fountain. The Lilly Library will be directly across from the fountain, on the right side.

3. Introductions should be courteous and polite. They should supply information about the person being introduced. Make sure that you have enough information about the person before you begin. If you need more information, interview the person.

> Today's speaker is Mr. Brad Keating. Mr. Keating sings professionally in the Chicago area. Last year he was a finalist in the San Francisco Opera auditions. He is here to speak to you about careers in music. Please welcome Mr. Brad Keating.

4. Demonstrations should be well organized. Each step should be performed for the audience and explained as it is performed. Suppose you wanted to demonstrate how to change a bicycle tire. You would actually change a tire, describing each step while performing it. You will find it helpful to practice with such objects before giving the demonstration.

Check It Out   Read this situation.

> Someone stopped Helene on the street and said, "Excuse me. I am from out of town. Will you please direct me to the Post Office?" Helene replied, "Oh, sure, the Post Office is a couple blocks from here. You go that way. It's a big building. You can't miss it."

- What is wrong with the directions given by Helene?

Try Your Skill   Interview one of your classmates. Ask questions about your classmate's interests, activities, and accomplishments. Write a brief introduction using information from the interview. Share your introduction with your classmates.

Keep This in Mind

- Before giving an informal talk, know exactly what you want to say.
- Gather all the information you need. Put this information in logical order.
- Do not leave out any necessary steps or details.

Now Speak   Imagine that one of your favorite entertainers or sports figures is coming to your community. Prepare an announcement telling about this event. Make sure that you include *who, where, what, when,* and *why.* Then, imagine you have been chosen to introduce this person. Write a good introduction. Share your announcement and introduction with your classmates.

A Formal Engagement

Preparing a Formal Talk

Here's the Idea Have you ever been asked to give an oral report? If so, you have already given at least one type of formal talk. In the future you will probably give many such talks. Formal talks are common in classes, at club meetings, and at school assemblies.

When planning a formal talk, follow the pre-writing steps you use when planning a composition.

1. Select an interesting topic. The topic should be of interest to you and to your audience. Try to choose a topic that is fresh and unusual. It should be a subject that you know something about.

2. Narrow your topic. Make sure that your topic fits the time available for your talk. It should not be too broad or too narrow. For example, the topic "Ancient Egypt" would be too broad for a five-minute talk. However, "How Mummies Were Made" would probably be just right.

3. Determine your purpose. The purpose is the reason for your talk. Your purpose may be to inform, to persuade, or to entertain. Your purpose will help you to decide what ideas you will include and what points you will stress in your talk.

4. Identify your audience. Consider the ages, interests, and backgrounds of your audience members. Find out how much they know about your subject. Then, tailor your speech to suit them. Avoid talking about subjects that your audience will not understand or will not be interested in.

Check It Out Read the following topics.

> Why the United States Should Continue Its Space Program
> How Comic Books Are Made

- What purpose is indicated by each of these topics?
- Which topic is appropriate to an audience of children?
- Which topic is appropriate to an audience of adults?

Try Your Skill   Read each of the following broad topics for formal talks.

television	hobbies
games	pets
myths	space
school	music

Choose any four topics from this list. Narrow each one for a five-minute talk. Write each narrowed topic. Tell whether the topic is for a talk that informs, persuades, or entertains.

Keep This in Mind

- Choose a topic that interests both you and your audience.
- Choose a topic that you know something about.
- Narrow your topic to fit the available time.
- Decide whether your purpose is to inform, persuade, or entertain.
- Identify your audience before writing your talk.

Now Write   Choose one of your narrowed topics from **Try Your Skill.** Divide a piece of paper into three columns labeled *Topic, Purpose,* and *Audience.* Under *Topic,* write the topic you have chosen. Under *Purpose,* write the purpose of your talk. Under *Audience,* give the average age of people in your class. Then tell why you think your audience will find your talk interesting. Label your paper **A Formal Engagement,** and save it in your folder.

Source Sorcery

Gathering and Organizing Information

Here's the Idea   After you have identified your topic, purpose, and audience, you are ready to write a sentence stating the main idea of your talk. This sentence can guide you as you gather the information you need to develop the main idea.

Gathering Information for a Formal Talk

1. Look for information related to your main idea. Information can come from personal experiences, other people, books, magazines, newspapers, encyclopedias, and dictionaries.
2. Take notes on note cards. Write only one piece of information on each card.
3. Organize your notes. Divide the cards into groups of related ideas. If a note is not related to the main idea, leave it out.
4. Organize your groups of note cards. Place them in the order that you want them to appear in the talk. The following orders are common:
   order of importance   spatial order   chronological order
5. Do more research to fill in gaps in your information.

Check It Out   Hector was asked to give a formal talk in his English class. He knew that his own last name, *Calderon,* meant "kettle" or "cauldron" in Spanish. He decided to do a talk on the origins and meanings of last names.

- How could Hector state his main idea?
- What sources could he check for information?

Try Your Skill Read the following notes for a talk on the meanings of last names. Copy each note onto a note card. Then, divide these notes into groups of related ideas. Leave out any notes not related to the main idea.

–A *smith* is someone who works with metals.

–Some last names are names of places.

–*Clark* used to mean "priest."

–A *miller* is a person who grinds grain into flour.

–Some common English names are *Hill, Brook, Rivers, Lake, Stone,* and *Field.*

–The name *Taylor* comes from *tailor,* a person who makes clothes.

–The name *Amy* means "beloved."

–The name *Deborah* comes from the Hebrew word for "bee."

–Some names tell about occupations.

–*Lamb* is a common English name.

–The following names are common in English—*Carpenter, Cook, Baker.*

–*Rosenthal* means "red (rosen) valley (thal)."

–Some names, such as *Swan* or *Wolf,* come from animals.

Keep This in Mind

- The main idea is the subject of your talk. It should be stated in a single sentence.
- The information you gather should be related to your main idea.
- Information may be gathered from personal experience, other people, or written sources.
- Information should be put in a logical order.

Now Write Write a main idea statement for the topic you chose in **A Formal Engagement.** Do research for a talk on this topic. Take notes for your talk. Put these notes in a logical order. Save your notes in your folder.

Together at Last

Writing a Formal Talk

Here's the Idea After you have organized your notes, you are ready to put together your talk. To do this, you must write an introduction, a body, and a conclusion.

The Parts of a Formal Talk

1. The **introduction** should be short. It should hold the attention of your audience. It should end with a statement of your main idea. There are many ways of introducing a talk:
   a. State an interesting fact.
   b. Ask an interesting question.
   c. Make an interesting comparison.
   d. Tell an interesting story.
   e. Show an interesting object.
2. The **body** should support your main idea. It should present the bulk of your information from your note cards. This information should be organized logically.
3. The **conclusion** can restate your main idea in different words. It can also summarize major points made to support the main idea. If you are speaking to entertain, the conclusion may be a high point of entertainment. It could also be a lesson drawn from the experiences described in the body.

Check It Out Read the following conclusion to a talk.

I hope that Congress and the President will continue our exploration of space. Then we can continue to enjoy the many new inventions the space program has given us. People will continue to find jobs in space-related fields. Most importantly, our knowledge of the universe will continue to grow. Eventually, we shall make new worlds available for mining and colonization.

- Which sentence restates the main idea?
- What major points are summarized in this conclusion?

Try Your Skill   The following sentences could be the final sentences for the introductions of two talks. Each states the main idea of a talk. Write introductions for each of these main ideas. Use the techniques discussed in **Here's the Idea.**

1. This is a typical example of the slanted view of teenagers presented by television.

2. Similarly, you can't become an Olympic athlete without lots of dedication and practice.

Keep This in Mind

- The introduction should state the main idea of your talk. It should also capture the attention of your audience.
- The body should develop your main idea with details.
- The conclusion should restate your main idea. It may also summarize the important points in your talk.

Now Write   Using the notes gathered in Part 4, **Source Sorcery,** write a formal talk. Include an introduction, a body, and a conclusion. Then, revise your first draft. Make sure that each part of your talk contains the information described in **Here's the Idea.** Label your first and final drafts **Together at Last.** Save them in your folder.

Special Delivery

Presenting Yourself to an Audience

Here's the Idea   Before a movie director shoots a scene, he or she must plan it carefully. Many questions must be answered. How should the actors act and speak? What clothes should they wear? What gestures should they make? What expressions should they have on their faces? Before you give a talk, you must ask yourself the same questions. You must plan how to present yourself to your audience. The following guidelines will help you:

1. Appearance. Wear clothes that are right for the occasion. Stand up straight, but not rigidly. Try to appear relaxed and confident.

2. Eye Contact. Look directly at audience members or slightly above their heads. This will help keep the attention of your audience. Do not stare at your notes or props.

3. Voice. Speak clearly. Make sure that you can be heard. Pronounce each word precisely. Do not rush. Do not speak in a monotone. Instead, vary your volume, pitch, and rate of speech. Make sure that your tone fits the content of the speech. Pause for emphasis before important points.

4. Gestures and Facial Expressions. Use appropriate gestures and facial expressions. They will relax you and increase your confidence. They will also help you express your feelings. Smile when you talk about something wonderful. Look concerned when you talk about something upsetting. Use your hands to stress important points. Make sure that your gestures and facial expressions are natural.

Check It Out Study the following situations.

1. Pennie gave a speech about safety rules for swimmers. Her written speech was three pages long. However, she gave the entire speech in about one minute.

2. Ron gave a speech on how to do clown makeup. He felt embarrassed as he spoke. He mumbled and kept his head down. His audience had to lean forward to hear him.

- What problems did each speaker have?
- How could these problems be corrected?

Try Your Skill Practice speaking clearly. Read the following statements aloud. Pronounce all of the words clearly.

1. The six guests sang show tunes.
2. Thelma's father and brothers seem particularly healthy.
3. Bill broke the blue glass fruit bowl.
4. The jeweler filled the kettle with golden, molten metal.

Keep This in Mind

- Whenever you speak, try to look and sound your best.
- Stand up straight. Look at your audience. Speak loudly enough to be heard.
- Use natural gestures and facial expressions to communicate feelings.

Now Write Study the talk you wrote for **Together at Last.** Make two columns on a piece of paper. Label one column *Gestures.* Label the other *Facial Expressions.* Make a list of facial expressions and gestures that you could use in your talk. Label your list **Special Delivery.** Save it in your folder.

Mirror, Mirror

Practicing a Talk

Here's the Idea   There's more than a bit of truth in the expression "Practice makes perfect." Sports figures, actors, dancers, musicians, and artists all depend upon regular practice to perfect their skills. Practice is also important to giving a successful talk. The more you practice a talk, the better it will be.

Before you can begin to practice, you must decide how you are going to present your talk. There are two possibilities:

1. Memorize the entire talk. Use the following method.
   a. Read one sentence.
   b. Recite the sentence several times without looking at it.
   c. Read the next sentence.
   d. Recite both sentences without looking at them.
   e. Go through the entire talk in this manner. When you miss a sentence, start all over again.
2. Memorize the introduction and conclusion. Then, make an outline or notes for the body. When you give the talk, refer to your outline or notes as necessary. If you use an outline or note cards, practice with these. Avoid looking at them too often.

To practice your talk, say it aloud several times. If possible, use a tape recorder to check your voice and a mirror to check your posture, facial expressions, and gestures. Make sure you follow the guidelines for giving a talk explained in **Special Delivery.** Ask friends or relatives to listen to your talk. Ask for suggestions for improvement.

Check It Out   Kim Li wanted to run for class president. She wrote a campaign speech. She memorized the introduction and conclusion of her talk. Then, she made an outline of the body. She practiced her talk many times in front of a mirror.

- What did Kim Li do to make her talk a success?
- What else could she have done?

Try Your Skill   Practice giving the sample introduction from Part 2, **Look Before You Leap.** Write the answers to the following questions.

1. What tone of voice is appropriate for this talk?
2. What facial expressions and gestures could a speaker use when giving this talk?

Keep This in Mind

- You should practice your talk several times before giving it.
- You may memorize the entire talk. You may also memorize just the introduction and conclusion and use notes or an outline for the body.
- Consider your voice, gestures, and facial expressions when practicing a talk.
- Ask your friends or relatives to listen to your talk. Ask them to make suggestions for improvement.

Now Speak   Practice the talk you wrote in Part 5, **Together at Last.** Memorize the introduction and conclusion. Use note cards or an outline for the body. Practice your talk alone and then for a relative or friend. List any improvements that you can make on a piece of paper. Label the paper **Mirror, Mirror.** Place it in your folder. If your teacher wishes you to do so, give your talk to your class.

Have You Heard?

Listening to and Judging Talks

Here's the Idea An audience should listen closely to a speaker. These guidelines will help you to become a good listener:

Guidelines for Good Listening

1. Sit where you can see and hear. Pay attention.
2. Avoid distracting the speaker. Don't make unnecessary noises or movements.
3. Show the speaker your interest. Look at the speaker as he or she talks. Keep an interested expression on your face.
4. Think about what the speaker is saying. Listen for main ideas and supporting details. You may want to take notes.
5. Be open-minded. Don't judge the speaker's ideas before you hear how they are supported.

If you are asked to judge a talk, use these guidelines:

Evaluating a Talk

CONTENT

Topic:	Was the main point of the talk clear?
Purpose:	Was the purpose of the talk clear? Did the speaker accomplish this purpose?
Audience:	Did the talk suit its audience?
Development:	Did the speaker present enough information? Was any of this information unnecessary?
Organization:	Were the speaker's ideas presented logically?
Introduction:	Did the introduction capture your interest? Did it state the main idea?

Body:	Did the body offer details to support the main idea? Were the important points clear?
Conclusion:	Was the conclusion of the talk satisfactory?

PRESENTATION

Eye Contact:	Did the speaker look at the audience? Did the speaker look at his or her notes too often?
Posture:	Did the speaker appear confident and relaxed?
Voice:	Was the speaker easy to hear and understand? Did the speaker vary his or her voice?
Gestures:	Were the speaker's gestures natural?
Facial Expressions:	Were the speaker's facial expressions natural? Did they fit the content of the talk?
Preparation:	Had the speaker practiced the talk?

Check It Out   Di gave a talk on women in the space program. Later, she asked Joe about her talk. Joe said he liked the talk because it seemed that Di was interested in her subject.

- Why should speakers seem interested in their subjects?
- How could Joe's comments have been more specific?

Try Your Skill   Copy the main headings of the checklist for evaluating talks. Practice the talk that you wrote for Part 7, **Mirror, Mirror.** How can you improve it? Write your ideas next to the correct headings.

Keep This in Mind

- Good listeners show their interest. They don't distract the speaker.
- Good evaluators are polite and specific.

Now Listen   Evaluate a talk in class. Use the checklist for evaluating talks. Compare your ratings with those of your classmates. Label your evaluation **Have You Heard?**

Handbook

Section	1	**The Sentence and Its Parts**	**343**
Section	2	**Avoiding Fragments and Run-on Sentences**	**372**
Section	3	**Using Verbs**	**380**
Section	4	**Using Irregular Verbs**	**403**
Section	5	**Using Troublesome Pairs of Verbs**	**419**
Section	6	**Using Nouns**	**429**
Section	7	**Using Pronouns**	**453**
Section	8	**Using Adjectives**	**478**
Section	9	**Using Adverbs**	**496**
Section	10	**Using Prepositions**	**514**
Section	11	**Using Conjunctions**	**532**
Section	12	**Using the Parts of Speech**	**538**
Section	13	**Sentence Patterns**	**545**
Section	14	**Using Verbals**	**555**
Section	15	**Making Subjects and Verbs Agree**	**574**
Section	16	**Using Compound Sentences**	**592**
Section	17	**Using Complex Sentences**	**607**
Section	18	**Capitalization**	**631**
Section	19	**Punctuation**	**651**
Section	20	**Spelling**	**692**

A detailed Table of Contents for the Handbook appears in the front of this book.

The Sentence and Its Parts

When you speak to someone, you don't always use complete sentences. For example, you can answer a question with a word or two:

Yes.   No.   Tomorrow.

You can even ask a question without using what are usually considered complete sentences:

Whose car?   Which girl?   What record?

However, when you write, you must use complete sentences to make your meaning clear. Your reader is not able to ask you to explain what you mean.

Sentences are clear when all the parts are correctly put together. In this section you will study the parts of sentences.

Part 1 The Parts of a Sentence

A sentence is a group of words that expresses a complete thought.

A sentence makes a statement, asks a question, tells someone to do something, or expresses strong feeling. A sentence has two parts. One part names someone or something that the sentence is about. This is the **subject.** The second part tells *what is* or *what happens.* This is the **predicate.**

Subject (Who or what)	Predicate (What is or what happens)
Jeff	smiled.
The girl	is captain of the team.
The two cars	nearly collided.
Students in math class	write programs for the computer.

The subject of a sentence tells who or what the sentence is about.

The predicate of a sentence tells what *is* or what happens.

Every sentence must have a subject and a predicate. If one of these parts is missing from a group of words, it is not a complete sentence. It is a **fragment.**

Read these sentence fragments. Notice why each is not a sentence.

Dashed across the finish line. (Who dashed?)
Two girls with a huge banner. (What happened?)

Exercises **Find the subjects and predicates.**

A. Write each of the following sentences. Draw a vertical line between each subject and predicate.

Example: A flock of geese | flew overhead.

1. Nancy collects foreign postage stamps.
2. Joe's Labrador retriever jumped the fence.
3. Thunder rumbled in the distance.
4. The boy across the street raises rabbits.
5. Terry saw the musical on Channel 4.
6. A large crowd watched the faculty-varsity basketball game.
7. Janet designed the costumes for the play.
8. Karen wrote the weekly sports news.
9. One swimmer broke the school record.
10. The yardstick snapped in two.

B. Copy these sentences. Draw a vertical line between the subject and the predicate.

Example: The architect | checked her blueprints.

1. Greg's brother builds historical model boats.
2. The girl in the yellow slicker missed the bus.
3. Condors are large vultures.
4. My sister graduated from high school this year.
5. Several students at Central School drew the posters for the blood drive.
6. A monkey chattered in the treetops.
7. An alligator slid into the water.
8. Elaine threw the ball to home plate.
9. The roses in our garden bloom all summer.
10. Two boys from our neighborhood went on a canoe trip.

Part 2   Kinds of Sentences

You use language for several purposes. Sometimes you want to tell something. Sometimes you want to ask something. Sometimes you want to tell someone to do something. Sometimes you want to show how strongly you feel about something. There is a different kind of sentence for each of these purposes.

1. A sentence that makes a statement is a **declarative sentence.**

   Her story was short.   Tom called the store at noon.

2. A sentence that asks a question is an **interrogative sentence.**

   Was the play a success?   Are you going to camp?

3. A sentence that tells someone to do something is an **imperative sentence.** The subject is not usually stated but is understood to be *you. You* is the person or group spoken to.

   (you) Be here at nine o'clock.   (you) Please open the window.

4. A sentence that is used to express strong feeling is an **exclamatory sentence.**

   How Sherry yawned!   What fun we had!

Punctuating Sentences

Every sentence begins with a capital letter. Every sentence ends with a punctuation mark. Notice the marks at the ends of the sentences above. Remember these rules:

1. Use a period after a declarative sentence.
2. Use a question mark after an interrogative sentence.
3. Use a period after an imperative sentence.
4. Use an exclamation mark after an exclamatory sentence.

Exercises **Learn the kinds of sentences.**

A. Number your paper from 1 to 10. For each of the following sentences, write *Declarative, Interrogative, Imperative,* or *Exclamatory* to show what kind it is. Add the punctuation mark that should be used at the end of each sentence.

1. Hold my books for a minute, please
2. Yes, we took first place in the debate
3. Pour the water into the test tube
4. Have you been here before, Sara
5. We found kindling for our fire in the woods near the lake
6. What is the address of that company
7. Is your watch running
8. How frightened I was
9. Kate, look out
10. Move to the rear of the bus, please

B. Follow the directions for Exercise A.

1. Please don't erase this message
2. Have you heard the new song by Kansas
3. Dad always trims the lilac bush in the fall and in the spring
4. Tell the joke about the elephant again
5. Where did you put the Christmas tree lights
6. What big eyes you have
7. Keep your elbow stiff and watch the ball
8. When do the miners' shifts change
9. Willie, watch out
10. Have a good day

C. Writing Write three declarative, three interrogative, three exclamatory, and three imperative sentences.

Part 3 Simple Subjects and Predicates

In every sentence a few words are more important than the rest. These are the key words that make the group of words a sentence. Study these examples:

A cold, steady **rain**	**fell** throughout the night.
Rain	**fell.**

The subject of the first sentence is *A cold, steady rain*. The key word in this subject is *rain*. You could simply say *Rain fell throughout the night*. *Rain* is the **simple subject** of the sentence.

The predicate in the first sentence is *fell throughout the night*. The key word is *fell*. You could simply say *A cold, steady rain fell*. *Fell* is the **simple predicate.**

The key word in the subject of a sentence is called the simple subject. It is also called the subject of the verb.

The key word in the predicate is called the simple predicate. The simple predicate is the **verb.**

To find the simple subject in a sentence, first find the verb. Some verbs tell about action.

    Tom *paddled* the canoe.   Ann *caught* the ball.

Sometimes the action shown is an action you cannot see.

    Miki *had* a good idea.   Jim *remembered* the story.

Some verbs tell that something *is* or *exists*. Such verbs are **state-of-being verbs.**

    The doctor *is* here.   The test *seemed* easy.

To find the verb in a sentence, look for the word that shows action or state of being.

Exercises   **Find the verbs and their simple subjects.**

A.   For each sentence, write the verb and its subject.

   Example: The bus arrived early today.
      Verb: arrived   Subject: bus

1. Julie caught the baseball easily.
2. The co-pilot radioed the information to the tower.
3. Nancy plays the flute in the school band.
4. Careful beekeepers wear protective masks.
5. Jack worked at the ice rink after school.
6. The two boys built a chicken coop.
7. A robin built a nest in our cherry tree.
8. The swimmers waited for the starter's signal.
9. Tall elms lined the avenue.
10. The three girls walked home together.

B.   For each sentence write the verb and its subject.

1. Martha balanced on the high diving board.
2. The fans in the bleachers roared.
3. The compass pointed north.
4. The coach asked for a timeout.
5. A high fence enclosed the yard.
6. The pilot adjusted his headphones.
7. The helicopter landed on the hospital roof.
8. A heavy rain flattened our tomato plants.
9. Our group gave a report on solar energy.
10. A new member of the club made several suggestions.

Diagraming Verbs and Their Subjects

A diagram helps you see how the parts of a sentence work together. A sentence diagram always begins on a horizontal line. A vertical line cuts the horizontal line in two. It separates the subject from the verb. The subject is placed to the left of the vertical line. The verb is placed to the right.

Example: Gerry laughed with his friends.

Gerry	laughed

Exercises   Find the verbs and their subjects.

A.   Show the verb and its simple subject in each of the following sentences. Use diagrams or any other method your teacher may suggest.

1. Watermelon tastes good in hot weather.
2. Dr. Harvey's cat wore a tin bell.
3. A squirrel in the attic started a nest.
4. The clock in the hallway needs a new spring.
5. The blower on the furnace stopped.
6. The photographs fell out of the album.
7. Barbara's dresser fit next to the window.
8. The top drawer of the cabinet stuck.
9. A large, colorful umbrella shaded the chairs.
10. Curt wore his favorite sweatshirt.

B.   Write the verb and its simple subject in each sentence.

1. A judge read all the contest rules.
2. The students in our class made a model spaceship.
3. Her pocket bulged with pennies.
4. Fireworks exploded in the sky.
5. Unexpectedly, the engine stalled.
6. John visited the planetarium in Chicago last summer.
7. The Moores go to the photography show every year.
8. Maria's mother raises vegetables.
9. The end of vacation came too quickly.
10. We met Judy at the movie.

Part 4 Main Verbs and Helping Verbs

In some sentences, the verb is one word.

> Meg *visited* Boston.

In other sentences, the verb is two or more words.

> Meg *will visit* Boston.

In this sentence, *visit* is the **main verb.** *Will* is a **helping verb.**

A verb may consist of a main verb and one or more helping verbs.

Certain words are often used as helping verbs.

am	was	has	do	will	could	may	being
is	were	have	does	shall	should	must	been
are	be	had	did	can	would	might	

Some of these verbs can be used alone. Sometimes they are used as **helping verbs** with other verbs:

> The neighbors *have* a new car.   Bill *is* a painter.
> The girls *have finished* their work.   Sue *is going* home.
> We *have been looking* for Tom.

Exercises   Find helping verbs and main verbs.

A. Write the verb for each sentence. Make one column for helping verbs (HV) and one column for main verbs (MV).

> Example: Phil is keeping a journal.
>
> **HV**   **MV**
>
> is   keeping

1. The weather is becoming cooler.
2. The next players are waiting for the badminton court.

3. Four students were serving refreshments.
4. Lou has returned your tape recorder.
5. My brother did arrive after the thunderstorm.
6. Ted is writing the script for the skit.
7. The President has visited several countries this year.
8. I have gone to the dentist's office twice this week.
9. Patrick has eaten spaghetti for lunch.
10. The key for the garage is hanging by the back door of the kitchen.

B. Follow the directions for Exercise A.

1. Two ducks were huddling near the pond.
2. The Mulligans have had a good time at Six Flags.
3. The price will include the cost of lunch.
4. The director will select the cast this afternoon.
5. The sky has looked stormy all afternoon.
6. Twice recently the car has needed a new front tire.
7. Really, I do try.
8. At four o'clock the plumber was working on the bathtub drain.
9. Kathy had been ready for over an hour.
10. The outcome had seemed uncertain.

C. Writing Write five sentences. Each sentence should have a main verb and a helping verb. Underline each main verb once. Underline each helping verb twice.

Separated Parts of a Verb

Sometimes the parts of a verb are separated from each other by words that are not part of the verb. These words usually tell **when** (*often, always, never*) or **how** (*slowly, scarcely, hardly*). *Not* and the *n't* in contractions are never part of the verb, although they do change the meaning of the verb.

Notice how the parts of verbs can be separated.

That bus **has** *often* **been** late.
During the night, the temperature **had** *suddenly* **dropped.**
We **had** *not* **seen** the accident.

Exercises   Find the verbs.

A.   Write the verbs and their simple subjects in these sentences. Underline the subject once and the verb twice. Your teacher may ask you to use diagrams instead.

Example: My cousin had never seen snow before.
<u>cousin</u>   <u>had seen</u>

1. Sara has probably finished the poster by now.
2. Her friend had already opened the window.
3. That class is always going on field trips.
4. Several customers had angrily asked for the manager.
5. Ron was patiently sewing a patch on his jeans.
6. My family has never been to Los Angeles.
7. The dog was carefully burying its bone.
8. The painter had carelessly tossed the brushes away.
9. With little effort, the salmon were leaping the rapids.
10. Under the circumstances, we will certainly help you.

B.   Follow the directions for Exercise A.

1. We have never gone to the Milwaukee Zoo.
2. Jane's spirits were obviously rising.
3. The deer have often grazed in that field.
4. I do believe in life on other planets.
5. She had recently photographed the Florida Everglades.
6. Larry will not tell anyone his plans.
7. Trade between the two countries had not begun.

353

8. The waves were constantly pounding the deck.
9. The school is probably closed because of the snow.
10. We have often taken the train to the city.

Part 5   Compound Subjects and Compound Verbs

Look at these two sentences. How do they differ?

> Two girls tied for first place.
> Kara and Liz tied for first place.

In the first sentence, the subject is *girls*. What is the subject of the second sentence? Both *Kara* and *Liz* are subjects. When a subject has two or more parts, it is called a **compound subject.** The word *compound* means "having more than one part."

Verbs can be compound, too. How do these two sentences differ?

> He directed the movie.
> He directed and produced the movie.

In the first sentence the verb is *directed*. In the second, the verbs are *directed* and *produced*. The words *directed* and *produced* are called a **compound verb.**

Predicates may also be compound. Notice the parts in the following **compound predicate.**

> Dad *assembled the bookcase* and *painted it.*

In the compound subject above, the word *and* joins *Kara* and *Liz*. In the compound verb, *and* joins *directed* and *produced*. In the compound predicate, *and* joins *assembled the bookcase* and *painted it.* Words that join words and groups of words in this way are called **conjunctions.** The word *and* is a conjunction.

When any compound construction has more than two parts, separate the parts with commas.

Carol, Ted, and *Becky* entered the race.
Vince *washed, peeled,* and *chopped* the fruit.
Jan *went home, did her homework,* and *played tennis.*

Diagraming Compound Subjects and Verbs

To diagram the parts of a compound subject, split the subject line. Put the conjunction on a connecting dotted line.

Example: Dean and Mr. York have arrived.

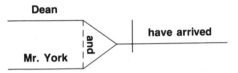

Compound verbs are similarly diagramed.

Example: Cheryl ran, swam, and rested.

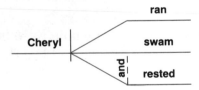

Exercises   Find the compound subjects and compound verbs.

A.   Write these sentences. Underline the subjects once and the verbs twice.

1. Thunder and lightning preceded the rain.
2. The width and depth of the stage were unusual.
3. The clerk totaled the sale, collected the money, and bagged the groceries.

4. Everyone swam, played ball, and then ate lunch.
5. The speaker's character and energy impressed the students.
6. Phil and Jerry carried water for the garden.
7. Marie and her father skate and ski together.
8. Ruth and Phil stood on the corner and waited fifteen minutes for the bus.
9. The wind and the tide were perfect for the race.
10. Jack's boat rounded the buoy and finished first.

B. Follow the directions for Exercise A.

1. Ann took some grapes and passed the bowl.
2. The lamp and the candles threw shadows on the wall.
3. Wonderful aromas and happy voices drifted from the kitchen.
4. His knees and ankles were weak from the long climb.
5. The football players pushed and shoved with their shoulders.
6. Trumpets and trombones accompanied the woodwinds.
7. By that time Tracy and Luanne were home.
8. Jeff walked to the front, looked briefly at his notes, and began his speech.
9. The ice-cream vendor rang the bell and pedaled slowly.
10. The contestants roped and tied the calves.

Part 6 Subjects in Unusual Order

In most of the sentences that you have looked at in this book, the subject has come before the verb. All sentences, however, do not follow this same order. Sometimes the subject comes after the verb.

Giving Variety to Sentences

Sometimes, you may want to emphasize certain words in a sentence. Then you may write sentences with the subject after the verb.

Subject Verb

Usual Order: A strange *sound came* from the attic.

Verb   **Subject**

Unusual Order: From the attic *came* a strange *sound.*

Unusual order does not change the positions of subjects and verbs in diagrams.

Example: Out of the hat popped a rabbit.

rabbit	popped

Exercises   Find the subjects and verbs.

A. Show, as your teacher directs, the subjects and verbs in the following sentences.

1. On the other side of the tracks stood the church.
2. High above our heads stretched the Bay Bridge.
3. At the meeting were boys and girls from every class.
4. Behind his sleepy face was a quick, intelligent mind.
5. From one end of the pipe scampered a frightened squirrel.
6. Close behind the horse trotted a pony.
7. Into Mr. Bevan's office strolled my playful dog.
8. From the sand along the shore came a curious glow.
9. In the corridor were models of boats and a special nautical exhibit.
10. Across the valley stretched fields of beautiful flowers.

B. Follow the directions for Exercise A.

1. Beyond the spaceship streamed the stars.
2. From the river rose three flamingoes.
3. Beyond the line of hills stood the crimson forest.
4. Suddenly out of the shrubs zoomed our cat.
5. Over the car lot flapped colorful banners.
6. Under the table lurked the gerbil.
7. Far below our campsite lay the rapids.
8. Into the light of the campfire fluttered a moth.
9. Near the barge bobbed a tugboat.
10. Behind the kitchen was the entrance to the cellar.

C. Writing Write five sentences in which the subject comes after the verb.

Part 7 Subjects and Verbs in Questions and Exclamations

Some interrogative sentences (questions) are written in normal order: the subject comes first, and the verb second.

Which team won the World Series?

(*Team* is the subject; *won* is the verb.)

Who bought the hamburgers?

(*Who* is the subject; *bought* is the verb.)

Not all questions follow this order. Read the following:

Do you know Mike?

(*You* is the subject; *do know* is the verb.)

Here the subject comes between the parts of the verb.

Some exclamatory sentences also have the subject after the verb.

Was that movie beautiful!   Are you late!

To find the subject and verb in a question or exclamation, try putting the sentence in normal order.

Has Julie repaired the TV?   Was I upset!
Julie has repaired the TV.   I was upset.

Diagraming Questions and Exclamations

To diagram a question or exclamation, put the subject and verb in normal order.

Example: Will you please answer the telephone?

you	Will answer

Exercises **Find subjects and verbs in questions and exclamations.**

A. Make two columns on your paper labeled *Subject* and *Verb*. Write the subject and verb for each sentence.

1. Does Marilyn study in the library?
2. Have you heard the news?
3. Were we thrilled by the news!
4. Did you watch the television special last night?
5. Does Andrea help in the print shop?
6. Do Mike and Pam work at the pharmacy?
7. Is Jim moving to Arizona?
8. Do the members of the committee know the date?
9. Do we need practice!
10. Do raspberries grow wild in the Midwest?

B. Follow the directions for Exercise A.

1. Has Pedro given his speech?
2. Which movie played first?
3. Do I have a surprise for you!
4. Are winters warmer in Tallahassee than in Corpus Christi?
5. Did the officer question the suspects?
6. Have you had dinner yet?
7. Have you gone to the dentist yet?
8. Are your parents going to the meeting?
9. Which magazine came in today's mail?
10. Who gave the message to Nancy?

Part 8 Sentences That Begin with *There*

Study this sentence. What is the simple subject?

There are some pencils in my locker.

The subject is *pencils*. The word *there* is not the subject. When the word *there* comes at or near the beginning of a sentence, it often serves just to get the sentence started.

        Verb   **Subject**

There *are* some *pencils* in my locker.

Study the following sentences. Notice that the subject is not first when *there* comes near the beginning of the sentence. Point out the subjects.

1. **Are** there any **grapes**?
2. There **are** some **apples** in the bag.
3. There **are** two **birds** at the feeding station.
4. **Were** there many **families** at the picnic?
5. There **were** two **people** in the car.

Diagraming Sentences with *There*

There is usually just an "extra" word. It is placed on a separate line above the subject in a sentence diagram.

Example: There were many students at the track meet.

There
_____

| **students** | **were** |

Exercises **Find the subjects and verbs in sentences with *there*.**

A. Write the subjects and verbs in these sentences.

1. There was a line at the theater.
2. Are there any blossoms on the apple tree?
3. There were several questions after Helen's report.
4. There were two skunks near our cabin.
5. Are there any newspapers in the cellar, Mother?
6. There are some new notices on the bulletin board near the library.
7. Are there any Canadian dimes here?
8. There were two gulls on the pier.
9. Was there any more salad?
10. There are new chairs in the science room.

B. Write the subjects and verbs in these sentences.

1. There are a few rust spots on our car.
2. There is a charge for children over five.
3. There were several eggs in the basket.
4. Is there anyone home?
5. There have been hornets on the porch again.
6. There is really no reason for concern.

7. Were there any problems at the meeting?
8. There was an old bicycle in our garage.
9. Are there pickles in the sandwich?
10. Were there telescopes in the tower?

C. Writing Write lively sentences using the following beginnings. Add the correct punctuation.

1. There is
2. There would often be
3. There has never been
4. Has there ever been
5. Will there be
6. Were there
7. There has been
8. There will be
9. Have there been
10. Would there ever be

Part 9   Subjects and Verbs in Imperative Sentences

Imperative sentences (commands) usually begin with the verb. For example, in the command *Pay the cashier,* the verb is the first word, *Pay.* What is the subject? There doesn't seem to be any, does there? The subject in the sentence is *you,* even though it is not stated. *You* is the person or group spoken to. The subject *you* is understood.

One-Word Commands

Some imperative sentences consist of only one word—a verb. *Think. Go. Stop.* These are single-word sentences. The subject is the same: *(you) Think. (you) Go. (you) Stop.*

Diagraming Imperative Sentences

When the subject of an imperative sentence is understood, show it in a diagram by writing *(you)*.

Example: Hurry.

(you)	Hurry

Exercises Find the subjects and verbs in imperative sentences.

A. Write the subjects and verbs in the following sentences. Use whatever method your teacher suggests.

1. Tear along the dotted line.
2. Hold this for a moment.
3. Put some spruce branches under your sleeping bag.
4. Stack the dishes in the sink.
5. Try a bottle opener.

B. Follow the directions for Exercise A.

1. Have the rest of the casserole for supper.
2. Ask Nicole her opinion.
3. Dismount from the parallel bars to your right.
4. Look this over before the meeting.
5. Take another apple.

C. Writing Write a paragraph on how to get to your house from school. Use only imperative sentences. Underline the verb in each sentence.

ADDITIONAL EXERCISES

The Sentence and Its Parts

A. Subjects and Predicates Number your paper from 1 to 10. Copy these sentences. Draw a vertical line between the subject and the predicate.

1. Tom found some wood for the fire.
2. Acorns from red oaks have dark shells.
3. The girl in the red jersey won the race.
4. Students crowded around the bulletin board.
5. Vinegar softened the eggshell.
6. The gray fish eats algae.
7. Two of the players left the game with injuries.
8. Jerome's aunt writes books for children.
9. Shadows from the clouds moved across the football field.
10. Maria kept score for us.

B. Kinds of Sentences Number your paper from 1 to 10. For each of the following sentences, write *Declarative, Interrogative, Imperative,* or *Exclamatory* to show what kind it is. Add the correct end mark for each sentence.

1. How did the game end
2. How the movie scared him
3. Set the popcorn on the table
4. Cork comes from the bark of the cork tree
5. Why was the practice session cancelled
6. Ramon, may I ask you something
7. Sandy, ask that woman for directions
8. What is this knob for
9. What a close call we had
10. I asked Mr. Loy for help with my history project

C. Verbs and Simple Subjects Number your paper from 1 to 10. For each sentence write the verb and its subject.

1. Angela draws cartoons for the school paper.
2. A thick fog rolled into the harbor.
3. The sparrows chirped furiously at the dog.
4. The pitcher hurled a no-hitter.
5. Our goalie saved the game.
6. Most students bring their lunches.
7. Our basketball team beat the Dolphins.
8. Some Siamese cats sound like babies.
9. Snowflakes clung to Rosie's hair.
10. A koala bear eats two pounds of leaves each day.

D. Verbs Number your paper from 1 to 10. Write the verb in each of the following sentences.

1. The barber cut Jacob's hair last week.
2. Holly wore a turquoise shirt.
3. This clay hardens quickly.
4. Carolyn removed the film from the camera.
5. Winter came early this year.
6. Tracy's hands were cold.
7. I wonder.
8. You sit at the head of the table.
9. Nick daydreamed all morning.
10. Those slides of onion cells are for my science project.

E. Main Verbs and Helping Verbs Make one column for helping verbs (HV) and one column for main verbs (MV). Find the helping verbs and main verbs in the following sentences. Write them in the proper columns. Some sentences have more than one helping verb.

1. Ryan is joining an archery club.
2. The test papers will be collected in five minutes.

3. I am saving money for a pair of skates.
4. Jessie did understand you.
5. The fish should be fed once a day.
6. I do surprise myself sometimes.
7. Somebody is listening at the door.
8. Our gym class has been practicing backflips.
9. Brenda will be told about the new schedule.
10. Jake had been thinking about the problem.

F. Separated Parts of a Verb Write the verb and its simple subject for each of the following sentences. Underline the subject once and the verb twice.

1. Soccer has recently become a popular game in the United States.
2. Natalie has again won the trophy.
3. Many children have never been to a dentist.
4. Jim was carefully wrapping the glasses.
5. Amy has not missed one rehearsal.
6. Red blood cells will usually live for four months.
7. Bob is probably babysitting tonight.
8. Ms. Koperski does not often speak sharply.
9. Sharon could not remember the lock's combination.
10. The bus had just left.

G. Compound Subjects and Compound Verbs Underline the subjects once and the verbs twice in the following sentences.

1. Records and cassettes were scattered around the room.
2. The mascot and the band marched onto the field.
3. Marty's boots and socks were soaked.
4. The nurse weighed and measured the patients.
5. The ball bounced and rolled into the street.
6. Seedless tangerines and grapes are in the next aisle.

7. The pilot sighted the runway and landed the plane.
8. Both Garfield and Snoopy are popular cartoon animals.
9. The girls waded and splashed across the stream.
10. Detectives and spies think and act fast.

H. Subjects in Unusual Order
Underline the subjects once and the verbs twice in the following sentences.

1. Into the alley dashed the child.
2. In the center of the ring stood Chuck.
3. From the ceiling hung colorful banners.
4. In my locker was the library book.
5. On the rose perched a butterfly with yellow wings.
6. Up the ladder went Kay with a bucket in her hand.
7. Almost beyond belief were Houdini's stunts.
8. Far out past the breakers swam the lifeguard.
9. Onto the trampoline leaped Ann.
10. All through the night whined the lonely puppy.

I. Subjects and Verbs in Questions and Exclamations
Make two columns on your paper. Write *Subject* at the top of one column and *Verb* at the top of the other. Write the subject and verb for each of the following sentences.

1. Do the Carsons live in the basement apartment?
2. Did we have fun!
3. Are the handlebars too high?
4. Do you smell smoke?
5. Was Amelia Earhart ever found?
6. Which teacher sponsors the club?
7. Does that fish have teeth?
8. How happy we were!
9. Did those runners go fast!
10. Did Barb and Thaddeus choose the props?

J. Subjects and Verbs in *There* Sentences Write the subjects and verbs in the following sentences.

1. There was a rainbow over the mountain.
2. Are there rough spots on the ice?
3. There is a penalty for lateness.
4. Is there another exit?
5. There was only one act in the play.
6. Are there cranberries in these muffins?
7. Were there any calls for me?
8. There is really no excuse.
9. There will certainly be fireworks at the picnic.
10. There were several volunteers for the job.

K. Subjects and Verbs in Commands Write the subjects and verbs in the following imperative sentences. Underline the subject once and the verb twice.

1. Use a red pencil.
2. Change the station.
3. Forget it.
4. Wear boots on the hike.
5. Help yourself to some lemonade.
6. Keep your arm perfectly straight.
7. Please pass the salad.
8. Never put the sun behind the subject in a photograph.
9. Keep your eyes on the magician's hands.
10. Always obey traffic laws on a bike.

MIXED REVIEW

The Sentence and Its Parts

A.   Identifying subjects, predicates, simple subjects, and verbs   Copy the following sentences. Draw a line between each subject and predicate. Underline each simple subject once and each verb twice. Remember that a verb can be more than one word.

1. Greg has missed the first inning.
2. Cindy caught a small brown toad.
3. Many athletes study ballet.
4. The man in the white car obviously caused the accident.
5. The grocery store closes at six o'clock.
6. A family of cats is living in that old barn.
7. Most of my friends live nearby.
8. The flowers near the garage need water.
9. The members of our club toured the Smithsonian Institute.
10. The bright moon lit the lake.

B.   Finding subjects and verbs   Copy the following sentences. Underline each simple subject once and each verb twice. Some subjects and verbs may be compound. Some subjects may be in unusual order. Verbs may include helping verbs.

1. Print your name in the space below.
2. Is this event sponsored by the PTA?
3. An exhibit of Mexican art will be displayed in the library.
4. Before today, Ben didn't know anyone in our class.
5. This machine chops and grates vegetables.

6. Who designed the magazine cover?
7. Trish sold twenty magazine subscriptions.
8. Are there any apples in the refrigerator?
9. The members of the team washed and waxed the gym floor.
10. Jim and Sal have started their science projects.

C. Identifying fragments and kinds of sentences Read the following groups of words. If a group of words is a fragment, write *Fragment*. Copy any sentences and punctuate them correctly. Then write *Declarative*, *Interrogative*, *Imperative*, or *Exclamatory* to show what kind of sentence it is.

1. A long, brisk walk in the woods
2. Where is my apartment key
3. Rodney, Kay, and all of their friends
4. This brand of paint costs less
5. We videotaped the program
6. The shiny, new van in the driveway
7. Don't forget your wallet
8. Waited impatiently for the bus
9. Gretchen collects dolls from foreign countries
10. Where is the Lincoln Memorial
11. Stop that noise
12. Your camera might need a new battery

USING GRAMMAR IN WRITING
The Sentence and Its Parts

A. You are a biologist studying life in the Antarctic. One day you are out collecting samples. A sudden blizzard blows up. When you finally get back to your tent, you find that there is a radio message for you. It has been recorded directly onto a cassette. When you play the tape, you find that the message was interrupted by static. Below are the fragments that you hear. Try to make sense out of the message. Supply the missing sentence parts.

> _____ when you get back to the tent. We suggest _____. When the storm clears, _____ to get your samples. _____ emergency supplies. Do not, repeat, do not _____.

B. An android is a robot that looks like a human being. Pretend you are a reporter who is doing a story on an android. Complete the following interview. For each question, write the android's answer. For each statement by the android, write the question you might have asked. At the end, write a command you would like to give the android. Give the android a name and use it in the interview.

> Q: What kind of music do you enjoy?
> A: _____
> Q: _____
> A: I consume three deep-dish pizzas a day.
> Q: What are your plans for the future?
> A: _____
> Q: _____
> A: Most androids get plenty of exercise.
> Q: Is it difficult to make friends with human beings?
> A: _____
> Command: _____

Avoiding Fragments and Run-on Sentences

Sentences tell about facts, ideas, and feelings. When you write sentences, you have the chance to tell about whatever is important to you. You want to make your sentences as clear as you can.

Some sentences are not clear. Confusion may be caused when part of a sentence is left out. Such a group of words is called a **sentence fragment.** Confusion may also be caused when two or more sentences are written as one. Such a group of words is called a **run-on sentence.** In this section you will learn how to avoid these two errors.

Part 1   Avoiding Sentence Fragments

A group of words that is not a complete sentence is called a **sentence fragment.** A fragment is only a part of something. Avoid sentence fragments in your writing.

In a sentence fragment, something important has been left out. Sometimes the subject is missing. Sometimes the verb is left out. As you read a fragment, you may wonder either *What is this about?* or *What happened?*

Fragment: The can of paint (*What happened?*)
Sentence: The can of paint *spilled*.

Fragment: Left the house early (*Who* or *what?*)
Sentence: *I* left the house early.

Exercises   Recognize sentences.

A. Number your paper from 1 to 10. Write *Sentence* or *Fragment* for each of the following groups of words.

1. The parrot is asleep on its perch
2. Arrived before the end of the game
3. Grandfather in our backyard
4. At the pharmacy in the middle of the block
5. In the yard the leaves
6. We can rent a canoe
7. Came up and spoke to us
8. Suddenly a fire siren screamed
9. Rain, wind, and hailstones
10. The branch landed on the garage roof

B.   Writing Correct each of the following fragments by adding the words needed to make a sentence.

1. practiced for two hours

2. earned ten dollars
3. walked cautiously through the dark corridors
4. really likes to sing
5. the mailbox next to the street light
6. designed the yearbook cover
7. near the football field
8. Eliot and his father
9. across the hall from the cafeteria
10. hiked through the hills and valleys

Part 2 Avoiding Run-on Sentences

A **run-on sentence** is two or more sentences written incorrectly as one. Here are some examples:

> Incorrect: (*run-on*): Pam arrived, we went cycling.
> Correct: Pam arrived. We went cycling.

> Incorrect: (*run-on*): Aren't you through let me help.
> Correct: Aren't you through? Let me help.

Run-on sentences confuse your readers. Without a period and a capital letter to guide them, they believe they are reading just one thought. Then the words stop making sense.

You can correct run-on sentences by using the proper capitalization and punctuation. Do not use a comma where one is not needed.

Exercises Correct the run-on sentences.

A. Correct the following run-on sentences.

1. We stayed at Elinor Village we were only two blocks from the ocean.
2. The noise stopped they finished the rest of the work.
3. The refrigerator was broken water was dripping from the freezer.

4. Kay is the sports editor, she is my sister.
5. Everyone was busy we all had assignments to complete.
6. It rained for days, the soccer field was soaked.
7. There were many balloons strung from the ceiling, they were torn down afterwards.
8. We skated for one hour, we came in to get warm.
9. I have read several biographies, I find them very interesting.
10. Monica and I aren't going skiing the snow is too slushy.

B. Follow the directions for Exercise A.

1. It snowed throughout the night, most schools were closed the next day.
2. The skyline of Chicago is beautiful the city has many unusual buildings.
3. Rachel and I ate dinner then we rushed to the movies.
4. We had basketball practice until noon we have a game tomorrow.
5. Our class had a bake sale it was very successful.
6. Ken and Lynn are co-editors, they manage our school newspaper.
7. The doctor X-rayed my arm she then put a cast on it.
8. Our plane arrived early, we took a bus into the city.
9. Anne is on the volleyball team she is the captain.
10. The plumber fixed the sink, then he checked the main water pipe.

ADDITIONAL EXERCISES

Avoiding Fragments and Run-on Sentences

A. Sentences and Fragments Number your paper from 1 to 10. Write *Sentence* or *Fragment* for each of the following groups to show what each group is.

1. Carried a radio with a long antenna
2. The lights are operated by an electric eye
3. Enormous stone statues with seashell eyes on Easter Island
4. Look at that motorcycle
5. Is there a difference between a diary and a journal
6. Is often at the recreation center
7. The pastor spoke at the ceremony
8. Students with early lunch periods
9. Straighten the ruler
10. Straightened his tie

B. Sentences and Run-ons Number your paper from 1 to 10. Write *Sentence* or *Run-on* for each of the following groups of words to show what each group is.

1. Dig for clams at low tide they are easier to find then
2. Football helmets are required, they prevent injuries to the players
3. Sue raised the seat, oiled the chain, and got on the bike
4. With one quick motion Laura captured the monarch butterfly
5. The man felt for the curb with his white cane
6. Sara has cousins in New York she will stay with them during her visit

7. Lou used watercolors, oil paints would have been better
8. James walks to school and takes the bus home
9. What are you staring at
10. Ted works at the supermarket he bags groceries

C. Sentences, Fragments, and Run-ons Number your paper from 1 to 10. Write *Sentence, Fragment,* or *Run-on* for each of the following groups of words to show what each group is.

1. People with a lot of free time and nothing to do
2. The waters around Antarctica contain many strange life forms
3. Sally left, however
4. The movie was about Australia, it showed the Great Barrier Reef
5. Lacrosse, the national sport of Canada
6. Luke added mushrooms to the spaghetti sauce
7. A dumbwaiter is a tiny elevator it carries food
8. Called just before the game
9. The stage crew built the scenery, they painted it, too
10. Music blared from a radio outside

MIXED REVIEW

Avoiding Fragments and Run-on Sentences

A. Identifying sentences, fragments, and run-on sentences Write *Sentence*, *Fragment*, or *Run-on* for each of the following groups of words. Then correct any fragments by adding words to make complete sentences. Correct any run-ons by adding capitalization and punctuation to show where each complete thought begins and ends.

1. Andy ruined the cake, he used salt instead of sugar
2. Carol can't play tennis she twisted her ankle
3. Geese and ducks overhead
4. That phone number has been disconnected
5. Is this Room 208
6. That's my older brother, he's a sophomore in college
7. The runner tried to steal second but was called out
8. Darci missed the bus she didn't hear the alarm
9. Chris picked a bushel of apples
10. Pesty flies, curious ants, and busy bees

B. Correcting fragments and run-on sentences Copy the following paragraph. Correct any fragments or run-ons.

My brother and I had one purpose in mind. When we visited Everglades National Park in Florida, We wanted to see an alligator with our own eyes on our second day there we spotted a seventeen-foot long creature floating lazily along the channel We knew by the short, blunt snout that this was it We kept our distance, this large animal looks slow and sluggish but can move very quickly The park ranger reminded us That it's against the law to tease alligators, I found that law easy to obey an alligator will eagerly eat anything it can swallow!

USING GRAMMAR IN WRITING
Avoiding Fragments and Run-on Sentences

A. After winning the Olympic gold medal for the downhill ski race, you breathlessly make this statement to the reporter.

> I can't believe I did it, this is a dream come true. All that practice. Really did pay off, I'd like to thank my parents and my coach for their support and help, my friends were behind me too. The most exciting moment of my entire life, I'll never forget it. As long as I live, see you all again. In four years,

The reporter who interviewed you rewrote your statement. She corrected all fragments and run-on sentences. Write the statement as it appeared in the newspaper.

B. You are reviewing a new local restaurant, The Round Table, for your school paper. These are the notes you secretly jotted down on a paper napkin. Use them to construct complete sentences. Avoid all fragments and run-ons. Write the review.

> had a twenty minute wait
> a noisy, bustling room
> waiters friendly and attentive
> interesting decorations, looked like a king's court
> the best char-broiled burgers in town
> rich, gooey desserts
> live music is very loud it makes conversation difficult

Using
Verbs

If you do not have a verb, you cannot have a sentence. Even the shortest sentences contain verbs:

Go.   Look.   Try.

You know that the verb is a key word in a sentence. A verb tells of an action or a state of being. Since verbs are so important, you should use them correctly.

In this section you will review what a verb is. You will also learn more about what verbs do. You will learn how verbs work with other words to express your ideas.

Part 1 The Work of Verbs

The verb is one of the main parts of every sentence.

Compare these groups of words. Look at the difference a verb makes.

Without Verbs	With Verbs
The school band well	The school band played well.
Lee over the hoe	Lee tripped over the hoe.
Dan angry	Dan seems angry.

The verb may tell what the subject of the sentence does or what happens. This kind of verb is an **action verb**. The action of the verb may be seen or unseen. Read the following examples:

She *danced*.	Donna *wanted* a job.	I *have* a cold.
Ramon *laughed*.	We *enjoyed* the show.	We *ate*.

A verb may tell that something exists. This kind of verb is a **state-of-being verb**.

Cheryl *is* here.	Jack *seems* happy.
The star *grew* brighter.	The music *sounded* lively.

State of being verbs include *am, is, are, was, were, seem, look, feel, grow, taste, sound, become*, and *appear*.

A verb shows action or state of being.

Use these clues when you look for the verb in a sentence:

- Look for a word that shows action (*ran, walked*).
- Look for a word that shows action you cannot see (*want, have*).
- Look for a word that shows a state of being (*am, is, are, was, were, seem, look, feel, grow, taste, sound, become, appear*).

Examples: Judy *walked* to my house.   We *are* good friends.

Rob *wants* a chance.   You *seem* nervous.

When you are looking for verbs, remember that the parts of a verb may be separated. Remember also that the sentence may be in unusual order.

Will he *cook?*   Down the aisle *came* the bride.

Exercises   Find the verbs.

A.   Find the verb in each sentence.

1. The orchestra played country music.
2. Emily is a very good artist.
3. The fire nearly destroyed the fieldhouse.
4. Our class decorated the hall for the bazaar.
5. Marcy hit the ball over the fence.
6. Keith was very quiet.
7. Here is a dozen eggs.
8. Mark's cat climbed the maple tree.
9. Last Sunday we hiked in the woods.
10. During intermission, Erin told us about her canoe trip.

B. Writing   The following groups of words have subjects but no verbs. Make each group a sentence by adding a verb. Write your sentences and underline the verbs. Add the correct punctuation at the end of each sentence.

1. The library at noon today
2. A car radio in the background
3. We all Saturday afternoon
4. Dave a letter to his cousin in Texas
5. The boys the back steps
6. Randy very well
7. The bumper sticker off
8. Miriam in a play at school
9. Several of my friends to the rink every Saturday
10. The jet into the air

Part 2   Parts of the Verb

A verb often consists of more than one word. A two-word verb consists of one helping verb and the main verb. Helping verbs include *is*, *do*, and *has*. Some other helping verbs are shown below.

> **will** go   **may** go   **could** go   **must** go
> **should** go   **would** go   **might** go   **can** go

Three-word verbs consist of a main verb and two helping verbs. *Have* is often the middle verb.

> will *have* gone   would *have* played   must *have* taken
> could *have* gone   can *have* heard   should *have* gone

Do not use *of* for *have*. *Of* is not a helping verb.

> Wrong: I could *of* gone   Right: I could *have* gone

Separated Parts of the Verb

The words that make up a verb are not always right next to each other, like *could have done* and *might have seen*. Sometimes the helping verbs and the main verbs are separated by words that are not verbs. *Not* and the ending *n't* are not verbs.

> **can** hardly **wait**   **could** not **have come**
> **didn't understand**   **may have** already **arrived**

Exercises   **Find helping verbs and the main verb.**

A.   Label two columns *Helping Verbs* and *Main Verb*. Find all the parts of the verb in each of the following sentences. Write them in the proper columns.

> Example: We must have waited for an hour.

Helping Verbs	Main Verb
must have	waited

383

1. I should be ready by then.
2. Henry would not have forgotten my birthday.
3. Jeff could have told you that.
4. The driver may have put the package there.
5. Vicki would like more blankets.
6. You could have fooled me.
7. Who would have told him?
8. Shall I bring my art supplies?
9. The team could never have played in all that mud.
10. We will never forget his kindness.

B. Follow the directions for Exercise A.

1. We must not delay any longer.
2. We cannot go without him.
3. Do you have the letter with you?
4. Our neighbors are always helping us.
5. The secretary would have taken the message.
6. Didn't you hear the explosion?
7. I could not possibly have thrown out my Disneyland T-shirt.
8. The coin may have fallen through the crack.
9. We have been planning the party for weeks.
10. The parade must be on Central Street.

Part 3 Verbs and Direct Objects

In many sentences, a verb and its subject are enough to state a complete thought.

Subject	Verb
Snow	fell.
Everyone	laughed.

In other sentences the thought is not complete unless more words are added.

Roger cut _____.   Linda met _____.

You wonder *what* Roger cut and *whom* Linda met. You could complete the sentences as follows:

Roger cut the *rope*.   Linda met *Alice*.

In the first sentence, the word *rope* receives the action of the verb *cut*. *Rope* is the **direct object** of the verb.

In the second sentence, *Alice* receives the action of *met*. *Alice* is the **direct object** of the verb.

The direct object tells who or what receives the action of the verb.

Recognizing Direct Objects

To find the direct object in a sentence, first find the verb. Then ask *what* or *whom* after the verb.

Read these examples.

The engineers studied the plans.

Verb: studied
          studied *what*? plans
Direct object: plans

A reporter interviewed Donna.

Verb: interviewed
          interviewed *whom*? Donna
Direct object: Donna

Direct objects only answer *what* or *whom* after the verb. They do not tell *when* or *where* or *how*. You will see that there are no direct objects in the following sentences.

Kelly studies in the afternoon.
They drove around the block.
Andrew whistled sharply.

Exercises   Find the direct objects.

A. Copy the following sentences. Underline the verb twice and circle the direct object.

Example: Rita explained her plan.

1. A huge puddle hid the path.
2. The players rushed the goalie.
3. Suddenly a breeze puffed the sail.
4. Mud splattered the windshield.
5. Dandelions covered the lawn.
6. He always starches his collars.
7. Allison designed the covers.
8. Pete mopped the floor.
9. Ms. Marshall lost her watch.
10. Judge Harvey takes the bus to the courthouse.

B. Number your paper from 1 to 10. Find and write the direct objects in these sentences.

1. The dam produces electricity.
2. The eagle guarded her nest.
3. Why did Tina crumple all that newspaper?
4. The store pipes music into every department.
5. Don't forget your appointment.
6. Did you call Tony about track practice?
7. Give an example.
8. Have you finished your project yet?
9. Mr. White was constantly wiping his brow.
10. Bob raised his eyebrows.

Exercises   Add direct objects.

A. Number your paper from 1 to 5. Write direct objects to complete each of the following sentences.

1. The girls ordered the _____ .
2. The farmer drove his _____ into the field.
3. The police car carried a _____ .
4. Helicopters make short _____ .
5. Do you watch many television _____ ?

B. Writing On a sheet of paper, write sentences using the following verbs. Put a direct object in each sentence. Circle each direct object.

1. will build
2. photographed
3. is sending
4. invented
5. has made
6. buys

Part 4   Transitive and Intransitive Verbs

A verb that has a direct object is called a **transitive verb.** A verb that does not have a direct object is called an **intransitive verb.** The following pairs of sentences show you the difference between transitive and intransitive verbs.

Some birds sing beautiful songs. (*Sing* is transitive; the direct object is *songs.*)

Some birds sing beautifully. (*Sing* is intransitive; it is used without an object.)

Matt paints houses. (*Paints* is transitive; the direct object is *houses.*)

Matt paints with watercolors. (*Paints* is intransitive; it is used without an object.)

If there is a word in the sentence that answers the question *whom?* or *what?* after a verb that shows action, that word is a direct object, and the verb is transitive.

Notice that *sing* and *paints* in the sentences above are used both as transitive and as intransitive verbs, depending on whether there is a direct object or not.

Some verbs are always used as transitive verbs. They must always have a direct object to complete the thought. An example is *bring*.

Other verbs are always used as intransitive verbs. They can never have a direct object. An example is *arrive*.

Most verbs can be used with or without direct objects. They can be transitive in one sentence and intransitive in another. Here are more examples.

Transitive	Intransitive
Maurita practices her dives.	Maurita practices daily.
Larry ate lunch.	Larry ate already.
Kim reached first base.	Kim reached for the ball.

A transitive verb is an action verb that has a direct object.

An intransitive verb is an action verb that does not have a direct object.

Exercises Find transitive and intransitive verbs.

A. Make two columns marked *Transitive* and *Intransitive*. Find the verb that shows action in each of the following sentences. If the verb has an object, write the verb under *Transitive* and put its object in parentheses after it. If the verb has no object, write it under *Intransitive*.

Example: John read the map.

Transitive	Intransitive
read (map)	

1. Al built a bookcase.

2. The zookeeper fed the seals.
3. Mark collects coins.
4. Bonnie has just moved to Richmond, Virginia, from Tallahassee, Florida.
5. The stamps are lying on the table.
6. Craig admired his grandmother.
7. Jennifer and I ordered a pizza.
8. His brow wrinkled.
9. Melanie wrinkled her nose.
10. A good architect designed this house.

B. Follow the directions for Exercise A.

1. Ned returned the books this morning.
2. Kay took the newspaper.
3. Mr. Thomas laid the keys on the TV.
4. Rake the front lawn.
5. We are eating pancakes with fresh blueberries for breakfast.
6. Darcy swam across the pool.
7. I was unpacking my suitcase.
8. Do you like cheesecake?
9. Barbara stayed at home.
10. Wind rippled the water.

C. Writing Each of the following verbs can be used either as a transitive verb or as an intransitive verb. For each verb write two sentences. Label the first of the two sentences (*a*) and the second (*b*). Make the verb transitive in the first of the two sentences and intransitive in the second. Write *Transitive* after the first sentence and *Intransitive* after the second.

Example: 1. (a) Jack dried his hands. Transitive.
(b) The paint dried. Intransitive.

1. study   2. turn   3. write   4. fly   5. crumble

Part 5 Linking Verbs

Verbs that show a state of being are often called **linking verbs.**

Cindy *is* a member.   The soup *tastes* good.

Linking verbs connect the subject with a word in the predicate. The word in the predicate tells something about the subject. In the examples given, *member* tells about *Cindy* and *good* tells about *soup. Is* and *tastes* are linking verbs.

The words *is, am, are, was, were, be,* and *become* are often used as linking verbs. The words *seem, look, appear, feel, grow, smell, taste,* and *sound* are sometimes used as linking verbs.

The same verb may be used to show action in one sentence and state of being in another. Notice the following examples:

We *smelled* smoke.   The children *looked* in the box.
The soap *smelled* sweet.   Jean *looked* happy.

Predicate Words

The words that follow linking verbs and tell something about the subject are called **predicate words.** Nouns that follow linking verbs are **predicate nouns.**

Anne *is* a good swimmer.   Larry *was* my classmate.

Adjectives that follow linking verbs are **predicate adjectives.**

The plant *seems* healthy.   David *is* very successful.

Do not confuse linking verbs and predicate words with transitive verbs and direct objects. Remember: A **direct object** answers the question *whom* or *what* after a **transitive verb.**

Connie painted the picture.   Ron won the prize.

A **predicate word** tells something about the subject of a **linking verb.**

Connie is a painter.   Ron was lucky.

Exercises   Find the linking verbs.

A.   At the top of three columns write: *Subject, Linking Verb,* and *Predicate Word.* Find the three parts in each sentence. Write them in the proper columns.

Example: The chili tasted spicy.

Subject	Linking Verb	Predicate Word
chili	tasted	spicy

1. The new store was open for business.
2. Margo is a volunteer.
3. Thursday was Diane's birthday.
4. The temperature is unbearable!
5. Do you ever feel lonesome?
6. Carlos is an ambitious worker.
7. Tracy feels fine today.
8. Soon Bill became sleepy.
9. The air feels warmer.
10. Sam was by far our best pitcher.

B.   Follow the directions for Exercise A.

1. The cost of the space station seemed tremendous.
2. Mrs. Meredith became the new principal.
3. Sue and Linda seemed anxious at first.
4. The orchids were beautiful.
5. Were you late for the races?
6. Before the game the team was restless.
7. Tony looks a little pale this morning.
8. Kristen is the manager of the tennis team.
9. Do be careful!
10. Water is essential to life on earth.

C.   Copy each of the following sentences. Circle the linking verbs. Underline the transitive verbs.

1. Robin packed the picnic.

2. Am I late?
3. Pete has the measles.
4. The new puppies seem content.
5. The sky became dark during the last inning.
6. Dale arranged the meeting.
7. The crowd seemed upset.
8. These walnuts taste good.
9. Jan tasted the pecans.
10. The lake appeared calm.

Part 6 Tenses of Verbs

Verbs change their forms to show the time when an action or state of being occurs. These changes are called **tenses.**

> The **present tense** shows present time: *I am. I see.*
> The **past tense** shows past time: *I was. I saw.*
> The **future tense** shows future time: *I shall be. You will see.*

Tense changes are made in three ways:

1. By changes in spelling: *sing, sang, sung*
2. By changes in ending: *walk, walked*
3. By adding helping verbs: *has walked, will walk*

Here are five important tenses:

Present Tense:	She talks.	We know.
Past Tense:	She talked.	We knew.
Future Tense:	She will talk.	We shall know.
Present Perfect Tense:	She has talked.	We have known.
Past Perfect Tense:	She had talked.	We had known.

You can see that three tenses are used to show different kinds of past time: *past, present perfect,* and *past perfect.* You will learn two things about them:

1. The past tense forms of a verb are used alone. They are never used with helping verbs.

> we cleaned   you ran   they brought   she slid

2. The present perfect tense uses the helping verbs *has* and *have*. The past perfect tense uses the helping verb *had*.

Present Perfect	**Past Perfect**
he has cleaned	you had run
they have brought	she had slid

Exercises   Learn to recognize and use tenses.

A.   Name the tense of the verb in each sentence.

1. The pitcher caught the ball.
2. Terry has seen the Painted Desert.
3. Seth has taken his bicycle.
4. Toss the ring.
5. Gayle is happy.
6. Mr. Gray has an antique car.
7. Has Rick already gone?
8. Shall we go too?
9. You will find it on the table.
10. We have eaten lunch already.
11. We almost froze yesterday.
12. My father had spoken to the club.

B.   Number your paper from 1 to 10. Write the verb tense asked for. Check by reading the sentence to yourself.

1. The hamster (past of *eat*) the food.
2. My mother (present of *work*) for that company.
3. The ship (past of *touch*) the iceberg.
4. The plants (past perfect of *grow*) much taller.
5. The PTA (future of *buy*) three new typewriters.
6. I (past of *win*) the prize.
7. Sue (future of *pick*) up the package tomorrow.
8. The bird (past of *fly*) away.
9. We (present perfect of *choose*) new band uniforms.
10. Tim (past perfect of *do*) twenty pushups.

Part 7   The Principal Parts of Verbs

Verb tenses are formed from three basic parts of the verb. These parts are called the **principal parts** of the verb. The principal parts are the **present,** the **past,** and the **past participle.**

Present	Past	Past Participle
paint	painted	painted
ring	rang	rung
throw	threw	thrown

By using the principal parts of a verb and different helping verbs, you can make any of the five important tenses.

The principal parts of a verb are the present, the past, and the past participle.

One other part of the verb that is helpful for making verb tenses is the **present participle.** The present participle is the **-ing** form of the verb as in *painting, ringing,* or *throwing.* You use the present participle with helping verbs (*am painting, is ringing, are throwing*).

Learning Principal Parts

There are several thousand verbs in the English language. You won't have any problems using most of them in any tense. They are **regular verbs.** This means that the past is formed by adding *-ed* or *-d* to the present. The past participle is the same as the past form and is always used with a helping verb.

Present	Past	Past Participle
march	march**ed**	(have) march**ed**
plant	plant**ed**	(have) plant**ed**
arrive	arriv**ed**	(have) arriv**ed**

There are a few commonly used verbs, however, whose past forms do not follow this pattern. They are **irregular verbs.**

The list on page 396 gives the principal parts of many irregular verbs. The past participle is always used with a helping verb.

When you use irregular verbs, remember these two important things:

1. The past form is always used by itself, *without* a helping verb.

> Jon *took* our picture.

2. The past participle is always used *with* a helping verb.

> Jon *has taken* our picture.

As you study the list on page 396, you may want to say *have* or *has* in front of each past participle. Then you will not confuse tenses and say, "he seen it," "he done it," "she had stole it," or "she had broke it."

The helping verbs that you will use most often include *has, have, had, is, are, was,* and *were.*

Using a Dictionary To Find Principal Parts

If you are not sure about a verb form, look it up in a dictionary. If the verb is regular, usually only one form will be listed.

If the verb is irregular, the dictionary will give the irregular forms. It will give two forms if the past and past participle are the same: *say, said.* It will give all three principal parts if they are all different: *sing, sang, sung.*

Dictionary Entry for *begin*

present
|
be·gin (bi gin′), **v.** to start being, doing, acting, etc.; get under way
[Work *begins* at 8:00 A.M. His cold *began* with a sore throat.]
—**be·gan′,** *p.*; **be·gun′,** *p.p.*
| └─────── **past participle**
|
past

Irregular Verbs

Present	Past	Past Participle
begin	began	(have) begun
break	broke	(have) broken
bring	brought	(have) brought
choose	chose	(have) chosen
come	came	(have) come
do	did	(have) done
drink	drank	(have) drunk
eat	ate	(have) eaten
fall	fell	(have) fallen
freeze	froze	(have) frozen
give	gave	(have) given
go	went	(have) gone
grow	grew	(have) grown
know	knew	(have) known
ride	rode	(have) ridden
ring	rang	(have) rung
rise	rose	(have) risen
run	ran	(have) run
say	said	(have) said
see	saw	(have) seen
sing	sang	(have) sung
sit	sat	(have) sat
speak	spoke	(have) spoken
steal	stole	(have) stolen
swim	swam	(have) swum
take	took	(have) taken
teach	taught	(have) taught
throw	threw	(have) thrown
wear	wore	(have) worn
write	wrote	(have) written

In **Section 4, Using Irregular Verbs,** you will practice using these verbs correctly.

ADDITIONAL EXERCISES

Using Verbs

A. Finding Verbs Number your paper from 1 to 10. Write the verb in each sentence.

1. Johnny tells that story very well.
2. The usher tore the tickets in half.
3. Janet clamped the new pencil sharpener onto the library desk.
4. Dead leaves whirled past.
5. There was a police officer by the meter.
6. She ticketed Mr. Crawford's car.
7. The ball crashed into the pins.
8. For a few minutes Carla seemed uneasy.
9. Good memories are valuable possessions.
10. In the last quarter of the game, Pam had better luck.

B. Main Verbs and Helping Verbs Label two columns *Helping Verbs* and *Main Verbs*. Find all the parts of the verb in each of the following sentences. Write them in the proper columns.

1. Nobody has used your camera.
2. Tony was boiling some eggs.
3. We had spread our beach towels too close to the water's edge.
4. Megan will probably remember the address.
5. Did you watch the eclipse?
6. The car was just entering the tunnel.
7. Are your parents really selling their van?
8. Carl would certainly not quit the team.
9. Shouldn't I melt the butter first?
10. I have often been told that.

C. Verbs and Direct Objects Write the verb and the direct object for each sentence. Underline the verb and circle the direct object.

1. A lightning bolt hit the tree.
2. Nelson collected the papers.
3. The judge thanked the jury for their hard work.
4. Nobody ever guessed the truth.
5. Did the puppy chew its leash?
6. Dan called Ruth to the phone.
7. Mr. Barnes finally signed the petition.
8. I sometimes enjoy the commercials.
9. The computer probably made a mistake.
10. Measure the shelves carefully.

D. Adding Direct Objects Number your paper from 1 to 5. Write direct objects that will complete each of the following.

1. Tricia opened the mysterious _____.
2. Snow covered the _____.
3. Arthur donated a _____ to the rummage sale.
4. Diane plays the _____ in the band.
5. Joey made a _____ for his mom.

E. Transitive and Intransitive Verbs Label two columns *Transitive* and *Intransitive*. Find the verb in each of the following sentences. If the verb has an object, write it under *Transitive* and put its object in parentheses after it. If the verb has no object, write it under *Intransitive*.

1. A guard stopped the children.
2. A taxi stopped in front of our apartment building.
3. The ice cubes melted in a few minutes.
4. The sun melted the tar on the roof.
5. The alligator covered its nest with leaves.
6. The firefighter swung an ax.
7. The street fair ended with a barbeque.

8. Lisa's words ended the discussion.
9. The mayor presented medals to the rescuers.
10. Write your name on the list.

F. Linking Verbs and Predicate Words At the top of three columns write: *Subject, Linking Verb,* and *Predicate Word.* Find the three parts in each sentence. Write them in the proper columns.

1. The full moon was bright.
2. Caged animals are often nervous.
3. Green vegetables are one source of iron.
4. Joyce seems happy about something.
5. Last Friday was the deadline for the contest.
6. The old school became a community center.
7. The cheerleaders sounded hoarse by the end of the game.
8. Sometimes the weather turns chilly overnight.
9. Those berries don't taste ripe to me.
10. The cornbread smells wonderful.

G. Verb Tenses Write the verb in each sentence. Then write the tense of the verb.

1. Our school has new computers.
2. Jeff bought a bag of sunflower seeds.
3. The parakeet flew out the window.
4. I had a bad cold last week.
5. Lauren will be home soon.
6. Janie has fished for trout before.
7. Will you sit at our table?
8. The driver had started the bus.
9. Is Teresa a baseball fan?
10. Bill has had a wonderful summer.

MIXED REVIEW

Using Verbs

A. Identifying verbs Number your paper from 1 to 10. Write the verb from each sentence. Then write whether it is an *Action* or *State-of-Being* verb. If it is an action verb, write whether it is *Transitive* or *Intransitive*.

1. Harvey cut the paper into long strips.
2. Jan found the key in the bottom of her purse.
3. Mr. Thomas works on weekends.
4. The film has not been developed yet.
5. Rain fell steadily throughout the night.
6. Has the TV been on channel 2 or channel 5?
7. Donna filled the vase with zinnias and asters.
8. John's brother ran in the marathon.
9. This camera seems broken.
10. The apple pie tastes delicious with cheddar cheese.

B. Recognizing verbs, direct objects, and predicate words Copy the following sentences. Underline the verbs. If a verb is a linking verb, draw an arrow from the verb to the predicate word. If the verb is an action verb, circle the direct object, if there is one.

1. Scott was the best pitcher in the league.
2. Your forehead feels hot.
3. Laura did not hear the question.
4. These plums are very ripe.
5. I have written to the editor of the magazine.
6. Mrs. O'Malley is our algebra teacher.
7. Have you ever seen a bullfight?
8. The rocket soared into outer space.
9. That man looks familiar.
10. Gwendolyn Brooks is a famous poet.

C. Using verb tenses correctly Copy the following sentences, using the verb and tense given in parentheses.

1. Dad (present perfect of *miss*) his train.
2. The spout on the teapot (past perfect of *break*).
3. The committee (future of *listen*) to each request.
4. Laura (past of *forget*) the important dates.
5. Dan (present perfect of *fill*) the basket with strawberries.
6. Floyd (present of *listen*) to classical music.
7. During the night the pond (past perfect of *freeze*).
8. Mike (present perfect of *write*) a one-act play.
9. The mayor (past of *throw*) out the first ball of the season.
10. The players on our team (present of *wear*) blue and white jerseys.

USING GRAMMAR IN WRITING
Using Verbs

A. Congratulations! You answered ten trivia questions correctly on the radio. Your prize is a ninety-second free shopping spree in any section of your favorite discount department store. Describe your frantic race to fill the shopping cart. Circle each verb. Label each verb *T* or *I* for transitive or intransitive. Underline each direct object once and each indirect object twice.

B. You are at a carnival. Walking along, you see a mysterious booth draped in black. A sign says "Have Your Future Read by Madame Nozall and Her Crystal Ball." You decide to use your last ticket to have your fortune told. Write a paragraph about some of the things that Madame Nozall tells you about your future. Use verbs in the future tense. Next imagine it is ten years in the future. Write a second paragraph about whether or not the predictions were right. Use the past tense for the verbs in this paragraph.

C. You are applying for a job selling the latest miracle gadget, the Kitchen Shark. To get the job, you have to memorize a list of the things it can do, and the features that it has. Use at least five action words that describe what the gadget can do to different vegetables and fruits. Perhaps it can also open cans and boil eggs. Be as inventive as you want to be. Then use three state-of-being verbs to describe how the object looks or feels.

Using Irregular Verbs

In Section 3, you learned about verbs, especially regular verbs. In this section you will practice using irregular verbs.

When you use irregular verbs, remember these two things:

1. The past tense is always used by itself, *without* a helping verb.

> I *rode* the subway.   Jean *wrote* a poem.

2. The past participle is always used *with* a helping verb.

> I *have ridden* the subway.   Jean *has written* a poem.

Practice Pages on Irregular Verbs

Irregular verbs can cause problems in writing as well as in speaking. Use the exercise on the next page as a test to show how well you can handle these irregular verbs.

If the exercise shows that you do know these verbs, you may refer to this section simply for review. If the exercise shows that you need practice with certain verbs, your teacher may ask you to practice those verbs. For each verb there are sentences that will help you to "say it right," "hear it right," and "write it right." Oral practice is an important way to learn these verbs. Review the oral sections before you do the written work.

Exercise Number your paper from 1 to 22. For each sentence, write the correct word from the two given in parentheses.

1. Dennis (bring, brought) cider for the party.
2. Joe has (broke, broken) the school track record.
3. Ruth had (came, come) to the meeting with us.
4. Rosita has (chose, chosen) a biography for her report.
5. After we had (did, done) the work, we went home.
6. Have you (drank, drunk) all the lemonade?
7. When I came home, everyone had (ate, eaten) dinner.
8. The shallow lake had already (froze, frozen).
9. Mrs. Lorenzo has (gave, given) us our assignment.
10. All of us have (went, gone) to the science fair.
11. Have you (grew, grown) strawberries or raspberries?
12. How long have you (knew, known) the MacArthurs?
13. Sara and Rick have (ran, run) in the relay race.
14. At camp, the dinner bell (rang, rung) every night.
15. I have never (rode, ridden) in a helicopter.
16. Robert had (sang, sung) at the Summer Festival.
17. I have (saw, seen) *E. T.* three times.
18. Ms. Bell has (spoke, spoken) to me about a job.
19. Ginny has (swam, swum) in the Pacific.
20. The umpire (thrown, threw) him out.
21. Have you ever (wore, worn) hiking boots?
22. Mark has finally (wrote, written) his report.

**Break
Broke
Broken**

**Bring
Brought
Brought**

Say It Right   Hear It Right

A. Say these sentences over until the correct use of *broke* and *broken* sounds natural to you.

1. Maria broke the glass.
2. The dish is broken.
3. The window had been broken.
4. Break the seal first.

5. The clock was broken.
6. They broke the news.
7. Did Jason break his arm?
8. Christie broke the lamp.

B. Say these sentences over until the correct use of *bring* and *brought* sounds natural to you.

1. Jeff has brought the album.
2. Bring an umbrella.
3. I brought mine.
4. Keith brought his lunch.

5. Laura will bring a camera.
6. Did you bring the tickets?
7. I wish I'd brought my jacket.
8. We brought you a gift.

Write It Right

Write the correct word from the two words given.

1. Did you (bring, brought) the salad?
2. Steve (bring, brought) the badminton set.
3. Have you (bring, brought) the reports to class?
4. I have (bring, brought) a friend along.
5. I have (bring, brought) you a surprise.
6. Haven't you (bring, brought) anything?
7. Peg (bring, brought) her new racket to class.
8. The paramedics had (bring, brought) him to the hospital.
9. Julie has (broke, broken) her wrist.
10. Allen may have (broke, broken) the typewriter.
11. We have (broke, broken) five dishes.
12. Our car had (broke, broken) down on the expressway.
13. That clock has been (broke, broken) for over a year.
14. Ted's fishing pole was (broke, broken) in half.
15. The runner has (broke, broken) the previous record.

Use the Right Word

Say It Right   Hear It Right

A. Say these sentences over until the correct use of *chose* and *chosen* sounds natural to you.

1. The team was chosen.
2. Fred chose a poem.
3. The class chose these books.
4. Ann has been chosen.
5. Choose a record.
6. Dick chose a yellow shirt.
7. Have you been chosen?
8. Was Liz chosen?

B. Say these sentences over until the correct use of *came* and *come* sounds natural to you.

1. Sue came to the meeting.
2. Will he come with us?
3. He should have come home.
4. Amy and Tad came with me.
5. Has the mail come yet?
6. They came yesterday.
7. Eric has come for his book.
8. Did you come to dinner?

Write It Right

Write the correct word from the two words given.

1. Loud cheers (came, come) from the fans.
2. The exhibit will (came, come) to the museum in July.
3. I wondered why the mail carrier (came, come) so early.
4. They had arrived long before we (came, come).
5. I saw the accident just as I (came, come) along.
6. My sister has (came, come) home from college this week.
7. She (came, come) last weekend, too.
8. We (chose, chosen) to go camping this summer.
9. I (chose, chosen) watermelon instead of pie for dessert.
10. Have you (chose, chosen) the color you want on your walls?
11. The team has (chose, chosen) Chris as captain.
12. We have (chose, chosen) new books for our library.
13. At camp we (chose, chosen) Pablo as our group leader.
14. Ruth has been (chose, chosen) class president.
15. I (chose, chosen) to work on the posters.

Do
Did
Done

Say It Right Hear It Right

Drink
Drank
Drunk

A. Say these sentences over until the correct use of *did* and *done* sounds natural to you.

1. Sam did his chores.
2. Ellen has done hers.
3. I did the dishes.
4. Lee has done ten problems.
5. Kim did only three.
6. Mark has done only one.
7. Tim did his work quickly.
8. Jim has done the laundry.

B. Say these sentences over until the correct use of *drank* and *drunk* sounds natural to you.

1. I have drunk the juice.
2. Ann has drunk three glasses.
3. Lynn had drunk only one.
4. Carol drank iced tea.
5. Chris drank root beer.
6. Kim and Lisa drank milk.
7. Tim had drunk water.
8. Carla drank ginger ale.

Write It Right

Write the correct word from the two words given.

1. Have you (did, done) the math exercises yet?
2. Juan (did, done) a good job on the model airplane.
3. Have you (did, done) your homework?
4. The team (did, done) the best it could.
5. The school band has never (did, done) so well before.
6. No one could have (did, done) those problems.
7. Jane (did, done) that scale model of a pyramid.
8. The performers (did, done) an excellent job.
9. I have (drank, drunk) eight glasses of water today.
10. Jamie and Steve (drank, drunk) the last soda.
11. Have you ever (drank, drunk) coconut milk?
12. The baby has (drank, drunk) all the juice in the bottle.
13. We (drank, drunk) ginger ale at the picnic.
14. Josh has never (drank, drunk) iced tea.
15. The hikers (drank, drunk) water from the well on the farm.

Use the Right Word

Say It Right   Hear It Right

A. Say these sentences over until the correct use of *ate* and *eaten* sounds natural to you.

1. Ted ate the salad.
2. Dana has eaten breakfast.
3. Jim ate later.
4. Beth ate slowly.

5. Shelly had eaten a lot.
6. We had eaten dinner.
7. I eat at noon.
8. We ate hot dogs.

B. Say these sentences over until the correct use of *froze* and *frozen* sounds natural to you.

1. Bus windows were frozen.
2. The fish was frozen.
3. The milk had frozen.
4. Rain froze into hail.

5. It may freeze tonight.
6. Mother froze the meat.
7. The fruit was frozen.
8. The pond froze.

Write It Right

Write the correct word from the two words given.

1. Todd had (ate, eaten) before the game.
2. Stephanie (ate, eaten) the yogurt.
3. I (eat, eaten) too fast sometimes.
4. Scott has (ate, eaten) all the peanut butter.
5. Lucy had (ate, eaten) lunch at a friend's house.
6. She has (ate, eaten) there lots of times.
7. Dave had (ate, eaten) slowly.
8. We (ate, eaten) at my cousin's last night.
9. The lake was (froze, frozen) halfway out from shore.
10. Jan's tears were almost (froze, frozen) on her cheeks.
11. We have (froze, frozen) the leftovers.
12. Waiting for the school bus, we nearly (froze, frozen).
13. Linda's toes were almost (froze, frozen).
14. This is the first winter the river has (froze, frozen).
15. The water pipe has (froze, frozen).

**Give
Gave
Given**

Say It Right   Hear It Right

**Go
Went
Gone**

A. Say these sentences over until the correct use of *gave* and *given* sounds natural to you.

1. Liz has given me a gift.
2. Jo gave her speech today.
3. Will you give me a hand?
4. My aunt gave me a watch.
5. I was given the day off.
6. I gave the baby a toy.
7. She has given a party.
8. Sue gave Bob a rare stamp.

B. Say these sentences over until the correct use of *went* and *gone* sounds natural to you.

1. Lisa went home.
2. John had gone last winter.
3. I went to the museum.
4. We went swimming.
5. Did Dee go, too?
6. Mom went to play golf.
7. Have you gone to the zoo?
8. I went there last summer.

Write It Right

Write the correct word from the two words given.

1. We (give, gave) our teacher a present.
2. You should have (gave, given) better directions.
3. Sally (gave, given) me a jigsaw puzzle.
4. Their team seemed to have (gave, given) up.
5. Our coach has always (gave, given) us praise when we win.
6. Sometimes he has (gave, given) us a lecture.
7. Mrs. Hanke (gave, given) us a spelling test.
8. Ann has (went, gone) away for the summer.
9. Jonathan and Liz have (went, gone) fishing.
10. I have (went, gone) fishing only once.
11. Rob has (went, gone) fishing every day this summer.
12. Mary has always (went, gone) to the show on Saturday.
13. The children (went, gone) down the street to get ice cream.
14. My sister has always (went, gone) to summer camp.
15. Jeremy and Beth (went, gone) to the meeting.

Use the Right Word

Say It Right   Hear It Right

A. Say these sentences over until the correct use of *grew* and *grown* sounds natural to you.

1. The sunflower grew tall.
2. We grew our own lettuce.
3. Did you grow beets?
4. The tree has grown tall.
5. The night grew cold.
6. I had grown tired of weeding.
7. The grass grew quickly.
8. We have all grown a lot.

B. Say these sentences over until the correct use of *knew* and *known* sounds natural to you.

1. Have you known Kim long?
2. I have known her for years.
3. Do you know the results?
4. I had known Jim at camp.
5. Jeff knew Sue from school.
6. I knew the owner.
7. Kay knew her well.
8. They knew it would rain.

Write It Right

Write the correct word from the two words given.

1. Our class (grew, grown) flowers for the army hospital.
2. We have (grew, grown) radishes every summer.
3. Anna (grew, grown) ten kinds of plants for her experiment.
4. George has (grew, grown) two inches since last fall.
5. The Jeffersons (grew, grown) their own vegetables.
6. Mother (grew, grown) catnip for our cat.
7. The corn has (grew, grown) six feet tall.
8. They have (knew, known) each other since fifth grade.
9. I have never (knew, known) a busier person.
10. The hikers (knew, known) they were lost.
11. Kathy (knew, known) how to read at four years old.
12. We (knew, known) the Jacksons.
13. Clara has (knew, known) how to swim since the age of three.
14. We hadn't (knew, known) the game was postponed.
15. Mike had never (knew, known) anyone from Japan before.

Run
Ran
Run

See
Saw
Seen

Say It Right   Hear It Right

A. Say these sentences over until the correct use of *ran* and *run* sounds natural to you.

1. The dog ran outside.
2. Has our time run out?
3. They ran out of ice cream.
4. Al had run very fast.
5. Steve has run three miles.
6. The joggers ran for miles.
7. Barb ran the school store.
8. Has the relay been run yet?

B. Say these sentences over until the correct use of *saw* and *seen* sounds natural to you.

1. Michelle has seen the play.
2. Have you seen my new puppy?
3. Jay saw the All-Star game.
4. Chris saw it, too.
5. Can you see the screen?
6. Eve saw us at the pool.
7. I saw you yesterday.
8. We haven't seen him.

Write It Right

Write the correct word from the two words given.

1. Ruth had (ran, run) until she was exhausted.
2. When my brother saw Dad, he (ran, run) to meet him.
3. The race was (ran, run) at the high school.
4. Who (ran, run) in the relays?
5. The car has (ran, run) out of gas.
6. Katie and Jeff (ran, run) four miles today.
7. Have you ever (ran, run) in a three-legged race?
8. We (saw, seen) the World Series on television.
9. I (saw, seen) Mr. and Mrs. Barton at the Auto Show.
10. My family (saw, seen) the Olympic Games.
11. Darcy has (saw, seen) the film before.
12. We (saw, seen) an exhibit of American Indian art.
13. I have never (saw, seen) a big league baseball game.
14. Have you (saw, seen) the movie *The Right Stuff?*
15. Ian (saw, seen) the President last week.

Use the Right Word

Say It Right   Hear It Right

A. Say these sentences over until the correct use of *sang* and *sung* sounds natural to you.

1. They sang with the band.
2. Who sang at the concert?
3. We sang in chorus yesterday.
4. She had sung that before.
5. The choir had sung.
6. Can you sing that song?
7. George had sung one song.
8. Have you ever sung here?

B. Say these sentences over until the correct use of *spoke* and *spoken* sounds natural to you.

1. Has Don spoken to you?
2. He spoke to Julie.
3. The principal spoke to us.
4. We had spoken to her.
5. Mother spoke to my teacher.
6. The baby spoke one word.
7. Lou has not spoken to me.
8. Who spoke at the meeting?

Write It Right

Write the correct word from the two words given.

1. The quartet (sang, sung) in the mall last weekend.
2. Have you ever (sang, sung) in a chorus?
3. Her cousin had (sang, sung) just before she did.
4. We (sang, sung) around the campfire.
5. Sara, Lois, Sam, and Chuck (sang, sung) a medley.
6. Ginny (sang, sung) beautifully in her recital.
7. Paul (sang, sung) a solo.
8. Roger and Donna had (sang, sung) a duet.
9. I have (spoke, spoken) to three movie stars.
10. The first speaker (spoke, spoken) on solar energy.
11. The second speaker (spoke, spoken) on nuclear energy.
12. They had both (spoke, spoken) to us before.
13. Tim (spoke, spoken) to the new students.
14. The coach (spoke, spoken) to us enthusiastically.
15. He has often (spoke, spoken) to us that way.

Use the Right Word

Ride
Rode
Ridden

Ring
Rang
Rung

Say It Right   Hear It Right

A. Say these sentences over until the correct use of *rode* and *ridden* sounds natural to you.

1. Josh rode the ferris wheel.
2. I have ridden it often.
3. We rode our minibikes.
4. We have ridden them before.
5. Did you ride the train?
6. Have you ridden a mule?
7. Pat has ridden a horse.
8. I rode one last summer.

B. Say these sentences over until the correct use of *rang* and *rung* sounds natural to you.

1. Who rang the doorbell?
2. The mail carrier rang it.
3. Has the bell rung yet?
4. I thought it rang.
5. The church bells rang.
6. Ring the bell for class.
7. The victory bell rang.
8. It had rung earlier.

Write It Right

Write the correct word from the two words given.

1. That jockey has (rode, ridden) in many races.
2. Have you ever (rode, ridden) in a rodeo?
3. Our club (rode, ridden) in the bike-a-thon.
4. My uncle (rode, ridden) his bicycle to work.
5. Gary has (rode, ridden) in many horse shows.
6. Have you ever (rode, ridden) a horse?
7. My brother (rode, ridden) in a dirt bike race Saturday.
8. The telephone (rang, rung) at midnight.
9. The student (rang, rung) the fire alarm.
10. When the ceremony ended, all the bells (rang, rung).
11. The doorbell (rang, rung) three times.
12. All the church bells had (rang, rung).
13. The fire alarm (rang, rung), but it was a false alarm.
14. The cathedral bells (rang, rung) at Christmas.
15. The camp dinner bell had (rang, rung) twice.

413

Use the Right Word

Say It Right   Hear It Right

A.   Say these sentences over until the correct use of *swam* and *swum* sounds natural to you.

1. Roy swam in the river.
2. Dozens of fish had swum by.
3. We swam after school.
4. Mandy swam for an hour.

5. I can swim three laps.
6. The salmon swam fast.
7. Wayne swam in the pool.
8. Sherry has swum there.

B.   Say these sentences over until the correct use of *threw* and *thrown* sounds natural to you.

1. The mayor threw the ball.
2. He threw his cap in the air.
3. Luzinski was thrown out.
4. Bench threw him out.

5. Who threw that pass?
6. Have you thrown it away?
7. I can't throw that far.
8. The pitcher threw a curve.

Write It Right

Write the correct word from the two words given.

1. Curt has (swam, swum) in races for years.
2. The trout (swam, swum) toward the bait.
3. We have (swam, swum) in that race every year.
4. Sally (swam, swum) faster than I did.
5. Only one goldfish (swam, swum) in the bowl.
6. Sharks (swam, swum) in those waters.
7. Our team (swam, swum) laps for an hour.
8. Dolphins (swam, swum) around our boat.
9. Our newspaper had been (threw, thrown) into the bushes.
10. The cargo was (threw, thrown) out of the train by the blast.
11. We (threw, thrown) rice at the bride and groom.
12. Lynn (threw, thrown) the ball to Tanya.
13. The wrestler has (threw, thrown) his opponent.
14. Kent (threw, thrown) the winning pass.
15. They had (threw, thrown) out bread for the birds.

Wear
Wore
Worn

Say It Right   Hear It Right

Write
Wrote
Written

A. Say these sentences over until the correct use of *wore* and *worn* sounds natural to you.

1. They had worn T-shirts.
2. I have worn out my pen.
3. José wore glasses.
4. Gail wore out the battery.

5. May I wear your hat?
6. We all wore sandals.
7. I wore out my shoes.
8. Ryan had worn his jacket.

B. Say these sentences over until the correct use of *wrote* and *written* sounds natural to you.

1. Amy has written a letter.
2. Who wrote this song?
3. Who wrote that play?
4. Shakespeare wrote it.

5. Sue has written a song.
6. We wrote the assignment.
7. I had written two letters.
8. Did you write this poem?

Write It Right

Write the correct word from the two words given.

1. My sister (wore, worn) her new blazer.
2. We had (wore, worn) our heavy gloves to shovel snow.
3. Holly and Juanita were (wore, worn) out from the hike.
4. My sandals (wore, worn) out.
5. I have already (wore, worn) out my jeans.
6. We all (wore, worn) costumes to the party.
7. I have never (wore, worn) roller skates before.
8. To whom have you (wrote, written)?
9. How many letters have you (wrote, written) now?
10. Adam (wrote, written) a science fiction story.
11. We had (wrote, written) to our friends in Indiana.
12. Emily Dickinson (wrote, written) many poems.
13. Have you ever (wrote, written) to the President?
14. Who (wrote, written) "The Raven"?
15. Edgar Allan Poe (wrote, written) it.

ADDITIONAL EXERCISES

Using Irregular Verbs

Irregular Verbs   Write the correct verb from the two forms given.

1. The guests had (bring, brought) food to the party.
2. The doorbell has been (broke, broken) for weeks.
3. Our dog has (come, came) back home.
4. Mike had (chose, chosen) a window seat.
5. The wreckers had (did, done) their job.
6. I (did, done) most of the planning.
7. The robin (drank, drunk) from the puddle.
8. Chip has (ate, eaten) all of the apples.
9. The lock had (froze, frozen).
10. The mayor should have (gave, given) you a medal.
11. Most of the summer workers have (went, gone).
12. Tasha (went, gone) to a gymnastics camp.
13. Mr. Novy has (grew, grown) a beard.
14. Lee (knew, known) the words to every song.
15. Althea has just (ran, run) out of patience.
16. The telephone (rang, rung) only once.
17. Jake had never (rode, ridden) the subway alone.
18. Our choir has often (sang, sung) in other cities.
19. Have you ever (saw, seen) a salt marsh?
20. Many people (saw, seen) strange lights in the sky.
21. The witness had (spoke, spoken) the truth.
22. Nina (swam, swum) from the raft to the pier.
23. I've (threw, thrown) the letter away.
24. I wish I'd (wore, worn) a sun visor.
25. Someone had (wrote, written) to the manager.

MIXED REVIEW

Using Irregular Verbs

A. Using irregular verbs correctly Number your paper from 1 to 12. Write the correct verb from those in parentheses.

1. Brett (chose, chosen) the striped wallpaper.
2. Who (ate, eaten) the last piece of pizza?
3. Jan (broke, broken) her new camera.
4. The runners have (drank, drunk) all the lemonade.
5. Chuck has (went, gone) to the art exhibit.
6. I have (bring, brought) my basketball.
7. Houston has (grew, grown) rapidly.
8. Lynn has (come, came) for her violin lesson.
9. Has Chris ever (ran, run) for president?
10. Walt (did, done) the most work for the homecoming dance.
11. Miss Temple has (rode, ridden) the Orient Express.
12. I (saw, seen) the Big Dipper.

B. Identifying principal parts Number your paper from 1 to 10. Label three columns *Present, Past,* and *Past Participle.* List the three principal parts of the following irregular verbs.

1. speak
2. wear
3. know
4. throw
5. give
6. go
7. swim
8. freeze
9. sing
10. write

USING GRAMMAR IN WRITING
Using Irregular Verbs

A. Two astronauts have been to your school to talk about their trip into space. When you leave school that day, your best friend is waiting to hear all about the talk. Retell some of the things you heard, using at least five of the following irregular verbs. Some of the verbs should be in the past participle form.

choose	have	see
do	go	sing
eat	ride	run
give	say	take
begin	wear	write

B. Many young people dream of becoming great athletes. Imagine that you have just completed your first big competition. You may pick any sport you like. Write about your experience. How had you felt before the competition began? How did you feel during your performance? Use several of the following verbs in your paragraph. Some should be in the past tense. Some should use the past participle form.

teach	grow	run	throw
break	know	see	wear
bring	ring	steal	take
fall	rise	swim	drink

Using Troublesome Pairs of Verbs

Sometimes people confuse certain verbs. For example, they don't know whether to say, "Let me help" or "Leave me help." They aren't sure whether "She lay her books on the table" or "She laid her books on the table" is correct.

In this section you will study six pairs of verbs that are often confused. Learn to use these verbs correctly.

Part 1 Using *Learn* and *Teach*

1. *Learn* means "to gain knowledge or skill." Example: I will *learn* French.

2. *Teach* means "to instruct or educate." Example: Kelly *teaches* her friends sign language.

The principal parts of these verbs are:

learn, learned, learned   teach, taught, taught

You use these verbs like this:

Learn

Present: Runners learn to breathe properly.
Past: Britt learned her sister's secret.
Past participle: Lee has learned some words in Spanish.

Teach

Present: That guard teaches the lifesaving course.
Past: Julia Child taught us French cooking.
Past participle: Mr. Mill has taught hundreds of music classes.

Exercise   Use *learn* and *teach* correctly.

Write the correct word from the two words given.

1. Will you (learn, teach) me the new plays before Saturday?
2. We (learned, taught) about dinosaurs at the museum.
3. We (learned, taught) of Ms. Moore's illness.
4. I (learned, taught) myself to play a banjo.
5. Mr. Good has (learned, taught) math for thirty years.
6. The actress had not (learned, taught) her lines.
7. My sister (learns, teaches) people to make clay pots.
8. My camp counselor (learned, taught) us water safety.
9. This course (learns, teaches) woodworking skills.
10. A flight student (learns, teaches) from a trained pilot.

Part 2 Using *Let* and *Leave*

1. *Let* means "to allow or permit." Example: *Let* me go.
2. *Leave* means "to go away (from)." Example: They will *leave* the party early. Leave also means "cause to remain." Example: Leave the books on the table.

The principal parts of these verbs are:

let, let, let   leave, left, left

You use these verbs like this:

Let

Present:	This window lets in plenty of air.
Past:	Sue's parents let her go on the trip.
Past participle:	We have let you win.

Leave

Present:	Don always leaves early.
Past:	Nora left the breakfast dishes in the sink.
Past participle:	Have they left us any chocolate cake?

Exercise   Use *let* and *leave* correctly.

Write the correct word from the two words given.

1. Please (let, leave) me help you with that.
2. (Let, Leave) me hold one of the new puppies.
3. Please (let, leave) these paintings dry.
4. We will (let, leave) a note for him.
5. Will you (let, leave) Ralph and Trisha go with you to the movies?
6. (Let, Leave) me take those packages.
7. Shouldn't we (let, leave) the others come?
8. Randy will (let, leave) the package in the hallway.
9. Did you (let, leave) your jacket in your locker?
10. The Jansens will (let, leave) us stay at their house.

Part 3 Using *Lie* and *Lay*

1. *Lie* means "to recline or rest." It never has a direct object. Its principal parts are *lie, lay, lain.* Example: I *will lie* down for a while.

2. *Lay* means "to put or place." It takes a direct object. Its principal parts are *lay, laid, laid.* Example: *Lay* down your pencils.

Look again at the principal parts of these verbs:

lie, lay, lain   lay, laid, laid

You use these verbs like this:

Lie

Present:	My dog rarely lies on the porch.
Past:	The cyclist lay under the tree for a rest.
Past participle:	How long has that shovel lain there?

Lay

Present:	Jan always lays her coat on this chair.
Past:	He laid his books on the table.
Past participle:	She has laid aside her work.

Exercise   Use *lie* and *lay* correctly.

Write the correct word from the two words given.

1. The nurse advised me to (lie, lay) down for a while.
2. Jill's skateboard is (lying, laying) in the driveway.
3. I'm going to (lie, lay) on the beach for an hour or so.
4. Where did you (lie, lay) the scissors?
5. The kittens like to (lie, lay) under the rocking chair.
6. We found a wallet (lying, laying) on the front walk.
7. Please (lie, lay) those photographs on the table.
8. Litter was (lying, laying) all over the picnic area.

9. Several runners (lie, lay) down after the strenuous race.
10. (Lie, Lay) all of the drawings on this counter.

Part 4 Using *May* and *Can*

1. *May* is a helping verb. It is used to show permission. Example: The guard said that we *may* enter. It also shows possibility. Example: According to the forecast, it *may* rain tomorrow. Another form of the verb *may* is *might*. Example: Debbie *might* join the swim team.

2. *Can* is also used as a helping verb. It shows ability to do something. Example: Jim *can* repair bicycles. *Could* is another form of the verb. Example: We *could* hear a strange noise.

The verbs *may* and *can* have no principal parts.

Exercise Use *may* and *can* correctly.

Write the correct form from the two words given.

1. The owner said we (may, can) use his rowboat.
2. Glass and metal (may, can) conduct electricity.
3. I (may, can) see that Anna is angry.
4. Ms. Tower, (may, can) I turn in the paper tomorrow?
5. Ted's parents said that he (may, can) go to the carnival.
6. Now that I've taken swimming classes, I (may, can) do the backstroke.
7. (May, Can) we please stay out late tonight?
8. If you (may, can) jump higher, you will win.
9. If you make noise, the baby (may, can) wake up.
10. Ed is so strong that he (may, can) lift two hundred pounds.

Part 5 Using *Rise* and *Raise*

1. *Rise* means "to get up or to move upward." It has no direct object. Example: The player *rose* from the bench.

2. *Raise* means "to lift." It also means "to grow something." It always takes a direct object. Example: Pam *raised* her arms and cheered.

Look at the principal parts of these verbs:

rise, rose, risen   raise, raised, raised

These verbs are used like this:

Rise

Present: Bread rises because of yeast.

Past: One boy rose from his seat and walked out.

Past participle: After the sun had risen, we began our work.

Raise

Present: Sam raises the curtain at every show.

Past: The rancher raised cattle.

Past participle: The cadets have raised the flag.

Exercise   **Use *rise* and *raise* correctly.**

Write the correct form from the two words given.

1. Smoke (rose, raised) from the burning building.
2. Ms. Scott (rises, raises) Venus' flytraps in her garden.
3. My parents (rose, raised) my allowance.
4. When Jackson hit a home run, a cheer (rose, raised).
5. The curtain (rose, raised), but the stage was empty.
6. The waves (rose, raised) to a height of five feet.
7. Linda (rises, raises) her voice when she gets angry.
8. Please (rise, raise) the picture higher on the left.
9. A young player (rose, raised) to the major leagues.
10. The thief (rose, raised) the window and looked in.

Part 6   Using *Sit* and *Set*

1. *Sit* means "to be seated." It has no direct object. *Sat* is the past tense of *sit*. Example: We *sat* on the stage.

2. *Set* is a different word entirely. It means "to put or place." *Set* has a direct object. Example: *Set* the package on the counter.

The principal parts of these verbs are:

sit, sat, sat   **set, set, set**

You use these verbs like this:

Sit

Present: Our cat always sits in the window.
Past: Jay sat in the first row.
Past participle: I have sat there many times.

Set

Present: Ned usually sets the table.
Past: I set the packages there last night.
Past participle: Carol has set the plants on the back porch.

Exercise   **Use *sit* and *set* correctly.**

Write the correct word from the two words given.

1. Tim and Michelle will (sit, set) near the fifty-yard line.
2. Will you (sit, set) the luggage on the curb, please?
3. Please (sit, set) the groceries on the table.
4. We (sat, set) in the front row for the outdoor concert.
5. Do you want to (sit, set) on the front porch?
6. I would prefer to (sit, set) on the main floor.
7. I thought I had (sit, set) my lunch on this table.
8. The drivers (sat, set) waiting for the race to begin.
9. Won't you (sit, set) down and join us for dinner?
10. Sandy (sit, set) the mail on the buffet.

ADDITIONAL EXERCISES

Using Troublesome Pairs of Verbs

Troublesome Verbs Write the correct verb from the two forms given.

1. Ms. Sims (learned, taught) us how to use a table saw.
2. The lab mice (learned, taught) to run the maze.
3. The mice (learned, taught) themselves to run the maze.
4. Bob (learns, teaches) dances from his sister.
5. That will (learn, teach) him a lesson.
6. Curt (let, left) me play his xylophone.
7. (Let, Leave) Jan stay home if she wants to.
8. Don't (let, leave) your little sister at home.
9. I (let, left) Craig have first choice.
10. The turtle (lay, laid) on its back.
11. Sheila (lay, laid) the turtle right side up.
12. The cat was (lying, laying) in a pile of sweaters.
13. Sue had (lain, laid) her purse on the counter.
14. (May, Can) I please use your pocketknife?
15. JoAnn (may, can) write with either hand.
16. The snake (might, could) be a copperhead.
17. Nobody (might, could) understand why.
18. Steam (rose, raised) from the radiator.
19. The dentist (rose, raised) the chair.
20. Let the pizza dough (rise, raise) for thirty minutes.
21. (Rise, Raise) your left leg.
22. I will (sit, set) in the back seat.
23. Ben had (sat, set) his stopwatch.
24. Jackie (sat, set) down on the diving board.
25. Let's (sit, set) in the shade.

MIXED REVIEW

Using Troublesome Pairs of Verbs

A. Using the correct verb   Number your paper from 1 to 12. Write the correct verb from those given in parentheses.

1. (May, Can) you ski down the highest slope?
2. Mrs. Green (teaches, learns) English to adults.
3. (Let, Leave) the child dress herself.
4. (May, Can) we please borrow that tape?
5. I (learned, taught) needlepoint from my sister.
6. The sun is (rising, raising) over the lake.
7. (Lie, Lay) your packages on the table.
8. Paul (let, leave) me use his golf clubs.
9. Gina (raised, rose) guppies last year.
10. The mechanic is (lying, laying) under the car.
11. Ken (sat, set) on the balcony.
12. Gary has (sat, set) the sprinkler in the yard.

B. Using troublesome verbs correctly   Five of the following sentences contain errors in their use of verbs. Rewrite correctly any sentences that contain errors. If a sentence is already correct, write *Correct*.

1. Dad said that I may wear his parka.
2. Mr. Meyer is leaving us use his typewriter.
3. Ken set in the rocking chair.
4. Tina can do many kinds of magic tricks.
5. Ms. Kelly learned us the Morse Code.
6. Jerry let us use his stopwatch.
7. The dog has lain on the patio all day.
8. The audience raised up and cheered.
9. Sharon lay her bike on the grass.
10. The builders have raised the roof of the house.

USING GRAMMAR IN WRITING
Using Troublesome Pairs of Verbs

A. Do you remember your first week of school this year? Did you feel unsure of yourself in some ways? Did you have to ask an older student or a teacher for directions or advice? What have you learned about the school that you think a younger student should know? Write a paragraph of good, sound advice for the incoming students. The advice may be funny or serious. In your paragraph, use the following sets of verbs correctly.

> learn—teach   let—leave   may—can

B. You have been changed into a sales item in a large department store. Are you an appliance, a piece of sporting equipment, a toy, or a computer? You may choose to be anything that would be sold in a department store. As soon as someone buys you, the spell is broken. You become yourself again. Write about your experiences on the shelf. Write about the customers who look at you and perhaps try you out. In your paragraph, use the following sets of verbs correctly.

> rise—raise   lie—lay   sit—set

Using Nouns

Part 1 What Are Nouns?

Nouns are used to name persons, places, and things.

Persons: friend, pilot, driver, Chris Evert Lloyd
Places: Charleston, beach, field, Disney World
Things: shoe, football, cloud, bread, Oldsmobile

Things named by nouns may be things you can see:

bike   belt   guitar   spoon

Other things named by nouns may be things you cannot see:

pain   science   language   law

Still other things named by nouns are ideas:

friendship   courage   honesty   sadness
freedom   poverty   religion   Christianity

A noun is a word used to name a person, place, or thing.

Exercises   Find the nouns.

A. Number your paper from 1 to 10. List the nouns in each of the following sentences.

1. Two waiters shoved the chairs and tables against the wall.
2. The wind blew the snow into enormous drifts.
3. The rains made a pond by the side of the road.
4. An hour and ten minutes had passed.
5. The words were on the tip of his tongue.
6. Put your foot on the ladder.
7. A fuzzy orange caterpillar crept up the tree.
8. The meadow behind the barn was covered with flowers.
9. There is a wide porch along the back of the house.
10. The company pumps 80,000 barrels of oil a day.

B. Follow the directions for Exercise A.

1. Add up the last column again.
2. That news calls for a celebration.
3. The crowd had already left the auditorium.
4. On a clear day you can see the islands.
5. Temperatures in the Antarctic are rarely above zero.
6. The bread was made with bananas.
7. Matthew asked the clerk for change.

8. Tina waited for the bus for fifteen minutes in the rain.
9. The truth of the matter is another story.
10. Two sparrows took baths in the puddle.

Part 2 Common Nouns and Proper Nouns

What do you notice about the italicized words in the following sentence?

One *boy*, *José Rodriguez*, and one *girl*, *Jenny Collins*, come from a nearby *city*, *Lansing*.

The italicized words are nouns. The words *boy*, *girl*, and *city* are called **common nouns.** A common noun is a general name. It does not name a particular boy, girl, or city.

The words *José Rodriguez*, *Jenny Collins*, and *Lansing*, on the other hand, name specific people and a specific city. They are called **proper nouns.** A proper noun always begins with a capital letter.

A common noun is a general name for a person, place, or thing.

A proper noun is the name of a particular person, place, or thing.

Common Nouns	Proper Nouns
team	Georgia Bulldogs
bridge	Golden Gate Bridge
encyclopedia	World Book
company	Jordan Marsh Company
nation	Finland

As the above list shows, a noun may consist of more than one word.

Exercises   Find the proper nouns.

A. Number your paper from 1 to 10. Write the proper nouns in each sentence. Capitalize them correctly.

1. We saw governor garfield in town.
2. I have never been to the everglades in florida.
3. My family visited toronto, montreal, and niagara falls during our vacation.
4. It was john glenn who became the first american sent into orbit.
5. She was an employee of atlanta national bank.
6. My aunt, vivian taylor, arrived yesterday on the train.
7. The clerk was talking to dan and sheila.
8. The schubert theater has closed.
9. Last night georgetown beat newport in basketball.
10. My parents took a cruise to puerto rico.

B. Follow the directions for Exercise A.

1. The jefferson public library was open yesterday.
2. We used to go to a library on michigan avenue in chicago.
3. The village called blue hills is near three small lakes.
4. Last summer we went camping near bear lake in rocky mountain national park.
5. We visited sequoia national park in california.
6. I live near the choctawatchee river in florida.
7. We stayed at the holiday inn on market street in san francisco.
8. Our school is on the corner of north street and hickory avenue.
9. We saw the san diego chargers play the green bay packers.
10. That's ellis island and the statue of liberty over there.

C. Writing On a sheet of paper, write each of the following common nouns. Next to each common noun, write the proper noun it suggests to you. Then write a sentence using the proper noun.

> Example: street   Market Street
> We went to the new theater on Market Street.

1. school	3. building	5. book	7. ocean
2. car	4. country	6. magazine	8. company

Part 3   Nouns Used as Subjects

The subject of a sentence tells who or what is being talked about. Nouns are often used as subjects.

> The goalie stopped the ball.
> (The noun *goalie* is the subject of the verb *stopped*.)
>
> Into the room came Ken and Martha.
> (The nouns *Ken* and *Martha* are subjects of the verb *came*.)

In some sentences, the subject may not be right next to the verb. Other words may separate them.

> The edge of the rink melted.
>
> What melted? Not the whole rink, just the edge.
> *Edge* is the subject of *melted*.

Exercises   Find the nouns as subjects.

A. Number your paper from 1 to 10. Write the nouns used as subjects in each of the following sentences.

1. My mother drove slowly around the detour.
2. The kittens were playing with the yarn.
3. The heavy rains forced many cars off the road.

4. Our troop is sponsoring a party for the children in the hospital.
5. His pocket was full of nails and washers.
6. The handle of the screwdriver was yellow.
7. The jets thundered off the deck of the carrier.
8. The steps could have been slippery.
9. The bottom of the bag was wet.
10. John Steinbeck wrote the novel *Of Mice and Men.*

B. Follow the directions for Exercise A.

1. The Incas built a great walled city in Peru.
2. The voices of the speakers did not carry to the rear of the gym.
3. At the concert Ms. Maney sat near us on the main floor of the auditorium.
4. In the morning his headlights were still on.
5. The game was delayed because of rain.
6. In England many people like marmalade.
7. Our cafeteria serves the best lasagna.
8. Mercury is the planet nearest to the sun.
9. Which singer is your favorite?
10. The canary in the cage sang continuously.

Part 4 Nouns Used as Direct Objects

A noun used as a direct object receives the action of a transitive verb. A direct object answers the question *whom?* or *what?* after the verb.

The arrow hit the *target.*   Peggy threw the *basketball.*

The nouns *target* and *basketball* are direct objects. They answer the questions: *Hit what?* and *Threw what?*

Now study these examples.

You can buy magazines at the corner store.

> Verb: *can buy*
> Buy *what:* *magazines*
> Direct object: *magazines*

Ramona directed Tom to the turnpike.

> Verb: *directed*
> Directed *whom:* *Tom*
> Direct object: *Tom*

You have learned that subjects and verbs may be **compound,** which means "having more than one part." Direct objects may also be compound. Look at this example.

We saw *Donna, Linda,* and *Pat*.

> Verb: *saw*
> Saw *whom:* *Donna, Linda, Pat*
> Direct objects: *Donna, Linda, Pat*

Diagraming Sentences Containing Direct Objects

When you diagram a sentence, place a direct object on the horizontal line following the verb. Separate it from the verb by a vertical line that does not cut through the subject-verb line.

Example: Shari enjoys music.

For compound direct objects, split the horizontal line after the verb. Make as many parallel direct object lines as you need. Put the vertical line before the split, to show that all the words that follow are direct objects.

Example: We saw Ralph, Sam, and Ed.

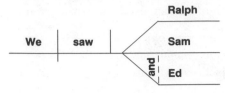

Exercises   Find the nouns used as direct objects.

A. Find the direct objects in the following sentences. Use diagrams or whatever method your teacher suggests.

1. Judy prepared the spaghetti.
2. Our coach clocked the race.
3. The vaporizer cleared my stuffed nose.
4. Adam took a big piece of pizza.
5. Barb suggested a possible solution.
6. The mechanic installed a new muffler.
7. Did you wash the car?
8. I've heard that song before.
9. Bob dropped the book into the return slot.
10. Brenda took a swing at the ball.

B. Follow the directions for Exercise A.

1. You should always use caution in shop class.
2. We climbed the stairs of the lighthouse.
3. Release the clutch slowly.
4. Mozart composed music when just five years old.
5. David could have found the way blindfolded.
6. Polish the candlesticks carefully.
7. Doris bought a coat and a dress.
8. The worker removed the lid from the manhole.
9. Erica and her two cousins solved the puzzle.
10. During the storm, three tugboats entered the harbor.

Part 5 Nouns Used as Indirect Objects

So far you have learned three basic parts of the sentence: *subject-verb-object*. Now you will learn several other parts of the sentence. You will see that nouns can be used in all of these other sentence parts. The part you will learn about first is the **indirect object** of the verb.

The indirect object tells to whom (or to what) or for whom (or for what) about the verb.

Subject	Verb	Indirect Object	Direct Object
Paula	told	her parents	the news.
Linda	showed	Sam	the pamphlet.
Carl	gave	his jade plant	some water.
I	brought	my sister	the tape.

A sentence contains an indirect object only if there is also a direct object. The indirect object comes between the verb and the direct object. The words *to* or *for* never appear before the indirect object.

Nouns used as indirect objects may also be **compound.**

The coach gave *Andy* and *Tim* new equipment.

Diagraming Sentences Containing Indirect Objects

An indirect object is shown on a line below the main line of the sentence.

Alice showed Pat her camera.

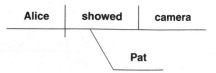

Notice that the indirect object is connected to the verb by a slanted line.

For compound indirect objects, continue the slanted line a little farther down. Then make as many parallel indirect object lines as you need.

Bob wrote Chris and Jean a letter.

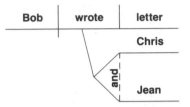

Exercises   Find the nouns used as indirect objects.

A.   Find the indirect objects in the following sentences. Use diagrams or whatever method your teacher suggests.

1. Tracy threw Mike a curve.
2. My grandmother taught her parakeet two new words.
3. Bill gave Eileen the directions.
4. Carl took the guests their coffee.
5. Ms. Meyers gave the boys a few tennis pointers.
6. Vicki sent Joe and Jim an invitation to the party.
7. We should have offered Sam a ride.
8. The class gave Mr. Collins a gift.
9. Have you given the chair a second coat of paint?
10. Alice sent Ginny several postcards from Texas.

B.   Find any indirect and direct objects in these sentences.

1. Last week Rhoda showed her dog at the dog show.
2. Give Linda a hint.
3. Beth showed signs of progress.
4. Ms. Jamison showed the class some beautiful slides.
5. They sent Mr. McCall flowers.

6. Mr. Hoffman sent Pete and Phil to the store.
7. Cindy gave the subject some thought.
8. Have you showed Jack your new watch?
9. My little brother pestered Jim.
10. Terry baked Nancy some brownies for her birthday.

Part 6 Predicate Nouns

You remember that a linking verb links the subject to some word in the predicate. If that word is a noun, it is called a **predicate noun.** It usually means the same thing as the subject. It may explain the subject.

> This machine is a *drill.*
> Jade is a very hard *stone.*
> Sally became *president* of the class today.
> Sylvia has been my best *friend.*

The nouns *drill, stone, president,* and *friend* are predicate nouns. In many sentences, the predicate nouns and the subject can be reversed without changing the meaning. The two parts are roughly equal.

> The boy is *Jack.*   Jack is the *boy.*

Predicate nouns may also be compound, as in this example:

> Rick is a good *singer* and *musician.*

Diagraming Sentences Containing Predicate Nouns

The diagram for a sentence containing a predicate noun is different from that for a sentence containing a direct object.

Janet was the leader.

| Janet | was | \ leader |

Notice that the predicate noun is on the horizontal line in the same position as the direct object. But the line that separates the predicate noun from the verb slants back toward the subject. This is to show the close relationship between the predicate noun and the subject.

For sentences containing compound predicate nouns, use parallel lines. Place the slanted line before the split in the main line.

Amy is a fine athlete and a loyal friend.

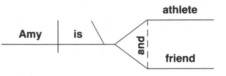

Exercises   Find the predicate nouns.

A. Find the predicate nouns in these sentences. Your teacher may ask you to diagram the sentences.

1. The course was a challenge for everyone.
2. Cory McCowan was one tough customer.
3. *Nova* is my favorite television program.
4. The library is the old building on the corner of Orrington Avenue and Church Street.
5. The piano was a Steinway.
6. Muncie is not the capital of Indiana.
7. Rhode Island is the smallest state in the Union.
8. Dr. Patterson is a veterinarian.
9. My sister is a teller at this bank.
10. Dr. Rebecca Barth is our dentist and our neighbor.

B. Some sentences below contain linking verbs, which are completed by predicate nouns. Some sentences contain action verbs, which are completed by direct objects. Find the predicate nouns and direct objects in these sentences.

Examples: Julie *ate* a big *lunch*.
        Ate is an action verb.
        Lunch is the direct object.

        Julie *is* a dancer.
        Is is a linking verb.
        Dancer is a predicate noun.

1. Willie became my best friend.
2. Marlene seems an excellent organizer.
3. A job at the pool might be Brad's chance.
4. The council proposed two new laws.
5. Polo is a game for horseback riders.
6. Darren closed the shutters and waited.
7. My father watched the basketball game on TV this afternoon.
8. The Lions Club donated the money for the new children's park.
9. She is the manager at the Holiday Inn.
10. The mayor's action caused an uproar among the city councilmen at the meeting.

Part 7 The Plurals of Nouns

When a word stands for one thing, it is **singular.** These are singular forms: *girl, city, classroom,* and *child.* When a word stands for more than one thing, it is **plural.** These are plural forms: *girls, cities, classrooms,* and *children.*

Here are seven rules for forming the plurals of nouns:

1. To form the plural of most nouns, just add -s:

| pencils | cows | buildings | friends |
| trees | games | roads | logs |

2. When the singular ends in s, sh, ch, x, or z, add -es:

gases	losses	brushes	churches	boxes
buses	waltzes	rashes	porches	foxes

3. When the singular ends in o, add -s:

studios	sopranos	Eskimos	solos
radios	altos	egos	silos

Exceptions: For a few nouns ending in *o* with a consonant before it, add -es:

potatoes	tomatoes	heroes	echoes

4. When a singular noun ends in y with a consonant before it, change the y to i and add -es:

baby—babies	country—countries	hobby—hobbies
army—armies	cry—cries	courtesy—courtesies

When a vowel comes before the *y*, do not change the *y* to *i*. Just add -s to the singular.

boy—boys	play—plays	day—days
valley—valleys	monkey—monkeys	tray—trays

5. For most nouns ending in f, add -s. For some nouns ending in f or fe, however, change the f to v and add -es or -s:

roof—roofs	leaf—leaves	half—halves	self—selves
belief—beliefs	elf—elves	calf—calves	shelf—shelves

6. Some nouns are the same for both singular and plural:

deer	sheep	trout	salmon	moose
tuna	bass	pike	grouse	elk

7. Some nouns form their plurals in special ways:

child—children	foot—feet	woman—women
mouse—mice	tooth—teeth	man—men

Using a Dictionary To Find Plurals

Here is a dictionary entry for the word *knife*. Notice that the entry shows the plural, *knives*. Most dictionaries show the plural of a noun if the plural is formed in an irregular way. When you are in doubt about plurals, check a dictionary.

---

plural

knife (nīf) **n., pl. knives** [OE. *cnif*: for IE. base see KNEAD] **1.** a cutting or stabbing instrument with a sharp blade, single-edged or double-edged, set in a handle **2.** a cutting blade, as in a machine —**vt. knifed, knif'ing 1.** to cut or stab with a knife ☆**2.** [Colloq.] to use underhanded methods in order to hurt, defeat, or betray —☆**vi.** to pass into or through something quickly, like a sharp knife —☆**under the knife** [Colloq.] undergoing surgery —**knife' like' adj.**

Exercises   Form the plurals of nouns.

A.   Write the plural of each of these nouns.

1. tomato	5. echo	9. table	13. company
2. thief	6. loaf	10. dress	14. stay
3. key	7. lady	11. deer	15. dormouse
4. daisy	8. coach	12. woman	16. way

B.   Read the following plural nouns. If the plural has been formed incorrectly, write the correct form. If the plural is correct, write *Correct*.

1. tattoos	6. selfs	11. churches	16. skies
2. joys	7. boxes	12. parties	17. donkies
3. buses	8. patchs	13. crashs	18. citys
4. babys	9. potatos	14. firemans	19. knifes
5. twos	10. wolves	15. moose	20. flies

Part 8   Possessive Nouns

Nouns can show ownership or possession.

Laura's house   *Bill's* lunch   *Jill's* car

Nouns can also show that something is a part of a person.

Jane's sincerity   *Barbara's* ability   *Tom's* face

The *italicized* words above are called **possessive nouns** because they show possession of the noun that follows.

Forming Possessives of Singular Nouns

Do you see what it is about *Jane's* and *Barbara's* that is a sign of possession? It is the ending—the apostrophe and the *-s*.

To form the possessive of a singular noun, add an apostrophe and -s.

Singular Noun	Possessive Form
Sharon	Sharon's
Ms. Hernandez	Ms. Hernandez's
waitress	waitress's
Charles	Charles's

Forming Possessives of Plural Nouns

There are two things to remember in writing the possessive of a plural noun:

If the plural noun ends in s, simply add an apostrophe.

Plural Noun	Possessive Form
teams	teams'
drivers	drivers'
runners	runners'
waitresses	waitresses'

If the plural noun does not end in s, add an apostrophe and s.

Plural Noun	Possessive Form
children	children's
men	men's
women	women's

Diagraming Sentences Containing Possessive Nouns

In a diagram, possessive nouns are written on lines slanting down from the nouns with which they are used.

Larry is Jeff's teammate.

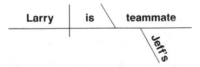

Exercises **Show the possessive forms of nouns.**

A. Write the possessive forms of these nouns.

1. secretaries
2. banker
3. James
4. Peggy
5. artist
6. photographer
7. Mr. Briggs
8. Ms. Holmes
9. Charles Smith
10. customers
11. day
12. hours
13. Lee
14. Ms. Voss
15. designers

B. Write the possessives of the following nouns.

1. journalist
2. driver
3. women
4. ruler
5. group
6. ministers
7. girl
8. principal
9. father
10. Indians
11. mothers
12. teacher
13. Smith
14. leaders
15. Choctaw

ADDITIONAL EXERCISES

Using Nouns

A. Identify Nouns   Number your paper from 1 to 10. Write the nouns in each of the following sentences.

1. The mushrooms grew under a log.
2. Dead leaves clogged the sewers on our street.
3. Turn up the radio, Bridget.
4. Jason played his guitar at the assembly.
5. Last year our class took a tour of Gettysburg.
6. Leah saw a game in the new stadium recently.
7. Some students disagreed about the moral of the story.
8. My grandmother has an excellent memory.
9. The mayor asked her aides for an explanation.
10. Floods caused damage throughout the state.

B. Proper Nouns   Number your paper from 1 to 10. Write the proper nouns in each sentence. Capitalize them.

1. Is egypt part of africa?
2. In july we visited storm lake in iowa.
3. On monday the public pools will open.
4. The eagle scouts camped in shawnee national forest.
5. Does chicago have two baseball teams?
6. The city is the home of the cubs and the white sox.
7. Only one yellow chevy was parked on the street.
8. On the front page of the *herald* was a photo of ann.
9. Isn't twelfth street now rosa parks boulevard?
10. The potomac river winds through virginia.

C. Nouns as Subjects   Number your paper from 1 to 10. Write the nouns used as subjects in each of the following sentences. Some subjects may be compound.

1. Sticky liquid oozed from the battery.

2. A long, red car rounded the curve.
3. Beside the basket was a note.
4. Piled on the shelf were hats of all kinds.
5. Liz tied a string to the light switch.
6. The dusty floor showed footprints.
7. There is a picture of Ed in the yearbook.
8. During the movie Bobby and Ray dozed.
9. On the table was a small bell.
10. Does the referee need glasses?

D. Nouns as Direct Objects   Number your paper from 1 to 10. Write the nouns used as direct objects in each of the following sentences. Some direct objects may be compound.

1. Caroline bought a folder.
2. He put the report on her desk.
3. Use exact change.
4. The smoke detector alerted the family.
5. Some reptiles lay eggs.
6. Cass wears bright colors and big hats.
7. Some people really prefer leftovers.
8. She cracked the shell with her teeth.
9. Have you heard the score?
10. Winter turned the rocks into ice castles.

E. Nouns as Indirect Objects   Number your paper from 1 to 10. Write the indirect objects in the following sentences. Some indirect objects may be compound.

1. Chris got Ben a chair.
2. The clerk gave Cheryl and me a funny look.
3. The Red Cross found the family another home.
4. Offer Judy some lemonade.
5. Did Rick lend Jean his umbrella?
6. The class wrote the President a letter.
7. Ms. Carver bought the school a new projector.

8. Tell Vince the rest of the story about the haunted house across the road.
9. Rita tossed Alice a pillow.
10. A nurse taught Ms. Pardo and the troop first aid.

F. Predicate Nouns   Number your paper from 1 to 10. List the predicate nouns in these sentences. Some predicate nouns may be compound.

1. The truck's cargo was gasoline.
2. That tiny dog is a chihuahua.
3. *Barney Miller* was a popular television show.
4. The math teacher is also the track coach at the community center.
5. Her sister is her best friend.
6. Leslie is an expert in judo.
7. This beach is not private property.
8. Saturday is always a very short day.
9. Are the Riordans your neighbors?
10. Hank's first customers at his lemonade stand were his aunt and uncle.

G. Plurals of Nouns   Number your paper from 1 to 30. Write the correct plural form of each word.

1. scratch	11. fox	21. tooth
2. radio	12. potato	22. branch
3. child	13. moss	23. foot
4. deer	14. stereo	24. inch
5. sky	15. county	25. self
6. wrench	16. elf	26. lobby
7. alley	17. reef	27. cross
8. spy	18. bay	28. butterfly
9. hero	19. dish	29. maze
10. mirror	20. player	30. gentleman

H. Possessives of Nouns Write the following phrases, adding the possessive forms asked for in parentheses.

> Example: the (plural-possessive of *team*) schedules
> the teams' schedules

1. the (singular possessive of *city*) budget
2. (singular possessive of *Amy*) loafers
3. the (plural possessive of *class*) field trips
4. the (singular possessive of *glass*) rim
5. (singular possessive of *Jess*) plans
6. (plural possessive of *deer*) habits
7. (plural possessive of *man*) shirts
8. the (singular possessive of *show*) theme song
9. the (plural possessive of *country*) leaders
10. Mr. (singular possessive of *Ross*) car
11. the (plural possessive of *sandwich*) crusts
12. the (singular possessive of *woman*) hands

MIXED REVIEW

Using Nouns

A. Identifying common and proper nouns Label two columns on your paper *Proper Nouns* and *Common Nouns*. Find the nouns in the following paragraph. List them in the correct columns.

In 1983, workers began a big project in New York City. They cleaned and repaired the Statue of Liberty. The statue, designed by Frederic Bartholdi, was a gift from France to the United States in 1884. After nearly a hundred years of service as a symbol of freedom, the statue, made of copper, showed serious signs of age. The Statue of Liberty was closed to visitors during this work. When the job was completed the famous monument once again lit the way into New York Harbor for people seeking freedom.

B. Identifying nouns and their uses Write the nouns from the following sentences. After each, write *Subject, Direct Object, Indirect Object,* or *Predicate Noun* to show how each is used.

1. Your photograph won first prize.
2. Barbara sent her aunt a get-well card.
3. Does Ms. Alvarez teach history?
4. Mrs. Barclay is a detective.
5. Trini served the guests sandwiches and cake.
6. Captain Simon is the pilot.
7. Len and his brother paid the vendor five dollars.
8. Give the baby her bottle.
9. Your jeans need a patch.
10. Eric has two brothers and one sister.

C. Using plural and possessive nouns correctly The following sentences contain ten errors in the use of plural and possessive nouns. Copy the sentences, correcting any errors in the use of plurals and possessives. If a sentence is already correct, write *Correct*.

1. Ellen likes comedys better than dramas.
2. The traines will be late today.
3. Jan's arm was fractured in two places.
4. The childs' shoes are too tight.
5. Martha caught two bass and three trouts.
6. The magazine's editor's read the contest entrys.
7. Michael bought four loafs of French bread.
8. The school's library is being remodeled.
9. Amy and Susan peeled the potatoes and sliced the tomatoes.
10. The womans' garden contains many varieties of flowers.

USING GRAMMAR IN WRITING
Using Nouns

A. Your class is turning an unused locker into a time capsule. The locker will be filled with carefully selected items that reflect the students' lives today. It will remain locked until your class's twenty-year reunion. Each class member must submit a paragraph that tells what items he or she thinks should be placed in the time capsule. Write your own paragraph. Include some specific names of records, tapes, books, magazines, and clothing brands. Circle each common noun. Underline each proper noun.

B. Imagine that you are a scientist who lives one hundred years in the future. You are visiting the site of an excavation. A house from the 1980's has been discovered there. The excavation team has asked you to analyze some of the odd items that have been found within the house. What do you think each item is? How was it used? Who might have used it?

Write down your comments for four of the items. For each object, first describe what the item looks like. Then answer each of the questions above. Remember that your guesses may be entirely wrong. You may, for example, decide that an egg beater was some sort of noisemaker. When you are finished with your comments, underline the nouns. Label each one S (subject), D.O. (direct object), or I.O. (indirect object).

Using Pronouns

Part 1 What Are Pronouns?

Study these sentences:

> When Roger saw Wendy, Roger spoke to Wendy.
> When Roger saw Wendy, he spoke to her.

The words *he* and *her* are pronouns. They stand for the nouns *Roger* and *Wendy*.

A pronoun is a word used in place of a noun.

A pronoun is a very useful word. It helps you write and talk smoothly and easily without losing track of your ideas and without repeating the same words too often.

453

How Pronouns Differ from Nouns

Nouns change only to show possession and number.

Pronouns differ from nouns. They change form according to their use in a sentence. Study these pairs of sentences to see how pronouns change form and how they differ from nouns.

Nouns	Pronouns
1. *Jerry* pruned the tree.	1. *He* pruned the tree.
2. Mr. Barnes helped *Jerry*.	2. Mr. Barnes helped *him*.
3. Mr. Barnes is *Jerry's* father.	3. Mr. Barnes is *his* father.
4. The *books* came yesterday.	4. *They* came yesterday.
5. Mr. Frank brought the *books*.	5. Mr. Frank brought *them*.

The Forms of Pronouns

Pronouns have three forms: *subject, object,* and *possessive.* Notice how the pronoun *she* changes as its use changes:

> *She* left. (*She* is the subject.)
> I saw *her*. (*Her* is the direct object.)
> It is *hers*. (*Hers* is the possessive.)

The pronouns listed below are all called **personal pronouns**. Here are the forms you should know.

	Subject	Object	Possessive
Singular:	I	me	my, mine
	you	you	your, yours
	she, he, it	her, him, it	her, hers, his, its
Plural:	we	us	our, ours
	you	you	your, yours
	they	them	their, theirs

Notice the pronoun chosen for each of the following sentences. See how the form of each pronoun depends upon the use of the pronoun in the sentence.

1. The girls are here. *They* arrived early. (subject)
2. The workers left later. Ann saw *them*. (direct object)
3. Sean was early. Terry showed *him* the new aquarium. (indirect object)
4. The Boyles have moved. Caryl has *their* address. (possessive)
5. Karen is my sister. *She* is older than I am. (subject)

Exercise   Use pronouns correctly.

You will study many pronoun forms in the remaining parts of this section. The following sentences use pronouns correctly. Read each sentence aloud.

1. *We* tried the mushroom pizza.
2. The girl on the left is *she*.
3. Sam's friends congratulated *him* for winning the speech contest.
4. John sent *her* a valentine.
5. *We* girls are the winners.
6. *Our* friends are coming today.
7. Tom keeps *his* room clean.
8. The candidates made *their* speeches on cable television last night.
9. *Everybody* liked the movie.
10. *Everybody* has *her* own book.
11. *He* and *I* auditioned for the spring play.
12. The only volunteers were *she* and *I*.
13. Kim saw Todd and *her* together at the movies last Saturday afternoon.
14. Ms. Finch gave *him* and *me* extra help.
15. The yearbook editor gave *us* reporters a new deadline to meet.

Part 2 Subject Forms of Pronouns

The subject forms of pronouns are used as **subjects** of the verb. Most of the time you use these pronoun forms correctly without difficulty.

The subject forms of pronouns are also used as **predicate pronouns**. A predicate pronoun is a pronoun that follows a linking verb and is linked by the verb to the subject. You may be confused by predicate pronouns because you may often hear the wrong forms used.

The correct use of predicate pronouns is not difficult. But you must be sure that you understand what these pronouns are and how they are used.

Study these examples. Read the sentences aloud.

Subject		Predicate Pronoun	
She and *I*	went	The students were	*she* and *I*
You and *he*	came.	The visitors were	*you* and *he*.

If you have trouble recognizing predicate pronouns, remember these points:

1. Predicate pronouns follow linking verbs, such as *is, was, were,* and *will be.*
2. The predicate pronoun usually means the same thing as the subject.
3. A sentence with a predicate pronoun will usually make sense if the subject and the predicate pronoun are reversed. Study the following example.

Subject	Verb	
He	was	the visitor.
The visitor	was	he.

Always use the subject form of a pronoun for subjects and predicate pronouns.

Exercises   Choose the correct pronoun.

A.   Number your paper from 1 to 10. Choose the correct pronoun in each of the following sentences. Check your work by reading the sentences aloud.

1. (We, Us) and the Bradleys play touch football every Saturday.
2. It was Todd and (me, I) to the rescue.
3. The base runners were Mark and (I, me).
4. The boys are Al's brothers. Al and (they, them) live next door.
5. Kathy and (I, me) work together.
6. Chris and (her, she) are coming.
7. It is (her, she).
8. There are Ginny and (I, me) on TV!
9. (Him, He) is the boy at the door.
10. The baseball experts are (they, them) and their brothers.

B.   Follow the directions for Exercise A.

1. Michael and (he, him) are always together.
2. (Her, She) and (I, me) will see you tonight at the movies.
3. The winners are Trudy and (me, I).
4. Scott and (her, she) are cousins.
5. Robin and (she, her) both roasted marshmallows over the campfire.
6. (Us, We) and about half the class were tennis players.
7. The Big Hawk Pack and (us, we) became friends at camp.
8. The boy on the right is (he, him).
9. Michele and (they, them) kept movie scrapbooks about their favorite actors.
10. Peter and (us, we) were almost late to homeroom because we missed our bus.

Part 3 Object Forms of Pronouns

Always use the object form of a pronoun for direct objects and indirect objects.

Direct object: Ted saw *him* and *her*.

Indirect object: Lynn asked *me* a question.

Pronouns in Compound Objects

A compound object may consist of two pronouns joined by *and, or,* or *nor*. A compound object may also consist of a noun and a pronoun. The object form of pronouns is used in all compound objects.

Direct object: They saw *Terry* and *me*.
  Virgil questioned *him* and *her*.

Indirect object: Please give *Alice* and *me* your address.
  She gave *us* and *them* the records.

Exercises   Use the correct pronoun as object.

A.   Choose the correct pronoun from the two given in parentheses in each of the following sentences. Remember to use the object form of a pronoun for direct and indirect objects.

1. Have you seen John and (he, him) this morning?
2. My uncle sent (he, him) and (I, me) a frisbee.
3. June saw Rosa and (she, her) at the county fairgrounds yesterday.
4. Tim bought (them, they) and their friends ice cream and lemonade.
5. Juan was teaching (he, him) and his sister Spanish.
6. The snow slowed (they, them) and the other hikers down.
7. Tell Linda and (she, her) to wait.

8. Mother gave (they, them) and (us, we) a ride to school.
9. The old man told Jack and (me, I) about the Louis-town flood.
10. Give (he, him) and his friend tickets for the tourna-ment.

B. Choose the correct pronoun from the two given in parentheses in each of the following sentences.

1. Kirk helped (he, him) and (she, her) with the dishes.
2. Curtis gave Barry and (I, me) his promise.
3. The architect drew (they, them) and the onlookers a brief sketch.
4. Will you give (she, her) and (I, me) some help with this ladder?
5. The lawyer brought the jury and (her, she) positive proof.
6. Will you give Mary and (me, I) some apples?
7. Mrs. Folette asked (they, them) and Kent to dinner.
8. The parade delayed my grandmother and (we, us).
9. You should have seen (he, him) and (me, I) in our costumes.
10. My mother will call Jim and (they, them) tomorrow.

Part 4 *We Girls* or *Us Girls;* *We Boys* or *Us Boys*

When do you say *we boys* and *we girls*? When do you say *us boys* and *us girls*? You will make the correct choice if you try the pronoun alone in the sentence.

(We, Us) boys walked ten miles.

(*We* walked. Therefore, *We boys walked ten miles* is correct.)

The music director chose (we, us) sopranos.

(The music director chose *us*. Therefore, *The music director chose us sopranos* is correct.)

Exercises   Use the correct pronoun.

A.   Choose the correct pronouns in the following sentences.

1. (We, Us) boys were selected as the finalists.
2. Ms. Gianetti picked (we, us) two for the parts.
3. Take (we, us) boys with you.
4. The winners were (we, us) girls.
5. At first (we, us) receivers were dropping the passes.
6. Give (we, us) members a break!
7. Do (we, us) students have a spelling test today or tomorrow?
8. (We, Us) girls were chosen as representatives.
9. (We, Us) girls are all on the team.
10. Did you see (we, us) boys in the pool?

B.   Choose the correct pronouns in the following sentences.

1. (We, Us) girls have all seen the movie.
2. Please take (we, us) boys on the boat, too.
3. (We, Us) two are in the play-offs Saturday.
4. (We, Us) three did all the cleaning up.
5. Give (we, us) boys some help with wrapping these presents.
6. You never told (we, us) class representatives.
7. (We, Us) girls are from Lincolnwood.
8. He is watching (we, us) boys on the bridge.
9. (We, Us) girls have waited half an hour for the school bus.
10. (We, Us) girls are the best.

Part 5   Possessive Forms of Pronouns

The possessive forms of pronouns are these:

my, mine	our, ours
your, yours	
his, her, hers, its	their, theirs

Notice that possessive pronouns have no apostrophes.

Its and It's. Many people confuse the contraction *it's* (meaning *it is* or *it has*) with the possessive *its*. *It's* with an apostrophe always means *it is* or *it has*.

> The dog lost *its* collar. (*its* = the collar belongs to the dog)
> *It's* been raining. (*it's* = it has)
> The horse turned *its* head. (*its* = the head is part of the horse)
> Now *it's* clear again. (*it's* = it is)

Exercises   Use *its* and *it's* correctly.

A. Copy the following sentences and insert apostrophes where they are needed.

1. Its about time for the news.
2. The bear could not find its cubs.
3. Its a little too hot for practice today.
4. The long run by the quarterback brought the crowd to its feet.
5. Its either yours or hers.
6. See if its melted yet.
7. The airline will page us when its cargo plane arrives at the loading dock.
8. Its raining again.
9. Give the dog its bath.
10. Its an old story.

B. Follow the directions for Exercise A.

1. Its good to know a foreign language.
2. Bill thinks its his football, but its mine.
3. That bat is theirs. Its much newer than ours.
4. The robin left its nest too soon.
5. According to the weather report, its supposed to rain all weekend.
6. Its not an impossible dream.
7. The marathon is Sunday; its distance is 26 miles and 385 yards.
8. The new record shop opens Saturday, and all of its albums will be on sale.
9. Its usually warm in San Diego.
10. The kitten was lying on its back.

Part 6 Pronouns and Antecedents

The **antecedent** of a pronoun is the noun or pronoun that it replaces or to which it refers.

1. *Larry* came today and brought *his* tools.
   (*Larry* is the antecedent of *his*.)
2. *Debbie* and *Tom* came in. *They* were laughing.
   (*Debbie* and *Tom* are the antecedents of *they*.)

The antecedent usually appears before the pronoun. Sometimes, as in the second example, the antecedent is in the sentence before it.

Singular and Plural Pronouns

Use a singular pronoun for a singular antecedent. Use a plural pronoun for a plural antecedent.

The *runner* talked about *his* Olympic medals.
(*Runner* is singular; *his* is singular.)

The *actors* learned *their* lines.
(*Actors* is plural; *their* is plural.)

Exercises   Find the antecedents.

A.   Number your paper from 1 to 10. Make two columns, and label one *Pronouns* and the other *Antecedents*. Place the pronouns in one column and their antecedents in the other.

Example: Aunt Carol and Uncle Jim like Susan. They told her many stories about the old mining town.

Pronouns	Antecedents
they	Aunt Carol
	Uncle Jim
her	Susan

1. Mr. Mulligan planted more soybeans last year. They brought him a good price.
2. That tree lost all its berries overnight.
3. Tim and Rick didn't bring their raincoats.
4. Here is the tent Bill's grandparents lent him. He brought it with his sleeping bag.
5. Steel mills can create a serious problem. They pollute the air.
6. The thief erased his fingerprints from the windowsill and the door handle.
7. Owen had the injured sparrow with him. He carried it carefully.
8. Joan has had her bike repaired.
9. Rex showed Al his hockey trophy. They talked about the championship game.
10. Ann won the citizenship award. It was given to her at the city council meeting.

B. Follow the directions for Exercise A.

1. Jim and Liz brought their dog. They kept it on a leash.
2. Wayne sanded and painted the birdhouse. He had made it in shop class.
3. My father held the needle at arm's length. Then he poked the thread at it.
4. Marsha and Jack are here now. She is washing the apples, and he is peeling them.
5. Even before Mary got there, Jay and Frank had started their breakfast.
6. Carla grabbed her end of the rope.
7. The boys saw Nancy. They asked her how she liked the movie.
8. Peter left his camera on Sheila's desk. When she came in, she found it.
9. Mrs. Foster bought all those bananas for a dollar. They were certainly worth it.
10. Ann let Ned try her skateboard. He couldn't keep his balance on it.

Part 7 Compound Personal Pronouns

A **compound personal pronoun** is formed by adding -*self* or -*selves* to certain personal pronouns.

myself	ourselves
yourself	yourselves
himself, herself, itself	themselves

Here are some examples.

	We always do the repairs *ourselves*.
(You)	Read the story *yourself*.
	She weighs *herself* every day.

Exercise **Use compound personal pronouns.**

Number your paper from 1 to 10. Beside each number write the correct compound personal pronoun for each of the following sentences. After it, write the noun or pronoun to which it refers.

> Example: She made (pronoun) a big breakfast. (herself, She)

1. Nancy thought of (pronoun) as everyone's friend.
2. She bandaged the cut (pronoun).
3. The wolves threw (pronoun) against the cage in an attempt to escape.
4. A motor-driven robot can walk by (pronoun).
5. Cut (pronoun) another piece of cake.
6. We made (pronoun) at home.
7. Jim looked at (pronoun) in the mirror while putting on a tie.
8. You made this sled (pronoun), didn't you?
9. Kevin pushed (pronoun) to run farther and faster around the track.
10. The campers arranged (pronoun) in a circle around the fire.

Part 8   Demonstrative Pronouns

The pronouns *this, that, these,* and *those* are used to point out which persons or things are referred to. They are called **demonstrative pronouns**.

This and *these* point to persons or things that are near. *That* and *those* point to persons or things farther away.

This is our campsite.	**These** should be packed.
That was a rattlesnake.	**Those** are pine trees.

Exercise   Use demonstrative pronouns.

Number your paper from 1 to 10. Write the correct demonstrative pronoun for the blank space in each sentence.

1. _These_ on my feet are wooden shoes from Holland.
2. _Those_ were the days when cowboys roamed the West.
3. Now _these_ is the moment I have been waiting for.
4. _____ in my hand are rare coins.
5. _____ that we saw yesterday were counterfeit bills.
6. Look over there. _____ must be a gold nugget.
7. _____ is his picture, right there.
8. Right here, _____ is the spot where they landed.
9. _Those_ over there are Jonathan's boots.
10. Is _____ Mt. Rainier in the distance?

Part 9   Interrogative Pronouns

The pronouns *who, whose, whom, which,* and *what* are **interrogative pronouns.** Interrogative pronouns are used to ask questions.

Who plays tennis?   *Which* came first?
Whose is this bike?   *What* is the answer?
Whom did you call?

Exercise   Find the interrogative pronouns.

Find the interrogative pronoun in each sentence.

1. Who made these delicious tacos?
2. Of the two sweaters, which do you prefer?
3. What is the best way to learn to ski?
4. Who planned the picnic?

5. If that bike is Jack's, whose is this?
6. Whom did you invite to the party?
7. Which of the players scored the goal?
8. Whose are these?
9. What caused the explosion?
10. Who invented the parachute?

Using *Who* and *Whom*

The interrogative pronouns *who* and *whom* are often confused. Study these examples. They will help you to use *who* and *whom* correctly.

Use *who* as the subject of the verb.

> *Who* is coming today?   *Who* gave you that sweater?

Use *whom* as the direct object of the verb and as the object of the preposition.

> *Whom* were you describing?   With *whom* did you dance?
> *Whom* did Jim call?   To *whom* was she talking?

Exercise   Use *who* and *whom*.

Choose the correct interrogative pronoun from the two given in parentheses.

1. (Who, Whom) recorded that album?
2. At (who, whom) did the bus driver yell?
3. (Who, Whom) ate all the bananas?
4. (Who, Whom) did Emily invite to the dance?
5. To (who, whom) did Eva pass the ball?
6. (Who, Whom) plays first base?
7. (Who, Whom) did Ramon ask?
8. (Who, Whom) was Butch Cassidy's sidekick?
9. For (who, whom) are you babysitting?
10. (Who, Whom) did the Emmy winner thank?

Part 10 Indefinite Pronouns

Some pronouns do not refer to a particular person. They are called **indefinite pronouns**. The following indefinite pronouns are singular:

anybody	each	everything	no one
anyone	everybody	neither	somebody
anything	everyone	nobody	someone

Because they are singular, use the singular possessive pronouns *his, her,* or *its* to refer to them. Perhaps these sentences will help you to remember. Read each of them aloud.

Everybody took *his* turn.   Something had *its* burrow here.
Someone left *her* raincoat.   No one had *his* or *her* ticket.

Notice that the phrase *his or her* may be used when the person referred to could be either male or female.

A few indefinite pronouns are plural. They refer to more than one person or thing:

both   many   few   several

Both raised *their* hands.   Few stopped *their* cars.
Many of the fans left *their*   Several offered *their* help.
    seats.

Four indefinite pronouns may be either singular or plural, depending on their meaning in the sentence:

all   any   some   none

All of the salad *was* eaten. (singular)
All of the seats *were* empty. (plural)

Does any of this newspaper need to be saved? (singular)
Do any of these songs sound familiar? (plural)

Some of the jewelry *is* missing. (singular)
Some of the plants *need* direct sunlight. (plural)

None of the food *was* left. (singular)
None of the planes *were* taking off. (plural)

A. Choose the correct possessive pronoun for each sentence from those in parentheses. Write the pronoun. Then read each sentence aloud, using the correct form.

1. Somebody lost (his or her, their) hockey stick.
2. Both of the referees blew (his or her, their) whistles.
3. Many of the runners clocked (his or her, their) best times.
4. All of the snakes shed (its, their) skins.
5. Did everyone bring (his or her, their) permission slip?
6. Each of the boys displayed (his, their) drawing.
7. Some of the plants dropped (its, their) leaves.
8. No one raised (his or her, their) hand.
9. Can anyone touch (his or her, their) toes?
10. Neither of the twins remembered (her, their) locker number.

B. Follow the directions for Exercise A.

1. Each of the panthers must stay in (its, their) cage.
2. Did any of the truck drivers stop (his or her, their) rigs?
3. All of the photographers snapped (her, their) shutters.
4. Will somebody lend me (his or her, their) compass?
5. Both of the police officers jumped in (his, their) cars.
6. Somebody broke (his or her, their) leg on the ski slope.
7. All of the campers cooked (his or her, their) own food.
8. Several of my teammates offered (his, their) help.
9. Everyone brought (her, their) favorite record to the party.
10. Some of the punch has lost (its, their) flavor.

ADDITIONAL EXERCISES

Using Pronouns

A. Pronouns Rewrite the following sentences, changing all the words in italics to pronouns.

1. *Susan* looked up *Greg's* address.
2. *Matthew* enjoyed reading *the book*.
3. *Janet* and Mary waded across Blue Creek.
4. *Mr. and Mrs. Bailey* sent *Dan* a telegram.
5. The award was given to *Ellen* by Mr. Scott.

B. Subject Pronouns Number your paper from 1 to 10. Choose the correct pronoun in each of the following sentences.

1. Carmen and (she, her) crossed the swinging bridge.
2. Ellis and (me, I) are in the same history class.
3. Marsha and (he, him) set up the badminton net.
4. Jenny and (them, they) are the backup singers.
5. (I, Me) was the only survivor.
6. The Browns and (us, we) share the garage behind the apartment building.
7. Connie and (her, she) are at the counter.
8. (Them, They) were the winners of the relay race.
9. Shawn and (she, her) were on the bus.
10. Bill and (he, him) went ice skating this afternoon.

C. Predicate Pronouns Choose the correct pronoun from the two given in parentheses.

1. The team captains were Lonny and (he, him).
2. Our choice for class president is (she, her).
3. The starting forwards in Friday night's game will be (we, us).

4. Tubman High's newest National Honor Society members are (they, them).
5. The auto shop teachers are Ms. Rodriquez and (he, him).
6. The ushers for the school musical will be the Key Club and (we, us).
7. Our best wide receiver is (he, him).
8. The winner of this year's perfect attendance award was (she, her).
9. The homecoming dance committee includes Mr. and Mrs. Nelson and (they, them).
10. Ms. Jacob's secretary is (he, him).

D. Object Pronouns Choose the correct pronoun from the two given in parentheses.

1. The director gave Tony and (me, I) our cues.
2. The principal congratulated Vicky and (he, him).
3. The dog was chasing Bonnie and (them, they).
4. Ms. Tesser knitted Ron and (she, her) sweaters for Christmas.
5. We soon spotted Carol and (they, them).
6. Show Gwen and (I, me) the photograph from the party.
7. Are you following Mike and (me, I)?
8. Ask Charles and (he, him) for the information.
9. The manager gave Nina and (we, us) refunds.
10. An usher seated Jackie and (she, her).

E. *We and Us* Choose the correct pronoun from the two given in parentheses.

1. (We, Us) girls are in the same homeroom.
2. The waiter gave (we, us) girls another table.
3. (We, Us) people in the back can't hear you.

4. Mr. Nakai chose (we, us) three for the judo demonstration.
5. Are (we, us) boys still on the team?
6. (We, Us) swimmers must wear lifejackets, too.
7. Watch (we, us) boys at the track meet.
8. Don't forget (we, us) girls.
9. (We, Us) patients can get very lonely.
10. The teacher saved (we, us) latecomers some seats.

F. *Its* **and** *It's*   Copy these sentences. Insert apostrophes where needed. If the sentence is correct, write *correct*.

1. The spider spun its delicate web.
2. Its a soccer ball.
3. Jody caught the duck and banded its leg.
4. Its mane was braided.
5. Its a grand old flag.
6. The pine was shedding its needles.
7. I can't find its leash.
8. Riley put the album back in its cover.
9. We know its snowing.
10. Surely its a joke of some kind.

G.   Pronouns and Antecedents   Number your paper from 1 to 10. Make two columns. Label one column *Pronouns* and the other *Antecedents*. Place the pronouns in one column and their antecedents in the other.

1. Darlene displayed her collection of arrowheads.
2. Several animals escaped from their cages.
3. A hurricane destroyed the shed, but Grandpa rebuilt it.
4. Karen watched the robin gather twigs for its nest.
5. Clark never looks at his opponent during a match.
6. Lucy and her sister share a room. They divide the space.

7. Marvin pushed his sunglasses up.
8. Where have you been, Rachel?
9. Stephen lost his gloves. He can't remember where he left them.
10. Paul asked Angie if she remembered their zip code.

H. Compound Personal Pronouns

Number your paper from 1 to 10. Beside each number write the correct compound personal pronoun for each of the following sentences. After it, write the noun or pronoun to which it refers.

1. Ken forced (pronoun) to dive.
2. The squirrels found (pronoun) a new tree.
3. The referee (pronoun) will keep score during the basketball game.
4. Ms. Sedik drove (pronoun) to the emergency room after the accident.
5. Don't cut your hair (pronoun), Molly.
6. We appointed (pronoun) leaders.
7. I (pronoun) called the station.
8. The store calls (pronoun) a junior department store.
9. Runners time (pronoun), don't they?
10. Andrew weighed (pronoun).

I. Demonstrative Pronouns

Number your paper from 1 to 10. Add the correct demonstrative to the blank in each sentence.

1. _____ is the bus stop across the street.
2. Isn't _____ Sal way over there?
3. Are _____ the Blue Ridge Mountains ahead?
4. _____ is the best place right here.
5. _____ were harder times back then.
6. _____ over here are for pierced ears.
7. Wasn't _____ your cousin that I met last week?
8. _____ is a shortcut that I'm showing you.

9. _____ is what you said last month.
10. _____ is a garter snake I am holding.

J. Interrogative Pronouns Choose the correct interrogative pronoun from the two given in parentheses.

1. (Who, Whom) scored the last touchdown?
2. For (who, whom) is the flag at half-mast?
3. You asked (who, whom) to the dance?
4. With (who, whom) was Ralph walking?
5. To (who, whom) should I give the note?
6. (Who, Whom) did you meet?
7. (Who, Whom) solved the Rubik's cube?
8. (Who, Whom) talked with Milo last?
9. With (who, whom) were you talking?
10. At (who, whom) is Gayle smiling?

K. Possessive Pronouns with Indefinite Pronouns Number your paper from 1 to 10. Choose the correct possessive pronouns from those given in parentheses.

1. Nobody knows (his or her, their) topic yet.
2. Somebody was muttering (his, their) locker combination.
3. Both of the men overcame (his, their) handicaps.
4. Neither of the teams regained (its, their) standing.
5. Some of the cake had mysteriously lost (its, their) icing.
6. Anyone can lose (his or her, their) job.
7. All the girls carried (her, their) own luggage from the airport to the car.
8. Everybody made a tape of (his or her, their) speech.
9. Some of the swimmers broke (her, their) own records.
10. Several of the musicians rent (his or her, their) instruments.

MIXED REVIEW

Using Pronouns

A. Using personal pronouns For each of the following sentences, write the correct pronoun from the two given in parentheses. Then, write the antecedent if one is given.

1. Emma and (I, me) couldn't stay for lunch.
2. (We, Us) disagree with your position on this issue.
3. After lunch, Mr. Regis gave (I, me) a tour of the stables.
4. Kara read her lines. The director asked (she, her) to repeat them.
5. Kelly took the keys from Vera and (her, she).
6. Jamie met (we, us) at the bus station.
7. Give the final copy of the report to (he, him) before you leave.
8. (We, Us) and they worked extra hard.
9. The most reliable babysitters are Liz and (her, she).
10. Chris and Tom read the telegram. (They, Them) were shocked.

B. Using the correct pronoun Write the correct pronoun from those given in parentheses.

1. (My, Mine) idea was not very practical.
2. Kelly's dog has chewed (its, it's) leash.
3. (We, Us) girls helped decorate the cafeteria.
4. Mr. Jeffers chose (we, us) debaters to represent our school.
5. (It's, Its) not your turn to bat.
6. The blue woolen mittens are (her, hers).
7. (We, Us) runners never break training.
8. Jill told us her story, and (it's, its) unbelievable.

9. The fields beyond this fence are (theirs, their's).
10. Give the job to one of (us, we) boys.

C. Using pronouns For each sentence, write the correct pronoun from those given in parentheses.

1. (Who, Whom) locked the cabin door?
2. To (who, whom) do you wish to speak?
3. They built the campfire (themselves, theirselves).
4. (Those, These) planes over there are flying awfully low.
5. Many of my friends earn (his, their) own spending money.
6. He helped (hisself, himself) to another burrito.
7. (Who, Whom) brought these ice skates?
8. (This, That) player at third base is my cousin.
9. These ovens can turn (themselves, theirselves) off.
10. Everybody in the class cast (his or her, their) ballot.

D. Choosing pronouns correctly Number your paper from 1 to 11. Read the following paragraph. Write the correct pronouns from those given in parentheses.

(Who, Whom) said that bees are busy? (We, Us) know that a queen bee has a lazy existence. (She, Her) only lays eggs and lets the worker bees feed and care for (her, she). The workers are females, too, but (they, them) are smaller. (Their, They're) chores are many: caring for the nest, gathering nectar, and waiting on the queen. But (who, whose) fate can be worse than that of the drone? (He, Him) is the male honeybee. In autumn, the workers let (he, him) starve. (They, Them) are afraid (he, him) will eat too much of the stored honey.

USING GRAMMAR IN WRITING
Using Pronouns

A. Write six questions for use on a game show. In each question, use one of these subject form pronouns: *I, he, she, we, it,* and *they.* Then use other pronouns as necessary. Exchange papers with a partner. See if you can answer each other's questions.

> Examples: *I* am a famous baseball player. *My* home run record is better than Babe Ruth's. Who am *I?* (Answer: Hank Aaron)
>
> *It* is the largest mammal in the world today. *Its* home is the ocean. What is *it?* (Answer: a whale)

B. Pronouns make our language flow more naturally and easily. This is especially true in poetry. The following poems have been rewritten incorrectly without pronouns. Correct them by replacing the italicized words with pronouns.

The Moon (use feminine pronouns)

The moon was but a chin of gold
 A night or two ago,
And now *the moon* turns *the moon's* perfect face
 Upon the world below.

EMILY DICKINSON

Paper Dragons

In March, kites bite the wind
and shake *kites'* paper scales.
Kites strain against *kites'* fiber chains
to free *kites'* dragon tails.

SUSAN ALTON SCHMELTZ

Using Adjectives

Part 1 What Are Adjectives?

Nouns and pronouns name and identify people and things. Verbs tell what the people and things are or what they do.

Adjectives describe people and things.

When you write the noun *hills*, you probably have a picture of certain kinds of hills in your mind. Will your reader have the same picture? He or she may not. Do you mean *rolling* hills, *distant* hills, or *steep* hills? Do you mean *purple* hills, *bare* hills, or *rocky* hills? Each one of the words in italics describes the word after it. Each word in italics is an adjective.

Adjectives help to give your readers a clear picture of what you are writing about. They add to the meaning of another word. They make the meaning more exact. When one word adds to the meaning of another word, it *modifies* that word. It is called a **modifier.**

An adjective is a word that modifies a noun or a pronoun.

Adjectives can tell three things about the words they modify.

Which one or ones?
this book, *that* jet, *these* shoes, *those* passengers

What kind?
blue sky, *hot* oven, *small* jar, *old* house, *beautiful* sunrise

How many?
four bicycles, *several* cars, *many* people, *few* children

Look at the adjectives in italics in these sentences:

This street is the *dividing* line.
One lucky day they found *buried* treasure.

You can see that some adjectives come from verbs and have verb endings. *Dividing* and *buried* are two examples. Here are three more:

running water   *toasted* muffin   *broken* glass

Most adjectives from verbs have *-ing* and *-ed* endings. Some have irregular forms, as *broken* does.

Proper Adjectives

Proper adjectives are adjectives formed from proper nouns.

Proper adjectives are always capitalized. Here are some examples:

a Chinese puzzle   the Atlantic coast   a Swedish ship
a Mideast peace   the French language   a Roman coin

Articles

The adjectives *a, an,* and *the* are called **articles.**
The is the **definite article.**

> This is *the* shirt that I want. (one specific shirt)

A and *an* are **indefinite articles.**

> I would like to ride *a* horse. (any horse)
> Please bring me *an* orange. (any orange)

Use *a* before a consonant sound (*a* horse, *a* jar, *a* leg). Use *an* before a vowel sound (*an* orange, *an* ounce, *an* umbrella).

The sound, not the spelling, makes the difference. Do you say *a* honorable man or *an* honorable man? *a* hour or *an* hour?

Diagraming Sentences Containing Adjectives

In a diagram, write an adjective on a line that slants down from the noun it modifies.

An elm tree shades the front porch.

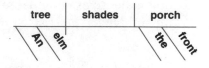

Exercises   Find the adjectives.

A.   Find the adjectives in the following sentences. Show in writing, as your teacher directs you, how they modify nouns.

1. The red car had a flat tire.
2. Sherry is an early bird.
3. The sheep and their lambs went in the empty shed.
4. Our old car needs new brakes.
5. Rob whipped up a hot, peppery sauce.
6. The fat, laughing clown led the parade.

7. Black soot coated the old fireplace.
8. The ancient Dutch windmill made a screechy sound.
9. A young otter splashed in the small pond.
10. A playful young husky pranced ahead of the sled.

B. Writing Copy the following sentences. Write a clear, exact adjective in place of each blank.

1. A _____ statue stood at the _____ intersection.
2. The sky was filled with _____ stars.
3. The _____ clock has a _____ dial.
4. Have you ever seen such a _____ collection of bottles?
5. The _____ town had _____ buildings.
6. A _____ string dangled from the light fixture.
7. The _____ basket was full of _____ clothes.
8. The _____ ship sailed rapidly through the _____ sea.
9. _____ gophers sat upright in the _____ pasture.
10. A _____ car was parked near the _____ house.

Part 2 Predicate Adjectives

When a noun follows a linking verb and refers to the subject of the sentence, that noun is called a predicate noun.

> Mark is our *treasurer.* (The noun *treasurer* follows the linking verb *is* and modifies the subject *Mark. Treasurer* is a predicate noun.)

When an adjective follows a linking verb and modifies the subject of the sentence, that adjective is called a **predicate adjective.**

> Nancy is *funny.* (The adjective *funny* follows the linking verb *is* and modifies the subject *Nancy. Funny* is a predicate adjective.)

481

Here are some more sentences that contain predicate adjectives. What is the predicate adjective in each sentence? What word does it modify?

The windows were dirty.
This room smells musty.
Rich looks sick.
Sean appears calm.

A predicate adjective is an adjective that follows a linking verb and that modifies the subject.

Exercises **Find the linking verbs and predicate adjectives.**

A. On your paper, label three columns *Subject, Linking Verb,* and *Predicate Adjective.* Find these words in each sentence below. Write them in the column where they belong.

Example: This water is salty.

Subject	Linking Verb	Predicate Adjective
water	is	salty

1. My shoes felt tight.
2. The possibilities are endless.
3. After the rain, the basement smelled damp.
4. The plant looked dry.
5. The spinach tastes gritty.
6. His story sounds fishy to me.
7. This cocoa tastes bitter.
8. Does the old rug look clean?
9. Emily seemed happy tonight.
10. That mosquito is pesky.

B. Follow the directions for Exercise A.

1. This board still feels rough.
2. The rice looks sticky.

3. That siren sounds close.
4. On Thursday my mother is busy with her patients.
5. Your topic sounds good to me.
6. Is the knife sharp?
7. The applause seemed endless after her performance.
8. On stage Sharon felt confident.
9. That canoe appears unsafe.
10. These flowers smell good in the spring.

Diagraming Sentences Containing Predicate Adjectives

Show predicate adjectives in diagrams just as you show predicate nouns. Place them on the horizontal line following the verb. Separate them from the verb with a slanted line that points back toward the subject.

The slanting line shows the relationship between the predicate adjective and the subject.

The morning was cool.

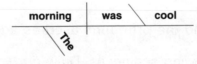

Exercise   Find the predicate adjectives.

Copy these sentences. Show the relationship of the predicate adjective to the subject as your teacher directs.

Example: John is musical.

1. That room seemed stuffy.
2. Does the raft look safe?
3. That milk is sour.
4. Is your pencil sharp?

5. The teams appeared unequal in strength and speed.
6. In response to my question, Glenda's reply was frank.
7. The lake seems rough today.
8. During the race, his knees felt wobbly.
9. Under the microscope, the ant looked huge.
10. The Johnsons were nervous after the accident.

Part 3 Pronouns Used as Adjectives

Possessive pronouns are used as adjectives. As you can see from the following examples, a possessive pronoun is a modifier because it makes the meaning of a noun more exact.

my book	*our* room
your game	*your* trophies
his house, *her* ruler, *its* foot	*their* school

The words *my, your, his, her, its, our,* and *their* are possessive pronouns used as adjectives.

Exercise   Find the pronouns used as adjectives.

Copy the following sentences. Draw arrows from the possessive pronouns to the words they modify.

1. Dick and Elsie brought their stamps.
2. My new book has a red leather cover.
3. The horse has losts its rider.
4. My watch is on the mantel.
5. Did you wash your car?
6. The girls are repairing their bicycles.
7. These pants should have their cuffs fixed.
8. Our bicycles were chained to the parking meter.
9. The computer stored its information.
10. Jane left her bracelet on the chair.

Part 4   Demonstrative Adjectives

The words *this, that, these,* and *those* may be used as modifiers with nouns to point out specific things.

> I liked *this* book, but I really didn't like *that* one.
> *These* peas are fine, but *those* beans are tasteless.

When used as modifiers, these four words are called **demonstrative adjectives.** They tell *which one* or *which ones* about the nouns they modify. (When they are used by themselves, instead of as modifiers, these words are called **demonstrative pronouns:** I like *that. This* is better.)

Demonstrative Adjective	**Demonstrative Pronoun**
I liked *this* book.	I liked *this.*
We saw *that* play.	We saw *that.*

Exercise   **Find demonstrative pronouns and demonstrative adjectives.**

On your paper make two columns: *Demonstrative Adjectives* and *Demonstrative Pronouns.* Write the demonstrative words in these sentences in the correct columns.

1. These are my friends Terry and JoAnn.
2. That was my final trip to the orthodontist.
3. This is the field where we play softball.
4. That woman told my fortune.
5. This moped runs well.
6. That motor should be oiled.
7. Don't these pictures remind you of summertime?
8. This is the second time I've lost my bike.
9. Do you see those airplanes flying in formation over the lake?
10. Can you knock over those bowling pins all at once?

Part 5 Adjectives in Comparisons

Comparing people and things is one way of learning about the world. You often compare new things with things you already know. You might say, for example, "These new stereo speakers are *better* than the old ones. The sound is *clearer,* but they are *more expensive.*" Or you might say, "The new singer is the *best* one in the group."

In comparisons, adjectives have special forms or spellings.

The Comparative

When you compare one person or thing with another, use the **comparative** form of the adjective.

> Rob is *taller* than John.
> My dog is *smarter* than yours.

The comparative form is made in two ways:

1. For short adjectives like *calm* and *slow,* add -er.

   calm + er = calmer   slow + er = slower
   happy + er = happier   bright + er = brighter

2. For longer adjectives like *delicious,* use *more.*

   more delicious   more enjoyable

Most adjectives ending in *-ful* and *-ous* form the comparative with *more.*

   more thoughtful   more gracious

The Superlative

When you compare a person or a thing with all others of its kind, use the **superlative** form of the adjective. In fact, whenever you compare a person or thing with more than one other person or thing, use the superlative.

Lynn is the *tallest* person in the class.

The tiger seems to be the *most ferocious* animal in the zoo.

The superlative form of adjectives is made by adding *-est* or by using *most*. For adjectives that take *-er* in the comparative, add *-est* for the superlative. Those that use *more* to form the comparative use *most* for the superlative.

Adjective	Comparative	Superlative
full	fuller	fullest
dim	dimmer	dimmest
pretty	prettier	prettiest
practical	more practical	most practical
courageous	more courageous	most courageous

Remember three things in using adjectives for comparison:

1. Use the comparative to compare two persons or things. Use the superlative to compare more than two.

This year's model is *sleeker* than last year's.

Jenny is the *youngest* member of our family.

2. Do not leave out the word *other* when you are comparing something with everything else of its kind.

Wrong: I like Mark Twain better than any author.
(This sentence says that Mark Twain is not an author.)

Right: I like Mark Twain better than any *other* author.

Wrong: Sequoias grow taller than any tree.
(Are sequoias trees?)

Right: Sequoias grow taller than any *other* tree.

3. Do not use both *-er* and *more* or *-est* and *most* at the same time.

Wrong: Lead is more softer than steel.
Right: Lead is *softer* than steel.

Wrong: Science is the most easiest subject for me.
Right: Science is the *easiest* subject for me.

Irregular Comparisons

You form the comparative and superlative of certain adjectives by changing the words:

	Comparative	Superlative
good	better	best
well	better	best
bad	worse	worst
little	less *or* lesser	least
much	more	most
many	more	most
far	farther	farthest

Exercises **Use the correct form of the adjective.**

A. Write the correct form of the adjective.

1. My suitcase is (heavier, heaviest) than yours.
2. It was (warmest, warmer) in Texas than in Florida.
3. Wilson's store was always the (busiest, busier) in town.
4. Of the two parks, I like this one (best, better).
5. This is the (worse, worst) program I've ever seen.
6. Jill was the (youngest, younger) of the two.
7. These socks are the (softer, softest) of all.
8. This traffic is the (worst, worse) in the area.
9. That was the (shorter, shortest) night of the year.
10. Jan's room is (more cluttered, most cluttered) than mine.

B. Write the correct form of the adjective, following the directions in parentheses.

> Example: He runs (comparative of *fast*) than I.
> Answer: faster

1. We need a (comparative of *narrow*) board than this.
2. Lunch was (comparative of *good*) than breakfast.

3. The lake was (comparative of *rough*) than usual.
4. It was the (superlative of *funny*) movie I've ever seen.
5. No school in town has (comparative of *beautiful*) grounds than ours.
6. Greg politely took the (comparative of *small*) piece.
7. That's the (superlative of *bright*) star in the whole sky.
8. This soda tastes (comparative of *creamy*) than that.
9. He was (comparative of *underweight*) than his brother.
10. The bus driver was (comparative of *careful*) than most I have seen.

Part 6   Special Problems with Adjectives

Them and *Those*

Them is always a pronoun. It is used as an object.

Those is an adjective if it is followed by a noun. It is a pronoun if it is used alone.

> We asked *them* for a ride. (pronoun)
> *Those* cans fell to the floor. (adjective)
> *Those* are my books. (pronoun)

Never substitute *them* for *those*.

> **Wrong:**   *Them* boys brought the canoe.
> **Right:**   *Those* boys brought the canoe.

The Extra *Here* and *There*

Have you ever heard someone say, "This here pen" or "That there car"? The word *this* includes the meaning of *here*. The word *that* includes the meaning of *there*. Never use *this here* or *that there* before a noun.

Kind and *Sort*

Kind and *sort* are singular. Use *this* or *that* to modify *kind* and *sort*.

Kinds and *sorts* are plural. Use *these* or *those* to modify *kinds* and *sorts*.

I enjoy *this* kind of movie.   *Those* kinds of games tire Spot.

Exercises   Use modifiers correctly.

A.   Choose the right word from the two given in parentheses in each of the following sentences.

1. (This, This here) cake is made from carrots.
2. Did (them, those) raccoons raid the garbage cans?
3. Have you seen (them, those) magazines?
4. (That, That there) biplane crossed the Atlantic.
5. Our gym class does (that, those) kinds of exercises.
6. (Them, Those) plums look fresh and juicy.
7. Actors wear (that, those) kind of makeup.
8. I like (them, those) commercials better than the show.
9. (That, That there) roller coaster goes very fast.
10. (This, These) kinds of tapes don't have good sound.

B.   Choose the right word in these sentences.

1. Lola can do (that, those) kind of back dive.
2. Someone should wash (them, those) windows.
3. Football players wear (this, these) kind of shoe.
4. (Them, Those) sponges grow on the ocean floor.
5. Campers use (this, these) kinds of wood for fires.
6. The forest ranger spotted (them, those) bears.
7. (That, That there) bicycle belongs to Brian.
8. (This, This here) train runs between here and Boston.
9. Terry's stereo has (that, those) kinds of speakers.
10. The Dodgers train at (that, that there) stadium.

ADDITIONAL EXERCISES

Using Adjectives

A.   Adjectives   Number your paper from 1 to 10. Make two columns. Put the adjectives in one column and the nouns they modify in the other. Ignore any articles.

1. The fence had sharp spikes on top.
2. The two hikers dropped the heavy backpacks.
3. These books have good photographs.
4. The gym echoed with the lively beat of the music.
5. You need a lighter hammer for those tiny nails.
6. The bright sun melted the snow despite the low temperature.
7. A weary young man was picking the ripe berries.
8. I bought Swiss cheese and one loaf of French bread.
9. The moon made a narrow gold path on the water.
10. We packed the fragile glasses in a sturdy crate.

B.   Predicate Adjectives   Label three columns *Subject, Linking Verb,* and *Predicate Adjective.* Find these words in each sentence below, and write them in the appropriate columns.

1. Your map is too old.
2. Lake Huron was once clear.
3. The butter knife is smaller.
4. These drums are African.
5. My closet is full of junk.
6. Maybe that box is empty.
7. Sandy's balance has always been poor.
8. The child star grew too tall for the part.
9. Her remarks sounded rude.
10. The stars were visible last night.

C. Pronouns Used as Adjectives Number your paper from 1 to 10. Label two columns *Possessive Pronoun* and *Word Modified.* Put the possessive pronouns and the words that they modify in the correct columns.

1. Our kite soared above the trees.
2. The siren screamed its warning.
3. Ducklings follow their mother almost everywhere.
4. Betsy bought some buttons for her shirt.
5. The students cleaned out their lockers before vacation.
6. Mr. Cabrera usually enjoys his job.
7. The janitor washed our windows.
8. The garter snake raised its head and looked around.
9. Did you finish your math yet?
10. I found my scarf at Kitty's house.

D. Demonstrative Adjectives Number your paper from 1 to 10. Label two columns *Demonstrative Adjective* and *Word Modified.* Put the demonstrative adjectives and the words that they modify in the correct columns.

1. This splinter will be hard to remove.
2. Did you see that motorcycle?
3. Take these clothes to the dry cleaner's.
4. Those holes in the net won't hurt the game.
5. That song gets on my nerves.
6. Our doctor has an office in this building.
7. Doesn't that van belong to the school?
8. Some of those horror movies are funny.
9. Shall I give out these booklets?
10. Throw away those rags with paint on them.

E. Adjectives in Comparisons Number your paper from 1 to 10. Choose the correct form of the adjective from the two given in parentheses.

1. That was the (hottest, most hottest) day of summer.

2. Tara is the (more athletic, most athletic) of the twins.
3. Does an album or a cassette cost (more, most)?
4. Gold is (heavier, more heavier) than silver.
5. Mr. Ridolfi tells the (worse, worst) jokes.
6. Of the three dogs, Scout is the (shyer, shyest).
7. Of these two books, which is (best, better)?
8. Pete is (courteouser, more courteous) when he's happy.
9. This roller coaster is the (most best, best) I've ridden.
10. That is the (least, leastest) of my worries.

F. Special Problems with Adjectives Number your paper from 1 to 10. If there is a mistake with the way an adjective is used, write the sentence correctly. If the sentence is correct, write *Correct*.

1. I will send them this here card.
2. Them seeds should be planted in the shade.
3. These kinds of moccasins wear out quickly.
4. Some of them electronic eyes can identify colors.
5. This here is your seat.
6. That there door leads to the basement.
7. Not many of them Canadian Mounties still ride horses.
8. The dentist recommended this sort of toothbrush.
9. Don't give him those kind of gift.
10. Don't them there peaches look good?

MIXED REVIEW

Using Adjectives

A. Finding adjectives Write all of the adjectives in the following sentences. Include proper adjectives, articles, pronouns used as adjectives, and demonstrative adjectives. After each adjective, write the word it modifies.

1. The tourists ate in a small Chinese restaurant.
2. An entire city was buried by the huge volcano.
3. The students, rested and prepared, took the exam.
4. The mountaintops were snowy.
5. That magazine has a wide circulation.
6. My mother will be running in our local marathon.
7. This sauce tastes delicious.
8. Your music is disturbing my sleep.
9. Are my books in the cafeteria?
10. A colorful quilt covered the old brass bed.

B. Using adjectives correctly The following paragraph contains nine errors in the use of adjectives. Rewrite the paragraph, correcting any errors you find.

The firstest question people ask me about mine dog, Pedi, is always the same: "What breed of dog is that there dog?" I don't enjoy this kinds of questions. You see, breeds are a delicate subject for me. Don't misunderstand. I'm not ashamed of Pedi's poodle, spaniel, and terrier background. He's bright, obedient, and healthier. With his shiny black coat, Pedi is the handsomer dog I know. Like most mixed breeds, he's calmest and good-natured. To show how much I care for him, I named him Pedigree. It's the only pedigree he'll ever have, but he's the bestest dog in this here world.

USING GRAMMAR IN WRITING
Using Adjectives

A. The things we own and the way we dress often tell others a lot about us. For example, a guitar, frayed jeans, and a short-wave radio might be clues to someone's personality and interests. What do you own that tells something about you? What might someone learn about you if he or she peeked into your closet or your school locker? Write a paragraph that tells what this person might see and what conclusions he or she might draw. Use plenty of adjectives to describe your closet or locker and its contents.

B. Imagine that you have been chosen as a set designer for the class play. The setting for this one-act play is the attic of a large, old house. You must create an atmosphere of mystery and suspense. Before visiting the prop room, you make a list of items you might need. Rewrite the list, using adjectives to further describe these key elements of the setting.

trunk	barrel of clothes	doll
mannequin	chair	boxes
newspapers	lamp	painting
phonograph	mirror	rocking horse

Using Adverbs

Part 1 What Are Adverbs?

You have already studied adjectives, which modify nouns and pronouns. In this section you will learn about a second kind of modifier: **adverbs.** Adverbs modify verbs, adjectives, and other adverbs.

In order to make your meaning clear, vivid, and complete, you often use words that tell *how, when, where,* or *to what extent.* These words are called adverbs.

Adverbs Modify Verbs.

We *walked*.

How?   We walked *slowly*.

When?   We walked *yesterday*.

Where?   We walked *out*.

Adverbs Modify Adjectives.

It was a *clear* day.

How clear?   It was a *fairly* clear day.

The problem was *difficult*.

How difficult?   The problem was *too* difficult.

I was *late*.

To what extent?   I was *very* late.

Adverbs Modify Other Adverbs.

Joe talked *fast*.

How fast?   Joe talked *extremely* fast.

The senators agreed *enthusiastically*.

How enthusiastically?   The senators agreed *most* enthusiastically.

The ball rolled *away*.

To what extent?   The ball rolled *far* away.

Adverbs are words that modify verbs, adjectives, and other adverbs.

Exercises   Find the adverbs.

A.   Copy each sentence. Draw an arrow from the adverb to the word it modifies.

Example: Ms. James came home early.

1. Our puppy barked eagerly.

2. Sandra and Andy play tennis regularly.
3. Rain fell heavily during the night.
4. They ran swiftly from the car to the house.
5. The Warners had parked nearby.
6. Ben scored easily from mid-court.
7. The water rose steadily.
8. He will leave tomorrow for San Francisco.
9. Have you skied lately?
10. The skiers raced daringly down the slopes.

B. Follow the directions for Exercise A.

1. The movie was terribly funny.
2. Chris and Bruce are definitely running for office.
3. The gymnast gracefully performed her floor exercise.
4. Scott was extremely quiet during the class discussion.
5. A performance by that symphony orchestra is always beautiful.
6. To our surprise, Luanne's speech was quite short and very interesting.
7. The cowboy hat looked simply ridiculous on him.
8. The closet is cleaner now.
9. His report on the battles of the Civil War was very long.
10. The base runner easily stole second.

The Position of Adverbs

When an adverb modifies an adjective or another adverb, it usually comes before the word it modifies:

very hot   *quite* still   *not* often

But when an adverb modifies a verb, its position is not usually fixed:

I see *now.*   *Now* I see.   I *now* see.

Diagraming Sentences Containing Adverbs

Adverbs, like adjectives, are shown in diagrams on lines slanting down from the words they modify. The following diagram shows an adverb modifying a verb.

Finally the shy boy asked a question.

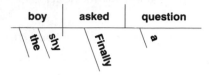

Notice that *Finally*, the first word in the sentence, keeps its capital *F* in the diagram.

That fairly young boy plays the violin quite well.

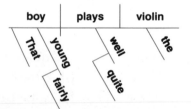

This diagram shows an adverb modifying a verb (*plays*). It shows an adverb (*fairly*) modifying an adjective (*young*). It also shows an adverb (*quite*) modifying another adverb (*well*). Notice how *fairly* is attached to *young*. Notice how *quite* is attached to *well*.

Exercises   Use adverbs.

A.   Rewrite the following sentences, supplying adverbs that answer the questions in parentheses.

Example: Wash the dishes. (*When?*)
Wash the dishes *now*.

1. Bring your books. (*When?*)

2. The monkey climbed. (*How?*)
3. The elevator stopped. (*Where?*)
4. Did your cousin arrive? (*When?*)
5. The bird flew. (*Where?*)
6. The runners rounded the turn. (*How?*)
7. Jack slept soundly. (*How soundly?*)
8. The small deer raised up its head and looked. (*Looked where?*)
9. The sunset was beautiful. (*How beautiful?*)
10. The damaged plane arrived. (*When?*)

B. Writing Write sentences using the following adverbs. You have seen that certain adverbs may appear in three positions: after the verb (I see *now*), at the beginning of a sentence (*Now* I see), and just before the verb (I *now* see). Try to experiment with the position of these adverbs in the sentences you write.

1. closely	5. finally	9. quietly	13. fairly
2. speedily	6. forcefully	10. often	14. quite
3. now	7. nearly	11. sometimes	15. soon
4. never	8. loudly	12. always	16. lately

Forming Adverbs

Many adverbs are made by adding *-ly* to an adjective:

plain + -ly = plainly
brave + -ly = bravely

Sometimes the addition of *-ly* involves a spelling change in the adjective:

noisy + -ly = noisily (*y* changed to *i*)
terrible + -ly = terribly (final *e* dropped)
dull + -ly = dully (*ll* changed to *l*)

Exercise   Form adverbs.

Change the following adjectives into adverbs by adding -*ly*.
Use a dictionary to check your spelling.

pure	nice	large	gloomy
crazy	open	merry	speedy
full	shy	evil	loose
thoughtful	double	capable	playful

Part 2   Adverbs in Comparisons

Adverbs are used to compare one action with another. You
might say, "This engine runs *smoothly*, but that one runs *more
smoothly*."

Or you might say, "Julie planned her exhibit *more carefully*
than any other student in the class."

Adverbs have special forms or spellings for use in making
comparisons, just as adjectives do.

The Comparative

When you compare one action with another one, use the
comparative form of the adverb. The comparative form is made
in two ways:

1. For short adverbs like *high* and *early*, add -er.

The rocket soared *higher* into space.
Betsy left the party *earlier* than Sue.

**2. For most adverbs ending in -ly, use *more* to make the
comparative.**

Stores handle eggs *more carefully* than other foods.
The instructor skied *more smoothly* than his pupils.

The Superlative

When you compare one action with two or more actions of the same kind, use the **superlative** form of the adverb.

> Of all the clerks, Debbie works *most efficiently.*
> Connie and Dave try hard, but Joe tries *hardest.*

The superlative form of adverbs is formed by adding *-est* or by using *most.* Adverbs that form the comparative with *-er* form the superlative with *-est.* Those that use *more* for the comparative use *most* for the superlative.

Adverb	Comparative	Superlative
late	later	latest
fast	faster	fastest
fiercely	more fiercely	most fiercely
softly	more softly	most softly

In using the comparative and superlative forms of adverbs, keep in mind the following three points.

1. Use the comparative to compare two actions and the superlative to compare more than two.

> Jenny runs *faster* than Emmy.
> Of all the runners, Jenny moves the *fastest.*

2. Do not leave out the word *other* when you are comparing one action with every other action of the same kind.

> Wrong: A cheetah travels faster than any animal.
> Right: A cheetah travels faster than any *other* animal.

3. Do not use both *-er* and *more* or *-est* and *most* at the same time.

> Wrong: Bill sprints more faster.
> Right: Bill sprints *faster.*

Irregular Comparisons

Some adverbs make their comparative and superlative forms by complete word changes. For example:

Adverb	Comparative	Superlative
well	better	best
much	more	most
little	less	least

Exercises Use the correct forms of adverbs.

A. For each of the following sentences, write the correct form of the adverb from the two given in parentheses.

1. I walked into the library (more quietly, most quietly) than before.
2. Nobody can count money (best, better) than she.
3. My mother exercises (more regularly, most regularly) than I do.
4. Our relay team could run the (faster, fastest) of all.
5. He wrapped my package the (more carefully, most carefully) of all.
6. Watch this film (more closely, most closely) than that.
7. Mark ran (best, better) than anyone in the group.
8. Ray cleared the jump (most easily, more easily) than I.
9. My dog drinks (less, least) than any other dog I know.
10. Sally tried (hardest, harder) than anyone.

B. For each of these sentences, write the correct form for the adverb, following the directions in parentheses.

1. Ted usually wakes up (superlative of *early*).
2. A snail walks (comparative of *fast*) than Joe.
3. Our friends stayed (comparative of *long*) than usual.
4. Dr. Parr arrived home from Brazil (comparative of *soon*) than her postcards.

5. That package took the (superlative of *long*) time to arrive.

6. No one draws (comparative of *well*) than Sue.

7. I reread the short story (comparative of *carefully*) the second time.

8. She speaks (comparative of *distinctly*) than he does.

9. That driver approached the bridge (comparative of *cautiously*) than anyone.

10. This door opened (comparative of *easily*) than the other.

Part 3   Adjective or Adverb?

An adverb tells	An adjective tells
how	what kind
when	how many
where	which one
to what extent	
about a verb, adjective, or adverb.	**about a noun or pronoun.**

Study the following sentences. Which sentence sounds right to you?

> Our team won *easy.*
> Our team won *easily.*

The second sentence is the correct one. An adverb (*easily*) should be used, not an adjective (*easy*).

It is sometimes difficult to decide whether an adjective or an adverb should be used in sentences like the two given above. When you are not sure which modifier to use, ask yourself these questions:

1. Which word does the modifier describe? If it describes a verb (like *won* in the sentences above), it is an adverb. It is also an adverb if it describes an adjective or another adverb. If it describes a noun or a pronoun, it is an adjective.

2. What does the modifier tell about the word it describes? If the modifier tells *how, when, where,* or *to what extent,* it is an adverb. If it tells *what kind, how many,* or *which one,* it is an adjective. In the sentences above, the modifier tells *how* our team won. Therefore, it must be an adverb: *easily.*

Exercises   **Find the adjectives and adverbs.**

A.   Number your paper from 1 to 10. Make two columns. Label one *Adjectives* and one *Adverbs.* List the adjectives and adverbs from each sentence in the proper columns. Do not list articles.

1. The sportscaster talked endlessly about the new season.
2. A single sailboat drifted on the peaceful lake.
3. Suddenly, a heavy rainstorm flooded the streets.
4. The tiny car left a gray cloud of smoke as it quickly pulled away.
5. This salesperson seems too pushy.
6. An extremely deep hit by Garvey scored two runs.
7. Rapidly and skillfully, the farmer steered a huge tractor through the fields.
8. The gray horse responds more gently than the brown one.
9. Jed was pleasantly surprised by very good grades last semester.
10. Kris usually studies in the quietest room in the house.

B.   Follow the directions for Exercise A.

1. Of the fifty jumpers, Molly leaped highest.

2. The confused driver mistakenly dumped gravel in our front yard.
3. The boys mowed the tall grass swiftly but neatly.
4. It was a cold and rainy day, and we walked quickly to the bus stop.
5. Carrie smiled broadly as she happily held the trophy in her hands.
6. Jeff finally bought the dark brown boots.
7. The sunbathers lay on the hot beach and slowly sipped lemonade.
8. The teacher quietly opened the door, and the class calmly filed in.
9. One canteen is almost empty, and the other is nearly full.
10. The parachute billowed and then slowly drifted to the ground.

Exercises Choose the right modifier.

A. Write the correct word for each of the following sentences. Be ready to tell why it is correct.

> Example: White's Pond looks (clean, cleanly) enough for swimming.
> *Clean* is a predicate adjective modifying *White's Pond.*

1. He lined up his airplane collection (neat, neatly).
2. May plays the piano (good, well), doesn't she?
3. This way is (more quickly, quicker).
4. That's a (real, really) tough question.
5. The bread smells (fresh, freshly).
6. Are you (near, nearly) through?
7. The new girl watched the preparations (shy, shyly).
8. The puppy appeared (hungry, hungrily).

9. The graduates walked (proud, proudly) through the corridors to the auditorium.
10. Mr. Murphy argued (more strongly, stronger) than Ms. Kimball about the council's decision.

B. Follow the directions for Exercise A.

1. My dog soon became (smarter, more smarter).
2. John felt (bad, badly) about the accident.
3. This building is (bigger, more bigger) than that one.
4. Your centerpiece looks (beautiful, beautifully).
5. Ms. Becket answered (more gently, more gentle).
6. The squad looked (envious, enviously) at the trophy.
7. The auctioneer gave the (most brief, briefest) nod to the bidder.
8. That pie smells (wonderfully, wonderful)!
9. He didn't do so (good, well) this time.
10. The students moved (quiet, quietly) through the halls.

Part 4 Special Problems with Modifiers

Good and *Well*

Good is used only as an adjective to modify nouns and pronouns. It is used after linking verbs.

> This book is *good.*   I feel *good.*

Well is an adjective when it means "in good health." *Well* is used as an adverb to modify an action verb when it means that the action was performed properly or expertly.

Adjectives	Adverbs
I feel *well.*	The baby walks *well* now.
Karen looks *well.*	The battery works *well.*

Bad and Badly

Bad is used only as an adjective to modify nouns and pronouns.

This tape sounds *bad*.   Karen felt *bad*.

Badly is an adverb. It is used with action verbs.

The orchestra played *badly*.   The gymnast performed *badly*.

The Double Negative

A **double negative** is the use of two negative words together when only one is needed. Good speakers and writers take care to avoid the double negative.

Wrong: This orange *doesn't* have *no* seeds.
Right: This orange doesn't have any seeds.

Wrong: I *haven't never* missed a football game.
Right: I haven't ever missed a football game.

Wrong: After his dental work, Keith *couldn't* eat *nothing*.
Right: After his dental work, Keith couldn't eat anything.

The most common negative words are *no, none, not, nothing, never,* and contractions with *n't* (for *not*).

After contractions like *hasn't* and *didn't*, use words such as *any, anything,* and *ever*. Do not use *no, nothing, never,* or any other negative words with such contractions.

The motel *hasn't any* empty rooms.
The team *didn't* score any hits.
Laura *hadn't ever* eaten curry.
The mechanic *didn't* fix *anything*.

Hardly, barely, and *scarcely* are often used as negative words. Do not use them with contractions like *haven't* and *didn't*.

Wrong: Megan *couldn't hardly* wait for her fifteenth birthday.
Right: Megan could hardly wait for her fifteenth birthday.

Wrong:	The man *hadn't barely* any friends.
Right:	The man had barely any friends.
Wrong:	Kevin *couldn't scarcely* remember his first day of school.
Right:	Kevin could scarcely remember his first day of school.

Exercises Use modifiers correctly.

A. Choose the correct modifier in these sentences.

1. The teacher knew her subject (good, well).
2. That new paint job looks (bad, badly).
3. Cindy types (good, well).
4. A (good, well) photo tells a story.
5. Oil doesn't mix (good, well) with water.
6. Terry asked a (good, well) question.
7. Danny felt (bad, badly).
8. John pitches as (good, well) as Lee.
9. Kim had a (good, well) chance to win the election.
10. The papers we wrote in class were quite (good, well).

B. Number your paper from 1 to 10. Write the following sentences, correcting the double negatives. If a sentence contains no double negative, write *Correct.*

1. Connie hadn't never flown in an airplane.
2. The injured horse couldn't barely walk.
3. Some people don't eat any meat.
4. The car didn't stop for no stoplights.
5. Bert won't read no love stories.
6. We can't barely hear the speaker.
7. Seniors don't have nothing to complain about.
8. We don't have no time for lunch.
9. The deep-sea divers couldn't find the sunken ship.
10. The band didn't play hardly any popular music.

ADDITIONAL EXERCISES

Using Adverbs

A. Adverbs Number your paper from 1 to 10. Write the adverbs in the following sentences. After each adverb, write the word it modifies. Some sentences have more than one adverb.

1. The referee quickly blew her whistle.
2. Denny could hardly open his eyes.
3. Cynthia is swimming too far from the boat.
4. The laundry flapped gently in the breeze.
5. I feel lucky today.
6. The angry customer walked away.
7. Fortunately, a taxi finally appeared.
8. Tim walked very slowly on his crutches.
9. A hubcap fell off the old car.
10. Justine strolled lazily down the sunny boardwalk.

B. Adverbs in Comparisons For each sentence, write the correct form of the adverb from the two given in parentheses.

1. Cocoa is (more better, better) than cider on cold days.
2. Can the fullback run (faster, more fast)?
3. Hold the racquet (more firmly, firmlier).
4. Jessica played (least often, less often) than the other drummer.
5. Of the four girls, Sara draws (better, best).
6. Tie the tourniquet (tightlier, more tightly).
7. Hank exercises (less, littler) than Perry.
8. Of the two boys, Vic bowls (better, best).
9. Lynn sang (more beautifully, most beautifully) than any other contestant.
10. Of all the debaters, Ron spoke (less confidently, least confidently).

C. Adjective or Adverb? Choose the correct word from the two given in parentheses in each of the following sentences. Write whether you have chosen an adjective or an adverb.

1. Penny looked (careful, carefully) for her lost contact lens.
2. Skateboarding appears (easier, more easily) than it is.
3. The last problem was (real, really) difficult.
4. Ken speaks (quick, quickly) when he is nervous.
5. Shellfish are becoming (scarce, scarcely) in the bay.
6. Rescuers worked (desperate, desperately) to save the miners.
7. The tunnel had collapsed (sudden, suddenly).
8. Line up the numbers in (even, evenly) columns.
9. Ginger (scarce, scarcely) had time for lunch.
10. Ocean breezes smell (salty, saltily).

D. Special Problems with Modifiers Number your paper from 1 to 10. If the sentence is correct, write *Correct*. If there is an error, write the sentence correctly.

1. The cottage looks well with new shutters.
2. Our goalie defends the goal good.
3. He couldn't hardly squeeze through the trapdoor.
4. Tammy sings good in the school musical.
5. I can't pedal any faster.
6. Mel's idea sounds well to me.
7. Erin saw nothing she liked at the store.
8. I didn't say nothing.
9. Don't never forget to wear your safety glasses in wood shop.
10. You won't find prices as good anywhere else.

MIXED REVIEW

Using Adverbs

A. Finding adverbs Write all of the adverbs in the following sentences. After each adverb, write the word it modifies. Then write *how*, *when*, *where*, or *to what extent* to show what each adverb tells.

1. Kyle read the material slowly and carefully.
2. The paramedics arrived very quickly.
3. I'll frost the cake now.
4. Dana looked up and smiled warmly.
5. This instrument measures more exactly than that one.
6. The box of cereal was almost empty.
7. Occasionally we have ice cream for dessert.
8. These shoes are too tight.
9. The jazz band practices daily.
10. George speaks well before a group.

B. Using adverbs correctly The following paragraph contains errors in the use of adverbs. Rewrite the paragraph, correcting any errors.

The runner training serious for the 26-mile marathon must be dedicated and determined. He begins by increasing his daily running distance. This is done gradual. Then he works on his speed. A potential marathon runner should be able to run ten miles in an hour easy. He carefully must also pace himself. The first few miles pass quick. But energy and willpower are needed desperate for that twenty-sixth mile.

USING GRAMMAR IN WRITING
Using Adverbs

A. Your friend Tracy has maintained a perfect driving record during her first year behind the wheel. The following paragraph states some of the things Tracy does when she drives. Rewrite the paragraph, adding one of the following adverbs to each sentence. *Note:* The fifth and seventh sentences won't make sense in your story until you add the adverbs:

> Adverbs: often   usually   slowly   rarely
> never   always   carefully

> Tracy wears her seatbelt. She asks her passengers to buckle up, too. Tracy backs the car up. She watches the road. Tracy exceeds the speed limit. She checks the mirrors. She laughs and jokes while she drives.

B. You just got home from an exciting movie. It was called *Superchase*. Someone asks you what the movie was about. Who was chasing whom? Was the chase on foot? Did it involve bicycles, cars, or motorcycles? Maybe it was an inter-galactic space chase. Write a vivid description of the chase. Include adverbs in your description that answer *when, where, how*, and *to what extent* the action happened. Underline every adverb.

C. You are a junior reporter for a major newspaper. Your boss sends you to do a story on a fire in an old warehouse. Because you are inexperienced, he tells you that the story should be no longer than five lines. When you turn in your story, however, he is so pleased that he asks you to double its length.

Make a copy of both versions of your story. The first should contain only basic information. This information might include the time and place of the fire, who was involved, and when the firefighters arrived. Your second version should include striking and original adjectives that bring the scene to life.

Using Prepositions

Sometimes you are able to communicate an idea clearly by using short sentences.

> David won.   We will go.

Often you have to provide more information.

> David won first prize.   We will go there today.

You can add some information by using adjectives and adverbs (*first, there, today*).

Another way to express more information is to use words that show relationships.

> *At the science fair*, David won first prize.
> We will go there *by train* today.

In this section you will learn about a part of speech that shows relationships: **prepositions.**

Part 1 What Are Prepositions?

Prepositions are words that show how one word is related to another word. Read these sentences. Notice how each expresses a different relationship.

The radio is *on the table*.
The radio is *near the table*.
The radio is *beside the table*.

Dorothy pulled a muscle *before the final race*.
Dorothy pulled a muscle *after the final race*.
Dorothy pulled a muscle *during the final race*.

Katy spoke *to him*.
Katy spoke *for him*.
Katy spoke *against him*.

In the first group of sentences, you can see that the words *on*, *near*, and *beside* show the relationship of *table* to *radio*. In the next group, *before*, *after*, and *during* show the relationship of *race* to *pulled a muscle*. In the last group, *to*, *for*, and *against* relate *him* to *spoke*.

You can see that prepositions do not show relationships by themselves. They begin a **phrase,** a group of words that belong together but do not have a subject and verb. *On the table*, *before the final race*, and *to him* are examples of the prepositional phrases in the sentences above.

A preposition is a word used with a noun or pronoun, called its *object,* to *show how* the noun or pronoun *is related to* some other word in the sentence.

A prepositional phrase consists of a preposition, its object, and any modifiers of the object.

Here is a list of words often used as prepositions. Most of these prepositions show relationships of place or time. Some show other relationships among people and things. Study the prepositions and see the relationship that each shows.

515

Words Often Used as Prepositions

about	before	down	of	throughout
above	behind	during	off	to
across	below	except	on	toward
after	beneath	for	onto	under
against	beside	from	out	until
along	between	in	outside	up
among	beyond	inside	over	upon
around	but (*except*)	into	past	with
at	by	like	since	within
		near	through	without

Exercises   Find the prepositional phrases.

A.   Write all the prepositional phrases you find in the following sentences.

> Example: He ran out the door without his shoes.
>
> out the door, without his shoes

1. Attach the shells to the frame with this glue.
2. Gail was waiting for the special dessert with raspberry sauce.
3. The picture fell off the wall during the night.
4. Behind the garage is a row of sunflowers.
5. The Cullens went from Seattle to San Diego by train.
6. A batting cage is behind home plate.
7. Terry slid into second base.
8. There was dust under the bed.
9. The sailboat was drifting toward the breakwater.
10. Brad is waiting for you in the lobby.

B.   Follow the directions for Exercise A.

1. Juanita fed the dollar into the change machine.

2. The program began after a brief announcement by the principal.
3. They built their Fourth of July bonfire by the light of the moon.
4. Go through that door and up the stairs, and leave the package there.
5. The group of skiers was taking the bus to Aspen.
6. The band marched briskly down the street toward the reviewing stand.
7. We visited Lincoln's home in Springfield, Illinois.
8. Under the bridge the river flowed swiftly.
9. My brother was babysitting with Drew.
10. Never look a gift horse in the mouth.

Part 2   Objects of Prepositions

Objects of prepositions are the nouns or pronouns within prepositional phrases. Objects complete the meaning of prepositions. Objects may or may not be modified.

Using Nouns as Objects of Prepositions

You have seen that nouns are used as subjects, direct objects, and indirect objects of the verb. Nouns are also used as objects of prepositions. Look at the nouns used as objects in the following prepositional phrases.

> behind *Jenny*   without a *doubt*
> in the *World Series*   by *Thanksgiving*

Like nouns used in other ways, objects of prepositions also may be compound. Look at these examples:

> to *teachers* and *students*
> toward her *house* and the new *library*
> like *Paul* and *Danny*

In these sentences nouns are used as objects of prepositions. Write the prepositional phrases in each sentence. Circle
the object of each preposition.

1. Joan climbed up the ladder and onto the roof.
2. After school, we went to the pool.
3. Pat and Leslie walked along the beach with their dog.
4. Kevin looked closely at the big bluefish.
5. The jet landed on the runway and taxied to the
   terminal.
6. They walked along the edge of the lagoon.
7. Jay rushed into the waiting room with the timetable.
8. Bob sat beside the fire and talked to Christine.
9. A spider crawled across the ceiling and down the basement wall.
10. Ten kinds of tropical fish were swimming in the huge
    tank.

Using Pronouns as Objects of Prepositions

Pronouns are also used as objects of prepositions.
The object forms of pronouns are the only forms used for
objects of prepositions.
Here are the object forms of pronouns:

me	us	whom
you	you	
him, her, it	them	

Pronouns are used as objects in the following prepositional
phrases.

to *me*	with *whom*
through *us*	like *her*
from *them*	toward *you*

Compound Objects

You seldom make mistakes in using a single pronoun directly after a preposition. But you may be confused when the object of a preposition is compound.

Simple Object	Compound Object
Take it to *her.*	Take it to *Mary* and *her.*
Come with *me.*	Come with *her* and *me.*
We worked for *him.*	We worked for *Homer* and *him.*

Here is a way to know if you are using the correct pronoun in a prepositional phrase with a compound object. First say the pronoun alone after the preposition. If it sounds right, then that is the correct pronoun to use in the compound object.

These tickets are for Pam and (he, him).

These tickets are for *him.*
These tickets are for *Pam* and *him.*

Exercises Use pronouns as objects of prepositions.

A. Choose the correct pronoun from the two given in parentheses. Write the prepositional phrase.

1. The Junior Achievement presentation was given by Sara and (her, she).
2. Nobody was there except Mr. Parks and (I, me).
3. Finally the nurse looked at Bill and (I, me).
4. Beside Karen and (he, him) were their parents.
5. I almost fell over Amy and (she, her).
6. Ms. Sims bought tickets for Judy and (I, me).
7. Hal stood behind Tracy and (we, us).
8. We gave the winners' score sheets to the coach and (he, him).
9. The ball fell between Steve and (he, him).
10. Roger was talking about Robin and (she, her).

B. Choose the correct pronoun from the two given.

1. to him and (I, me)
2. past them and (we, us)
3. for you and (we, us)
4. between Joy and (she, her)
5. beside them and (we, us)
6. toward Sally and (I, me)
7. between Carl and (he, him)
8. near Ellen and (I, me)
9. to Jim and (he, him)
10. at Sam and (I, me)

Part 3 Prepositional Phrases as Modifiers

A modifier may be a group of words as well as a single word. Frequently a prepositional phrase is a modifier. Prepositional phrases do the same work in a sentence as adjectives and adverbs.

A prepositional phrase that modifies a noun or pronoun is called an adjective phrase.

> The procession passed the statue *of Lincoln*.
>
> He was washing the window *over the sink*.
>
> A room *on the third floor* is available.

Like adjectives, adjective phrases tell *which one, what kind,* or *how many.*

A prepositional phrase that modifies a verb is called an adverb phrase.

> The crowd ate *in shifts*.
>
> The geyser erupted *at noon*.
>
> They swam *under the bridge*.

Like adverbs, adverb phrases tell *how, when, where,* and *to what extent* about verbs.

Often you will find two prepositional phrases in a row. Sometimes the second phrase is an adjective phrase modifying the object of the first phrase.

The grocer put a sign *on the basket of apples.*

(*On the basket* is an adverb phrase telling *where* about the verb *put.*)

(*Of apples* is an adjective phrase modifying *basket.* It tells *which* basket.)

The car streaked away *in a cloud of smoke.*

(*In a cloud* tells *how* the car streaked.)

(*Of smoke* modifies *cloud.* It tells *what kind* of cloud.)

Diagraming Sentences Containing Prepositional Phrases

Since a prepositional phrase does the work of an adjective or an adverb, you diagram it like an adjective or an adverb. Write the preposition on a line slanting down from the word modified. Then, on a horizontal line attached to the preposition line, write the object. Anything modifying the object slants down from it. Notice in the following diagram that the object of a preposition (*rim*) may be modified by another phrase (*of the volcano*).

In the morning we walked to the rim of the volcano.

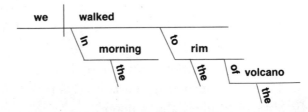

A prepositional phrase containing a compound object is diagramed in a similar way.

Trucks with fruits and vegetables attracted the passers-by.

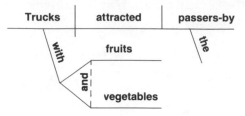

In this sentence, the phrase *with fruits and vegetables* is an adjective phrase modifying the noun *trucks*. The preposition line therefore slants down from the word *trucks*. Because of the compound object, the line for the object of the preposition is split.

Exercises   **Find adjective and adverb prepositional phrases.**

A.   Make three columns marked *Phrase, Word Modified,* and *Kind of Phrase*. For each prepositional phrase in the following sentences, fill in the information under the three columns. (Before you begin the exercise, review what questions adjectives and adverbs answer.)

> Example: Under the planks, Gary could always find
> worms for bait.

Phrase	Word Modified	Kind of Phrase
under the planks	could find	adverb
for bait	worms	adjective

1. The buttons on his sleeve caught in the door.
2. I saw a strange Siamese cat in the alley.
3. At the corner they built a new sign.
4. The bacon sizzled in the frying pan.
5. Someone called about noon.
6. The hikers without maps returned at sunset.
7. Gulls flocked around the fishing boats.

8. The Mannings went through the Blue Ridge Mountains on their trip.
9. Dad had already put the pizzas in the oven.
10. On his birthday, he has cake with chocolate icing.

B. Find the prepositional phrases in the following sentences. Tell whether each phrase is used as an adjective or adverb. Write the answers as your teacher indicates.

1. Put Jack's books behind the big chair.
2. In the afternoon, the class went to a museum.
3. Sheila waited patiently on the landing.
4. After a while, the cars moved at a snail's pace.
5. Four girls on the team waited in the office.
6. The Brown County art colony in Indiana is famous.
7. He didn't look under the couch.
8. The closet beneath the stairs is full.
9. In the greenhouse, they grew three kinds of violets.
10. In the fifth inning, the first batter for the Tigers hit a home run.

Part 4 Putting Prepositional Phrases in the Right Place

Sometimes, the position of a prepositional phrase makes a great deal of difference in the meaning of the sentence.

> The trainer signaled the dolphins on the platform.
> The trainer on the platform signaled the dolphins.

The first sentence is unclear because the phrase *on the platform* seems to modify *dolphins*. The second sentence brings the phrase where it should be: closer to *trainer*, the word it modifies. As with other modifiers, a prepositional phrase should be placed as close as possible to the word it modifies.

Exercises Place prepositional phrases correctly.

A. Writing The following sentences are awkward. Change the position of one phrase in each sentence to make the meaning clear. Rewrite each sentence.

1. The boys hurried after the ice-cream truck on their bikes.
2. Jean wrote several long letters to the director on her typewriter.
3. John stood on tiptoe and reached for the string beans with raised arms.
4. David mailed his request to the senator at the post office.
5. With his big straw stomach Al laughed at the scarecrow.
6. There is some orange juice for the boys in the refrigerator.
7. We saw a big white horse beside a brook with a long tail.
8. Alice searched for rare birds with powerful binoculars.
9. A rabbit ran across the street with long ears.
10. Grandpa picked up the baby with his pipe in his mouth.

B. Follow the directions for Exercise A.

1. The baby wanted its mother in the highchair.
2. Kathy has a letter from a friend in her desk.
3. That tall girl caught the ball with the striped T-shirt.
4. The game was played at the stadium between Detroit and Cleveland.
5. The clock stopped by the water fountain at 3:30.
6. Was he the only one who could do cartwheels on the gymnastics team?
7. Dan told everyone about his high dive at breakfast.

8. The woman looked at the garden in the green jacket.
9. Carol and I startled the mail carrier in our costumes.
10. That money is for the tollbooth on the dashboard.

Part 5 Preposition or Adverb?

Many words used as prepositions may also be used as adverbs. A preposition never appears alone. It is always followed by its object, a noun or pronoun. If the word is in a phrase, it is a preposition. If it is not in a phrase, it is probably an adverb.

> The carpenter climbed *in the window.*
> Grandfather walked *in.*
>
> Uncle Frank fell *down the stairs.*
> Put your pencils *down*, please.
>
> *Outside the stadium* the crowd waited.
> The puppy followed the children *outside.*

Exercises Find prepositions and adverbs.

A. In each pair of sentences that follows, there is one adverb and one preposition. Number your paper from 1 to 10. After each number, write *a* and *b*. After each letter, write *Preposition* or *Adverb*, depending on which you find.

> Example: (a) He heard a noise below.
> (b) He heard a noise below the window.
> (a) adverb
> (b) preposition

1. (a) We climbed out. (b) We climbed out the window.
2. (a) The ball fell through the net. (b) The ball fell through.
3. (a) Terry walked along. (b) Terry walked along the shore.

4. (a) Behind came Joanne. (b) Behind us came Joanne.
5. (a) Above our heads shone the sun. (b) Above, the sun shone.
6. (a) The bear cub rolled over. (b) The cub rolled over its brother.
7. (a) We had not met before the game. (b) We had not met before.
8. (a) The red blanket goes beneath. (b) The red blanket goes beneath the saddle.
9. (a) Come up the stairs. (b) Come up.
10. (a) Bob stayed in the house all day. (b) Bob stayed in.

B. Follow the directions for Exercise A.

1. (a) They went inside the house. (b) They went inside.
2. (a) The train went through. (b) The train went through the mountain village.
3. (a) Beyond lay the Smoky Mountains. (b) Beyond the town lay the Smoky Mountains.
4. (a) The picture fell off. (b) The picture fell off the wall.
5. (a) The doctor is in. (b) Dr. Rayner is in her office.
6. (a) The dog ran beside the motorcycle. (b) The dog ran beside.
7. (a) They drove past. (b) They drove past the old theater.
8. (a) The boys waited outside the gym. (b) The boys waited outside.
9. (a) We went inside. (b) We went inside the gymnasium.
10. (a) I've heard that song before. (b) I've heard that song before today.

ADDITIONAL EXERCISES

Using Prepositions

A. Prepositional Phrases Number your paper from 1 to 10. Write the prepositional phrases in the following sentences. Underline the object of each preposition.

1. Simon drew boundary lines in the dust.
2. The empty highway stretched before us.
3. We inched our way to the back.
4. Trisha stepped carefully onto the roof.
5. During a storm, Mother unplugs the television.
6. Hang the blankets in the sun.
7. The rear wheel of the car was on the sidewalk.
8. Wait for me by the fountain.
9. Laura kept the news to herself without difficulty.
10. Monty talks about himself.

B. Pronouns as Objects of Prepositions Choose the correct pronoun from the two given in parentheses. Write it with the preposition.

1. The block party was planned by the Rays and (they, them).
2. Stacey dribbled past the forward and (I, me).
3. At the assembly we sat behind Jess and (she, her).
4. To (he, him), the news was a shock.
5. To (who, whom) do you wish to speak?
6. It sounds like (he, him).
7. Nobody admitted sending the Valentines to Ed and (I, me).
8. I ordered pizza for you and (her, she).
9. The Bellaks share the cottage with the Haines and (we, us).
10. The sponsor with (who, whom) I spoke liked the plan.

C. Adjective and Adverb Prepositional Phrases
Find the prepositional phrases in the following sentences. Write *adjective* or *adverb* to describe each phrase.

1. The woman in the trenchcoat is Ms. Lorca.
2. Cary put his earnings into the bank.
3. Our parrot escaped from its cage.
4. Neal boiled five pounds of potatoes.
5. The table was near the restaurant's kitchen.
6. The constant drone of the mosquitoes woke me up.
7. Don't swim past the rope.
8. We huddled under the canoe during the rain.
9. Dark clouds were massing in the east.
10. The boy in the blue jacket is a student from Brazil.

D. Correct Use of Prepositional Phrases
The following sentences are awkward. By changing the position of one prepositional phrase in each sentence, you can make the meaning clear. Rewrite each sentence in this manner.

1. The spaceship was aimed for the moon with an unusual wing design.
2. Joannie bit into the plum with a wide grin.
3. The headlights shined dimly in the fog on the jeep.
4. There is tuna casserole for your brother Chris in the oven.
5. Donald wore his new parka on the camping trip with the fur hood.
6. We sent the card to Grandma in a perfumed envelope.
7. A wrestling match was held in the gym between Ted and Vic.
8. The acrobat landed on the chair with the sequined tights.
9. The batter hit the ball out of the park in the red uniform.
10. Martha told me about the track meet in art class.

E. Preposition or Adverb? Decide whether the italicized words in these sentences are adverbs or prepositions. Write *Adverb* or *Preposition* for each sentence.

1. Derek flashed a light *around* the dark warehouse.
2. *In* strolled Marilyn.
3. Carrie vaulted *over* the hurdle.
4. Ivy grew *up* the brick walls.
5. Can we wade *across* the stream?
6. The bag of groceries toppled *over*.
7. *Down* the alley strolled the tomcat.
8. Flies were buzzing *around*.
9. Carter put the violets *in* a little pitcher.
10. The audience stood *up* and applauded.

MIXED REVIEW

Using Prepositions

A. Finding prepositions and adverbs Copy each sentence. Underline any prepositional phrases. Put an *O* over the objects of the prepositions. Circle any adverbs.

1. The judge walked in.
2. Please leave the air conditioner off.
3. The address book is in the top drawer.
4. Let's go inside.
5. The contest is over.
6. Janet stumbled and fell off the diving board.
7. Our plane flew over the Rocky Mountains.
8. The musicians put their instruments down.
9. We found shelter inside the old cabin.
10. Peter lives in the new building down the street.

B. Using adjective and adverb phrases Rewrite the following sentences, adding the prepositional phrases shown in parentheses. Be sure to place the phrase in the correct place. After each sentence, write *Adverb* or *Adjective* to show what kind of phrase you have added.

1. The new girl is in our homeroom. (from Tulsa)
2. The dog barked at me. (on the leash)
3. Josh captured a yellow and red butterfly. (in his net)
4. The new emergency center treats many patients. (on Washington Street)
5. My pencil broke. (before the test)
6. Susan frightened the children. (in a scary costume)
7. Marc told us about the secret. (in a whisper)
8. The books are on the second shelf. (about old coins)
9. Bill asked his boss during their meeting. (for a raise)
10. The crew saved the boat. (during the storm)

USING GRAMMAR IN WRITING
Using Prepositions

A. Imagine that you have just seen the magician David Copperfield. He pulled objects from many different places only to make them disappear again. Write a paragraph describing part of the routine in which the magician used several props. Tell how the props were used and how or where things were concealed from the audience. Underline prepositional phrases. Here are some prepositions you might use.

from	under	off	in
into	over	around	up
of	with	through	during
with	at	to	toward

B. The following story needs descriptive phrases to make it more interesting. Rewrite the paragraph, adding at least eight prepositional phrases. You may use some of the prepositions above. Underline the prepositional phrases. Label them *Adjective* or *Adverb* to tell how the phrases are used.

> It was almost dark. A full yellow moon hung low. Annette was walking. She heard a rustling noise.
> "It's nothing," she told herself.
> She began walking again, more quickly this time. The noise returned. Annette peered. There was something hiding. It was low and dark. It moved. Suddenly it jumped. Annette laughed.
> "OK, Pepper," she said, "you can come. You've scared me so much, I need a watchdog now!"

Using Conjunctions

You have learned that prepositions show relationships between words in a sentence. Relationships are also shown by another kind of word: **conjunctions.**

Read these examples:

> The students *and* the teacher laughed.
> Before the opening, the actors were nervous *but* happy.
> Jason *or* Brooke will know the answer.

In the examples, you can see how the conjunctions *and, but,* and *or* are used. *And* connects *students* and *teacher. But* connects *nervous* and *happy. Or* connects *Jason* and *Brooke.*

A conjunction is a word that connects words or groups of words.

Coordinating Conjunctions

Coordinating conjunctions join only words or groups of words that are of equal importance. The coordinating conjunctions are *and, but,* and *or.* The words joined by coordinating conjunctions are called **compound constructions.** These sentences show how coordinating conjunctions connect words of equal importance.

> **Mark** *or* **she** will fix it. (*Or* connects *Mark* and *she,* the compound subject of the verb *will fix.*)
>
> Kent **shot** *and* **scored.** (*And* connects *shot* and *scored,* verbs that form the compound verb.)
>
> We need **string** *and* **tape.** (*And* connects *string* and *tape,* the compound direct object of the verb *need.*)
>
> Give **Susan** *or* **her** the mail. (*Or* connects *Susan* and *her,* the compound indirect object of *give.*)
>
> The suitcase was **light** *but* **awkward.** (*But* connects *light* and *awkward,* compound predicate adjectives.)
>
> He spoke **briefly** *but* **well.** (*But* connects the adverbs *briefly* and *well.*)
>
> Send it to **Andrea** *or* **him.** (*Or* connects *Andrea* and *him,* the compound objects of the preposition *to.*)

Correlative Conjunctions

A few conjunctions are used in pairs:

both . . . and	neither . . . nor	not only . . . but (also)
either . . . or	whether . . . or	

Such conjunctions are called **correlative conjunctions.**

> Cal ordered *both* bacon *and* eggs.
> *Either* Debbie *or* Eric will win the election.
> *Neither* the drugstore *nor* the market had any cough drops.
> I like *not only* rock music *but also* classical music.
> The question is *whether* Karen *or* Beth should receive the award.

Exercises **Recognize conjunctions and compound constructions.**

A. Find the conjunctions in the following sentences. Be prepared to tell what words or word groups are connected by each conjunction.

1. In the past, people either hunted or went hungry.
2. The President or Vice-President will travel to Russia.
3. Candy has both a sled and ice skates.
4. Beth put on the horse's saddle and bridle.
5. Some stars appear both on television and in films.
6. Neither jokes nor riddles could make Lynn laugh.
7. The math test was long but easy.
8. Ernie reads sports stories or biographies.
9. Whether he is happy or sad, Tom always smiles.
10. Leslie takes not only ballet but also voice lessons.

B. Number your paper from 1 to 10. Write the compounds you find in each sentence. Circle the conjunction. Then write *Subject, Verb, Direct Object, Indirect Object, Predicate Adjective, Adverb,* or *Object of a Preposition* to identify each compound.

Example: Wear a dress or jeans.

dress ⊙ jeans: direct object

1. The lettering on the posters and banners is too small.
2. Slowly and thoughtfully he repaired the clock.
3. His story was unbelievable but true.
4. Lori carefully but quickly explained the answer.
5. The travelers waved and smiled.
6. Dad and Mother bought a rocking chair.
7. Janet found the address and telephone number.
8. We waited throughout the afternoon and evening.
9. The biggest tractor on the lot was green and yellow.
10. She could have given you or Pat a chance.

ADDITIONAL EXERCISES

Using Conjunctions

Conjunctions and Compound Constructions   Write the compound construction in each sentence. Underline the conjunction. Underline every word of a correlative conjunction.

1. Yvonne practiced on the parallel bars and the rings.
2. Cold nights and warm days are good for maple sap.
3. The fugitive either swam or rowed across the river.
4. I waited but got no answer.
5. The girls washed and waxed Mom's new car.
6. The hawk swooped toward Adam and me.
7. Red and yellow lights flashed on the control panel.
8. Neither aspirin nor rest helped his headache.
9. This peanut butter contains neither salt nor sugar.
10. Joy worked slowly but steadily on the model ship.
11. The hailstones destroyed not only the soybean crop but also the sweet corn.
12. This switch turns the furnace on and off.
13. I wonder whether the dust or the cat is making me sneeze.
14. We studied not only history but also geography.
15. Kip asked whether milk or juice had more calories.
16. Jerry reads well but writes poorly.
17. The team and the coach huddled during the timeout.
18. Is the snow wet or powdery?
19. Dwight neither knows nor cares.
20. Nicole washed not only the apples but also the grapes.
21. The detective was polite but persistent.
22. First, turn over the soil and then remove the stones.
23. Sacajawea guided Lewis and Clark.
24. The seahorse swims upright and grasps with its tail.
25. Both Brenda and Carol play softball.

MIXED REVIEW

Using Conjunctions

A. Identifying compound sentence parts Copy the following sentences. Underline the compound sentence parts. Circle the conjunctions. After each sentence, write what the compound part is.

> Example: Stephen wrote the letter quickly (but) neatly.
> Compound Adverb

1. Mr. Jacobs researched and wrote the article about vampire bats.
2. Marion or Colette will represent our neighborhood at the meeting.
3. The opposing team wore blue and gold uniforms.
4. I enjoy reading mysteries now and then.
5. Stu collects matchbooks and menus from famous restaurants.
6. The service in this store is slow but dependable.
7. Katherine said her lines smoothly and distinctly.
8. Neither he nor I actually saw the accident.
9. Beth designed and built an unusual doghouse.
10. Dad gave Sam and me haircuts.

B. Using conjunctions and compound sentence parts Write sentences using compound sentence parts according to the directions that follow.

1. Compound indirect object. Use a noun and a pronoun.
2. Compound predicate noun. Use proper nouns.
3. Compound object of a preposition. Use two pronouns.
4. Compound subject. Use *either, or.*
5. Compound verb. Use *but.*

USING GRAMMAR IN WRITING
Using Conjunctions

A. Following are instructions for making fresh applesauce. These instructions were written for a child. Therefore, the sentences are short and simple. Rewrite the instructions for an adult, combining ideas into compound constructions.

> Peel several apples. Core the apples. Slice the apples. Set the slices aside. Pour one-fourth cup of apple juice in a blender. You can use water instead. Add the apples one at a time. Blend the mixture until it is smooth. Pour it into a saucepan. Cook over low heat. Add some cinnamon to taste. Add some honey to taste. Add a dash of lemon juice.

B. The last ten seconds changed the outcome of the basketball game between your team, the Jays, and your arch rivals, the Falcons. Write a paragraph that describes the last ten seconds of the game. Use the following compound constructions in your sentences.

> shot and scored
> both the referee and the
>   coach
> missed the shot and
>   fouled
>
> tired but happy
> must either pass or shoot
> our forward and their
>   guard

C. You are listening to a speaker who tries to impress listeners by using long, involved sentences. Here is the first sentence of today's speech. Write out what you think the rest of it might be. Use the same style. When you are done, underline the conjunctions you used.

> "My friends <u>and</u> fans, I come before you today not as a celebrity <u>or</u> a star, <u>but</u> as a friend."

Using the Parts of Speech

Part 1   The Parts of Speech

You have studied verbs, nouns, pronouns, adjectives, adverbs, prepositions, and conjunctions. You have been learning to recognize words in these groups and to use them correctly in sentences.

In this section, you will learn about an eighth group of words called **interjections.**

The name used for all of these groups of words is **parts of speech.** Here are the eight parts of speech:

nouns	**verbs**	**adverbs**	**conjunctions**
pronouns	**adjectives**	**prepositions**	**interjections**

A word fits into one of the groups because of the way it is used in a sentence.

What Are Interjections?

In addition to the seven parts of speech you have studied, there is a group of words called **interjections.**

An interjection is a word or short group of words used to express strong feeling. It may be a real word or merely a sound. It may express surprise, joy, longing, anger, or sorrow. An interjection is usually followed by an **exclamation mark (!).**

Read these examples of interjections:

> *Hooray!* We won the game.
> *No way!* I'm not riding that roller coaster.
> *Congratulations!*
> *Ouch!* That hurts.

Exercises **Recognize the parts of speech.**

A. Read each sentence. Then write the italicized word. Beside each word, write what part of speech it is.

1. Margaret is locked *in* her room.
2. The hermit is irritable *and* unfriendly.
3. Jody *whistled* for her dog.
4. A *shaggy* dog ran through the yard.
5. Rain *gently* tapped on the windows.
6. A performer walked on broken *glass.*
7. *He* was not scratched or cut.
8. *Ugh!* This is disgusting!
9. *Marcus* saw a strange flying object.
10. A *silver* racer streaked around the curve.

B. Follow the directions for Exercise A.

1. The soccer players *scrambled* down the field.
2. These new rules are *strict.*
3. The *mayor* appointed a new aide.
4. Opera fans applauded *her* enthusiastically.

5. Vincent painted the sign *neatly*.
6. Two men escaped *into* the jungle.
7. Sunglasses *or* a visor shades the sun.
8. *Wow!* You dance so well!
9. The hikers *finally* found the waterfall.
10. Bonnie lit the charcoal *with* a match.

Part 2 Words Used as Different Parts of Speech

You cannot tell what part of speech a word is, of course, until you see how the word is used in a sentence. Many words may be used in different ways.

Read these examples:

Dennis took a *break* from his homework.
  (*Break* is used as a noun.)

Don't *break* the cookie jar.
  (*Break* is used as a verb.)

Money is kept in a *safe*.
  (*Safe* is used as a noun.)

Lexington is a *safe* town with little crime.
  (*Safe* is used as an adjective modifying *town*.)

The gymnast soared *high* into the air.
  (*High* is an adverb modifying the verb *soared*.)

Horses jumped the *high* hurdles.
  (*High* is an adjective modifying *hurdles*.)

The ice skater whirled *around*.
  (*Around* is an adverb telling *where* about the verb *whirled*.)

The sentry paced *around* the fort.
  (*Around* is used as a preposition.)

This is our lunch hour.
  (*This* is used as a pronoun, the subject of the sentence.)

We will take a field trip *this* week.
 (*This* is used as an adjective modifying *week*.)

The enemy will *free* its prisoners of war.
 (*Free* is used as a verb.)

Paula received a *free* T-shirt.
 (*Free* is used as an adjective modifying *T-shirt*.)

Exercises   Decide the part of speech.

A.   Write the italicized word in each sentence. After it, write its part of speech.

1. The center took one free *throw*.
2. Children *throw* peanuts to the elephant.
3. Your arrow came *close* to the bull's-eye.
4. *Close* friends talk honestly.
5. Monopoly uses *play* money.
6. We girls often *play* soccer.
7. *Which* is the best restaurant?
8. *Which* films are playing downtown?
9. Seagulls flew *by* the beach.
10. Suddenly a fire engine sped *by*.

B.   Follow the directions for Exercise A.

1. A huge jade *plant* grows in the greenhouse.
2. Did the gardener *plant* tulips?
3. The twins strolled *in*.
4. The freshman class held a party *in* the gym.
5. Put the *cover* on the jar.
6. *Cover* the flowers before winter.
7. I *long* for some privacy.
8. Beth wore a *long* scarf around her neck.
9. This wallet is *his*.
10. Lou threw *his* cards on the table.

ADDITIONAL EXERCISES

Using the Parts of Speech

Parts of Speech Number your paper from 1 to 25. Write the part of speech of the italicized word in each sentence.

1. Francine put a jacket *on*.
2. Sea holly grows *on* the beach.
3. *That* noise was thunder.
4. *That* sounded like thunder.
5. Dave's *curls* lay around the barber's chair.
6. Our terrier *curls* her tail when she's happy.
7. *Well!* Did you see that?
8. Leslie can't see that *well* without her glasses.
9. That mousey little animal is a miniature *Siamese* cat.
10. The *Chinese* are more likely to own bikes than cars.
11. Shirley made a good *move* with her pawn.
12. Jeff *moved* closer to the microphone.
13. *Flip* the coin again.
14. Juan did a *flip* from the high diving board.
15. Freddie waxed his new *leather* boots.
16. *Leather* has become expensive.
17. A satellite revolves *around* the earth.
18. The seeing-eye dog led its master *around*.
19. *Which* is the starter switch?
20. *Which* league is he in?
21. Mark *skated* across the pond.
22. Molly borrowed my *skate* key.
23. Lee found only one *skate* in the garage.
24. There was no *screen* on the window.
25. Ms. Washington *screened* all applicants.

MIXED REVIEW

Using the Parts of Speech

A. Identifying parts of speech Number your paper from 1 to 15. Copy the words in italics. Decide how each word in italics is used. Then write its part of speech.

1. Do you have *enough* warm clothing?
2. Carol worked *hard* on her acceptance speech.
3. Mom paid the *bill* promptly.
4. Ben's cat *scratches* the furniture.
5. We had a *great* day at the beach.
6. This small *print* is difficult to read.
7. *Dry* brown leaves rustled in the wind.
8. We must *clean* the stables before sundown.
9. Scott painted the fence with firm, even *strokes*.
10. A light shone *above* the door.
11. Your application is *complete*.
12. Move *over*, please.
13. The judges praised Dad's *giant* marigolds.
14. This pillow is stuffed with *goose* feathers.
15. The two sides reached a settlement by *morning*.

B. Using words as different parts of speech Write two sentences for each of the following words. In each sentence, use the word as a different part of speech. Underline the word, and then write what part of speech it is used as in that sentence.

1. thought
2. below
3. brush
4. lost
5. call

USING GRAMMAR IN WRITING
Parts of Speech

A. There are many kinds of codes. This one is based on words that can be used as different parts of speech. For example, you want to relay this message:

My <u>cover</u> is <u>broken</u>. I will <u>fly</u> to a <u>safe</u> area.
(N) (V)   (V) (Adj)

You could write it in code this way, using the underlined words as different parts of speech:

<u>Cover</u> the <u>broken</u> bed. The <u>fly</u> on the <u>safe</u> can be found.
(V) (Adj.)   (N)   (N)

The following are important messages. Write them in the code, using the underlined words as different parts of speech. Label what part of speech each of the code words is now used as.

1. Thieves may <u>break</u> into the <u>safe</u>. <u>Place</u> money in the <u>wall</u>.
2. They <u>demand</u> a raise. <u>Pay</u> by <u>check</u>.
3. <u>Leads</u> are few. Must <u>fly</u> <u>back</u>.
4. <u>Hit</u> the jackpot. Will <u>stop</u> at your <u>place</u>.

B. Each word below can be used as at least two different parts of speech. Some can be used as verbs, nouns, or adjectives. Some can be used as all three. Write two or three sentences for each word, using that word as a different part of speech in each sentence.

Example: <u>Place</u> the money over there.
     I hid in a safe <u>place</u>.
     My mother bought new <u>place</u> mats.

1. plant 4. safe
2. cover 5. sail
3. play   6. meet

Sentence Patterns

Part 1 Word Order and Meaning

Sentences are made up of words that are arranged in order. However, not just any order will do. To make sense, the words must be put together in order according to certain patterns. Read the groups of words below. Which groups make sense?

Rain fell heavily.   Ms. Parker hired Louis.
Fell heavily rain.   Ms. Parker Louis hired.

The first group in each pair makes sense because the words are in the right order for one of the patterns of an English sentence. The second group in each pair does not make sense because the words are not in the right order. From your experience with English sentences, you know what the right order is. You can see at once when the order is wrong.

Sometimes there is more than one right order for the words in a sentence. Each order makes sense and expresses an idea. However, when the order is changed, the ideas expressed may change, too. Read the following pairs of sentences.

Kathy held the baby.   Benson watched the creature.
The baby held Kathy.   The creature watched Benson.

The words are the same in each sentence, but the word order is not. The difference in word order makes a difference in meaning.

Exercise   Change word order to change meaning.

Read each sentence. Then change the order of the words to change the meaning. Write each new sentence on your paper.

1. Rachel ignored Albert.
2. The climbers saw Bigfoot.
3. That dog chased the jogger.
4. Mike burned the cookies.
5. Laura petted the cat.
6. Diane called the captain.

Part 2   The N V Pattern

In English sentences, words are arranged in a certain order to make sense. The word order of most sentences follows a pattern. In this section, you will study five **sentence patterns.**

One simple pattern for English sentences is called the **N V pattern.** Every sentence has a subject and a verb. The subject is usually a noun or a pronoun. In this chart, N stands for the noun (or pronoun) in the complete subject. V stands for the verb in the complete predicate.

N	V
The crowd	applauded.
Loretta	left.
She	walked slowly.

The word order above follows the N V pattern.

Exercises   Use the N V pattern.

A.   Make a chart for the N V pattern. Label one column *N*. Label the other *V*. Write these sentences on the chart.

1. Walter understands.
2. Spring arrives tomorrow.
3. Time flies.
4. New shoes may hurt.
5. The sink overflowed.
6. Madeline ran by.

B.   Copy this chart. Complete each N V pattern.

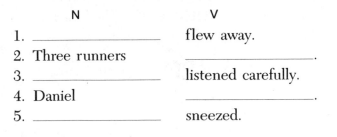

N	V
1. _____	flew away.
2. Three runners	_____.
3. _____	listened carefully.
4. Daniel	_____.
5. _____	sneezed.

Part 3   The N V N Pattern

A sentence in the **N V N pattern** has three parts. The first *N* stands for the subject noun or pronoun. The *V* stands for the verb. The second *N* stands for the direct object. The sentences in the following chart are in the N V N pattern.

N	V	N
Elizabeth	heard	a crash.
Many people	will see	that movie.
Everyone	wanted	a rest.

Exercises   Use the N V N pattern.

A.   Make a chart for the N V N pattern. Label the three columns *N*, *V*, and *N*. Write these sentences on the chart.

1. Terry has a cold.
2. My aunt built some shelves.
3. He climbed the ladder.
4. I cooked the hamburgers.
5. Roger borrowed my pen.
6. Thelma can fix your bike.

B.   Copy this chart. Complete each N V N pattern.

N	V	N
1. _____	dropped	the mirror.
2. Fran	sold	_____.
3. _____	caught	_____.
4. _____	_____	the boat.
5. _____	operated	the machine.

Part 4   The N V N N Pattern

A sentence in the **N V N N pattern** has four parts. The first *N* stands for the subject noun or pronoun. The *V* stands for the verb. The second *N* stands for the indirect object. The third *N* stands for the direct object. Read the sentences in the following chart. They are in the N V N N pattern.

N	V	N	N
Sue	gave	Joan	a scarf.
The waiter	brought	us	the menu.
I	sent	the company	a complaint.

Exercises **Use the N V N N pattern.**

A. Make a chart for the N V N N pattern. Label the four columns *N, V, N,* and *N.* Write these sentences on the chart.

1. Pollen gives me hay fever.
2. My aunt brought me an album.
3. Someone sent Caroline a note.
4. I made myself a sandwich.
5. Tom told Ted your secret.
6. The judges gave the winner a perfect score.
7. We sent Ms. Samuelson a get-well card.
8. Midnight snacks give Hubert nightmares.
9. The manufacturer sent me a replacement.
10. A victory will earn us the championship.

B. Copy this chart. Complete each N V N N pattern.

N	V	N	N
1. _____	gave	Lucille	_____ .
2. Rick	told	_____	_____ .
3. Someone	_____	_____	a gift.
4. _____	_____	me	two letters.
5. I	taught	_____	_____ .

C. **Writing** Make a chart of your own for the N V N N pattern. Write five sentences in the N V N N pattern.

Part 5 The N LV N Pattern

A sentence in the **N LV N pattern** has three parts. The first *N* stands for the subject noun or pronoun. *LV* stands for a linking verb. The second *N* stands for the noun or pronoun that follows the linking verb. The sentences in this chart are in the N LV N pattern.

N	LV	N
Rita	is	our pitcher.
She and I	are	co-captains.
The cold lemonade	was	a treat.

Exercises   Use the N LV N pattern.

A.   Make a chart for the N LV N pattern. Label the three columns *N*, *LV*, and *N*. Write these sentences on the chart.

1. Don was the winner.
2. They are the only volunteers.
3. This book is a thriller.
4. Betsy is a good bowler.
5. Soccer is my favorite sport.
6. Snakes are reptiles.

B.   Copy this chart. Complete each N LV N pattern.

N	LV	N
1. _____	is	the owner.
2. Babe Ruth	was	_____.
3. _____	are	_____.
4. Claudia and Bill	_____	marathon runners.
5. _____	were	_____.

C.   Writing   Make a chart of your own. Label the columns *N*, *LV*, and *N*. Write five sentences in the N LV N pattern.

Part 6   The N LV Adj Pattern

Sentences in the **N LV Adj pattern** have three parts. The *N* stands for the subject noun or pronoun. *LV* stands for the linking verb. *Adj* stands for the predicate adjective. The sentences in the following chart are in the N LV Adj pattern.

N	LV	Adj
Bald Mountain	is	steep.
Your brother	seems	certain.
Kathleen	sounds	quite worried.
Our pizza	will taste	superb.
You	have been	helpful.

Exercises   Use the N LV Adj pattern.

A.   Make a chart for the N LV Adj pattern. Label the three columns *N*, *LV*, and *Adj*. Write these sentences on the chart.

1. Marge looks curious.
2. These pickles are sour.
3. The crisp lettuce tasted fresh.
4. Snails are slow.
5. Joel seemed eager.
6. The movie was hilarious.
7. The sunrise was brilliant.
8. She will be busy.

B.   Make a chart like the one below. Complete each sentence in the N LV Adj pattern.

N	LV	Adj
1. _____	is	quiet.
2. The wind	became	_____.
3. Mustard	tastes	_____.
4. The shelves	_____	sturdy.
5. _____	sounded	_____.

C.   Writing   Make a chart of your own. Label the columns *N*, *LV*, and *Adj*. Write five sentences in the N LV Adj pattern.

ADDITIONAL EXERCISES

Sentence Patterns

Sentence Patterns Number your paper from 1 to 25. Write the pattern for each sentence. Each sentence fits one of these patterns:

N V   N V N   N V N N   N LV N   N LV Adj

1. Your brother will be furious.
2. The sign collapsed.
3. Harper caught the pass.
4. The rebels fought fiercely.
5. Randy became weary.
6. I recognized Sherry's voice.
7. The class bought the principal a birthday cake.
8. Marva Collins is a well-known teacher.
9. Freckles dotted his nose.
10. The judge gave the lawyer a lecture.
11. I passed Cara the ball.
12. Cara passed the ball to Jessica.
13. My aunt is a minister.
14. Somehow the flowers survived under the snow.
15. The hurricane season had begun.
16. Ashes from the volcano covered the streets.
17. San Juan is a seaport.
18. Kate is arguing with Mimi again.
19. The sergeant showed us her badge.
20. The street is noisy in summer.
21. People sat on the front porch.
22. Cheryl sounded sincere.
23. Bert sounded the alarm.
24. Donna walked slowly to the board.
25. I told you the truth.

MIXED REVIEW

Sentence Patterns

A. Finding sentence patterns Decide what sentence pattern is used in each of the following sentences. Write *NV, NVN, NVNN, N LV N,* or *N LV Adj.* Then write another sentence with the same pattern.

1. Meg knit Clara leg warmers.
2. The officer gave Dad directions.
3. The hamburgers burned.
4. Gail's sister is a dental hygienist.
5. The storm raged throughout the night.
6. My tennis shoes are clean.
7. I will be ready at ten.
8. Andrew mailed the invitations.
9. Todd showed the class pictures from his vacation.
10. These children are first graders.

B. Using sentence patterns Write two sentences using each of the following sentence patterns.

1. N V
2. N V N
3. N V N N
4. N LV N
5. N LV Adj

USING GRAMMAR IN WRITING
Sentence Patterns

A. You can use the different sentence patterns to write a nature poem. Choose a subject in nature and follow the sentence patterns given in this example.

Rain

NV	Clouds form.
NVN	The sun leaves the sky.
NVNN	The trees give the wind their branches.
N LV Adj	The rains are furious.
N LV N	The storm is a lion.

Your last sentence, the N LV N pattern, should compare your subject with something else. The comparison should not use the words "like" or "as." This kind of comparison, used often in creative writing, is called a *metaphor.*

B. When you apply for a job, you must usually state your qualifications. Think of a job for which you are qualified. Using each of the five basic sentence patterns, state your qualifications for that job. Remember, you may substitute personal pronouns for nouns.

Example: Job—announcer on the school's radio station, WIGH.

Radio interests me. (NVN)

My drama teacher gave me a recommendation. (NVNN)

My voice is clear. (N LV Adj)

I am a hard worker. (NLVN)

I can work after school. (NV)

Using Verbals

Many words are used as different parts of speech. You can determine the part of speech of a word only when you see how the word is used in a sentence.

In this section, you will study some special kinds of words that seem to be one part of speech but are used as a different part of speech. These words are called **verbals.**

A verbal is a word that is formed from a verb, but that acts as another part of speech. Verbals may look like the verbs in a sentence, but they are never used as verbs.

There are three kinds of verbals:

gerunds   **participles**   **infinitives**

You will study these three kinds of verbals in this section and learn how they are used in sentences.

Part 1   Gerunds

A gerund is a verb form that is used as a noun. Gerunds end in *-ing*. Gerunds can be used in any way that nouns are used.

Like nouns, gerunds may be used as subjects.

> *Running* is good exercise.
> (*Running* is a gerund, the subject of the verb *is*.)

Like nouns, gerunds may be used as objects.

> Kelly likes *reading*.
> (*Reading* is a gerund, the direct object of the verb *likes*.)

Like nouns, gerunds may be used as objects of prepositions.

> The time for *swimming* is too short.
> (*Swimming* is a gerund, the object of the preposition *for*.)

The Gerund Phrase

Gerunds are not always used alone. Because gerunds are formed from verbs, they can have objects. A gerund with its objects and modifiers is called a **gerund phrase.**

> *Playing the piano* relaxes me.
> (*Playing the piano* is a gerund phrase used as the subject of *relaxes; piano* is the object of *playing*.)

Because gerunds are formed from verbs, they can be modified by adverbs.

> *Parking here* is difficult.
> (*Parking here* is a gerund phrase used as the subject of *is; here* is an adverb modifying *parking*.)

Because gerunds are used as nouns, they can be modified by adjectives.

> *Careful planning* is necessary.
> (*Careful planning* is a gerund phrase used as the subject of *is; careful* is an adjective modifying *planning.*)

Gerunds can be modified by prepositional phrases.

> Mr. Lane allowed *talking after the test.*
> (*Talking after the test* is a gerund phrase used as the direct object of *allowed; after the test* is a prepositional phrase modifying *talking.*)

In all of these examples you can see that gerunds are verb forms, but they are never used as verbs. Because *running, reading, swimming, playing, parking, planning,* and *talking* are used as nouns in the example sentences, they are gerunds.

Exercises Find the gerunds and gerund phrases.

A. Write the gerund or gerund phrase in each of the following sentences. Then write whether the gerund or gerund phrase is used as a subject, a direct object, or the object of a preposition.

> Example: Shoveling snow is hard work.
> *Shoveling snow:* subject

1. Chasing rabbits is our dog's favorite pastime.
2. Digging for clams is done at low tide.
3. That team won by playing good defense.
4. Wearing contact lenses is convenient.
5. The coach recommended running.
6. Rebuilding engines is Janet's hobby.
7. Sewing clothes saves money.
8. There are trails for horseback riding.
9. Dancing builds grace and control.
10. After washing the walls, Chris painted them.

B. Follow the directions for Exercise A.

1. Melissa enjoys taking pictures of babies.
2. Bob is known for being friendly.
3. Craig earns money by moving furniture.
4. Sailing on rough water is dangerous.
5. Did you ever try tobogganing?
6. Inez stays informed by reading magazines.
7. The library is a place for quiet studying.
8. Flying is one method of travel.
9. We get to the island by taking a ferry.
10. Seeing a dentist regularly is important.

Part 2 Participles

A participle is a verb form that is used as an adjective.

You remember that one of the principal parts of the verb is the **past participle.** The past participle is formed by adding *-d* or *-ed* to the present tense: *walk–walked.* The past participles of irregular verbs do not follow this rule and have to be learned separately: *bring–brought, ring–rung.*

There is another kind of participle, called the **present participle.** All present participles are formed by adding *-ing* to the present tense of the verb: *bring–bringing, ring–ringing, walk–walking.*

Look at these additional examples.

Verb	Past Participle	Present Participle
talk	talked	talking
go	gone	going
give	given	giving
write	written	writing

(If you need more review, see **Sections 3** and **4** on verbs and irregular verbs.)

Participles are always used as adjectives. They can modify nouns or pronouns:

> *Laughing*, the speaker turned away.
> (*Laughing* is a present participle modifying the noun *speaker.*)

> The truck hit a *parked* car.
> (*Parked* is a past participle modifying the noun *car*.)

> *Waving*, the police officer signaled us to stop.
> (*Waving* is a present participle modifying the noun *officer*.)

The Participial Phrase

Participles are not always used by themselves. They may be part of a phrase. The participle with its objects and modifiers is called a **participial phrase.** Because participles are formed from verbs, they may have objects.

> *Wearing high boots*, the fisherman waded into the stream.
> (*Wearing high boots* is a participial phrase, modifying the noun *fisherman; boots* is the object of the participle *wearing.*)

Because participles are formed from verbs, they may be modified by adverbs.

> A *badly dented* bicycle was left at school.
> (*Badly dented* is a participial phrase modifying the noun *bicycle; badly* is an adverb modifying *dented.*)

Participles may be modifed by prepositional phrases.

> *Listening to the radio*, Tom heard the final score.
> (*Listening to the radio* is a participial phrase, modifying *Tom; to the radio* is a prepositional phrase modifying *Listening.*)

In all of these examples you can see that participles are verb forms, but they are never used as verbs. Because *laughing, parked, waving, wearing, dented,* and *listening* are used as adjectives, they are participles.

Exercises Find the participles and participial phrases.

A. Write the participle or participial phrase in each of the following sentences. Write the word modified.

> Example: Bowing, the lord greeted the queen.
> *Bowing:* modifies *lord*

1. Hearing the alarm, Toni jumped out of bed.
2. The boy pumping gas is my brother.
3. Bitten by a snake, Cara was rushed to the hospital.
4. Dribbling, the forward stalled for time.
5. The teacher found her class telling jokes.
6. Linda Ronstadt, singing sweetly, opened the show.
7. Kathy listened at the slightly opened door.
8. Salted popcorn is tasty.
9. Hitting a home run, Cruz tied the score.
10. The villain, played by Brian, twirled his moustache.

B. Follow the directions for Exercise A.

1. No one noticed the shooting star.
2. The expertly coached team won all its games.
3. Hoping for a victory, the team practiced daily.
4. The man riding a motorcycle stopped suddenly.
5. Circling, the plane was running out of fuel.
6. The person wearing the best costume wins a prize.
7. One patient, covered with a blanket, lay on the floor.
8. Sitting on the bench, Ted hoped he would play.
9. The woman campaigning for mayor shook my hand.
10. Cleverly drawn cartoons appear in the newspaper.

Gerund or Participle?

You have studied two of the three kinds of verbals. The gerund, like the present participle, is formed by adding -*ing* to the present tense of the verb. How can you tell whether a word is a gerund or a participle? It depends upon how the word is used. If it is used as a modifer, it is a participle. If it is used as a noun, it is a gerund. Study these examples:

> *Walking* is good exercise.
>   (*Walking* is a gerund, the subject of *is*.)
>
> *Walking*, we could take the shortcut.
>   (*Walking* is a participle modifying *we*.)
>
> *Climbing the stairs* is slower than taking the elevator.
>   (*Climbing* is a gerund, the subject of *is*.)
>
> *Climbing the stairs*, Ellen spotted a dollar bill.
>   (*Climbing* is a participle modifying *Ellen*.)

Exercise   **Distinguish between gerunds and participles**

For each sentence, write the gerund or participle and tell which it is. Be prepared to explain why it is a gerund or a participle.

1. After fixing the TV, the repairman left.
2. Lying on the beach, Willy read a book.
3. Training for the Olympics, Sarah skates each day.
4. Stamping her feet, the child would not move.
5. Exercising in gym class is required.
6. Taking the school bus saves time.
7. Walking to the bus stop, Shawn met a friend.
8. Throwing snowballs is against school rules.
9. Running daily built Ann's endurance.
10. Hosting the debate, the senator introduced her guests.

Part 3 Infinitives

The third kind of verbal is the **infinitive.**

An infinitive is a verbal that usually appears with the word *to* before it. *To* is called the **sign of the infinitive.**

The following are examples of infinitives.

to be	to give	to want	to run
to go	to have	to see	to ask

Note: You already know that the word *to* is often used as a preposition. *To* is a preposition if it is followed by a noun or pronoun that is its object. *To* is the sign of the infinitive if it is followed by a verb. Notice the difference in these examples:

Prepositional Phrases

We are going *to the game.*
Jim ran *to the door.*

Infinitives

Dee and Jim want *to go.*
I plan *to study.*

When you see the word *to,* look to see if it is used as a preposition or as a sign of the infinitive.

The Infinitive Phrase

Like the other verbals, the infinitive is not always used alone. The infinitive with its objects and modifiers is an **infinitive phrase.** Because the infinitive is formed from a verb, it is also like a verb in several ways. An infinitive may have an object.

> Kris wanted *to own a dog.*
> (*Dog* is the direct object of the infinitive *to own.*)
>
> Sue planned *to give her friends gifts.*
> (*Friends* is the indirect object and *gifts* is the direct object of the infinitive *to give.*)

Because the infinitive is formed from a verb, it may be modified by adverbs.

> The batter tried *to swing hard.*
> (*Hard* is an adverb modifying the infinitive *to swing.*)
>
> Sunshine helps plants *to grow quickly.*
> (*Quickly* is an adverb modifying the infinitive *to grow.*)

Infinitives may also be modified by prepositional phrases.

We'd like *to fly in a helicopter.*
> (*In a helicopter* is a prepositional phrase modifying the infinitive *to fly.*)

Ken volunteered *to work in the library.*
> (*In the library* is a prepositional phrase modifying the infinitive *to work.*)

Uses of the Infinitive Phrase

Unlike the other verbals, infinitives and infinitive phrases can be used as more than one part of speech. Infinitives can be used (1) as nouns, (2) as adjectives, or (3) as adverbs.

You remember that nouns are used as subjects and direct objects of verbs. Infinitives and infinitive phrases can be used as subjects, as direct objects, and in other ways that nouns are used.

Subject: *To become a mechanic* is Lou's goal.
> (*To become a mechanic* is the subject of *is.*)

Direct Object: The girls wanted *to eat pizza.*
> (*To eat pizza* is the direct object of *wanted.*)

Infinitives and infinitive phrases can also be used as modifiers. If the infinitive or infinitive phrase modifes a noun or pronoun, it is used as an adjective. If it modifies a verb, adjective, or adverb, it is used as an adverb.

Adjective: My friend brought a magazine *to read.*
> (*To read* modifies *magazine.*)

Adverb: Laughter is good *to hear.*
> (*To hear* modifies *good.*)

Adverb: The fans came *to hear a jazz concert.*
> (*To hear a jazz concert* modifies the verb *came.*)

Adverb: A lathe is hard *to use.*
> (*To use* modifies the adjective *hard.*)

In all of the examples given, you can see that infinitives are verb forms, but they are never used as verbs. Infinitives are used as nouns, as adjectives, or as adverbs.

The Split Infinitive

Sometimes a modifier is placed between the word *to* and the verb. A modifier in this position is said to split the infinitive. A split infinitive sounds awkward and should be avoided.

> Awkward:　Sue learned to *rapidly* type.
> Better:　Sue learned to type *rapidly*.

Exercises　Find the infinitives and infinitive phrases.

A.　Write the infinitive or infinitive phrase in each of the following sentences. Tell how it is used.

1. Sandra likes to fish on the lake.
2. Tracey learned to paddle a canoe.
3. To settle disputes is the referee's job.
4. Scheduling is the main issue to discuss.
5. The map showed the road to take.
6. To tell jokes well requires good timing.
7. Cary wanted to play darts.
8. The air controller watches to prevent accidents.
9. To get good grades takes effort.
10. Grapes are good to eat.

B.　Follow the directions for Exercise A.

1. A kiln is used to bake clay.
2. The engineer decided to stop the train.
3. Money is easy to spend.
4. The movers used dollies to carry the furniture.
5. A guitar is fun to play.
6. I bought pants to match the sweater.

7. Speakers are designed to amplify sound.

8. The lifeguard rushed to save the swimmer.

9. To level the street, the crew used a steamroller.

10. To see relatives is the purpose of a family reunion.

Part 4   A Review of Verbals

You have learned that verbals are special kinds of words. Verbals are verb forms, but they are never used as verbs in a sentence. Verbals are used as other parts of speech.

There are three kinds of verbals: gerunds, participles, and infinitives. All three verbals may be used by themselves. They may also be used in phrases. These phrases are gerund phrases, participial phrases, and infinitive phrases. Because they are like verbs, all three kinds of verbals may take objects and they may have modifers.

A **gerund** is a verb form used as a noun. (Gerunds end in -*ing*.) A gerund may be used in all the ways a noun used.

> *Reading* is fun.
> I enjoy *reading*.
> I enjoy *reading aloud*.
> I have a question about *your reading*.

A **participle** is a verb form used as an adjective. (Past participles of regular verbs end in -*d* or -*ed*. Past participles of irregular verbs must be learned individually. Present participles end in -*ing*.) Participles, like adjectives, modify nouns or pronouns.

> *Reading his assignment*, Jim fell asleep.
> *Reading too quickly*, Jim made a mistake.
> *Reading by the fire*, Jim fell asleep.
> *Reading by the fire*, he fell asleep.

An **infinitive** is the verbal that usually appears with the word *to* before it. Infinitives may be used as nouns, as adjectives, or as adverbs.

To read is fun.
To read a mystery is enjoyable.
I like *to read*.
The funniest book *to read* is this one.
This novel is hard *to read*.

Exercises   Find the verbals.

A. Find the verbal in each sentence. Write the verbal or verbal phrase. Tell whether the verbal is a gerund, participle, or infinitive.

1. John is likely to succeed.
2. Tired of the city, the Browns moved to the country.
3. The visitors hated to leave.
4. Expecting a call, Don waited by the phone.
5. Tanning makes leather flexible.
6. These paths are for snowmobiling.
7. Gliding gracefully, Wendy skied down the hill.
8. People opposing the new law held a rally.
9. Hang gliding is a new sport.
10. Lee learned to use sign language.

B. Follow the directions for Exercise A.

1. Working hard usually pays off.
2. Autumn is the time to harvest pumpkins.
3. Turning sideways, the model posed for a picture.
4. Casts allow bones to heal.
5. Recording an album is done in a studio.
6. The people standing in line were waiting for tickets.
7. The youth center is a place to meet friends.
8. Winning four straight games, the Yankees took the World Series.
9. Doing crossword puzzles can build your vocabulary.
10. Guided by radar, the shuttle landed on target.

ADDITIONAL EXERCISES

Using Verbals

A. Gerunds and Gerund Phrases Write the gerunds and gerund phrases in these sentences.

1. Collecting stickers is my little sister's hobby.
2. Teasing the cat is mean.
3. Hal did not enjoy weeding the garden.
4. Gwen was paid five dollars for addressing the envelopes.
5. Running has become a popular sport.
6. Bullfighting involves great risk.
7. Mr. Novo disapproves of bullfighting.
8. A blizzard hit without warning.
9. Before leaving, Cal washed the dishes.
10. Jeanie was saving bus fare by walking to school every day.

B. Participles and Participial Phrases Write the participles and participial phrases in these sentences. Some sentences have more than one participle or participial phrase.

1. The whining, injured dog was taken to the vet.
2. Have you ever seen a flying saucer?
3. Paul repaired the broken radio.
4. Taking a corner too fast, the cyclist skidded.
5. A driving rain flattened the plants.
6. A guard caught the boys climbing the tower.
7. The arresting officer wrote the report.
8. Does the city or the school pay crossing guards?
9. Blushing, Patrick joined in the laughter.
10. The ingredients include beaten eggs and sifted flour.

C. Gerund or Participle? Write the gerund or participle in each sentence, and write which it is. Tell what part of speech each is used as.

1. A winding staircase led to the attic.
2. Digital watches do not need winding.
3. William swept the dining room.
4. Dining out was a rare treat.
5. Blake waited at the starting line.
6. Try starting the motor again.
7. I still like wading in the creek.
8. A limp, plastic wading pool hung over the bench.
9. Grinding his teeth, Carl said nothing.
10. Grinding the peanuts takes a long time.

D. Infinitives and Infinitive Phrases Write the infinitives and infinitive phrases in these sentences.

1. These dogs are trained to attack.
2. Use a calculator to do the last problem.
3. Melissa had planned to put her stuffed animals away.
4. The old jeans are too comfortable to throw away.
5. Ms. Kung offered to drive me to the stadium.
6. To get there on time, Martha took a taxi.
7. To smile can take a lot of effort sometimes.
8. Judy likes to go out, but Mae prefers to stay home.
9. Curtis has yet to hit a home run.
10. After a tiring day at work, Mom does yoga to relax.

E. Kinds of Verbals Write the verbal in each sentence. Label the verbal *Gerund, Participle,* or *Infinitive*.

1. Cleaning my room will take an hour.
2. I didn't mean to forget you.
3. Feeling sick, Joe stayed home from work.
4. Whistling happily, Cathy started down the path.

5. A hiker noticed the rising river.
6. Ryan shoved his clenched fists in his pockets.
7. You can't use a stick to paddle a raft.
8. Rebecca forced herself to pay attention.
9. We passed the time by playing cards.
10. Learning English was hard for the refugees.
11. I want to eat lunch right now.
12. Playing tennis is strenuous exercise.
13. Looking for firewood, Alan came across a nest of mourning doves.
14. Hurrying through a job often causes mistakes.
15. Is Amy to meet you before or after school?
16. Laughing, Andy grabbed the pillow from his brother.
17. Bob got paid for mowing and then raking the yard.
18. The principal said that no one is allowed to run through the halls.
19. Our dog got out of the yard by pushing at the gate's lock with her paw.
20. The papers from Cyna's notebook went flying around the room.

MIXED REVIEW

Using Verbals

A. Identifying verbals Write the verbals and verbal phrases from the following sentences. Then write whether the verbal or verbal phrase is a *gerund, gerund phrase, participle, participial phrase, infinitive,* or *infinitive phrase.*

1. Asking questions is important for students.
2. The freshly painted car looks new.
3. Clutching the grocery bag, Martha ran to the car.
4. Talking to the counselor helped David.
5. Learning a new language is a challenge.
6. I want to learn that song.
7. Taking long walks relaxes me.
8. Dee plans to visit us this summer.
9. Smiling happily, Jenny told us the story.
10. I'd like to ask a question.

B. Using verbals in sentences Complete the following sentences by adding the verbal or verbal phrase asked for.

> Example: _____ is my favorite sport. (gerund)
> <u>Swimming</u> is my favorite sport.

1. Ms. Keene asked me _____. (infinitive phrase)
2. Susan wants _____. (infinitive phrase)
3. _____, Jeff scored a goal. (participial phrase)
4. _____, Denise told the joke. (participle)
5. _____ is a popular hobby. (gerund phrase)
6. _____ is important in any sport. (gerund)
7. _____, the gymnasts impressed the crowd. (participial phrase)
8. My favorite job is _____. (gerund phrase)

USING GRAMMAR IN WRITING
Using Verbals

A. Are you an excellent basketball player or a gymnast? Is a friend of yours a fine musician or artist? If you could pick any one skill to excel in, what would it be? Write a paragraph about it. Give reasons why you wish you had that particular skill. In your paragraph include at least one infinitive, two gerunds, and two participles. Underline the verbal phrases.

B. You are at the homecoming football game. The score of the game is tied. By the third quarter, almost everyone in the stands is hoarse. Describe the behavior of the fans during the last quarter. Use at least five of the following verbals in your paragraph. Use at least two as gerunds. Use at least two as participles. Your paragraph should convey plenty of excitement.

laughing	shouting	cheering	jumping
screaming	yelling	clapping	watching

C. If you could spend a day anywhere you like, doing whatever you want, how would you spend it? Use at least three infinitive phrases in your description. At least one should be the subject of a sentence. At least one should be a direct object.

CUMULATIVE REVIEW
The Parts of Speech

A. Identifying parts of speech There are twenty underlined words in the following paragraph. Decide what part of speech each word is used as. Number your paper from 1 to 20. Write *Noun, Verb, Pronoun, Adjective, Adverb, Preposition,* or *Conjunction* for each word. Be sure to notice *how* the word is used in the sentence.

Many people do not get enough exercise. It is
     1   **2**   **3**
important to get regular exercise in order to look good
4
and to feel good. Some people do not know how to
5
exercise to get the most benefit. You need at least
                  6   **7**
three thirty-minute sessions of exercise a week. A ses-
                    8
sion should consist of a five-minute warm-up, twenty
    9   **10**
minutes of vigorous exercise, and a five-minute cool-
         11
down. The best type of exercise is an aerobic exercise
     12   **13**   **14**
like walking, jogging, swimming, or jumping rope.
                      15
These exercises really get your heart and lungs work-
16   **17**
ing efficiently. A sweaty brow and a strongly beating
    18   **19**
heart are signs of a good workout.
              20

B. Recognizing how words are used Each of the following sentences contains an underlined word. Number your paper from 1 to 15. Write *Subject, Verb, Direct Object, Indirect Object, Object of the Preposition, Predicate Noun,* or *Predicate Adjective* to show what each word is.

1. Zeke made his brother an egg sandwich.

2. Running is not a good sport for people with back trouble.
3. That specimen box contains my insect collection.
4. A puffin is a bird with a short neck and a large, grooved bill.
5. The pilot landed the helicopter on the roof of the sky-scraper.
6. Rob gets around in a motorized wheelchair.
7. Have the pears ripened yet?
8. After the storm, the beach looked deserted.
9. Sam was revising his composition.
10. Marla wants to win the speech contest.
11. The marine gave his commanding officer a salute.
12. Virgil I. Grissom was one of the first astronauts.
13. The bulldozer leveled the building.
14. The clown's hair was pink.
15. Ross enjoys cross-country skiing.

Making Subjects and Verbs Agree

You have studied the sentence and its parts. In this section you will look closely at how subjects and verbs work together.

Part 1   Singular and Plural Forms

Here is a brief review for you:

When a noun stands for one thing, it is **singular.**

>   dog   student   city   classroom

When a noun stands for more than one thing, it is **plural.**

>   dogs   students   cities   classrooms

Verbs, too, have singular and plural forms:

> Singular: The class *votes.*   Plural: The classes *vote.*
> The team *practices.*   The teams *practice.*

The *s* at the end of a verb, such as *votes* or *practices*, shows that it is singular. Unlike nouns, most verbs drop the *s* to form the plural.

Special Forms of Certain Verbs

A few verbs have special forms that you should keep in mind. These verbs are used frequently.

Is, Was, Are, and Were:

The verbs *is* and *was* are singular. The verbs *are* and *were* are plural.

> Singular: Pat *is* here.   Plural: They *are* here.
> Pat *was* here.   They *were* here.

Has and Have:

The verb *has* is singular. The verb *have* is plural.

> Singular: She *has* a bicycle.   Plural: They *have* bicycles.

Does and Do:

The verb *does* is singular. The verb *do* is plural.

> Singular: He *does* the dishes.   Plural: They *do* the dishes.

Part 2   Agreement of Subject and Verb

When you say that a word is singular or plural, you are saying that the word tells about one or more than one thing or action. This is called the **number** of the word. When one word **agrees** with another, it is the same in number.

A verb must agree with its subject in number.

Singular: *She does* an excellent job.
Willy has a new car.
Was Dan at home?

Plural: *Students do* homework.
The *Yankees have* a good pitcher.
Were the *uniforms* clean?

Beware of Phrases

When you are making subjects and verbs agree, beware of phrases. Often a phrase appears between the subject and the verb. The subject is never part of such a phrase. Look for the subject outside the phrase.

The subject of the verb is never found in a prepositional phrase.

One of the glasses *was* broken.

The *pictures* on the desk *were* torn.

Phrases beginning with the words *with, together with, including, as well as,* and *in addition to* are not part of the subject.

The *principal*, in addition to the teacher, *is* here.

Mr. Casey, together with his children, *has* left.

The Pronouns *You* and *I*

Unlike other pronouns, *you* is the same for both singular and plural. But *you* is never used with a singular verb. It is always used with plural verbs.

> You have (*not* has) my best wishes.
>
> You were (*not* was) next on the list.

The pronoun *I* is also used with plural verbs.

> I *do* lawn work.
> I *have* a collie.

The only singular verb forms used with *I* are *am* and *was*.

> I *am* a member.
> I *was* in the band.

Exercises   Make the subject and verb agree.

A.   Choose the right verb for each sentence. Write the subject and the verb. Beware of phrases that come between the subject and the verb.

> Example: The vase of roses (were, was) lovely.
>
> vase, was

1. These sets of books (are, is) to be returned to the library.
2. You (was, were) late today.
3. The chances for a victory (is, are) good.
4. One of the motors (need, needs) oil.
5. The footprints in this cave (seem, seems) very large.
6. Several houses in our block (is, are) for sale.
7. This group of skiers (give, gives) lessons to beginners.
8. The pond by the willow trees (were, was) deep.
9. I (sing, sings) a solo in the second act.
10. The paper on the walls (was, were) silvery.

B. Follow the directions for Exercise A.

1. The bag of grapes (is, are) beside the nectarines in the refrigerator.
2. This kind of sundae (is, are) best.
3. I (was, were) the only person home.
4. The rungs in the ladder (was, were) loose.
5. Terri and Kate (works, work) at the dairy.
6. (Were, Was) you at the concert, too?
7. The boys in the park (has, have) a soccer ball.
8. This pair of gloves (look, looks) like yours.
9. The cars in the garage (needs, need) new tires.
10. (Has, Have) you any more paint?

Part 3 Verbs with Compound Subjects

You will remember that a compound subject is two or more subjects used with the same verb.

A compound subject that contains the conjunction *and* is plural. Therefore, a plural verb must be used with it.

Examples: Marie and Lynn *are* here.

He and she *work* at the supermarket.

The tomatoes and peppers *were* ripe.

When the parts of a compound subject are joined by *or* or *nor*, the verb agrees with the subject nearer to the verb.

Examples: Lisa or Ted *is* coming.

Neither Beth nor her sisters *are* here.

Three oranges or one grapefruit *makes* enough juice for the punch.

Exercises   Use the right verb with a compound subject.

A.   Choose the correct form of the verb, from the two given in parentheses.

1. The band and the chorus (is, are) performing tonight.
2. The older men and Jack (walk, walks) home along Plymouth Street.
3. Steve and I (is, are) both busy.
4. My mother or my older brothers always (meet, meets) Dad at the airport.
5. (Have, Has) either Carol or Brenda heard that record?
6. Either the Taylors or my parents (are, is) going with us.
7. Neither the mushrooms nor that chicken (is, are) fresh.
8. The cottonwood trees and the elm (is, are) budding out.
9. Ellen and her mother (was, were) here.
10. The president or the vice-president usually (takes, take) charge.

B.   Follow the directions for Exercise A.

1. Neither Jane nor her sister (is, are) at home.
2. Sarah's cat and puppy (don't, doesn't) like each other.
3. (Do, Does) your mobile and that poster always hang there?
4. Either my cousins or Kathy (phone, phones) every week.
5. (Do, Does) either Bob or Larry play soccer?
6. Neither Alicia nor I (believes, believe) in ghosts.
7. My bedspread and rug (match, matches) the curtains.
8. (Does, Do) either Colleen or her sisters practice on Tuesday?

9. Bob and his guitar (is, are) inseparable.
10. The treasurer's figures and the secretary's report (agree, agrees).

Part 4   Agreement in Inverted Sentences

In most sentences, the subject comes before the verb. A person is likely to say, for example, "The glider soars over the hill." For emphasis, however, a writer or speaker might say, "Over the hill soars the glider." The second sentence is called an **inverted sentence.** In each sentence the subject is *glider* and the verb is *soars*.

In inverted sentences, as in ordinary ones, the subject and verb must agree.

Examples: Up above *flutter* a thousand *flags*. (flags flutter)

Through the museum *stream tourists* by the thousands. (tourists stream)

In the yard *is* a *pile* of leaves. (pile is)

Exercises   Use the right verb in inverted sentences.

A.   Number your paper from 1 to 10. Read each sentence. Find the subject. Write the correct form of the verb for each sentence.

1. To each of you (go, goes) the speaker's thanks.
2. Down the stretch (thunder, thunders) the horses.
3. On and on (go, goes) the story.
4. After all that baking (come, comes) the best part.
5. Out of the birdbath (jump, jumps) one goggle-eyed frog.
6. After the Marshfield band (comes, come) the 4-H float.

580

7. Round and round (go, goes) the Ferris wheel.
8. Beside the bench (is, are) the toolbox.
9. With each of the games (go, goes) an instruction booklet.
10. Under the street (rumble, rumbles) the subway.

B. Follow the directions for Exercise A.

1. Between the cushions (was, were) some pennies and a key.
2. Around the bend (come, comes) two buses.
3. Over the fire (hang, hangs) an old iron pot.
4. On either side of Trisha (sit, sits) her brothers.
5. At the end of the two-by-fours (flap, flaps) a red flag.
6. After the chapter on oceans (come, comes) one on mountains.
7. Beside their house (flow, flows) the Wabash River.
8. Over the chimney (curls, curl) the smoke.
9. High above the peaks (soar, soars) two eagles.
10. There on the windowsill (lie, lies) the stopwatch.

Part 5   Verbs with *There*

The word *there* often comes where you expect the subject to be. As you will remember, *there* is often used simply to get a sentence started. When *there* begins a sentence, look for the subject farther on in the sentence.

> Examples: There is a book on the table.
>   (*Book* is the subject; *is* is the verb.)
>
>   There are no questions.
>   (*Questions* is the subject; *are* is the verb.)

In the first example, notice that the correct verb is *is*, because the subject, *book*, is singular. In the second example, *are* must be used because the subject, *questions*, is plural.

When *there* is used at the beginning of a sentence, be careful to make the verb of the sentence agree in number with the actual subject of the sentence.

Exercises   Use the correct verb with *there*.

A.   Read each sentence. Choose the correct form of the verb. Write the subject and verb for each sentence.

> Example: There (is, are) some new notices on the
> bulletin board.
>
> subject: notices
> verb: are

1. There (is, are) no reason for that.
2. Often there (is, are) people on the pier.
3. There (is, are) someone looking for you.
4. (Are, Is) there any toothpicks in the box?
5. (Was, Were) there no ushers?
6. There (is, are) a second-hand, three-speed bike for sale.
7. (Were, Was) there two windows in the stage set?
8. There (weren't, wasn't) many fans in the stadium.
9. (Is, Are) there any oranges?
10. Sometimes there (is, are) taxis waiting here.

B.   Follow the directions for Exercise A.

1. There (is, are) just two pages left in my notebook.
2. There (was, were) several witnesses to the accident.
3. (Is, Are) there four rows of seats in the balcony?
4. (Is, Are) there any strawberry jam left?
5. There (were, was) extra hangers in the closet.
6. (Are, Is) there a second for the motion?
7. (Was, Were) there a cap on the oil can?

8. (Weren't, Wasn't) there pyramids before the Egyptians?
9. There (wasn't, weren't) another marina on the lake.
10. There (is, are) a chance of rain.

Part 6 Indefinite Pronouns

Making subjects and verbs agree may be more difficult if the subject is an indefinite pronoun. You will remember that some indefinite pronouns are singular, some are plural, and some may be either singular or plural. Study these examples.

The indefinite pronouns in the list below are **singular:**

another	each	everything	one
anybody	either	neither	somebody
anyone	everybody	nobody	someone
anything	everyone	no one	something

Examples: *Each* of the customers *was* given a number.
Everybody has a report to do.
Neither of us *has* a good plan.

The indefinite pronouns below are **plural:**

both   few   many   several

Examples: *Both* of the boys *were* sick.
Several of us *have* vacations soon.

These indefinite pronouns are **singular** if they refer to one thing. They are **plural** if they refer to several things:

all   any   most   none   some

Examples: *All* of the paper *was* yellow.
All of the supplies *were* here.

Most of the work *is* mine.
Most of the books *are* new.

Some of the jewelry *has* diamonds.
Some of the cookies *have* walnuts.

Exercises   Make verbs agree with their subjects.

A.   Choose the verb that agrees with the subject, which is an indefinite pronoun.

1. Somebody (has, have) broken the window on the back porch.
2. Nobody (likes, like) being criticized.
3. All of the prizes (was, were) hidden.
4. Everything (seems, seem) peaceful.
5. Neither of the pictures (is, are) flattering.
6. (Was, Were) any of the food left?
7. One of my favorite programs (begins, begin) at eight o'clock.
8. Both of the boys (has, have) a soccer ball.
9. Most of the sophomores (takes, take) driver's education.
10. Either of the keys (opens, open) the front door.

B.   Follow the directions for Exercise A.

1. Both of her ears (was, were) red.
2. (Does, Do) everyone have a schedule?
3. Some of the clubs (sells, sell) refreshments.
4. Most of the record (sounds, sound) distorted.
5. (Has, Have) any of the exchange students from France or Germany arrived?
6. Many of my friends (wears, wear) braces.
7. Few of the tourists (climbs, climb) to the top of the monument.
8. Each of the club members (was, were) going to bake something for the sale.
9. Everybody (knows, know) the procedure for fire drills.
10. One of their starters (was, were) injured in last night's game.

ADDITIONAL EXERCISES

Making Subjects and Verbs Agree

A. Singular and Plural Forms Number your paper from 1 to 20. Write the subject and verb for each sentence. Tell whether they are singular or plural.

1. The steps were high and narrow.
2. Linda studies Spanish.
3. These vitamins contain no sugar.
4. The saber-toothed tiger is extinct.
5. Rory does the laundry at the laundromat.
6. A boomerang is an Australian weapon.
7. They do exercises every morning.
8. This horn sounds funny.
9. It was my mistake.
10. The picture needs a larger frame.
11. The telephone is in the kitchen.
12. The water is icy.
13. The picnic tables are near the shelter.
14. Miguel has the tickets.
15. Sarah was in a fashion show.
16. Ants live in colonies.
17. Bees have remarkable abilities.
18. Some bakeries sell milk.
19. Donna has a typewriter.
20. Melinda's toes were cold.

B. Agreement of Subjects and Verbs Number your paper from 1 to 10. Choose the correct form of the verb for each sentence.

1. Carly (does, do) a good routine on the balance beam.
2. The cords on the parachute (was, were) twisted.

3. A wreath of pine cones (hangs, hang) on our door.
4. The bouquet of flowers (was, were) from Darcy.
5. The patch of weeds (was, were) wet and tangled.
6. Two of the drains (is, are) clogged.
7. You still (is, are) missing that high note.
8. The coach, together with the players, (plans, plan) the strategy.
9. You (was, were) reading the wrong chapter.
10. All the students, including Judy, (seems, seem) glad.

C. Verbs with Compound Subjects Number your paper from 1 to 10. Choose the correct form of the verb for each sentence.

1. The leaves and the grass (is, are) turning brown.
2. The stars and moon (was, were) shining.
3. Flags and a banner (was, were) waving in the breeze.
4. The parrot and the parakeet (does, do) not talk to each other.
5. The McBrides and she (has, have) had some problems.
6. My mother or my brothers always (meets, meet) me there.
7. Neither Marge nor Stu (remembers, remember) the phone number.
8. Either sharks or dolphins (follows, follow) boats.
9. Popcorn or peanuts (is, are) for sale.
10. Either goggles or a face mask (is, are) required.

D. Agreement in Inverted Sentences Number your paper from 1 to 10. Use the correct form of the verb for each sentence.

1. Up the mountain (winds, wind) a narrow road.
2. Under the stone bridge (is, are) the rod and reel.
3. Around the corner (is, are) three apartment buildings.
4. In the cave (sleeps, sleep) hibernating skunks.

5. Behind the garage (is, are) the children's playhouse.
6. Behind the house (is, are) a spacious patio.
7. In the doorway (hangs, hang) wind chimes.
8. On the windowsill (is, are) a bowl of flowers.
9. At the top of the steeple (is, are) a big clock.
10. Over the dam (pours, pour) the torrents of water.

E. Verbs with *There* Choose the correct verb from the two in parentheses.

1. There (goes, go) the stock cars.
2. On holidays there (is, are) many relatives to visit.
3. (Is, Are) there a thirteenth floor in this building?
4. There (is, are) extra test booklets.
5. There (is, are) no ice cubes left.
6. (Is, Are) there bobcats in these woods?
7. There (is, are) no snakes in Ireland or New Zealand.
8. There (was, were) chicken and ham in the refrigerator.
9. There (was, were) no return address on the envelope.
10. (Was, Were) there complaints about the noise?

F. Verbs with Indefinite Pronouns Number your paper from 1 to 10. Write the correct form of the verb.

1. Someone in the audience (was, were) coughing.
2. Everyone (meets, meet) at the bus stop after school.
3. (Does, Do) anybody play the banjo?
4. (Has, Have) all of your friends seen the circus?
5. Another of my favorite television shows (has, have) been canceled.
6. Most of the records (is, are) on sale.
7. All of the snow (has, have) melted.
8. Several of the rescue workers (was, were) injured.
9. Either of those times (is, are) convenient.
10. (Do, Does) each of the pockets have a hole in it?

MIXED REVIEW

Making Subjects and Verbs Agree

A. Making subjects and verbs agree For each sentence, write the verb that agrees with the subject.

1. The hamsters in that cage (is, are) hungry.
2. The students at our school (study, studies) French.
3. (Do, Does) Amy live near you?
4. Joan (keep, keeps) her diary in her room.
5. Neither Brendan nor James (want, wants) to play.
6. Elephants (live, lives) longer than many animals.
7. Parts of London (was, were) rebuilt after the war.
8. One of my sisters (attend, attends) Wright College.
9. Only two people (fit, fits) in this canoe.
10. I (wake, wakes) up every morning at 6:30.

B. Using verbs correctly Six of the following sentences contain errors in subject-verb agreement. If a sentence contains an error, rewrite it correctly. If a sentence is already correct, write *Correct*.

1. The team members respect Coach Myers.
2. Dozens of apples remains unpicked.
3. There is a good reason for his error.
4. Ten rolls of film was needed to photograph the wedding.
5. Paperback books are less expensive than hardcover books.
6. Orange, purple, and green is secondary colors.
7. Most of my friends babysits on weekends.
8. With every ten-dollar purchase come a coupon.
9. On the shores of Lake Michigan stands Chicago.
10. There is several good comedians in the show.

USING GRAMMAR IN WRITING
Making Subjects and Verbs Agree

A. Do you have an opinion about how some part of the government should be run? There is probably at least one thing you wish the President or Congress would change. Write a letter to the President or your state representative. Tell him or her what you think needs improvement, and why. Suggest how the situation could be changed for the better. Begin at least one sentence with *There*. Also use at least four of the following indefinite pronouns in your letter. Be sure all verbs agree with their subjects.

anyone   each   everybody   nobody   somebody
few   many   several   all   most   none   some

B. This letter appeared in an Alison's Advice column:

Dear Alison,

My sister and I share a room. One of our biggest problems is that I am extremely neat and Chris is not. Her clothes cover the floor. Her books and records are thrown all over. Even our dog can't handle the mess. When he sees it, he whimpers and runs away.

I discuss this problem with Chris daily. She says she can't change. Our parents want us to solve this without their interference. What do you suggest?

Desperately,
Kara

Write a reply from Alison. Use the following as sentence subjects in the reply. Make sure the verbs you use agree with the subjects.

you	Chris	her belongings
you and your sister	your parents	you or Chris
either of you	the dog	every member of the family

CUMULATIVE REVIEW
Usage

A. Choosing the correct word Write the correct word from the two given in parentheses.

1. Surgeons wear (this, these) kinds of gloves.
2. Mrs. Casselli plays chess (good, well).
3. The kitten licked (its, it's) paws.
4. (May, Can) we (sit, set) in the front row?
5. Have you seen (them, those) new video games?
6. (Its, It's) my bicycle (laying, lying) on the front lawn.
7. This bread smells (fresh, freshly).
8. You should (let, leave) Jim (teach, learn) you guitar.
9. Our school colors look (good, well) together.
10. Clare hasn't (never, ever) seen (them, those) snap-shots.
11. (Lie, Lay) the packages under the Christmas tree.
12. The dog doesn't have (any, no) water in (its, it's) bowl.
13. Larry feels (bad, badly) about losing (them, those) papers.
14. (Let, Leave) Ida (rise, raise) the issue in Student Council.
15. You look (good, well) in (that, those) kind of sweater.
16. One of the bushes (were, was) in full bloom.
17. There (is, are) some tickets for the operetta for Mother and (I, me).
18. Everybody from the nearby high schools (was, were) there that day.

19. Neither the Halloween witches nor the ghost (look, looks) very realistic.
20. Behind the oak tree (run, runs) two small streams.

B. Using words correctly Twenty words are underlined in the following paragraph. Ten of the underlined words contain errors in the use of verbs, nouns, pronouns, adverbs, and adjectives. Ten of the words are correct. Proofread the paragraph. Rewrite it, correcting the errors.

Zack looked happily at the calendar and realized that it was the day he was going to the circus with his dad. When they arrived, Zack asked quick, "Can I have some of them peanuts?" The circus parade started the show. Zack thought the chain of elephants wouldn't never end. Finally the show begin. It were not possible to watch everything going on in all three ring at one time. Zack kept looking from the farther ring to the middle ring to the nearest ring. Zack's favorite act was the tigers. When they performed, each of the tigers had their own stand to sit on. "The tigers really move graceful," said Zack, "but there's no way you'd ever get me in the cage with those cats!"

Using Compound Sentences

You use sentences to communicate information, ideas, and feelings. You know that there are many differences among the sentences you use. In this section, you will learn about two kinds of sentences. The kinds of sentences you will study are called simple sentences and compound sentences.

Part 1 Review of the Sentence

Throughout this book you have been studying sentences. You know that a sentence has two basic parts, the **subject** and the **predicate.**

Subject	Predicate
Nancy	sang.
Kevin	shouted.
Winter	arrived.
Parrots	talk.
Actors	spoke.
The actors	spoke their lines.
The actors on the stage	spoke their lines with emotion.

The subject of a sentence names the person or thing that the sentence talks about. The predicate tells what the subject is, what the subject did, or what happened.

The **simple predicate** is the verb. The **simple subject** is also called the subject of the verb.

In the subject of a sentence, you will find the simple subject and words that modify it. In the predicate of the sentence, you will find verbs, objects, predicate words, and their modifiers.

Compound Parts in a Sentence

You also know that all of the parts of a sentence may be **compound.** That is, they may themselves have more than one part.

Compound Subject:	The *coach* and the *team* discussed strategy.
Compound Verb:	The girls *talked* and *laughed.*
Compound Object:	The store accepts *cash* or *credit.*
Compound Predicate Word:	The tacos were *hot* and *tasty.*

Definition of the Sentence

You can see that each of these sentences expresses one main idea. These sentences, like all of those you have been studying, are called **simple** sentences.

Now you are ready for a definition of the simple sentence:

A simple sentence is a sentence that contains only one subject and one predicate. The subject and the predicate, or any part of the subject or predicate, may be compound.

Exercises   Review simple sentences.

A. Find the subjects and verbs in each of the following simple sentences.

1. Sid brushed and groomed the horse.
2. My favorite place is a riverbank in the woods.
3. In our town, nothing ever happens.
4. Rain battered the windows.
5. Did Evan pass the test?
6. My family enjoys practical jokes.
7. The bullfighter shook the cape and waited for the bull to charge.
8. Katie rode her bike to the store.
9. In 1861 the Civil War began.
10. Several miners were trapped by a fall.

B. Follow the directions for Exercise A.

1. The club outing was a dinner and a hayride.
2. Someday humans will land on Mars.
3. Why do people explore caves?
4. The train of wagons headed west.
5. Ruth painted the walls and ceiling.
6. Each lighthouse flashes a different signal.

7. Geronimo was a leader and warrior.
8. Vegetables fill the basket.
9. Ray Bradbury is a science fiction writer.
10. The American cowboy is a folk hero.

Part 2 What Is a Compound Sentence?

Sometimes two sentences are so closely related in thought that you join them together. Then you have a different kind of sentence. You have a sentence that has more than one subject and more than one predicate. This is called a **compound sentence.**

A compound sentence consists of two or more simple sentences joined together.

The parts of a compound sentence may be joined by a coordinating conjunction or by a semicolon (;). Study the following examples.

> My uncle gave me a book, **and** I read it from cover to cover.
> We need scientists, **but** we need laboratory workers even
>   more.
> You can take the course now, **or** you can wait until next year.
> Mother threw the coat away; it was worn out.

All of the main parts of the compound sentences above could be written as separate sentences without conjunctions.

> My uncle gave me a book. I read it from cover to cover.
> We need scientists. We need laboratory workers even more.
> You can take the course now. You can wait until next year.
> Mother threw the coat away. It was worn out.

Why not, then, write only simple sentences? Why bother with compound sentences? You will see the answer as soon as you read this passage:

I earned four dollars last weekend. I decided to buy a Mother's Day present with it. My mother doesn't like candy. She does like flowers. My brother drove me into town. I went to the florist's shop. All the nice flowers cost too much. Finally, I decided to buy a box of candy for the whole family.

A long series of short sentences is monotonous and choppy. Joined into compound sentences, they sound much better.

I earned four dollars last weekend, *and* I decided to buy a Mother's Day present with it. My mother doesn't like candy, *but* she does like flowers. My brother drove me into town. I went to the florist's shop, *but* all the nice flowers cost too much. Finally, I decided to buy a box of candy for the whole family.

Diagraming Compound Sentences

It is not difficult to diagram compound sentences if you can already diagram simple sentences. A compound sentence is two or more simple sentences joined together. Therefore, you draw the diagram for the first half of the sentence, draw a dotted-line "step" for the conjunction, and then draw the diagram for the second half.

Example: Elaine ran swiftly, but she couldn't catch the other girls.

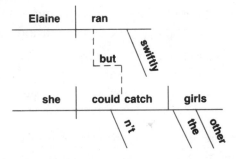

Exercises **Analyze compound sentences.**

A. Number your paper from 1 to 10. Label three columns *Subject/Verb, Conjunction,* and *Subject/Verb*. For each sentence, fill in the columns.

Example: Greg went to the library, but I stayed home.

Subject/Verb	Conjunction	Subject/Verb
Greg/went	but	I/stayed

1. The clouds are low, but it still isn't raining.
2. He's buying radish seeds, but I'm getting green beans.
3. Debby shut the curtain, and the crew changed the props.
4. Cheryl plays checkers, but she prefers chess.
5. The commercial came on, and we headed for the kitchen.
6. The bluejay called, and three other jays answered.
7. Five cars passed us, but we took our time.
8. Either I broke my watch, or it needs a new battery.
9. Tracy mowed the front lawn, and Jim weeded the garden.
10. Wendy washed the car, and Kim cleaned the garage.

B. Follow the directions for Exercise A.

1. The stars were out, but the southern sky was cloudy.
2. Scott flew to Miami, but we took the train.
3. He painted the wall yellow, and his brother liked it.
4. Kate arranged the meeting, but Sue organized it.
5. Mom and I played records, and Dad read the newspaper.
6. Bill painted the back porch, and he sanded the front steps.
7. The dog barked, but the cat just arched its back.

8. The program was on at eight, but we weren't home.
9. The paintings were mostly oils, but there were several watercolors.
10. The nozzle came off, and Terry got all wet.

Compound Predicate or Compound Sentence?

You should know the difference between a compound sentence and a simple sentence with a compound predicate. Read these sentences:

> s.　　　v.　　　　　　　　　　v.
> The girls *painted the posters* and *tacked them to the bulletin boards.*
> (This is a simple sentence. The conjunction *and* joins two parts of a compound predicate.)

> s.　　　v.　　　　　　　　　　　s.　　　v.
> *The girls painted the posters,* and *the boys tacked them to the bulletin boards.*
> (Here are two simple sentences, each with a subject and verb. They are joined by the conjunction *and* into a compound sentence.)

Exercises **Compound predicate or compound sentence?**

A. Number your paper from 1 to 10. Decide whether the following sentences are compound sentences or simple sentences with compound predicates. Write *Compound Sentence* or *Compound Predicate*.

1. They sat down and waited for the train.
2. We enjoyed the show, but it was too long.
3. Julia and Jerry cleaned the garage and went home at eight o'clock.
4. It is early, but we'd better leave anyway.
5. I enjoy movies but don't go often.
6. We started early for the game but got there late.

7. Jan likes dramatics, and she enjoys singing, too.
8. The llama looked very proud and kept his long neck stiff.
9. Larry rang the doorbell twice, but no one came to the door.
10. In no time the elephant reached out for the hay and stuffed it into his mouth.

B. Follow the directions for Exercise A.

1. The tank was empty, and we were far from a gas station.
2. Laura closed the window and locked it.
3. We rowed out to the middle of the lake and fished until noon.
4. We called twice, but there was no answer.
5. The whistle blew suddenly, and everyone in the room was quiet.
6. Our dog barks furiously at strangers, but he never bites.
7. Our bus was late, and we missed our flight.
8. Dave opened his wallet and took out his money.
9. Our wrestling team won the district meet, and we were second in the regionals.
10. Kristie and I went to the concert, but we missed the first group's performance.

Punctuating Compound Sentences

Since compound sentences are made up of two or more simple sentences, they may be long. To help the reader keep the thoughts in order, put a **comma** before the coordinating conjunction in a compound sentence.

> Patty did a routine on the parallel bars **,and**
> Liz and Amy performed on the trampoline.

Sometimes the parts of a compound sentence are joined by a **semicolon (;)** instead of by a conjunction and a comma.

> Patty did a routine on the parallel bars;
> Liz and Amy performed on the trampoline.

The only compound construction you have studied that requires a comma is the compound sentence. You do not need a comma to separate two subjects, two predicates, or two of any of the other compound constructions you have studied. Look at these examples.

> s.   s.
> The students from the seventh grade and those from the
> v.
> eighth formed a baseball team.

> s.   v.   v.
> We walked into the office and talked with the manager.

Finally, the comma is not necessary in a very short compound sentence, unless it is joined by *but*.

> We skated and we skied.
> You can play or you can watch.
> The movie was short, but it was fascinating.

Exercises   Punctuate compound constructions.

A.   In the following sentences, commas have been omitted from all the compound constructions. If a sentence is correct, write *Correct*. If it needs a comma, write the two words between which the comma belongs, and put in the comma.

> Example: The class was preparing a program and the
>   class sponsors were helping with it.
>
>   program, and

1. They took pictures of the activity groups and put them on display.

2. The Hiking Club has taken several training walks lately and it is planning a walkathon for next month.
3. We could hear the rumbling of thunder and see flashes of lightning across the lake.
4. Ms. Hart and the members of the camera club will be putting on an exhibit of indoor photography.
5. The program was interesting but we couldn't hear some of the speakers.
6. The walls were concrete and the windows were narrow.
7. The old bathtub had legs on it and its feet were imitation lion's paws.
8. The old pie safe had tin ends on it and Carrie was fascinated by the interesting designs cut through the tin.
9. I like all sports but I really enjoy baseball.
10. Dennis wears hip boots and fishes right in the stream.

B. Follow the directions for Exercise A.

1. We went to the drugstore for our photos but the film hadn't come back yet.
2. Carlos tuned his guitar but it still sounded flat.
3. A chain saw can be dangerous and can cause accidents.
4. A lion is a huge cat but a bobcat is rather small.
5. An electric typewriter is very sensitive and types at the slightest touch.
6. They folded the raft and Russ stowed it in the trunk.
7. Steve was the villain in the play and he wore a long brown cape.
8. The lawyer approached the bench and spoke with the judge.
9. We repaired our bikes and rode to the lake.
10. Our cat poked a hole in the screen door and mosquitoes flew in.

Combining Related Thoughts

You have learned that the parts of a compound sentence are related grammatically. That means they are simple sentences, each with a subject and a predicate. The parts of a compound sentence must also be related in thought.

Some pairs of sentences make good compound sentences, and some do not.

> It looked like rain. We went anyhow.
> > (Will these two simple sentences make a good compound sentence? Yes, because they are closely related in thought. Use *but* to join them.)
>
> I like horseback riding. Deep-sea fish are often big.
> > (The ideas are not related. These two sentences should not be joined into a compound sentence.)
>
> Pete flew his kite. The rain got the car wet.
> > (The ideas are not related. These two sentences should not be joined into a compound sentence.)
>
> Give me your boat. I'll give you my ski poles.
> > (These two may be joined into a compound sentence because they are related in thought. Use *and* to join them.)

Exercises   Make compound sentences.

A. Rewrite the following sentences as compound sentences. Pick the best coordinating conjunction for each.

1. Marilyn and Phillip were going to the carnival. The thunderstorm changed their plans.
2. Charlene was talking to Joey. Joey wasn't paying any attention.
3. The fan belt on the old Chevy was worn out. There was nothing wrong with the engine.
4. The car wash is finally open. Now the line is too long.
5. The wood in that pile is hickory. This pile is maple.

6. Builders use those concrete blocks for walls. My older brother uses them with boards for bookcases.
7. The swimming pool is crowded. The water is cold.
8. She put the test booklet on the desk. The students picked them up.
9. Ann went horseback riding every weekend. She rode in the annual horse show every summer.
10. Dad has gone to PTA. Mom is going to the League of Women Voters.

B. Writing Find the six pairs of sentences that are related in thought. Write them as compound sentences. Use a good coordinating conjunction. Remember to use commas correctly.

1. Elizabeth has the mumps. She is not very sick.
2. Most trees lose their leaves. Evergreens live up to their name.
3. Todd and Doug were the winners. It started to snow after the match.
4. Have a good time in New York. See all you can.
5. You can make it this way. You can try another way.
6. The potatoes were raw. Some of the meat was burned.
7. Arizona is a beautiful state. Rhode Island is on the east coast.
8. Lori and Jovita walked to the basketball game. Lori's mother picked them up when it was over.
9. The feature of the game was the raising of the flag. Our cheerleader sprained his ankle.
10. Cross-country skiing is a popular winter sport. Many Midwestern states provide excellent skiing trails.

ADDITIONAL EXERCISES

Using Compound Sentences

Compound Sentences Copy each sentence. Decide whether it is a compound sentence or a simple sentence with a compound predicate. Write *Compound Sentence* or *Compound Predicate* after each sentence. Add a comma in the right place for each compound sentence.

1. The telephone rang and Tara answered it.
2. Diana built a table but most of the class made lamps.
3. Jason listens to the radio but he doesn't read a paper.
4. The skater held one arm forward but kept the other back.
5. They live in town during winter but move to the shore during the summertime.
6. Shawn looked around the store but bought nothing.
7. The end reached for the pass but he missed it.
8. John either types his homework or he prints it neatly.
9. The school library didn't have the book but the public library did.
10. The diver saw an eel but she didn't see the octopus.
11. Everybody was clapping and dancing in the aisles.
12. Mom chose the pattern but I picked out the material.
13. He went home and sulked for a few hours.
14. I called Kevin but his phone was busy.
15. The portrait is beautiful but doesn't resemble her.
16. Julie makes up tongue-twisters and tries them on us.
17. Choctaw Indians used two sticks for lacrosse but some other tribes used one.
18. Food was scarce and there were long lines at stores.
19. The rabbit plucks her fur and lines the nest with it.
20. We brushed the snow off the car and scraped the ice from the windows.

MIXED REVIEW

Using Compound Sentences

A. Identifying simple and compound sentences Copy the following sentences. If a sentence is simple, write *S*. If a sentence is compound, write *C*. Underline all subjects once and all verbs twice. Add any necessary commas to compound sentences.

1. The boys sold hot dogs and hamburgers at the picnic.
2. Yvette and Cheryl teach arts and crafts on Saturdays.
3. Birds came to the feeder but none were cardinals.
4. Rita washed and dried her hair before the party.
5. The students write and edit our school newspaper.
6. Mr. Healy invented the device and he sold it.
7. Jorge took the exam and passed it.
8. We left the house on time but the snow delayed us.
9. The night air was damp and chilly.
10. Dad and I repaired the shutters and we painted them.

B. Combining sentences Combine the following simple sentences into compound sentences. Punctuate them.

1. We can wait for Bob's call. We can call him ourselves.
2. Camping is a fun vacation. It's inexpensive.
3. Ellen wants those boots. She can't afford them.
4. Jack chopped the wood. We stacked it on the porch.
5. Harold practiced the concerto. He made several mistakes.
6. Jodie wants to play by the rules. She won't play.
7. Dr. Hines examined my throat. It was not infected.
8. The senator campaigned vigorously. She won the election.
9. Dan can accept this. He can wait for a better offer.
10. Rick wound the old watch. It worked.

USING GRAMMAR IN WRITING
Using Compound Sentences

A. Your town officials are discussing the possibility of building an indoor ice rink. You and your friends are stopped by a reporter and asked for your opinions on this issue. Complete the five replies by making them compound sentences.

1. (Use *and*) It would encourage more people to skate
2. (Use *or*) We should improve our outdoor rinks
3. (Use *but*) It would increase taxes
4. (Use *and*) An indoor rink would attract skaters from other towns
5. (Use *but*) Ice skating is really an outdoor sport

B. Your best friend has decided to run for a class office. He or she has asked you to help write campaign slogans. These slogans will be put on posters. Write five campaign slogans for your friend. Your slogans may rhyme, and they may be funny or serious. Each one should be a compound sentence. Use the conjunction *or* in at least one slogan. Use *but* in at least one.

C. Old mail order catalogues contained many amusing ads for strange medicines and gadgets. These ads often made outrageous claims about the products. Help make the following ads more truthful by changing each claim into a compound sentence. Use the conjunctions *and, but,* and *or*.

> Example: Clark's Cleaning Compound removes any stain . . .
> *and* takes the material with it.

1. Dr. Doolittle's Elixer cures any sickness
2. The Kitchen Wizard was designed to do fifty tasks
3. Professor Clef's Band-in-One lets you sound like three instruments at once
4. Magic Brush will groom and clean your hair each morning
5. The Excel-Exerciser can change the way you look

Using Complex Sentences

You have studied simple sentences and compound sentences. Another kind of sentence that will help you to express your ideas is the **complex sentence**. In this section, you will learn about complex sentences.

Part 1 What Is a Complex Sentence?

Before you can know what a complex sentence is, you should know what a clause is.

A clause is a group of words that contains a verb and its subject.

From this definition you can see that a simple sentence is a clause. It has both a verb and a subject.

> s. v.
> We heard a loud explosion.

> s.   v.
> The blacksmith forged a horseshoe.

Your study of sentences will be clearer, however, if you think of a clause as a part of a sentence. A clause is a group of words containing a subject and a verb within a sentence.

Do compound sentences contain clauses? Do they contain groups of words that have a subject and a verb? Look at these examples:

> s. v.   s.   v.
> Tall tales are not true, but they are amusing.

> s.   v.   s.   v.
> Don walked into the store, and he asked for a job.

The answer is clear. Compound sentences do contain groups of words that have their own subjects and verbs.

See what happens when you divide the compound sentences above into their main parts.

> Tall tales are not true. They are amusing.

> Don walked into the store. He asked for a job.

Each one of the clauses in the compound sentences can become a sentence by itself.

Phrases and Clauses

Can you tell the difference between a *phrase* and a *clause?* Read these examples.

Phrases: in the river
            with friends

                  s.   **v.**
Clauses: when she was busy

              s.   **v.**
            who planned the party

A clause has a subject and a verb. A phrase does not.

Main Clauses

A clause that can stand as a sentence by itself is a **main clause**. All the clauses in compound sentences are main clauses. They can all stand as simple sentences by themselves. For that reason, they are sometimes called **independent clauses**.

Subordinate Clauses

Now look at clauses of a different kind.

          s.   **v.**
as the clock struck twelve

           s.   **v.**
after the movie was over

Neither group of words above is a complete thought. Each leaves you wondering: "Then what?"

Now, with your finger, cover the first word in each group of words. What happens? Each group of words becomes a complete sentence. You can see, then, that words like *as* and *after* are important in a clause.

When a word like *as* or *after* introduces a clause, it *subordinates* the clause. That is, it makes the clause depend on a main clause to complete its meaning. Words like *as* or *after* are called **subordinating conjunctions**. They introduce **subordinate clauses**.

Subordinate clauses are clauses that cannot stand alone as sentences.

Not every subordinate clause begins with a subordinating conjunction, but many do. The following words are used frequently as subordinating conjunctions.

Words Often Used as Subordinating Conjunctions			
after	because	so that	whatever
although	before	than	when
as	if	though	whenever
as if	in order that	till	where
as long as	provided	unless	wherever
as though	since	until	while

Caution: These words are subordinating words only when they introduce a clause. Some can be used in other ways.

Not all subordinate clauses begin with subordinating conjunctions. The following words can also introduce subordinate clauses:

that	who, whom, whose	which
what	whoever, whomever	how

Exercise   Make subordinate clauses.

Writing   Use a variety of subordinating words to make subordinate clauses out of these sentences.

1. My shoes are tight.
2. The bus pulled away.
3. The Ferris wheel stopped.
4. The cookies are done.
5. There is no answer.
6. The battery works.
7. Some insects bite.
8. We ate the cake.
9. The buzzer sounded.
10. It snowed last night.

Definition of the Complex Sentence

Now that you know about main clauses and subordinate clauses, you are ready to learn what a complex sentence is.

A complex sentence is a sentence that contains one main clause and one or more subordinate clauses.

Main Clause	Subordinate Clause
We left	before you came.
We'll go to the carnival	unless it rains tonight.
We were on the lake	when the storm began.

Exercises   Recognize subordinate clauses.

A. Find the subordinate clause in each sentence. Copy it. Underline the subject once and the verb twice.

1. The crowd cheered after the game ended.
2. Carlos wears a strange hat when he fishes.
3. People dream while they sleep.
4. Although she was tired, the mountaineer continued.
5. I have days when nothing goes right.
6. The diver who came ashore had seen a shark.
7. The trout is a fish that lives in fresh water.
8. The balloon rose when we filled it with helium.
9. David was scared, although he pretended not to be.
10. Jane pulled the parachute cord as she jumped.

B. Follow the directions for Exercise A.

1. The water is shallow here because the tide is out.
2. Call a plumber if the pipes leak.
3. Planes will land if the fog clears.
4. The audience hissed when the villain appeared.
5. Carolyn waved as the ship pulled out.

6. Aretha Franklin brings music to life when she sings.
7. We grilled the red snapper that Dave caught early this morning.
8. Bob left for basketball practice when it was four o'clock.
9. Mimes do not talk while they act.
10. Morse code, which was developed in 1840, was once used for sending telegrams.

Part 2 Adverb Clauses

You know that every complex sentence contains a subordinate clause. There are three kinds of subordinate clauses. The first kind you will study is the adverb clause.

An **adverb** is a word that modifies a verb, an adjective, or another adverb.

Adverb: A fire started *suddenly*.

An **adverb phrase** is a prepositional phrase used as an adverb. Adverb phrases usually modify verbs.

Adverb phrase: A fire started *in the forest*.

An adverb clause is a subordinate clause used as an adverb.

When an adverb clause begins a sentence, use a comma to separate the clause from the rest of the sentence.

Adverb clause: A fire started *when lightning struck*.

When lightning struck, a fire started.

Adverbs and adverb phrases or clauses tell *when, where, how,* or *to what extent* about the word they modify.

Remember that a *clause* contains a subject and a verb. A *phrase* has neither a subject nor a verb.

Exercises   Recognize adverb clauses.

A.   Copy the adverb clause from each sentence. Underline its subject once and its verb twice. Circle the subordinating conjunction.

> Example: Although the lights were on, no one was home.
>
> (Although) the lights were on

1. His nickname is Rocket because he moves fast.
2. Our dog barks if it sees strangers.
3. If I could move, I'd live in Australia.
4. Water looks blue since it reflects the sky.
5. I follow rules if they are necessary.
6. We awoke when the tent collapsed.
7. Dana shopped while Cathy waited.
8. When Liz can't sleep, she reads.
9. While everyone slept, snowplows cleared the main streets.
10. Ships send signals when they need help.

B.   Follow the directions for Exercise A.

1. Travelers were trapped when the blizzard hit without warning.
2. Although Tim hits well, his fielding is weak.
3. The door swung open when we knocked.
4. A siren screamed as the ambulance raced down the street.
5. Use candles if the electricity goes off.
6. We stopped where the road forked.
7. After the battle was lost, the army retreated through the forest.
8. Maureen tripped as she reached for the ball.
9. We sang carols while we decorated the tree.
10. The rookies were learning while they worked.

613

Part 3 Adjective Clauses

The second kind of subordinate clause is the adjective clause. An **adjective** is a word that modifies a noun or pronoun.

> a *delicious* lunch   the *exciting* book

An **adjective phrase** is a prepositional phrase that modifies a noun or pronoun.

> the message *in the mailbox*   the load *of gravel*

An adjective clause is a subordinate clause used as an adjective to modify a noun or pronoun.

Usually, an adjective clause comes immediately after the word it modifies. Study the examples.

> This drive-in has a computer *that takes food orders.*

> We learned the metric system, *which is used worldwide.*

> Anyone *who is late* will miss the field trip.

Some adjective clauses start with *where* and *when.*

> The cafeteria is the place *where friends meet.*

> September is the month *when school begins.*

Who and *Whom* in Clauses

The words *who, whose,* and *whom* are often used to begin adjective clauses. They tie the clause to the word it modifies in the main clause. When used in this way, *who, whom,* and *whose* are called **relative pronouns.** They relate the clause (called a **relative clause**) to the word it modifies. *That* and *which* may also be relative pronouns.

Relative Pronouns

who   whom   whose   that   which

Relative pronouns have three jobs:

1. They begin an adjective clause.
2. They relate the adjective clause to a word in the main clause.
3. They act as subject, object, predicate pronoun, or the object of a preposition in the adjective clause.

> Curtis is the player *who won the match.*
> (*Who* is the subject of *won.*)
>
> Is Gayle the girl *whom you met?*
> (*Whom* is the direct object of *met.*)
>
> That is the senator *to whom I wrote.*
> (*Whom* is the object of the preposition *to.*)

The subject form is *who*. The object form is *whom*. Which form you use depends upon how the word is used in the clause.

> Eric Heiden is an athlete (who, whom) I admire.
> (An object of the verb *admire* is needed. *Whom* is the object form.)
>
> Eric Heiden is an athlete *whom* I admire.

Exercises   Recognize adjective clauses.

A.   Copy the adjective clause from each sentence. Underline the subject once and the verb twice. Before the clause, write the word it modifies.

> Example: She is the guitarist who will perform with the Atlanta Symphony.
> (guitarist—who will perform with the Atlanta Symphony.)

1. Melissa wears clothes that are very stylish.
2. Someone who draws well will design the stage sets.
3. Nurses are people whom I admire.
4. Jenny is the only one who found a job.
5. The apples that we picked are crisp and juicy.

6. Zappo is a magician who does many amazing tricks.
7. The robber stole everything that was valuable.
8. Skateboarding, which was a fad years ago, is popular again.
9. Here is the newspaper that you wanted.
10. Jimmy Carter, who was the thirty-ninth President of the United States, wrote that book.

B. Follow the directions for Exercise A.

1. The fish that we catch with nets are smelts.
2. The class notes that I took are messy.
3. Mom brought plates that don't break easily.
4. Meryl Streep is an actress who has appeared on the stage, on television, and in movies.
5. One tribe that lives mainly in Oklahoma is the Cherokee.
6. The astronaut who returned from the moon gave a speech.
7. We rode the toboggan slide, which is very steep.
8. Mary Shelley is the author who wrote *Frankenstein*.
9. The doctor whom we consulted made a diagnosis.
10. The Milky Way is a group of stars that includes our sun.

Part 4 Noun Clauses

The third kind of subordinate clause is the noun clause.

You will remember that nouns can be used as subjects, as objects of verbs, as predicate words after linking verbs, and as objects of prepositions.

A noun clause is a clause used as a noun in a sentence. The noun clause can be used in any way that a noun is used. Noun clauses do not modify anything because nouns are not modifiers.

Uses of Noun Clauses

Subject:	*What the club needed* was a new president.
	Whoever guesses the correct number wins a prize.
Direct Object:	The teacher asked *who had read the story*.
	A beekeeper explained *how honey is made*.
Object of Preposition:	Tammy waved at *whomever she knew*. (The clause is the object of the preposition *at*.)
	A guide pointed to *where the exhibit was*. (The clause is the object of the preposition *to*.)
Predicate Noun:	His message was *that he would not be home for dinner*.
	The outcome is *what matters*.

You can see that a great many noun clauses are introduced by *that* and *what*. Some are introduced by *whatever, whoever,* and *whomever*. Other noun clauses are introduced by *who, whose,* and *whom*. Some are introduced by *where, when,* and *how*.

Exercises   Recognize noun clauses.

A.   Copy the noun clauses in these sentences. Underline the subject once and the verb twice. Tell how the clause is used.

Example: What I want is a warm hat.

What <u>I</u> <u><u>want</u></u> (used as subject)

1. No one knows how we won.
2. Merle never discovered who sent the Valentine.
3. Mike claims that horses have feelings.
4. Gene brought cupcakes for whoever wants one.
5. What Judy did was a surprise to everyone.
6. Where we sat was just fine.
7. Do you know where she works?

8. Connie laughs at whatever her baby brother does.

9. The lumberjack showed how he cuts down a tree.

10. I couldn't read what the billboard said.

B. Follow the directions for Exercise A.

1. Whoever wins the race will get a gold medal.
2. We didn't know who was in charge of the ballot box.
3. Whatever you decide is all right with me.
4. Save these coupons for whoever wants them.
5. Whoever finds Kathy's watch will receive a reward.
6. Why they chose me is hard to understand.
7. I was wondering how you did that.
8. Sally doesn't know where the supplies are.
9. Sign the papers for whoever needs them.
10. How you finished so quickly is beyond me.

Part 5   A Review of Subordinate Clauses

There are three kinds of subordinate clauses. They are the adverb clause, the adjective clause, and the noun clause.

You cannot tell the kind of clause from the word that introduces it. You can tell the kind of clause only from the way it is used in the sentence. If the clause is used as a noun, it is a noun clause. If the clause is a modifier, it is either an adverb or an adjective clause.

Exercises   Identify subordinate clauses.

A. Write each subordinate clause from the following sentences. If a clause is used as a noun clause, tell how it is used in the sentence. If a clause is used as an adjective or adverb clause, tell what it modifies.

1. The test, which was about the Civil War, was easy.

2. We went to the circus when it came to town.
3. The bait that worked best was shrimp.
4. Everyone who travels needs a map.
5. No one saw Diane after she left practice.
6. The wolf attacked because it was trapped.
7. The robot will do whatever you ask.
8. Len claims that he knows judo.
9. Amy blushed when she was announced as the winner.
10. What I like best is talking on the phone with friends.

B. Follow the directions for Exercise A.

1. Jeff's sister is the one who plays the guitar.
2. A person who designs buildings is an architect.
3. The champ beat whomever he fought.
4. Whoever returns the stolen jewels will get a reward.
5. The mutt followed Jeff wherever he went.
6. Although she prefers hockey, Grace plays baseball.
7. Many people watch television because they are bored.
8. We could see the lake from where we stood.
9. I don't know what you mean.
10. Radar, which locates distant objects, is used to track spacecraft.

Part 6   More About Sentence Fragments

The sentence fragments that you studied in Section 1 were easy to spot. They were fragments because they lacked a verb or the subject of a verb.

Another kind of sentence fragment is the subordinate clause. A subordinate clause has both a verb and a subject. By itself, however, it is still a fragment because its meaning is not complete. Look at the groups of words below. Which is a complete sentence? Which is a subordinate clause?

> The bell rang
> When the bell rang

A subordinate clause must not be written as a complete sentence. It must always be joined to a main clause.

> Fragment: When the bell rang
> Sentence: When the bell rang, the school emptied.
>
> Fragment: Although candy tastes good
> Sentence: Although candy tastes good, it causes tooth decay.

You can see that it is important to be able to recognize subordinating conjunctions.

Exercises   Recognize sentence fragments.

A.   Write each of the following groups of words. If the group of words is a sentence, write *S* and add the correct punctuation. If the group of words is a fragment, write *F*. Then add words to make each fragment a complete sentence. Punctuate and capitalize where necessary.

1. How the drill on the wall works
2. Smile for your picture
3. The attic holds many treasures
4. Have you seen this movie
5. Because the ending is a surprise
6. That manufactures fireworks
7. Where the trunk was hidden
8. That the doctor prescribed
9. The photos were blurry
10. When the waves hit the rocks

B.   Follow the directions for Exercise A.

1. Today machines make most goods
2. Until the judge rules

3. Because the pitcher balked
4. Where the icicles hung
5. Will the prisoner be released
6. Have a good day
7. In the United States bullfights are banned
8. Although they are popular events in Spain and Mexico
9. As everyone expected
10. The jury made its decision

Part 7   A Review of Sentences

In this section you have learned about three kinds of sentences that you use.

You know that a **simple sentence** contains one subject and one predicate. A simple sentence expresses one main idea. You will remember, however, that parts of the simple sentence may be compound.

              s.   **s.**   **v.**

The basketball team and the hockey team won yesterday.

   s.   **s.**   **v.**   **v.**

Mark and Donna read and discussed the history assignment.

You have learned that a **compound sentence** consists of two simple sentences. These simple sentences are joined by a coordinating conjunction or by a semicolon. A compound sentence expresses two main ideas that are related in thought.

              s.   **v.**   **s.**   **v.**

The basketball team won yesterday; the hockey team lost.

   s.   **v.**   **s.**   **v.**

Mark studied history, **but** Donna studied math.

You have also learned that a **complex sentence** contains one main clause and one or more subordinate clauses. (The subordinate clauses may be used as nouns, as adjectives, or as adverbs.) A complex sentence expresses one main idea and one or more ideas that depend on the main idea.

$$\overset{\text{s.}}{\text{Although the basketball team}} \overset{\text{v.}}{\text{won}} \text{ yesterday,} \overset{\text{s.}}{\text{the hockey team}}$$

Although the basketball team won yesterday, the hockey team

$$\overset{\text{v.}}{\text{lost.}}$$

lost.

$$\overset{\text{s.}}{\text{Tom}} \overset{\text{v.}}{\text{made}} \text{ a salad } \overset{\text{s.}}{\text{while Donna}} \overset{\text{v.}}{\text{grilled the hamburgers.}}$$

Tom made a salad while Donna grilled the hamburgers.

Exercises Recognize the kinds of sentences.

A. Number your paper from 1 to 10. For each sentence, write *Simple, Compound,* or *Complex* to show what kind it is.

1. If I close my eyes, a roller coaster doesn't scare me.
2. Do you know when vacation starts?
3. Have you ever seen a sunrise from a lighthouse?
4. Everyone who campaigns makes promises.
5. This area is perfect for cross-country skiing.
6. Kelly enjoys Monopoly, but she dislikes Scrabble.
7. Julie rode a unicycle in the parade.
8. The wind grew fierce, and several trees fell.
9. Mary washed the car, and Todd repaired his bike.
10. The cast and crew worked hard in rehearsal.

B. Follow the directions for Exercise A.

1. Molly owns and operates a ham radio.
2. Australia has summer when we have winter.
3. The tightrope walker fell, but she landed in a net.
4. We had fun when we were at camp.
5. Will you walk home, or do you have a ride?
6. The hermit loved animals but disliked people.
7. The talent show was scheduled for Friday and Saturday.
8. Our school newspaper has articles about student opinions.
9. A hurricane struck Florida, and then it moved south.
10. Migrant workers move to wherever there is work.

ADDITIONAL EXERCISES

Using Complex Sentences

A. Subordinate Clauses Copy the subordinate clause in each sentence. Underline the subject of the subordinate clause once and the verb twice.

1. Kelly hummed as she raked the leaves.
2. I will get a job when I am sixteen.
3. Whatever the problems are, Rob will do his best.
4. Lena is the one who is eating an apple.
5. When the alarm rings, the firefighters move fast.
6. People who believe in magic are superstitious.
7. That he won is exciting.
8. Since the buzzer had sounded, Chip's shot didn't count.
9. The dog that ran away is mine.
10. I looked more carefully for my contact lens than I had before.

B. Adverb Clauses Copy each adverb clause in the following sentences. Underline the subject of the clause once and the verb twice. Then write the word or words the clause modifies.

1. Because Rhonda was late, she missed lunch.
2. When autumn came, the birds flew south.
3. Since we had time, we saw the movie twice.
4. We could barely keep our balance when we walked on the ice.
5. Wherever Mary went, her dog and cat would follow her.
6. Everyone stood when the judge entered the courtroom.
7. Some people worry when they must give a speech.

8. Laura cried as she peeled the onions.
9. Until everyone is home, Dad cannot sleep.
10. Jack painted the house after we bought a new ladder.

C. Adjective Clauses Copy the adjective clauses in the following sentences. Underline the subject of the clause once and the verb twice. Write the word each clause modifies.

1. This is the school that won the championship.
2. The bicycle that you wanted has been sold.
3. Aaron, who is only five years old, found a dollar bill.
4. Do you know the name of the person who invented the television?
5. The bus that is parked at the corner only goes down State Street.
6. Do you remember the day that you met Emily?
7. Washington was a man who was known for his honesty.
8. Meet me at the shop that has a blue awning.
9. The plane, which was running short of fuel, landed.
10. This is my friend Davis, whom I told you about.

D. Noun Clauses Copy the noun clause in each sentence. Underline the subject of the clause once and the verb twice. Tell whether the clause is used as a subject, direct object, object of a preposition, or predicate noun.

1. How viruses make us sick is a mystery.
2. Vin asked if he could replace the broken window.
3. I wonder where fireflies go during the day.
4. Ms. Nolan does not agree with what you said.
5. Whoever comes in the room next wins the door prize.
6. That is what I would like.
7. Maria said that she had run four miles.
8. Marshall shouted that there was danger ahead.
9. Mom asked where we had been.
10. Whoever washed those windows did a good job.

MIXED REVIEW

Using Complex Sentences

A. Finding subordinate clauses Copy the subordinate clause from each of the following sentences. Underline the subject once and the verb twice.

1. After she practiced, Alice recited her lines smoothly.
2. Karl is the player who scored the winning touchdown.
3. Since we all agreed, we decided to work together.
4. Call me if you need advice.
5. Adam made the error because he didn't follow directions.
6. Aunt Susan will meet us in St. Paul if she can.
7. When we reached the top of the hill, we rested in the shade.
8. Students who lose their ID cards must pay for new ones.
9. If those gloves are too big, try this pair.
10. The hat that she wore attracted attention.

B. Identifying subordinate clauses Copy the subordinate clauses from the following sentences. Label each *Adverb, Adjective,* or *Noun* to show what kind of clause it is.

1. Pam took notes while she listened to the lecture.
2. That he won surprised us all.
3. I brought my boots because it might snow.
4. People who are busy must be well organized.
5. James cheered when he heard the news.
6. My little sister does whatever I do.
7. The fabric that I used is very inexpensive.
8. When Wendy studies, she needs complete quiet.
9. No one knew how the fire started.
10. Is she the woman who interviewed you?

C. Identifying fragments and kinds of sentences

Decide whether the following groups of words are sentences or fragments. Copy any sentences and punctuate them correctly. Then write *Simple, Compound,* or *Complex* to show what kind of sentence each is. If a group is not a sentence, write *Fragment.*

1. Whenever I hear a siren
2. We tried to make applesauce but it didn't taste right
3. No one who saw the movie liked it
4. This suitcase has not been claimed
5. I'd like to see how Brenda cuts hair
6. That we wanted for the display
7. London, Bristol, and Manchester were the main stops on their tour of Great Britain
8. The umpire who made the call admitted his mistake
9. Sandra started the job and Megan finished it
10. I called the doctor and made an appointment

D. Using subordinate clauses

Write a complex sentence for each of the following subordinate clauses.

1. while the snow fell
2. where this highway ends
3. what the symbols represent
4. that the storm is moving closer
5. which I applied for
6. when the band played
7. until the road is repaved
8. before the movie begins
9. whoever finds my ring
10. although the news was good

USING GRAMMAR IN WRITING
Using Complex Sentences

A.   In China, the most respected people are the oldest people. Grandparents have the most honored place in each family. Think of someone you know who is at least sixty years old. Write a paragraph that tells why you respect him or her. You might write about his or her accomplishments. You might mention some good advice this person gave you. Maybe you admire the way this older person treats other people. Include at least three complex sentences. Listed below are some subordinating conjunctions that you can use in those sentences.

although	if	whatever	while
as long as	so that	when	that
because	until	whenever	who, whom, whose
before	unless	wherever	which

B.   You are a famous mystery story writer. Your editor gives you the beginning of a mystery story. Complete the sentence as you wish. Then continue the story. Include at least four complex sentences in the story. Some of the subordinate clauses should be adjective and adverb clauses.

Although the windows of the old house were boarded up, ——————— .

C.   One of the differences between stories written for children and stories written for adults is word choice. Another is sentence length. Think of a famous fable, such as "The Tortoise and the Hare." First write it for children. Then write it for older readers. In your second version, use a more advanced vocabulary. Also use several complex sentences.

CUMULATIVE REVIEW
The Sentence

A. Identifying kinds of sentences Copy the following sentences. Insert the correct punctuation. After each sentence, write *D* for declarative, *INT* for interrogative, *IMP* for imperative, or *E* for exclamatory. Underline each subject once and each verb twice.

1. Plan your route carefully
2. Dr. Watanabe is a dentist
3. Where is the suntan oil
4. What a remarkable athlete he is
5. Brenda planted an herb garden
6. Prepare the outline for your speech tonight
7. Is that stone an emerald
8. Look out for those wasps
9. Waterfowl decoys are used by hunters
10. Turn on the projector, please

B. Understanding agreement in sentences Number your paper from 1 to 15. Write the correct word from the two given in parentheses.

1. There (was, were) forty members in Pep Club last year.
2. He and she (does, do) a skit about news anchor people.
3. The short stories in this book (is, are) all science fiction.
4. Here (is, are) the markers and the name tags.
5. Each of the men carried (his, their) own canoe.
6. You (was, were) the first runner to cross the finish line.
7. Either Bess or her brothers (walk, walks) the dog.
8. He (don't, doesn't) appreciate modern art.

9. Few of the movies (seem, seems) recent.
10. The pasta in those packages (is, are) homemade.
11. One of my friends (play, plays) the oboe in the community orchestra.
12. The grown chimpanzees shared (its, their) bananas with the baby chimps.
13. Where (was, were) the tickets to the play?
14. The piano and your desk (need, needs) polishing.
15. Have the ushers taken (their, its) places yet?

C. Correcting fragments and run-on sentences The following paragraph contains fragments and run-on sentences. Rewrite the paragraph. Use capitalization and punctuation to correct the fragments and run-ons. Do not add or change any words.

> The potato, a vegetable familiar to everybody, originally grew wild in South America. When the Spanish conquered the Incas in Peru in the 16th century. They introduced the potato to Europe. It is an amazing vegetable, it is quite nutritious. An average-sized potato, without rich toppings, contains only about 100 calories. And is 99.9 percent fat-free. One potato provides 50% of the daily adult vitamin C requirement, a potato also provides many of the B vitamins and iron. In addition, potatoes will grow almost anywhere. Except in a jungle. A potato crop. Matures faster than corn, wheat, or rice, the potato is a great bargain!

D. Writing good sentences Rewrite each of the following sentences. Follow the directions in the parentheses.

1. Belinda ordered two posters from the catalog. (Add the prepositional phrase *for her bedroom.*)
2. Mrs. Hopper peeled the apples. She made apple crisp. (Combine these two simple sentences into one with a compound predicate.)

3. Mr. Schwartz raced through the airport. His plane had already left.   (Combine these two simple sentences into a compound sentence using **,but**.)

4. Debby raked the leaves. Fred did, too.   (Combine these two simple sentences into one with a compound subject.)

5. The taxes must be raised. The educational programs will be cut back.   (Combine these two simple sentences into one compound sentence using **,or**.)

6. The Washington Monument is 555 feet, 5⅛ inches tall. It has 898 steps.   (Combine these two simple sentences into one complex sentence using *which*.)

7. Sally has found a summer job already. Kevin and Naomi have not.   (Combine these two simple sentences into one complex sentence using *although*.)

8. Johnny Morris reports on sports for a Chicago television station. He once played professional football.   (Combine these two simple sentences into one complex sentence using *who*.)

9. Peter studied last night.   (Change this NV sentence to one with a NVN pattern.)

10. Coach Jaworski is a patient man.   (Change this N LV N sentence into one with a N LV ADJ pattern.)

Capitalization

The use of capital letters is called **capitalization**. When you use a capital letter at the beginning of a word, you *capitalize* the word.

Capital letters are used to make reading easier. They call attention to the beginnings of sentences and to certain special words.

Proper Nouns and Adjectives

Capitalize proper nouns and proper adjectives.

A **proper noun** is the name of a particular person, place or thing.

    Victoria   Sweden   Congress

A **common noun** is the general name of a person, place, or thing. It is not capitalized.

    woman   nation   government

A **proper adjective** is an adjective formed from a proper noun.

    Victorian   Swedish   Congressional

Names of Persons

Capitalize the names of persons and also the initials or abbreviations that stand for those names.

    Linda S. Adams   William J. Franklin, Jr.
    Linda Susan Adams   William James Franklin, Junior

Capitalize titles used with names of persons and abbreviations standing for those titles.

    Doctor Maria A. Sandquist   Rev. M. R. Eaton
    Dr. John J. DeBender   President Lincoln

The titles Mr., Mrs., Ms., and Miss are always capitalized.

    Mr. Kotter   Miss Brooks   Ms. Gloria Thomas

Do not capitalize a title that is not followed by the name of a person.

    One of our police captains is Daniel Jeffries.
    The president was Mary Gomez.
    My mother is a doctor.

Capitalize titles of people and groups whose rank is very important.

Titles of important people, such as those of the President and Vice-President of the United States, are capitalized even though these titles are used without proper names.

The **V**ice-**P**resident presides over the sessions of the Senate. The **Q**ueen attended the opening of Parliament.

Family Relationships

Capitalize such words as *mother, father, aunt,* and *uncle* when these words are used as names.

Hello, **M**other. Is **D**ad home yet?

These words are not used as names when they are preceded by a possessive or by such words as *a* or *the*.

I talked with my **m**other about it.

The Pronoun I

Capitalize the pronoun I.

Did you get the postcard that **I** sent?

The Supreme Being and Sacred Writings

Capitalize all words referring to God, to the Holy Family, and to religious scriptures.

God	the **B**ible	the **T**orah
the **F**ather	the **G**ospel	the **T**almud
the **L**ord	**A**llah	the **K**oran
Jesus **C**hrist	the **H**oly **S**pirit	the **B**lessed **V**irgin

Exercises   Use capital letters correctly.

A.   Number your paper from 1 to 10. Write the following sentences, changing small letters to capital letters wherever necessary.

1. The president of the united states was there.
2. My mother said, "Ask dad if he brought the camera."
3. Four players in the baseball hall of fame are ernie banks, jackie robinson, sandy koufax, and mickey mantle.
4. Do you know the prince of monaco's last name?
5. We made french onion soup last night.
6. My sister linda is personnel director.
7. My favorite aunt is aunt ginny.
8. She is my father's sister.
9. Moslems study the koran; jews study the torah.
10. Two well-known women in the game of golf are babe didrikson zaharias and patty berg.

B.   Write the following sentences, changing small letters to capital letters wherever necessary. One sentence is correct.

1. Prince charles and queen elizabeth attended the reception.
2. On monday i had an appointment with the dentist.
3. The names on the door were dr. natalie j. sanders and martin able, jr.
4. Christopher columbus sailed under the spanish flag.
5. The coast was explored by portuguese sailors.
6. Edmund p. hillary climbed mt. everest.
7. The queen of england made him a knight.
8. Once he was a british spy.
9. Cheryl was elected president of our club.
10. Last spring, we saw hana mandlikova and chris evert lloyd play in several tennis tournaments.

Geographical Names

In a geographical name, capitalize the first letter of each word except articles and prepositions.

The article *the* appearing before a geographical name is not part of the geographical name. Therefore, it is not capitalized.

Continents:	North America, South America, Asia, Europe
Bodies of water:	the Indian Ocean, Lake Superior, the Jordan River, Cape Cod Bay, the Caspian Sea
Land forms:	the Rockies, the Sinai Peninsula, the Grand Canyon, the Syrian Desert
Political units:	Delaware, the District of Columbia, the British Isles, the Commonwealth of Massachusetts, the West Indies, San Francisco
Public areas:	Gettysburg National Park, Fort Niagara, Mount Rushmore, Statue of Liberty
Roads and highways:	Central Avenue, Route 66, Garden State Parkway, Van Buren Avenue, the Ohio Turnpike, State Street

Directions and Sections

Capitalize names of sections of the country.

Cotton was king in the South.
Cities in the Southwest are flourishing.
The legends of the West are fascinating.

Capitalize proper adjectives derived from names of sections of the country.

an Eastern school   a Western concept   Southern hospitality

Do not capitalize directions of the compass.

They flew east through the storm.
Sue lives on the north side of the street.
The hurricane moved northward.

Do not capitalize adjectives derived from words indicating direction.

a southerly course   an eastern route

Exercises   Use capital letters correctly.

A. Number your paper from 1 to 10. Find the words in the following phrases that should be capitalized. Write the words after the proper number, using the necessary capital letters.

1. near the gulf of mexico
2. represents the seventh congressional district
3. pike's peak near colorado springs
4. the pacific coast beaches
5. one block north of first avenue
6. in the catskill mountains
7. a street in paris, france
8. donner pass over the rockies
9. the transamerica pyramid in san francisco
10. across the great plains of the west

B. Follow the directions for Exercise A.

1. Colonel Powell explored the grand canyon in arizona.
2. The gateway arch in st. louis, missouri, is 630 feet high.
3. In the carolinas we found out about southern hospitality.
4. The southernmost continent is antarctica.
5. We drove from toronto to detroit on the macdonald-cartier highway.

6. We saw buffalo at custer national monument.
7. A toll bridge extends over the straits of mackinac.
8. The arlington memorial bridge extends across the potomac river to the lincoln memorial.
9. Our new neighbors come from southeast asia.
10. Is the united nations building on fifth avenue in new
    york city?

Names of Organizations and Institutions

Capitalize the names of organizations and institutions, including political parties, governmental bodies or agencies, schools, colleges, churches, hospitals, clubs, businesses, and abbreviations of these names.

General Motors Corporation   Stacy Memorial Hospital
Nichols Junior High School   Burns and White, Inc.

Do not capitalize words such as *school, college, church,* and *hospital* when they are not used as names.

the emergency entrance at the hospital
the basketball team at our school

Names of Events, Documents, and Periods of Time

Capitalize the names of historical events, documents, and periods of time.

Industrial Revolution   Bill of Rights
World War II   Middle Ages

Months, Days, and Holidays

Capitalize the names of months, days, and holidays.

February   Wednesday   Labor Day
April   Sunday   New Year's Day

Exercises   Use capital letters correctly.

A.   Copy the following, changing small letters to capitals or capitals to small letters where necessary.

1. the house of representatives
2. a Weekend in june
3. Eisenhower high school
4. the Battle of bunker hill
5. fire prevention Week
6. Industries and Colleges
7. Louisiana state university
8. the month of march
9. veterans' day, november 11
10. the civil war

B.   Write each sentence, using the necessary capital letters.

1. We saw the chicago bears play the new york jets.
2. One of the largest companies is xerox corporation.
3. The emancipation proclamation was written during the civil war.
4. The middletown team will play washington high.
5. In new orleans, mardi gras is celebrated with parades.
6. The first ten amendments to the constitution of the united states are called the bill of rights.
7. The first monday in september is labor day.
8. In our anthology, *Black Roots*, we read selections by maya angelou and anne moody.
9. Our class will visit the museum in april.
10. The period of the 1930's in the united states was known as the great depression.

Languages, Races, Nationalities, Religions

Capitalize the names of languages, races, nationalities, and religions, and also adjectives derived from them.

| Irish linen | German band | French language |
| Italian heritage | Lutheranism | African art |

School Subjects

Do not capitalize the names of school subjects, except course names followed by a number.

Algebra I   History of Civilization II   social studies

Remember that the names of languages are always capitalized.

English   Spanish   Hebrew   German

Ships, Trains, Airplanes, Automobiles

Capitalize the names of ships, trains, airplanes, and automobiles.

U.S.S. Constitution   *City of New Orleans*   *Concorde*
Firebird

Abbreviations

You know that an **abbreviation** is a shortened form of a word. You also know that abbreviations of proper nouns and proper adjectives are capitalized.

Capitalize the abbreviations *B.C.* and *A.D.*

Julius Caesar was born in the year 100 **B.C.**
Christopher Columbus landed on San Salvador in **A.D.** 1492.

You know that *B.C.* and *A.D.* are used to refer to time. *B.C.* is the abbreviation for *before Christ*. *A.D.* stands for Latin words meaning "in the year of the Lord."

Capitalize the abbreviations *A.M.* and *P.M.*

The bus leaves at 8:05 **A.M.** and returns at 5:30 **P.M.**

Exercises   **Use capital letters correctly.**

A.   Number your paper from 1 to 15. Copy each of the following groups of words. Wherever necessary, change small letters to capitals.

1. roman catholic
2. italian food
3. studying history I
4. bought a new ford
5. the spanish language
6. 2:30 p.m.
7. 10:00 a.m.
8. the year 40 b.c.
9. a.d. 300
10. the s.s. *france*
11. math problems
12. french bread
13. printed in english
14. a scottish writer
15. american citizen

B.   Number your paper from 1 to 10. Copy each of the following sentences. Wherever necessary, change small letters to capitals.

1. Although illinois is called the land of lincoln, abraham lincoln was born in kentucky.
2. A roman emperor gave his name to the month of august.
3. This year I am taking world history II, english, math, and art.
4. The sign said that banking hours are from 8:30 a.m. to 5:00 p.m.
5. We rode the *san francisco zephyr* to denver.
6. Every tuesday and thursday the german band plays polkas.
7. My sister can speak spanish, but she cannot write it.
8. We will see the *queen elizabeth II* the first weekend in may.
9. Mother will complete her master's degree at purdue university next august.
10. The datsun is a japanese automobile.

First Words

Sentences

Capitalize the first word of every sentence.

My sister plays basketball. **S**he is the captain of the team.

Poetry

Capitalize the first word in most lines of poetry.

> **A** word is dead
> **W**hen it is said,
>   **S**ome say.
> **I** say it just
> **B**egins to live
>   **T**hat day.
>   —EMILY DICKINSON

Sometimes, especially in modern poetry, the lines of a poem do not begin with capital letters.

Quotations

Capitalize the first word of a direct quotation.

When you use a **quotation,** you use the words of a speaker or writer. If you give the *exact* words of the speaker or writer, you are giving a **direct quotation**. If you change the words of the speaker or writer to your own words, you are giving an **indirect quotation**. Be sure that you can tell the difference between the two kinds.

Here are two examples of direct quotations:

"**C**lose the window, please," Ms. Smith said to Jerry.
Sarah said, "**M**y parents bought a new car."

Here are two examples of an indirect quotation:

> Ms. Smith asked Jerry to close the window.
> Sarah said that her parents had bought a new car.

Notice that the first word of an indirect quotation is not capitalized.

Sometimes a direct quotation is interrupted by explanatory words like *she said*. Here is an example

> "Well," she said, "you may be right."

Notice that the first word of the second part of this direct quotation is not capitalized since it is not the first word of a sentence. When a direct quotation is interrupted in this way, it is called a **divided quotation**.

If the second part of a divided quotation begins a new sentence, capitalize the first word as you would in any sentence.

> "I don't know," he said. "**Y**ou may be right."
> "We met Ellen," said Jane. "**S**he was with her father."

Exercises Use capital letters correctly.

A. Using correct capitalization, write the words that need capital letters.

1. sailing is a favorite sport for visitors to cape cod.
2. uganda, kenya, and chad are nations in africa.
3. thanksgiving is always the fourth thursday in november.
4. a harvest mouse goes scampering by
   with silver claws and a silver eye.
5. the doors open early. no one can enter after 2 p.m.
6. "hi," said bill. "we won. are mom and dad home?"
7. hope is the thing with feathers
   that perches in the soul,
   and sings the tune without the words,
   and never stops at all.

8. "you are late," said b. j. pate.
9. "there's no school tomorrow," said heather. "it's veterans' day."
10. what's that old saying about "a month of sundays"?

B. Follow the directions for Exercise A.

1. what do the shoppers want? they want more parking.
2. barton industries, inc., is constructing a new plant near chicago.
3. the grand canyon is a national park. It is in northwestern arizona.
4. you can see the colorado river from toroweap point.
5. some havasupai indians live at the foot of the gorge.
6. many years ago, mother shipton made rhymes about the future.
7. for every parcel i stoop down to seize,
i lose some other off my arms and knees.
8. call disc o. dan. ask him to play your favorite song.
9. "nurse," said dr. dee, "hold this while i get some alcohol."
10. it was many and many a year ago,
in a kingdom by the sea,
that a maiden there lived whom you may know
by the name of annabel lee;

Letters

Capitalize the first word, words like *Sir* and *Madam,* and the name of the person addressed in the greeting of a letter.

Dear Sir or Madam:	Dear Mrs. Cooper:	Dear Rick and John,
Dear Mr. Herrara:	Dear Ms. Ashley:	Dear Aunt Marge,

In the closing, capitalize the first word only.

Sincerely yours,   Yours very truly,

Outlines

Capitalize the first word of each line of an outline.

    II. Things to be considered
       A. Breed
          1. Kinds of dogs
          2. Uses of dogs
       B. Training

Titles

Capitalize the first word and all important words in chapter titles, titles of magazine articles, titles of short stories, essays, or single poems, and titles of songs or short pieces of music.

Chapter:	Chapter 2, "The First Settlers"
Magazine article:	"Taking Color Pictures"
Short story:	"To Build a Fire"
Essay:	"On the Importance of Friendship"
Poem:	"Richard Cory"
Song:	"The Star-Spangled Banner"

Capitalize the first word and all important words in titles of books, newspapers, magazines, plays, movies, titles of television and radio programs, works of art, and long musical compositions.

When you write titles like these, underline them. (When these titles are printed, they are *italicized*.)

Book:	*I Am the Cheese*
Newspaper:	*Boston Globe*
Magazine:	*Reader's Digest*
Play:	*The Miracle Worker*
Movie:	*Raiders of the Lost Ark*
Televison program:	*Today*
Work of art:	*Rodin's The Thinker*
Long Musical Composition:	*Amahl and the Night Visitors* *[opera]*

The words *a*, *an*, and *the* (called **articles**) are not capitalized unless they come at the beginning of a title. Conjunctions and prepositions (such as *and* and *of*) are not capitalized either, except at the beginning of a title.

Exercises **Use capital letters correctly.**

A. Copy the following, using the correct capital letters.

1. sincerely yours,
2. the poem, "my last duchess"
3. a *reader's digest* article
4. the painting, *blue boy*
5. *rocky*, the award-winning film
6. a *daily news* subscription
7. the magazine article "sailing the skies of summer"
8. the cast of *our town*
9. an early novel, *the deerslayer*
10. dear ms. martin

B. Follow the directions for Exercise A.

1. mother and dad went to see *the wiz* in chicago.
2. they sang "the sounds of silence" for an encore.
3. the *girl at the open half door* is in the Art Institute.
4. our copy of *the detroit free press* ended up on the roof.
5. during christmas vacation, we saw *the nutcracker suite*.
6. read "builders for a golden age" in *american heritage*.
7. dear mrs. gomez:
    your subscription to *national geographic* ends today.
8. "the outcasts of poker flat"
9. mother reads *the wall street journal*.
10. dear sir:
    have you read *the daily times* lately?

ADDITIONAL EXERCISES

Capitalization

A. Capital Letters Copy the following sentences. Change small letters to capital letters wherever necessary.

1. Some of harriet s. adam's pen names were laura lee hope, franklin dixon, and carolyn keene.
2. The atlanta falcons will play the new orleans saints on sunday, december 10.
3. They asked for god's blessing on their work.
4. Should i use an irish accent to read my lines?
5. Did you videotape the wedding of prince charles and princess diana?
6. Our family doctor is dr. lopez.
7. Maybe mr. and mrs. moss have no telephone.
8. On her patrols, sergeant pahls uses a two-way radio.
9. Did father sweeney read from the bible in latin?
10. My father got a letter from the president of the united states.

B. Capital Letters Copy the following sentences, changing small letters to capital letters wherever necessary.

1. The first nation in which women got the right to vote was new zealand.
2. Are the west indies in the caribbean sea?
3. The train crossed the rio grande into mexico.
4. Mr. davis now has an office on wall street.
5. Do people from florida have southern accents?
6. My cousin owns a farm in the midwest.
7. Villagers in uganda built a runway so that a doctor could visit by plane.
8. One seaport city in poland is named gdansk.

9. We drove south through the great smoky mountains.
10. Lake mead is near grand canyon national park.

C. Capital Letters Copy the following sentences, changing small letters to capital letters wherever necessary.

1. Jim is an orderly at community general hospital.
2. The fourth of july is a holiday celebrating the signing of the declaration of independence.
3. On the first monday in september, labor day is observed.
4. Sandra Day O'Connor was appointed to the supreme court on september 25, 1981.
5. When was the period of history known as the dark ages?
6. My mother is a student at savannah state college.
7. At sundown, passover will begin.
8. My uncle is a member of the urban league, a national organization.
9. When did that war become known as world war I?
10. April fool's day began as a celebration of spring.

D. Capital Letters Copy the following sentences, changing small letters to capital letters wherever necessary.

1. Next year I will take woodworking 200 and art 201.
2. Ty's favorite subjects are history and english.
3. The *invincible* is a british battleship.
4. The *cardinal* pulled out of the station at 6:00 p.m.
5. The Wailing Wall is part of a temple built in 515 b.c.
6. Is your jazz dance class at 8:00 a.m. or 8:00 p.m.?
7. A german ship sank the *lusitania*, a british ship, in 1915.
8. By a.d. 500, Ireland had become a christian country.
9. Mecca and Medina are holy places to moslems.
10. An early compact car was the volkswagen.

E. Capital Letters Copy the following sentences. Change small letters to capital letters wherever necessary.

1. a late blizzard struck. the first game was cancelled.
2. "we're lost," lee said. "who has a compass?"
3. "that," said betsy, "is none of your business."
4. dr. sanders said he would be happy to meet with us.
5. who said, "lafayette, we are here"? what did it mean?
6. "watch willy," said the coach. "he dribbles perfectly."
7. Cora asked if she could borrow my mexican necklace.
8. "nobody," said sonya, "is angry with you."
9. pandora promised that she would not open the box.
10. will there really be a morning?
    is there such a thing as day?
    could I see it from the mountains
    if I were as tall as they?

    −EMILY DICKINSON

F. Capital Letters Follow the directions for Exercise E.

1. the chapter in the manual is "know your computer."
2. dear ms. taylor:
    it's time to renew your subscription to *ebony*.
3. dear madam or sir:
    you can have *the herald* delivered to your doorstep.
4. the novel *the hobbit* is by j. r. r. tolkien.
5. there are many choruses to "yankee doodle."
6. the class discussed "the black madonna," a short story.
7. carl's essay was titled, "the end of summer."
8. here are your tickets to *a raisin in the sun*.

    sincerely yours,
    robert c. stone
9. "point of no return" is a short poem by mari evans.
10. III. kinds of religious art
    A. statues
    B. frescoes

MIXED REVIEW

Capitalization

A. Using capitalization correctly Copy the following sentences, changing small letters to capitals where necessary.

1. The dallas cowboys play at the silverdome.
2. The 1984 summer olympics were held in los angeles.
3. My uncle josh toured canada in a chevy van.
4. Turn south on freeport drive.
5. Marge wrote to howard l. byrne, jr., of greenleaf books.
6. We listened as reverend brooks read the gospel.
7. Diana, the princess of wales, is married to prince charles.
8. Sam and i met last summer at camp lincoln.
9. Can dad drive me to the dentist's office on saturday morning?
10. I haven't eaten at burger king since june.

B. Using capitalization correctly in proofreading Proofread the following paragraph. Copy it, using correct capitalization.

My favorite Baseball team resides in a city i've never visited. This may seem strange unless you know that the los angeles dodgers were once a brooklyn team. That's right, the brooklyn dodgers were our family team for generations. a simple move to the west coast couldn't change that tradition. Another california team, the oakland athletics, once hailed from kansas city, missouri. Professional Teams are bought and sold often. New owners can take the Team to another City in the united states. You never know when your loyalty as a Fan will be put to this test.

USING MECHANICS IN WRITING
Capitalization

A. The opening sentences of a news story contain the important facts of the story. The sentences often tell *who, what, where, when, why,* and *how*. Write the opening sentences for a story in each of the following sections of a newspaper. Follow the rules for capitalization.

> front page (include the names of a famous person and a country)
> sports section (include the names of a city and a team)
> food section (include a nationality, such as French)
> business section (include the name of a company and a quote by its president)
> entertainment section (include the name of a movie or play, the names of its stars, and a comment by a critic)

Example: **front page**
> In India this morning,
> Mother Teresa of Calcutta
> learned that she had won
> the Nobel Peace Price.

B. What is your favorite magazine? How would you convince others to buy and read it? Using a copy of the magazine, write a short paragraph that will "sell" your magazine. Tell what types of stories are included. Use titles of articles and authors' names in your paragraph. Quote satisfied readers. Remember to follow the rules for capitalization.

Punctuation

Punctuation is the use of commas, periods, semicolons, and other marks in writing. The marks used are called **punctuation marks.**

Good punctuation will help your readers understand what they read. It will show them where to pause or stop. It will tell them whether they are reading a statement, an exclamation, or a question.

End Marks

The punctuation marks that show where a sentence ends are called **end marks.**

There are three very important end marks: (1) the **period,** (2) the **question mark,** and (3) the **exclamation point.**

The Period

Use a period at the end of a declarative sentence.

A **declarative sentence** is a sentence that makes a statement. It is the kind of sentence you use when you want to tell something.

My sister plays the piano.

A declarative sentence is often shortened to one or two words, for example, in answering a question.

Where are you going to put the ladder?

Over there. (*I am going to put it over there.*)

Use a period at the end of an imperative sentence.

An **imperative sentence** is a sentence that requires or tells someone to do something.

Please open the window.

If the imperative sentence also expresses excitement or emotion, an exclamation point is used after it.

Look out!

Use a period at the end of an indirect question.

An **indirect question** is the part of a statement that tells what someone asked, but that does not give the exact words of the person who asked the question.

Judy asked *whether the movie was worth seeing*.

Now compare the indirect question with a **direct question:**

Judy asked, "Is the movie worth seeing?"

A direct question gives the exact words of the person who asked the question. It is always followed by a question mark, as in the above example.

Use a period after an abbreviation or after an initial.

An **abbreviation** is a shortened form of a word. You should know the correct abbreviations for many words.

in. *(inch or inches)*   Dr. *(Doctor)*

Sept. *(September)*   Tues. *(Tuesday)*

A name is often shortened to its first letter, or **initial.**

O. J. Simpson *(Orenthal James Simpson)*

Susan B. Anthony *(Susan Brownell Anthony)*

Sometimes an abbreviation is made up of two or more parts, each part standing for one or more words. A period is then used after each part.

B.C. *(Before Christ)*   S. Dak. *(South Dakota)*

Periods are omitted in some abbreviations. If you are not sure whether an abbreviation should be written with or without periods, look up the abbreviation in your dictionary.

FM *(frequency modulation)*   UN *(United Nations)*

Use a period after each number or letter that shows a division of an outline or that precedes an item in a list.

(Outline)	(List)
I. Trees	1. meat
A. Shade trees	2. potatoes
1. Elms	3. ice cream

The Question Mark

Use a question mark at the end of an interrogative sentence.

An **interrogative sentence** is a sentence that asks a question.

Has anyone seen my dog?

The above sentence gives the exact words of the person who asked the question. It is called a *direct question*. A question mark is used only with a direct question.

Do not use a question mark with an indirect question. Instead, use a period.

An *indirect question* is the part of a statement that tells what someone asked, without giving the exact words.

Kelly asked *whether anyone had seen her dog.*

The Exclamation Point

Use an exclamation point at the end of an exclamatory sentence.

An **exclamatory sentence** expresses strong feeling, such as excitement or fear.

What a terrific game that was!

An exclamation point is also used at the end of an imperative sentence that expresses excitement or emotion.

Hurry up!

Most imperative sentences, however, should be followed by a period.

Please shut the door.

Use an exclamation point after an interjection or after any other exclamatory expression.

An **interjection** is a word or group of words used to express strong feeling. It is one of the eight parts of speech. Words often used as other parts of speech may become interjections when they express strong feeling.

Oh! How beautiful! Wow! What an exciting movie!

Avoid using the exclamation point too frequently. Use it only when you are sure it is needed.

Exercises Use periods, question marks, and exclamation points correctly.

A. Copy these sentences. Supply the missing punctuation.

1. Help This carton is too heavy for me
2. On the card was printed "Dr Stephanie James, D D S"
3. Mr and Mrs T A Stock, Miss Sarah Temple, and Dr G B Torker spoke at the board meeting
4. How did the cat get into the birdcage
5. Write to J B Lippincott Co, publishers of the book
6. We listened to the news broadcast at 7:30 A M
7. Ms Sue M Horton teaches swimming at the Y M C A
8. Was Mr J E Edwards in Buffalo on June 19, 1985
9. Look out That shelf is falling
10. How peaceful it is here Is it always this way

B. Follow the directions for Exercise A.

1. Please let me see that book Is it yours
2. Pete asked me whether I had seen Dr M J Thomas
3. Wow That was an exciting race
4. Did Ms Bryant call Dr Loras about the appointment
5. How dare you say that
6. She lives at 1720 Pennsylvania Avenue, Washington D C

7. My plane left Boston at 11:45 A M and arrived in St. Louis at 2:15 P M
8. Do Mr and Mrs F L Schaefer live here
9. This map of Fresno, California, is drawn on a scale of 1 in to ¼ mi, isn't it
10. Sue asked Mr Cassini if he knew Ms Williamson or Mrs Marshall

The Comma

When you speak, you do not say everything at the same speed. You pause to show that there is a break in your thought. You put words into groups, pausing at the end of the group. You use the pause to help your listeners understand which words go together.

In writing, the comma is used to show which words go together. Commas also show your readers where to pause. If they read right on without pausing, they will be confused.

The Comma To Avoid Confusion

Some sentences can be very confusing if commas are not used in them. Read these two examples of such sentences:

In the morning mail is delivered.

After eating my dad takes a nap.

Now notice how much clearer a sentence is when a comma is used. Read the sentences again.

In the morning, mail is delivered.

After eating, my dad takes a nap.

Use a comma whenever the reader might otherwise be confused.

Exercise   Use a comma to avoid confusion.

Read each of the following sentences. Then write each
sentence, using commas to make the meaning clear.

1. When we approached the house was dark.
2. Before coloring her little sister put away all her toys.
3. After they had finished the table was cleared.
4. Sue ordered hot chocolate and Jo ordered ice cream.
5. By the time she woke up the neighborhood was very
    quiet.
6. Circling the airplane approached the field.
7. When we entered the room was empty.
8. When the climbers reached the top coats were neces-
    sary.
9. No matter what I do not want another milkshake.
10. While painting my sister accidentally broke a window.

Commas in a Series

Use a comma after every item in a series except the last.

In writing, a series consists of three or more items of the
same kind. These items may be nouns, verbs, modifiers,
phrases, or other parts of the sentence.

A comma is placed after every item in a series except the
last. Read these examples:

> We packed, ate, and left for home.
> (The three items in this series are verbs.)

> Tom, Mary, Eve, and Ray won prizes.
> (The four items in this series are nouns.)

> The arms of the machine moved up and down, in and out,
> and back and forth.
> (The items in this series are the groups of adverbs *up and
> down, in and out,* and *back and forth.*)

We could not decide whether to ride to the old mill,/to the
beach,/or to Sunset Park.
(The items in this series are the phrases *to the old mill, to
the beach,* and *to Sunset Park.*)

It was getting dark,/a wind blew down from the mountain,/
and Henry began to wonder where he was.
(The items in this series are sentences.)

Use commas after the adverbs *first, second, third*, and so on.

We had three reasons: first,/we weren't interested in fishing;
second,/we had no transportation; third,/we had other things
to do.

**When two or more adjectives precede a noun, use a comma
after each adjective except the last one.**

It was a bright,/brisk,/beautiful day.

Sometimes two adjectives are used together to express a
single idea made up of two closely related thoughts. Adjectives
used in this way are not usually separated by a comma.

A *little old* man knocked at the door.
A *big red* truck pulled into the driveway.

When you say the two sentences above, notice that you do
not pause between the adjectives.

Exercises   Use commas correctly to separate items.

A. Read the following sentences. Write each of the sentences, adding commas where they are needed.

1. These three girls were with us: Michelle Richards
   Martha Rose and Joanne Cary.
2. In his pockets Terry had a bent penny a pencil stub
   about a yard of string a comb and two rubber
   bands.

3. Mrs. Harrison ordered the ginger ale and cola checked on the supply of paper plates and cups and called the farmer to get permission for us to picnic.
4. Here are the kinds of sandwiches we had: peanut butter and jelly tomato and bacon ham and cheese and egg salad.
5. Last summer Ted helped with the haying fed the chickens went after the cows and hoed the garden.
6. Do three things: first get the book from the library; second make an outline; third write the report.
7. The three pairs were Bill and José Jim and Tony and Bob and Carl.
8. Please check the addresses of these persons: Ms. Sondra Jackson Dr. Joyce L. Rainer and Mr. and Mrs. George Abel.
9. That was a long hard train ride.
10. I saw them slide scramble and tumble down the slope.

B. Follow the directions for Exercise A.

1. About midnight I woke up. First there was a loud crash outside; second the dog barked; third things rustled on the table.
2. In the morning the sun rose over the hills the birds were singing in the trees and fish jumped in the lake.
3. You may go to the pool to the park or into town.
4. Karen Jack and Juanita went swimming; my mother my father and I went to the store.
5. For supper we had hot dogs pickles and baked beans.
6. That evening we unloaded the car set up the tent climbed into our sleeping bags and went to sleep.
7. When I looked out the garbage can was overturned, and two curious black-masked raccoons were on the picnic table.

8. Slowly quietly and thoroughly they investigated the house.
9. They nibbled the cookie argued over an apple and turned up their noses at a piece of pickle someone had dropped.
10. Dad said, "At least it wasn't a bobcat a skunk or a big bear."

The Comma After Introductory Words, Phrases, or Clauses

Use a comma to separate an introductory word, phrase, or clause from the rest of the sentence.

Yes, Paula is my sister.

Climbing down the tree, I ripped my jacket.

Because I studied hard, I passed the test.

The comma may be omitted if there would be little pause in speaking.

At first Nancy was frightened.

Commas with Interrupters

Use commas to set off words or groups of words that interrupt the flow of thought in a sentence.

This bike, however, is in better condition than that one.

The answer, I suppose, will never be known.

Exercises   Use commas to set off words correctly.

A.   Write the following, adding commas where necessary.

1. However Jan prefers to work on her own.

2. The library Bill had said was closed for the last two weeks.
3. Janet's absence is excusable I am certain.
4. The Safety Committee of course needs good equipment.
5. The test results I suppose will be posted tomorrow afternoon.
6. The Assembly Committee as I said earlier will meet on Thursday.
7. No I haven't seen that movie.
8. Several of the hikers nevertheless made the trip in an hour.
9. This paper for example has no watermark.
10. After all Maria is a college senior.

B. Write the following sentences, adding commas where necessary. (One sentence does not need any commas.)

1. Running to third base I tripped and sprained my ankle.
2. Maybe Sue will join us.
3. In slalom skiing on the other hand you use only one ski.
4. Mary has a Siamese cat I think.
5. Did you hear by the way that there was a sellout crowd at the game last night?
6. Pat I hope will make a better shortstop than Chris.
7. No you may not stay at Ellen's for dinner this evening.
8. Finally the last marathon runner entered the Olympic Stadium.
9. Yes the game has been postponed until we can find a referee.
10. While vacationing in Montreal Allison and I met many French-speaking people.

Commas with Nouns of Direct Address

Use commas to set off nouns of direct address.

When you are speaking to someone, you use that person's name. When you do, you use a **noun of direct address.**

Call me tonight, Jane, if you can.

In the above sentence, *Jane* is the noun of direct address. It names the person the speaker is addressing (speaking to).

If commas are omitted with nouns of direct address, the sentence may confuse the reader. Read this example of such a confusing sentence:

Help me bake Jon and you may have some cookies.

Now read the sentence with commas correctly placed:

Help me bake, Jon, and you may have some cookies.

Commas with Appositives

Use commas to set off most appositives.

Appositives are words placed immediately after other words to make those other words clearer or more definite. Most appositives are nouns. Nouns used as appositives are called **nouns in apposition.**

Our science teacher, Miss Bell, will not be back next year.

Karen and Maria, our co-captains, accepted the trophy.

When an appositive is used with modifiers, the whole group of words is set off with commas.

Joe, the boy in the blue shirt, is Dave's cousin.

When the noun in apposition is a first name, it is not usually set off by commas.

This is my friend Tony.

Exercises Use commas with nouns of direct address and with appositives.

A. Copy the following sentences. Add commas wherever necessary. After each sentence, give your reason for using commas in it.

1. Mrs. Harmon I'd like you to meet my sister Robin.
2. Mary this is my classmate Tanya Jefferson.
3. Mr. Ingram our English teacher is here now Dad.
4. Dad this is Mr. Ingram our English teacher.
5. Don Jenkins this is Cynthia my sister.
6. Mother have you met Mr. Gillespie our music teacher?
7. Carla Mantoya this is my father Ken Brown.
8. Mrs. Doyle our math teacher is from Alaska.
9. Beth dinner will be ready any minute now.
10. José this is my brother Larry.

B. Rewrite the following pairs of sentences. Combine each pair into a single sentence by using an appositive.

> Example: Jill Douglas is the mayor of our town. She will speak next.
>
> Jill Douglas, the mayor of our town, will speak next.

1. There was only one hit against Wills. It was a single.
2. Karen is on the swimming team. She is my classmate.
3. The author is Mark Twain. He knew a lot about people.
4. The girl in the third row is Paula. She likes to go camping.
5. The fastest runner is on the track team. She is Penny Tate.
6. We have a favorite horse. Her name is Daisy Belle.

7. The second largest city in the United States is Chicago. It was founded in 1803.
8. Our pitcher is Bill Phillips. He injured his arm.
9. Ms. Parsons is our music teacher. She plays the piano.
10. One of my favorite plays is *The Miracle Worker*. It's about Helen Keller and Annie Sullivan.

Commas with Quotations

Use commas to set off the explanatory words of a direct quotation.

Remember that when you use a quotation you are giving the words of a speaker or writer. You are *quoting* the words of the speaker or writer. If you give the *exact* words, you are giving a **direct quotation.** Usually you include explanatory words, like *Joyce said, Peggy answered,* or *Bill asked.*

Jeff said, "Mother and I are going to the store."

In the above sentence, the explanatory words come *before* the quotation. A comma is then placed after the last explanatory word.

Now look at this quotation:

"Let's visit the zoo," suggested Joe.

In the above sentence, the explanatory words come *after* the quotation. A comma is then placed after the last word of the quotation, as you can see.

Sometimes the quotation is separated into two parts.

"If it rains," he said, "it'll probably be just a shower."

The above sentence is an example of what is called a *divided quotation.* It is called "divided" because it is made up of two parts that are separated by the explanatory words. A comma is used after the last word of the first part. Another comma is used after the last explanatory word.

The quotations you have just looked at are all direct quotations. A quotation can be either *direct* or *indirect*. In an **indirect quotation** you change the words of a speaker or writer to your own words. No commas are used.

Ms. Mooney said *that she enjoyed visiting our class.*

Exercise **Use commas with direct quotations.**

Write each of the following sentences, adding commas where they are needed. If a sentence needs no commas, write the word *Correct* after it.

1. Jim said "Everyone has gone to the beach today."
2. Dr. Gonzales said that Sandy had broken her arm.
3. Liz asked "Won't your mother let you have a dog?"
4. "But London Bridge is no longer in London" Art said.
5. "Did you know" asked Angie "that Alpha Centauri is the nearest star?"
6. "I like the climate of Seattle best of all" answered Tom.
7. Denise asked "Have you ever flown in a helicopter?"
8. "I can fix that faucet in ten minutes" Mary boasted.
9. Ken asked if we could drop him off first.
10. "I believe" shouted the announcer "that we have a winner!"

The Comma in a Compound Sentence

You will remember that a **compound sentence** consists of two simple sentences joined together.

Use a comma before the conjunction that joins the two simple sentences in a compound sentence.

Chris got back from his trip, and now he's sleeping.

The comma is not necessary in very short compound sentences when the parts are joined by *and*.

> We were thirsty and we were hungry.

However, always use a comma before *but* or *or*.

> We were thirsty,/ but we weren't hungry.

Do not confuse a compound sentence with a sentence that has only a compound predicate. The two parts of a compound predicate are *not* joined by commas.

> We can stop here or go on to Toronto.

If a compound predicate has more than two parts, the parts are joined by commas.

> We came early,/ worked hard,/ and left late.

Exercises   Use commas correctly.

A.   Write each of the following sentences, adding commas where they are needed. Two sentences have compound predicates and need no commas. Write the word *Correct* after those sentences.

1. Can you stay for dinner or are you leaving early?
2. The coach drew a diagram and the players studied it.
3. We stopped on the side of the road and ate our lunch.
4. On the moon the temperature rises to over 200° in the daytime but it drops far below zero at night.
5. There was an annoying noise in the car but we could not locate the cause.
6. You can have two large containers or use three small ones.
7. I'd like to go to the show but I have too much work to do.
8. The movie was excellent but I didn't enjoy waiting in line.

9. We raked the leaves into neat piles but the wind blew them away.
10. Ellen played the piano and Laura performed a Mexican folk dance.

B. Follow the directions for Exercise A. (Here, also, are two sentences that have compound predicates and need no commas.)

1. The book wasn't very long but she couldn't finish it.
2. The mail carrier delivered two small packages and he asked me to sign for them.
3. I don't really want to go but I will if you come with me.
4. We went to the state fair yesterday and spent the day.
5. Is a meter shorter than a yard or is it longer?
6. Are you in a hurry or can you stop for some ice cream?
7. At first she couldn't dance at all but now she's pretty good.
8. He flew to San Francisco and took a bus from there.
9. Nancy brought lemonade but she forgot the glasses.
10. These jeans are too long and they don't fit at the waist.

Commas in Dates

Use commas to set off the parts of dates from each other.

Tuesday, November 9, 1978

If a date is used in a sentence, place a comma after the last part of the date.

February 20, 1962, was the day on which the first American orbited the earth.

Commas in Locations and Addresses

Use commas between the name of a city or town and the name of its state or country.

Des Moines, Iowa

London, England

Use commas to separate the parts of an address.

1943 Meech Road, Williamston, Michigan 48895

If an address is used in a sentence, also place a comma after the last part of the address.

From Omaha, Nebraska, we drove to Wichita, Kansas.

Please send the order to 125 West Lincoln Highway, DeKalb, Illinois 60115, as requested.

Commas in Letter Parts

Use a comma after the greeting of a friendly letter and after the closing of any letter.

Dear Dana,   Sincerely yours,

Exercises   Use commas correctly.

A. Write the following sentences, adding commas where they are needed.

1. Does this address say Gary Indiana or Cary Illinois?
2. My older brother was born on February 29 1968.
3. Sherlock Holmes lived at 221B Baker Street London.
4. Dear Diana
   Let me know if you can babysit on Friday.
   Yours truly
Margaret Findley

5. He was born on April 3 1967 so he's an Aries.
6. Ed lives at 4652 Orchard Street Oakland California.
7. We're going to the museum on Thursday May 5.
8. The first Boston Marathon was held on April 19 1897.
9. Are you talking about Kansas City Missouri or Kansas City Kansas?
10. Someday my address will be 1600 Pennsylvania Avenue Washington D. C.

B. Follow the directions for Exercise A.

1. Where were you on Friday June 24 1979?
2. Reno Nevada is farther west than Los Angeles California.
3. Eleanor Roosevelt was born on October 11 1884 and died on November 7 1962.
4. My cousins were both born on September 4 1964.
5. Why is 10 Downing Street London famous?
6. Saturday July 26 is Kathryn's birthday party.
7. The best hot dogs are at Petey's 110 Washington Street Elm Forest.
8. Dear Helen
   Thank you for the sweater. It fits perfectly.

   Love
   Marsha
9. We lived at 130 Rand Road Austin Texas from May 1 1973 to April 30 1977.
10. July 4 1776 is the only historical date I can remember.

The Semicolon

Use a semicolon to join the parts of a compound sentence when no coordinating conjunction is used.

Mother threw the coat away; it was worn out.

The Colon

Use a colon after the greeting of a business letter.

Dear Sir or Madam: Gentlemen:

Use a colon between numerals indicating hours and minutes.

9:30 A.M.

Use a colon to introduce a list of items.

We need the following items: paintbrushes, tubes of paint, a palette, and canvas.

Exercises Use semicolons and colons correctly.

Copy the word before and after the missing punctuation mark and add the correct punctuation mark.

1. Mary Ann is my sister Dan is my twin brother.
2. The last vote was counted Jane was elected by a large majority.
3. Class will be held at 2 15 P.M. in the music room.
4. The pupils with the highest marks are these Michael Karantz, Susan O'Brien, and Janet Newcombe.
5. Here is what Jack wants a compass, a pencil, and ink.
6. The game will begin at 1 00 P.M.
7. Sally decided against the 3-speed bike she's going to get a 10-speed instead.
8. My grandfather grows a lot of vegetables in his garden peas, lettuce, beets, carrots, and sweet corn.
9. Gentlemen

   The payment for your bill is enclosed.

   Sincerely,

   Jack Parsons
10. Which of the following flavors is your favorite boysen- berry, chocolate, vanilla, or strawberry?

The Hyphen

Use a hyphen to divide a word at the end of a line.

> My father gets extra pay when he has to work over-
> time at the office.

Only words of two or more syllables can be divided at the end of a line. Never divide words of one syllable, such as *school* or *worse*. A single letter must not be left at the end of a line. For example, this division would be wrong: *a-waken*. A single letter must not appear at the beginning of a line, either. It would be wrong to divide *slippery* like this: *slipper-y*.

Use a hyphen in compound numbers from twenty-one through ninety-nine.

> thirty-two seconds   forty-three pencils

Use a hyphen in fractions.

> We have a three-fourths majority.

Use a hyphen or hyphens in certain compound nouns.

> sister-in-law   commander-in-chief   great-aunt

Use a hyphen or hyphens between words that make up a compound adjective used before a noun.

> I rode my ten-speed bike to school.
> We have an up-to-date encyclopedia.

When a compound adjective comes after a noun, it is usually not hyphenated.

> The car engine has four cylinders.
> My sister is ten years old.

Exercise Use hyphens correctly.

Copy the words in each sentence that need hyphens and add them.

1. A two thirds majority vote by Congress is needed to override the President's veto.
2. Nora's great grandparents came here from Norway in 1892.
3. Today only, felt tip pens are reduced from eighty nine cents to fifty nine cents.
4. Marilyn's sister in law worked as a police officer before she became a lawyer.
5. The trip back to Bob's took forty five minutes by express bus.
6. I hope those money hungry, cattle rustling outlaws meet up with The Kid.
7. Eileen's mother bought her a peach colored blouse and a lime green jumper.
8. An eight cylinder engine has more power, but a six cylinder engine will burn less gas.
9. The Mason Dixon line, which divides the North and South, was surveyed by Charles Mason and Jeremiah Dixon.
10. The President is also commander in chief of the armed forces.

The Apostrophe

To form the possessive of a singular noun, add an apostrophe and an s.

girl + **'s** = girl's   man + **'s** = man's
boy + **'s** = boy's   Charles + **'s** = Charles's

To form the possessive of a plural noun that ends in s, add only an apostrophe.

friends + ' = friends'   countries + ' = countries'

To form the possessive of a plural noun that does not end in s, add an apostrophe and an s.

women + **'s** = women's   mice + **'s** = mice's

Exercises   Form the possessives of nouns correctly.

A. On a piece of paper, write the possessive form of the following nouns.

1. editor
2. counselor
3. producer
4. elephant
5. Dana
6. electrician
7. Ms. Prentiss
8. Randy
9. employee
10. architect
11. manager
12. conductor
13. artist
14. librarian
15. reporter
16. horse
17. doctor
18. writer
19. Mrs. Thomas
20. principal

B. On a piece of paper, write the plural form of each of the following nouns. After the plural form, write the plural possessive for each noun.

1. dentist
2. man
3. county
4. nurse
5. woman
6. optometrist
7. astronaut
8. teacher
9. bookkeeper
10. salesperson
11. company
12. family
13. student
14. accountant

15. city   18. journalist
16. lawyer   19. orthodontist
17. paramedic   20. carpenter

The Apostrophe in Contractions

Writing contractions is not at all difficult if you understand that the apostrophe simply replaces one or more omitted letters.

we're = we are   where's = where is
she's = she is   they're = they are
here's = here is   can't = cannot
there's = there is   couldn't = could not
I'd = I would   won't = will not
we'll = we will   wasn't = was not
they'll = they will   wouldn't = would not

Look out, too, for *it's* and *its*. Remember:

It's (with an apostrophe) always means *it is* or *it has*.
Its (without the apostrophe) is the possessive of *it*.

It's time for the dog to have *its* bath.

Remember, too, that no apostrophe is used with the possessive pronouns *ours, yours, hers, theirs*.

These magazines are *ours*.
Those on the table are *theirs*.

Look out for *who's* and *whose*. Remember:

Who's (with an apostrophe) means *who is* or *who has*.
Whose (without the apostrophe) is the possessive of *who*.

Who's going with you to the movie?
Whose house is that?

Two other contractions that you should watch are *you're* and *they're*. *You're* means *you are*. Do not confuse it with the possessive pronoun *your*. *They're* means *they are*. Do not confuse it with the possessive pronoun *their*.

> *You're* now in *your* own classroom.
> *They're* visiting *their* aunt.

Use an apostrophe to form the plurals of letters, figures, and words used as words.

> Children used to be told to mind their *p's* and *q's*.
> Carol should form her *3's* and *8's* more carefully.
> Pam's story was full of *but's*.

Exercises   Use apostrophes correctly.

A.   Copy these sentences, inserting apostrophes where they are needed.

1. Wheres the paint for the puppets faces?
2. Its on the garage shelf. Its Ms. Steins paint. Dont waste it.
3. Were going to keep working until weve finished.
4. Ill turn on Carls desk lamp. Wont that help?
5. Thats fine. Well work much faster now.
6. Jim cant go because hes helping his parents.
7. Its late. Havent you finished yet?
8. My puppet wont sit up. Its back isnt stiff enough.
9. Heres the book you wanted. Its been checked out in your name.
10. Wheres the paste? Im ready. Lets go.

B.   Write each of the following sentences. Choose the correct word from the two given in parentheses.

1. (You're, Your) the one (who's, whose) going to Mexico, aren't you?
2. Kathy and Peg are going to the play, but they (don't, dont) have (they're, their) tickets yet.
3. Which poster is (her's, hers)?

4. (It's, Its) hard to believe that the car has lost (it's, its) muffler already.
5. (Here's, Heres) the pump for (you're, your) tire.
6. (We'll, Well) all be happy if it (doesn't, doesnt) rain.
7. (Wasn't, Wasnt) Mr. Lopez (they're, their) teacher?
8. (Who's, Whose) going with you to the concert? I hope (you're, your) able to find someone.
9. Mrs. Larette (doesn't, doesnt) know (who's, whose) bike is in the driveway.
10. (They're, Their) team has had much more practice than (our's, ours).

Quotation Marks

Use quotation marks at the beginning and at the end of a direct quotation.

Quotation marks [" "] consist of two pairs of small marks that resemble apostrophes. They tell a reader that the exact words of another speaker or writer are being given.

Matt said, "I'm going to wash the family car."

Quotation marks are not used with indirect quotations:

Matt said *that he was going to wash the family car.*

Explanatory words before a direct quotation are followed by a comma. The period at the end of the sentence is placed *inside* the quotation marks.

My uncle answered, "I'll send you a postcard."

Explanatory words after a direct quotation are followed by a period. The words of a direct quotation are followed by a comma *inside* the quotation marks.

"I'll send you a postcard," my uncle answered.

Divided Quotations

Sometimes a direct quotation is divided into two or more parts by explanatory words. In such cases use quotation marks before and after each part of the quotation.

"If that team wins," Patty whispered, "I'll be surprised."

The second part of a divided quotation is not capitalized unless it is a proper noun or unless it starts a new sentence.

"If you're ready," said Paul, "we can leave now."

"I saw Mr. Prichard," said Amy. "He was in the supermarket."

After the first part of a divided quotation, place a comma *inside* the quotation marks.

"When you wash the car," Jan said, "use a soft cloth."

In a divided quotation use either a comma or a period after the explanatory words. Use a comma after the explanatory words if the second part of the quotation does not begin a new sentence. Use a period after the explanatory words if the second part of the quotation is a new sentence.

"Help me set the table," said Peter, "and then call the others."

"I've finished my homework," Dan said. "It was easy."

Exercise **Use quotation marks correctly.**

Writing Write each sentence three ways as a direct quotation.

> Example: Of course you can go.
> a. "Of course you can go," he said.
> b. He said, "Of course you can go."
> c. "Of course," he said, "you can go."

1. If you like, we will stay.
2. At least you like potatoes.

3. Well, there's another way to do it.
4. At noon the pool will open.
5. Aunt Mary is going to visit us.

Punctuating Direct Quotations

Place question marks and exclamation points inside quotation marks if they belong to the quotation itself.

> Mother said to Tim, "Have you finished the dishes?"
>
> "Look out!" Dad shouted.

Place question marks and exclamation points outside quotation marks if they do not belong to the quotation.

> Did Rachel say, "Meet me in the library"?
>
> The teacher said, "There is no homework tonight"!

Exercises **Punctuate correctly.**

A. Punctuate these quotations correctly. (There are three indirect quotations that only need periods.)

1. Did you notice Inspector Blaine asked anything peculiar about the suspect
2. Just that he wore a raincoat and a hat that hid his face I replied
3. Are you certain that he was tall and that he limped as he ran Blaine asked
4. Correct I answered I also believe he favored his left side
5. I reminded the Inspector that I had caught only a glimpse of the mysterious person
6. Oh by the way I added he was carrying a small suitcase too
7. Would you mind coming down to the station and making a statement Blaine asked

8. I told him that I wouldn't mind, but that I preferred to keep my name out of the newspapers
9. No need to worry he remarked as he opened the squad car door for me
10. I thanked him for his courtesy and got in

B. Writing Write each of the following sentences as a direct quotation. In some examples, put the quotation first. In others, put the quotation last. Also, for variety, divide some quotations.

Example: Next week I start my new job.

Possible Answers:
"Next week I start my new job," Sally said.
Sally said, "Next week I start my new job."
"Next week," Sally said, "I start my new job."

1. The shirts are dirty, but the slacks are clean.
2. By the way, that clock is ten minutes fast.
3. After lunch should we go to the movies?
4. Thank goodness my glasses didn't break!
5. Last night I had a terrible dream.
6. Walk three blocks and turn right.
7. Next summer my whole family is driving to California.
8. Perhaps poodles are smarter, but I still prefer collies.
9. Do green apples give you a stomachache?
10. All it takes to open that paint can is a screwdriver.

Punctuating Dialogue

Notice how the following quotation, which contains more that two sentences by one speaker, is punctuated.

"Can the repairman come tomorrow?" asked Jean over the telephone. "Mother needs to use the washing machine. She can't use it at all now."

Only one set of quotation marks would be needed if the example read as follows:

> Over the telephone Jean said, "Can the repairman come tomorrow? Mother needs to use the washing machine. She can't use it at all now."

In writing *dialogue* (conversation), begin a new paragraph every time the speaker changes:

> "Lynn invited us to the lake for the afternoon," said Jean.
> "How was it?" asked Barbara.
> "Well, the car broke down on the way. We had to walk three miles to the lake," replied Jean.

Exercise   **Punctuate dialogue correctly.**

Writing   Rewrite the following conversation. Make correct paragraph divisions and use the right punctuation.

> Home Run Reilly stepped up to the plate He was facing Lightning Louie the fastest pitcher in baseball The first pitch was a blur Strike one the umpire called Reilly gripped the bat and the second pitch streaked by Strike two the umpire said Reilly frowned as he heard the third pitch thunk into the catcher's mitt Strike three the umpire shouted You're out Reilly turned to the umpire and asked Could you see those pitches No the umpire confessed I couldn't either said Reilly but the last one sounded a little high to me

Using Quotation Marks for Titles

Use quotation marks to enclose chapter titles, titles of magazine articles, titles of short stories, essays, or single poems, and titles of songs or short pieces of music.

Chapter:	Chapter 8, "The Revolution Begins"
Magazine article:	"Space Age Tour"
Short Story:	"The Lady or the Tiger?"
Essay:	"The English Language Today"
Poem:	"The Raven"
Song:	"America"

Underline the titles of books, newspapers, magazines, plays, movies, titles of television and radio programs, works of art, and long musical compositions.

When you are writing or when you are typing, underline these titles, like this: Light in the Forest.

When these titles are printed, they are printed in *italics*, rather than underlined.

Book:	*The Pearl*
Newspaper:	*Los Angeles Times*
Magazine:	*Newsweek*
Play:	*Julius Caesar*
Movie:	*Butch Cassidy and the Sundance Kid*
Television program:	*Great Performances*
Work of art:	Grant Wood's *American Gothic*
Long Musical Composition:	*William Tell*

Exercises **Use quotation marks and underlining correctly.**

A. Copy the following sentences, adding quotation marks around titles or underlining titles where necessary.

1. The chorus sang My Old Kentucky Home.
2. The Catbird Seat is a funny story by James Thurber.
3. Karen's picture was in the local paper, the Leesburg Advance.
4. Did you read My Darling, My Hamburger for your book report?

5. The drama department is presenting The Miracle Worker as the spring play.
6. Our teacher assigned the second chapter, Families of Man, in our social studies book.
7. Robert Redford won the Academy Award as best director for Ordinary People.
8. Estelle used Time and Newsweek to write her report.
9. No one can even estimate the value of the Mona Lisa, which is in the Louvre museum.
10. The play Romeo and Juliet was the basis for the movie West Side Story.

B. Follow the directions for Exercise A.

1. One article in this month's Seventeen is Are You a Good Friend?
2. We are reading a science fiction novel, The Time Machine, in English class.
3. Shirley Jackson's story The Lottery has a shocking ending.
4. Before the game began, everyone sang The Star-Spangled Banner.
5. One Nova program explained sunspots.
6. My favorite poems are Dreams by Langston Hughes and Space Man by Babette Deutsch.
7. The longest running play is The Mousetrap by Agatha Christie.
8. We listened to the orchestra play Schubert's Unfinished Symphony.
9. Dan has seen Star Wars, The Empire Strikes Back, and The Return of the Jedi three times each.
10. My father reads the Chicago Tribune and the New York Times every Sunday.

ADDITIONAL EXERCISES

Punctuation

A. Periods, Question Marks, and Exclamation Points
Copy the following sentences. Supply the missing punctuation.

1. Donna explained why she was late
2. Please pull up a chair
3. What a hot day it is
4. What is the forecast for tomorrow
5. Wow Is it really 2:00 A M
6. The speaker is Bonita Pamatz, M D
7. Did you learn to swim at the Y W C A
8. Dr Hill and Ms Wirtz are the chaperones for the freshman dance
9. Chuck Berry recorded "Johnny B Goode" long ago
10. The Great Wall of China, built before 200 B C , is the only human structure visible from outer space

B. Commas Copy each of the following sentences. Use a comma to make the meaning clear.

1. Since Irv left Spot has been lonesome.
2. While juggling Mark talks to the audience.
3. Sandra can't stand cheese and Mimi dislikes milk.
4. Outside the lawn was being mowed.
5. While the turkey was roasting Kay opened a window.
6. Instead of moping around Kelly went biking.
7. Almost falling down Len regained his balance on his skateboard.
8. Running behind Nicole got her second wind.
9. When you finish the tests will be collected.
10. Tripping Lori stumbled into the Christmas tree.

C. Commas Copy the following sentences. Add commas where they are necessary.

1. We caught a bass a trout and a catfish.
2. Megan found a carton cleaned it out and packed the books.
3. The Barbary States were Algiers Tunis and Tripoli.
4. First slice the eggplant; second drain it; third brush it with oil.
5. I looked under the cushion beneath the rug and in the wastebasket.
6. The farm offers rides on a hay wagon a tractor or a horse.
7. Why did George sit through that long boring pointless movie?
8. Leon brought a red rubber ball Kristy brought a striped beach ball and Sabrina brought a Frisbee.
9. His plump freckled solemn face was on the front page.
10. Arlene and Vivian made up funny catchy campaign slogans.

D. Commas Copy these sentences. Add commas where necessary.

1. You are I'm sure telling the truth.
2. No the snow has not stopped.
3. The Packers however have an excellent chance of winning the championship.
4. For example Dracula movies are still being made.
5. Part of the mistletoe as you may know is poisonous.
6. Because Gerri is an usher she sees many plays.
7. Stuck under the viaduct the truck blocked traffic.
8. Helping himself to my popcorn Kent told me the ending of the movie.
9. Consequently the jury found her innocent.
10. Miriam yawning loudly looked at the clock.

E. Commas Copy these sentences. Add commas where necessary.

1. Danny where are you going?
2. Have you had lunch Maria?
3. Remember Charley to use hand signals.
4. Richard Pryor the comedian was the star.
5. Mrs. Owens this is my friend Nina.
6. Carol meet Olga Herrera my new neighbor.
7. I quickly spotted Al the only boy wearing a tie.
8. The award was presented by Gwendolyn Brooks the poet from Illinois.
9. Alice fed the garter snake a goldfish its favorite food.
10. Japanese children learn *origami* the art of folding paper.

F. Commas Copy these sentences. Add commas where necessary. If a sentence needs no comma, write *Correct*.

1. "Actually" said Jo "the sun is nearer the earth in winter."
2. Marla said that dinner would be late.
3. "I iron my own shirts" Art said.
4. Wendy asked if she was in the way.
5. Mr. Tijani asked "Do all of you see this line?"
6. "When I sing" said Laura "I forget myself."
7. "The coast is clear" Adrienne told us.
8. Walt told us that he was allergic to bee stings.
9. Michelle promised that she would shovel the walk.
10. Olsen promised us "I will not let you down."

G. Commas Copy these sentences. Add commas where necessary. If a sentence needs no comma, write *Correct*.

1. We practiced hard all week and our coach was pleased.

2. O. J. Simpson used to play football but now he's a sports commentator.
3. A rock hit the windshield and shattered it.
4. Carly and Lisa accepted but Nell declined the party invitation.
5. You'd better explain to Sid or he will be hurt.
6. Harry was talking fast and we were listening hard.
7. Jody and Fred were talking and laughing at the same time.
8. The ramps are meant to help people in wheelchairs but cyclists also like the smooth slopes.
9. Ian will wait in the car or walk around the block.
10. Did you mean that or were you joking?

H. Commas Copy the following sentences. Add commas where necessary.

1. There is a game preserve near Nairobi Kenya.
2. Hitler invaded Poland on September 1 1939.
3. On January 3 1959 Alaska joined the Union.
4. Contributions can be sent to UNICEF 331 East 38th Street New York New York 10016.
5. Wednesday April 8 was the night of the full moon.
6. Beverly Hills California is on the outskirts of Hollywood.
7. Our address will be 10 Sugar Pine Road Medford Oregon 97501 as of June 25.
8. Dear Sally
   I hope that I will be able to attend a performance of your play on Saturday January 20.
   Sincerely
   Linda
9. Ginger moved to Vose Farm Road Peterborough New Hampshire on May 1 1985.
10. Cairo Illinois is very different from Cairo Egypt.

I. Semicolons and Colons Copy these sentences, adding the missing punctuation mark.

1. The race was over the jockey jumped from her horse to accept the medal.
2. Bring the following supplies wood, nails, a hammer, and glue.
3. The plane didn't leave the runway until 5 30 P.M.
4. Dear Mrs. Kohl
   Your appointment is on March 12 at 9 00 A.M.
5. These students should report to the gym before the assembly Ben Evans, Josh Shapiro, and Lois Sims.
6. Stay on the right side of the road ride in a single file.
7. This is all you need salt, flour, and vinegar.
8. The hay got wet it might rot.
9. The clock struck 12 00 it was Christmas.
10. The camp will provide sheets and pillows you must bring your own towels, however.

J. Hyphens Copy the words that need hyphens and add the hyphens.

1. My great aunt is celebrating her ninety fifth birthday on January 23.
2. It was an attention catching sign.
3. The gravity of the moon is one sixth that of the earth's gravity.
4. My great grandmother rides a ten speed bike.
5. The living room has built in bookcases.
6. Reporters began predicting the winner when only one fourth of the votes were in.
7. The Vice President now has an official residence.
8. Gray brown dust was blowing everywhere.
9. Two thirds of the books are out of date reference works.
10. The co captains are half sisters.

K. Plurals and Possessives Write the plural form of each of the following nouns. After the plural form, write the plural possessive for each noun.

1. doctor	6. child	11. eagle
2. puppy	7. painter	12. mouse
3. heroine	8. contestant	13. lady
4. seamstress	9. panther	14. writer
5. man	10. member	15. electrician

L. Apostrophes Copy the following sentences, inserting apostrophes where they are needed.

1. Cant you see that Im busy?
2. Ill keep your secret.
3. Youre sure its a diamond, arent you?
4. The two girls mittens are missing.
5. Michaels dog isnt welcome here.
6. Europeans make their 7s differently.
7. Whose ice cream hasnt melted yet?
8. Whos playing those steel drums? Theyre Lizs.
9. Its feathers feel oily, dont they?
10. Ours has lost its cover. Yours hasnt.

M. Quotation Marks Copy and punctuate the following sentences.

1. I have homework to do Mother said
2. Charlene said that she was trying out for the cheerleading squad
3. Hal said That Harley-Davidson is a classic
4. Watch out for shaving cream Toby yelled It's Halloween
5. Chief Joseph told his warriors From where the sun now stands, I will fight no more forever
6. Mr. Rizal asked if we had any questions

7. Hattie asked Is the dolphin a mammal
8. When the snow thaws said Leah our street floods
9. Renault said that he would be here said Emma
10. I measured the doorway said Ann It's too narrow

N. Dialogue   Rewrite the following conversation. Make correct paragraph divisions and use the right punctuation.

Did you hear that storm last night asked Janet at breakfast Pam answered I certainly did not Well said Janet the thunder almost shook the house and lightning streaked right into our room I was afraid the hailstones would break the windows Why didn't you wake me up asked Pam indignantly You know I can't sleep during a storm

O. Titles   Copy the following and fill in the blanks. Punctuate the titles correctly.

1. My least favorite televison program is _____.
2. Joan has a subscription to _____ magazine.
3. The best movie that I ever saw was _____.
4. The title of Monty's essay was _____.
5. One book that held my attention was _____.

MIXED REVIEW

Punctuation

A. Using punctuation correctly Copy the following sentences, adding end marks, commas, apostrophes, and quotation marks, and underlining where necessary.

1. Pete Diane and Evan all have the flu
2. Have you read any poems by T S Eliot
3. Oh no I forgot the tickets
4. Laura has just finished the novel Little Women
5. Keep your eyes on the ball not on the pitcher
6. Before you leave said Dad clean your room
7. Yes I can go camping on Wednesday September 22
8. His argument I believe is logical
9. Sandra is a dancer a singer and an actress
10. There's a squirrel in the fireplace shouted Kevin

B. Using punctuation correctly in proofreading Proofread the following letter. Copy it, using correct punctuation.

Camp Willowbrook
P O Box 2112
Whitewater Wisconsin 51620

Dear Ellen

   You were so right? Being a camp counselor is better than babysitting. Where else could I teach swimming diving and gymnastics every day. The campers are, bright active kids. Sometimes however their creativity leads to some unusual pranks. I did have a reward last weekend when a camper said to her parents "Ill come back next year if Beverly does.

   Please write soon Ellen? I miss our phone calls.

Sincerely
Bev

USING MECHANICS IN WRITING
Punctuation

A. Marty was nervous but confident before the typing test. He knew he was faster and more accurate than anyone else in class. Fingers flying, he completed the test with a full minute to spare. But his heart sank as he reviewed his paper. He had forgotten to capitalize and punctuate. Rewrite Marty's test, making all necessary corrections.

> what do michelangelo ringo starr gerald ford and harpo marx have in common they all have one simple trait shared by millions of others theyre left-handed no one is sure why some of us prefer our left sides to our right sides many stories and superstitions have arisen because of the mystery the bible tells of sharp shooting left handed warriors in the middle ages some people even believed that left handed warriors had magic powers on the contrary lefties have problems with simple things such as cutting with scissors knitting and dining next to right handed people benjamin franklin an early champion of left handed people encouraged tolerance most lefties today are proud of their distinction for them its the right way.

B. A reporter has stumbled on an exciting story. She has discovered a scientist who has invented a machine that can control weather. The scientist is pleading with the reporter not to reveal the secret. He is afraid of what others might do with the knowledge. Write their conversation. Have each character speak at least four times. Include at least four divided quotations. Invent details to make the conversation interesting and realistic.

Spelling

It is important to have good spelling skills. You will use these skills when you write reports for school. You will use them when you write friendly letters and business letters, and you will use them when you fill out job applications. If you care what others think of you, you will want to be able to spell words correctly.

Being a good speller doesn't just happen. It takes practice, and you have to remember a few simple rules. If you do have trouble spelling, you may be relieved to know that generations of students have shared the same problem. Many of those students have learned to be good spellers. You can, too.

There is no simple way to teach you how to spell. However, there are several methods you can use to attack your spelling problems. These methods of attack are discussed in this chapter.

A General Method of Attack on Spelling

To improve your spelling, follow these helpful guidelines:

1. Find out what your personal spelling demons are and conquer them.   Go over your old composition papers and make a list of the words you misspelled on them. Keep this list and master the words on it.

2. Pronounce words carefully.   It may be that you misspell words because you don't pronounce them carefully. For example, if you write *probly* for *probably*, you are no doubt mispronouncing the word.

3. Get into the habit of seeing the letters in a word.   Many people have never really looked at the word *similar*. Otherwise, why do they write it *similiar?*

Take a good look at new words, or difficult words. You'll remember them better. Copy the correct spelling several times.

4. Think up a memory device for difficult words.   Here are some devices that have worked for other people. They may help you, either to spell these words or to make up your own memory devices.

princi**pal** (*pal*)	*The princi**pal** is my pal.*
fri**end** (*end*)	I will be your fri**end** to the *end*.
bus**i**ness (*i*)	*I* was involved in big business.
bel**ie**ve (*lie*)	There is a *lie* in bel**ie**ve.

5. Proofread everything you write.   In order to learn how to spell, you must learn to examine critically everything you write.

To proofread a piece of writing, you must read it slowly, word for word. Otherwise, your eyes may play tricks on you and let you skip over misspelled words.

6. Use a dictionary. You don't have to know how to spell every word; no one spells everything correctly all the time. A good dictionary can help you to be a better speller. Use a dictionary whenever you need help with your spelling.

7. Learn the few important spelling rules given in this chapter. Refer to these guidelines until you begin to follow them naturally on your own. You'll see that you will become a good speller.

A Method of Attack on Specific Words

To spell a specific word that is difficult for you, follow these steps:

1. Look at the word and say it to yourself. Be sure you pronounce it correctly. If it has more than one syllable, say it again, one syllable at a time. Look at each syllable as you say it.

2. Look at the letters and say each one. If the word has more than one syllable, separate the word into syllables when you say the letters.

3. Write the word without looking at your book or list.

4. Now look at your book or list and see whether you spelled the word correctly. If you did, write it again and compare it with the correct form again. Do this once more.

5. If you made a mistake, note exactly what it was. Then repeat steps 3 and 4 above until you have written the word correctly three times.

By following these steps, you will have mastered the difficult word. You will be able to spell it correctly whenever you use it.

Rules for Spelling

The Final Silent e

When a suffix beginning with a vowel is added to a word ending in a silent e, the e is usually dropped.

relate + -ion = relation   believe + -ing = believing
amaze + -ing = amazing   create + -ive = creative
fame + -ous = famous   continue + -ing = continuing

When a suffix beginning with a consonant is added to a word ending in a silent e, the e is usually retained.

hope + -ful = hopeful   waste + -ful = wasteful
state + -ment = statement   move + -ment = movement
noise + -less = noiseless   wide + -ly = widely

The following words are exceptions:

truly   argument   ninth   wholly

Words Ending in y

When a suffix is added to a word ending in y preceded by a consonant, the y is usually changed to i.

easy + -ly = easily   happy + -ness = happiness
sixty + -eth = sixtieth   clumsy + -ly = clumsily
city + -es = cities   marry + -age = marriage

Note the following exception: When *-ing* is added, the *y* does not change.

hurry + -ing = hurrying   worry + -ing = worrying
study + -ing = studying   copy + -ing = copying

When a suffix is added to a word ending in y preceded by a vowel, the y usually does not change.

enjoy + -ed = enjoyed   play + -ing = playing
employ + -er = employer   destroy + -er = destroyer

Exercises Spell words and their suffixes.

A. Find the misspelled words in these sentences. Spell them correctly.

1. Our class is competeing in the state science fair.
2. The magician's performance was truely amazeing.
3. My brother and I had an argument about rakeing the leaves.
4. The nurse placed the baby carfully against her shoulder.
5. By the seventh inning, the game was hopless for our team.
6. The troop leaders are arrangeing chairs for tonight's scout meeting.
7. The dareing circus performers walked easyly across the tightrope.
8. My grandparents were gratful for the pictures we sent them.
9. The chef's createion looked terrific but tasted awful.
10. It was truly exciteing to meet the actors and actresses backstage.

B. Add the suffixes as shown, and write the new word. Remember to change *y* to *i* wherever it is necessary.

1. silly + -ness
2. messy + -est
3. twenty + -eth
4. marry + -ing
5. crazy + -ly
6. relay + -ed
7. spray + -ing
8. beauty + -ful
9. glory + -ous
10. hasty + -ly
11. play + -ful
12. supply + -ing
13. employ + -ment
14. fly + -er
15. lazy + -er
16. dirty + -est
17. fancy + -ful
18. study + -ous
19. enjoy + -able
20. pretty + -er

The Suffixes -*ness* and -*ly*

When the suffix -*ly* is added to a word ending in *l*, both *l*'s are kept. When -*ness* is added to a word ending in *n*, both *n*'s are kept.

actual + -ly = actually	thin + -ness = thinness
real + -ly = really	even + -ness = evenness

The Addition of Prefixes

When a prefix is added to a word, the spelling of the word remains the same.

mis- + spell = misspell	mis- + place = misplace
il- + legal = illegal	im- + perfect = imperfect
im- + mobile = immobile	dis- + approve = disapprove
pre- + record = prerecord	ir- + regular = irregular

Exercise **Spell words with prefixes and suffixes.**

Find the misspelled words in these sentences and write them correctly.

1. Our car is parked legally, but yours is in an ilegal space.
2. The blue vase is slightly mishapen.
3. In English class we are learning about iregular verbs.
4. The uneveness of our sidewalk makes skateboarding dangerous.
5. We were practicaly finished eating when it began to rain.
6. The owner is disatisfied with the people who live up-stairs.
7. We received a thoughtfuly written thank-you note.
8. Scrooge's meaness was replaced by kindness and charity.

9. Dr. Martin's handwriting is almost ilegible.
10. I misspelled two words in my essay because I misspronounced them.

Words with the "Seed" Sound

Only one English word ends in *sede: supersede.*
Three words end in *ceed: exceed, proceed, succeed.*
All other words ending in the sound of *seed* are spelled *cede*:

    concede   precede   recede   secede

Words with *ie* and *ei*

When the sound is long *e* (*ē*), the word is spelled *ie* except after *c*.

I Before E

believe	shield	yield	fierce
niece	brief	field	pier

Except After C

receive	ceiling	perceive	deceit
conceive	conceit	receipt	

The following words are exceptions:

either	weird	species
neither	seize	leisure

Exercise   **Spell words with the "seed" sound and words with *ie* and *ei*.**

Find the misspelled words in these sentences and write them correctly.

1. My mother's salary excedes that of many people.
2. There are leaks on the cieling of the locker room.

3. I lost the reciept for the hockey equipment I rented.
4. Bikers should yeild the right of way to pedestrians.
5. The Student Council will procede with its plans.
6. The doctor gave me a prescription to releive my pain.
7. Niether Missouri nor Kentucky seceded from the Union during the Civil War.
8. My aunt bakes special cookies for all her neices.
9. The playing feild was too wet for the game to proceed.
10. The candidate did conceed the victory.

Doubling the Final Consonant

In words of one syllable that end with one consonant preceded by one vowel, double the final consonant before adding -ing, -ed, or -er.

bat + -ed = batted   bed + -ing = bedding
get + -ing = getting   grab + -ed = grabbed
big + -er = bigger   slim + -er = slimmer
put + -ing = putting   run + -er = runner

The following words do not double the final consonant because *two* vowels precede the final consonant:

treat + -ing = treating   loot + -ed = looted
feel + -ing = feeling   near + -er = nearer

Exercise   Doubling the Final Consonant

Add the suffixes as shown and write the new word. Remember to double the final consonant wherever it is necessary.

1. dig + -ing   6. hop + -ing
2. fear + -ing   7. bat + -er
3. fat + -er   8. creep + -ing
4. slap + -ed   9. wrap + -ed
5. pair + -ed   10. dim + -er

Words Often Confused

Study each group of words and meanings. Learn to spell these words that are often confused.

accept means "to agree to something" or "to receive something willingly."

except means "to exclude" or "omit." (As a preposition, *except* means "but" or "excluding.")

> Kay did *accept* the Hansens' invitation to go camping with them.
> The ninth grade will be *excepted* from locker inspection.
> Everyone *except* the team will sit in the bleachers.

all ready expresses a complete readiness or preparedness.

already means "previously" or "before."

> The pilots and their crew were *all ready* for the landing.
> We had *already* made arrangements to take the early train.

capital means "most important" or "most serious." It also refers to the city or town that is the official seat of government of a state or nation.

capitol is a building in which a state legislature meets.

the Capitol is the building in Washington, D. C., in which the United States Congress meets.

> Montpelier is the *capital* of Vermont.
> Use a *capital* letter to begin every line of poetry.
> The thief had previously been arrested for a *capital* offense.
> The committee held a special meeting at the *capitol* building.
> We visited the *Capitol* in Washington, D. C., last summer.

des'ert means "a wilderness or dry, sandy region with sparse, scrubby vegetation."

des·ert' means "to abandon."

dessert (note the change in spelling) is a sweet, such as cake or pie, served at the end of a meal.

The Mojave *Desert* is part of the Great American *Desert* in southern California.

When we ran out of fuel, we *deserted* our car to find gas.

Jon and Sue baked a strawberry pie for *dessert*.

hear means "to listen to" or "take notice of."

here means "in this place."

Because of a poor sound system, we couldn't *hear* the band.

We finally arrived *here* in Seattle after a flight delay in Denver.

its is a word that indicates ownership.

it's is a contraction for *it is* or *it has*.

The city lost *its* power during the thunderstorm.

It's almost noon, and I haven't finished my work.

lead (lēd) means "to go first."

led (lĕd) is the past tense of *lead*.

lead (lĕd) is a heavy, silvery-blue metal.

A circus wagon pulled by horses will *lead* the parade.

This wagon had *led* the parade for many years.

Lead is one of the heaviest metals, yet it melts at a very low temperature.

lose means "to misplay" or "suffer the loss of something."

loose means "free" or "not fastened."

Our car began to *lose* some of its power as we reached the top of Pike's Peak.

The hinges on the back gate are quite *loose*.

past refers to that which has ended or gone by.

passed is the past tense of *pass* and means went by.

Our *past* experience with that team has taught us to use a different defense.

We *passed* through the Grand Tetons on our vacation last summer.

piece refers to a section or part of something.

peace means calm or quiet and freedom from disagreements or quarrels.

> We cut each *piece* of lumber into several smaller *pieces*.
> I felt a certain *peace* as I sat and watched the sunrise.

plane is a flat, level surface or a carpenter's tool.

plain means clearly understood, simple, or ordinary. It can also refer to an expanse of land.

> In geometry, we learned how to measure a *plane*.
> In shop, we used a *plane* to smooth and trim boards.
> Milton likes *plain* foods; he won't try anything unusual.
> The farms were scattered across the *plain*.

principal describes something of chief or central importance. It also refers to the head of an elementary or high school.

principle refers to a basic truth, standard, or rule of behavior.

> The *principal* cities of France include Paris, Marseilles, Lyons, and Nice.
> The *principal* of our school presented the awards.
> We will study the *principles* of democracy in our American government class.

quiet refers to no noise or to something rather peaceful or motionless.

quite means really or truly, and it can also refer to a considerable degree or extent.

> Everyone was *quiet* during the graduation ceremony.
> We were *quite* sure that the school bus would be late.

stationary means fixed or unmoving.

stationery refers to paper and envelopes used for writing letters.

> The new digital scoreboard will be *stationary* in the large gym.
> Two students in my art class designed the school *stationery*.

there means in that place.

their means belonging to them.

they're is a contraction for *they are*.

> Please put the groceries over *there* on the counter.
> In 1803, the explorers Lewis and Clark led *their* expedition to the western United States.
> Sue and Pam are skiing, and *they're* going snowmobiling on Saturday.

to means toward, or in the direction of.

too means also or very.

two is the number 2.

> We all went *to* the zoo last weekend.
> It was much *too* cold to go cross-country skiing.
> *Two* television stations carried the President's last press conference.

weather refers to atmospheric conditions such as temperature or cloudiness.

whether helps to express choice.

> Daily *weather* reports are studied by meteorologists all over the world.
> *Whether* we call or write for our vacation reservations, we must do it soon.

whose is the possessive form of *who*.

who's is a contraction for *who is* or *who has*.

> Do you know *whose* bicycle is chained to the parking meter?
> *Who's* going to volunteer to help at the children's Christmas party?

your is the possessive form of *you*.

you're is a contraction of *you are*.

> Please take *your* books back to the library today.
> *You're* going there right after school, aren't you?

Exercises   Spell words often confused.

A.   Choose the correct word from the words in parentheses.

1. This (past, passed) year I had a special tutor to help me in math.
2. Three summers have (past, passed) since I went away to camp.
3. Be sure to check your paper for the correct use of (capital, capitol) letters.
4. This is no time to (desert, dessert) our baseball team!
5. We ran out of gas while crossing the (desert, dessert).
6. The weather (hear, here) has been extremely cold.
7. (It's, Its) hard to remember certain dates in American history.
8. Our puppy wags (it's, its) tail as soon as I enter the room.
9. Theodore Roosevelt (lead, led) the charge up San Juan Hill.
10. A drum majorette will (lead, led) the marching band.
11. The latch on the door is (lose, loose) and needs to be fixed.
12. Every winter I (lose, loose) at least two pairs of gloves.
13. All of the players (accept, except) the goalie were involved in the argument.
14. The refreshments are (all ready, already) for the parent-teacher meeting.
15. Loretta has (already, all ready) decided that she wants to be a veterinarian.

B.   Choose the correct word from the words in parentheses.

1. The carpenter used a (plane, plain) to trim the top of the door.
2. Would you like to try a (piece, peace) of pecan pie?

3. The two leaders signed a (piece, peace) treaty.
4. We studied the (principles, principals) of government in social studies.
5. The (principle, principal) actors took their bows.
6. Call us when (your, you're) ready.
7. The coach says (your, you're) the best hitter on the team.
8. Our neighbors never let (their, there) cat out at night.
9. (They're, There) widening Main Street to provide more parking places.
10. That movie was (to, too) funny for words.
11. If the (weather, whether) permits, we will have a picnic.
12. The police officer wondered (whose, who's) fingerprints were on the door.
13. (Whose, Who's) making all that noise?
14. I am (quiet, quite) nervous about going to high school.
15. I received a letter from the mayor on her official (stationery, stationary).

ADDITIONAL EXERCISES

Spelling

A. Spelling Find the misspelled words. Spell them correctly.

1. You surely don't beleive those stories!
2. The garden apartment is actualy the basement.
3. A rageing fire destroyed the department store.
4. Expressways are used heavyly at rush hour.
5. A referee shouted "ilegal motion."
6. Am I really mispronounceing that word?
7. As the tide receeds, we go digging for clams.
8. The arguement was completely silly.
9. Finaly my niece stopped crying.
10. Rose succedes when she tries.
11. Someone who recieves stolen goods is also a thief.
12. I could easyly give you a receipt.
13. The bus had stoped for the twentieth time.
14. I mistakenly thought I would become fameous overnight.
15. He beleives some truly amazing things.

B. Words Often Confused Choose the correct word from the two given in parentheses.

1. Everyone could attend (accept, except) Cal.
2. The concert is (all ready, already) sold out.
3. Rich didn't want to (loose, lose) your friendship.
4. We (past, passed) many vacant lots.
5. The empty gym was still and (quiet, quite).
6. My new (stationary, stationery) is gray with a black border.
7. I asked (whether, weather) the gerbils would bite.

MIXED REVIEW

Spelling

A. Spelling words correctly Pick out any misspelled words from the following sentences. Write them correctly. If there are no misspelled words in a sentence, write *Correct*.

1. There phone is out of order.
2. Our dog chewed it's leash.
3. Children except only sealed candy on Halloween.
4. Taylor had a piece of cake for desert.
5. Who's report was the most carefuly prepared?
6. Cheating on a test is against my principals.
7. Stan past his driveing test easily.
8. Our team suffered quiet a loss on Saturday.
9. Blair doesn't know whether she'll enter the contest.
10. Wayne lead the discussion.

B. Using spelling in proofreading Proofread the following paragraph. Copy it, spelling all words correctly.

Every amusement park from Six Flags too Great America boasts a thrilling roller coaster. Although simple gravity was and is the force that propels the ride, the first roller coasters would not seem exciteing today. An inclineed railway in Pennsylvania, once used too transport coal, became the first roller coaster in the United States. Called the Switchback, this ride chuged along at five miles per hour. In 1884, the Gravity Pleasure Railway at Coney Island, New York, had ten-passenger cars. The speed of this roller coaster did not excede six miles per hour. At midpoint, the cars had too be pushed up a hill until gravity could take over again. The only envyable thing about that old roller coaster was the price. Can you beleive it only cost five cents a ride?

USING MECHANICS IN WRITING
Spelling

A. Write a thank-you note to someone who has taken you on a wonderful weekend trip. Make up the details yourself, but use one of the following pairs of words in each sentence. One or both of the words in each pair is misspelled. Correct the misspelled words. Use all five pairs.

truely enjoied	createive planing	actualy studying
amazing citys	realy believe	

B. The following paragraph contains some words that are often confused. Those words are underlined. Some are spelled correctly, but others are not. Find the mistakes in this paragraph. Rewrite those sentences correctly.

I enjoy seeing disaster movies. The reel world seems so full of peace when compared to the events in these action-packed movies. Somehow the movie always ends with a happy seen, too. This happens whether heroes or heroines are trapped in a skyscraper, threatened by a fire, or surprised by an iceberg braking up a ship.

In one typical film, a hole is blown out of the rear of a plain by a passenger who hates airplane food. Of course, that causes the jet engines to become lose, too. And whose their to save everyone? That job falls to the quiet, misunderstood pilot who had been passed by for promotion. He excepts his assignment to save the passengers; he waists no time. The plane is already diving toward the dessert below. Its hard to believe, but the pilot saves everyone but the angry passenger who's plans are all waisted. If your depressed, go sea a disaster movie. It will cheer you up.

CUMULATIVE REVIEW
Capitalization, Punctuation, and Spelling

A. Using capitalization, punctuation, and spelling correctly Copy the following sentences, correcting the errors in capitalization, punctuation and spelling.

1. Étienne and joseph montgolfier launched the first hot-air balloon in france 200 years ago
2. Cary grant whose real name is alexander archibald leach is an american movie actor
3. Is you're reciept stapled to the bag
4. "jane fonda excepted the oscar for her father henry fonda said Mavis
5. "I beleive remarked larry that camels are called ships of the dessert"
6. Mike tryed a triple somersault but he didnt succeed
7. Jane bought copys of time newsweek and u s news and world report from the newsstand
8. "Ive typed you're business address on the office stationary said the secretary
9. The tourists visited coit tower and the transamerica building in san francisco california
10. What amazeing facts about tokyo japan are in this book
11. I drew a map showing how the strait of gibraltar connects the mediterranean sea and the atlantic ocean
12. Accept for Stephen everyone had all ready eaten desert
13. Our principle, ms Kahn gave me a copy of president Lincolns gettysburg Adress
14. Many of the worlds largest and most fameous diamonds come from the kimberly mine in cape province South Africa

15. "that is correct." said Mrs Dawes, "computors are not difficult to use if you follow there instructions carefully"
16. The Five Nations was a confederation of iroquoian Indians including the mohawks Oneidas, Cayugas, and senecas
17. "When we were in new mexico I saw an amazeing indian mound said Marsi"
18. They're is no place to put the radio that their fixing." said mother"
19. The president takes his oath of office on inauguration Day January 20
20. Michael jackson sang the song Thriller

B. Using proofreading skills Proofread the following paragraph. Copy it, correcting the errors in capitalization, punctuation, and spelling.

Have you ever been in a hot-air balloon. Well it is quiet an experience. my first flight was out in the colorado rocky mountains. The balloon that carryed me into the air was ninty feet tall. i had to stand in an open wicker gondola, or basket. "Your not getting me in their I cryed when i first saw it. When i finaly got in the pilot turned on the propane burner to warm the air in the balloon. We floated high above the ground and then we descended and skimed the treetops. what an exhilarating experience it was. the landing was the scaryest part. when we finaly bumped to a stop I shouted "lets do it again. that was realy great."

A

a, an, the. *See also* Articles.
   as adjectives, 480
   for alphabetizing, 266
   in book titles, 644–645
Abbreviations
   definition of, 639
   in dictionary entries, 24–25
   for note taking, 285
   punctuation of, 653
Accent mark, 28
accept/except, 700
Action verbs, 381–382
Additional exercises. *See* end of
   each lesson.
Addresses
   in business letters, 307–308
   on envelopes, 303–304
Adjectives, 478–495
   adverbs or, distinguishing,
      504–507
   articles as, 480
   in clauses, 614–616
   commas with, 658–659
   comparative forms of, 486–487
   definition of, 478–479
   demonstrative, 485
   in descriptive paragraphs, 122,
      126–127
   diagraming, 480
   predicate, 481–484
   pronouns as, 484
   proper, 479–481
   special problems with, 489–490
   superlative form of, 486–487
   that tell *how many*, 479
   that tell *what kind*, 479
   that tell *which ones*, 479
Adverbs, 496–513

adjectives or, distinguishing,
   504–507
in clauses, 616–618
comparisons with, 501–504
definition of, 496–497
diagraming, 499
forming, 500–501
position of in sentences, 498
prepositions or, distinguishing,
   525–526
Agreement of subject and verb,
   574–589
   compound subjects, 578–580
   in inverted sentences, 580–581
   prepositional phrases after sub-
      ject, 576
   pronouns, 583–584
   special forms of verbs, 575–576
   tricky subjects, 576
   using *I*, 577
   using *you*, 577
all ready/already, 700
Almanac, 271
Alphabetical order
   of dictionary words, 24–27
   of encyclopedia articles,
      268–269
   of fiction books, 262
   of titles in card catalog, 266
already/all ready, 700
Anecdotes in paragraphs, 70–71
Announcements, 324, 326
Antecedents, 462–464
Antonyms, 14–15
   in dictionary entries, 29
Apostrophe
   in contractions, 674–675
   to form plurals, 675

in possessives, 672–673
Articles, 266, 480
Assignments, understanding, 276–277
Atlas, 271
Audience
    of a composition, 166–167
    of a paragraph, 82–83
    of a speaker, 328
Author card in card catalog, 265
Auxiliaries. See Helping verbs.

B

bad/badly, 508
Base words, 16–17
be, forms of, 381, 390
    See also Irregular verbs.
Bibliography cards, 236–237
Bibliographies, 244–245
Biographical references, 271
Body
    of a business letter, 307–308
    of a composition, 160–161, 166–167, 184–185, 196–197, 218–219, 228–229
    of a friendly letter, 300–302
    of a report, 240–241
    of a speech, 332
Books, finding and using in the library. *See* Library, using the.
Borrowed words, 2
Brainstorming, 78–79
Bread-and-butter notes, 305–306
Business letters, 307–308

C

Call numbers, 262
can/may, 423
capital/capitol, 700

Capitalization, 631–650
    days, 637–638
    directions, 635–636
    direct quotations, 641–642
    events, 637
    family relationships, 633
    first words
        of outlines, 644
        of poetry lines, 641
        of quotations, 641
        of sentences, 641
    geographical names, 635
    holidays, 637–638
    I, 633
    initials, 632
    languages, 638
    in letters, 643
    months, 637–638
    names, 632–633
    nationalities, 638
    organizations and institutions, 637
    periods (of time), 637
    proper adjectives, 632
    proper nouns, 632
    races, 638
    religions, 638
    school subjects, 639
    and sections of the country, 635–636
    Supreme Being and sacred writings, 633
    titles of persons, 632–633
    titles of written works, 644
Card catalog, 265–266
Characters, 178–179
Charts, *See* Graphic aids.
Chronological order
    in narrative compositions, 180–181
    in paragraphs, 88–89, 108–109, 112–113, 198

Circular reasoning, 256–257
Clauses
  adjective, 614–616
  adverb, 612–613
  independent, 609–610
  main, 609–610
  noun clauses, 616–618
  relative, 614–615
  subordinate, 609–610, 618–619
Closing of letters, 300–302,
  307–308
  colons with, 307–308
  commas with, 300
Colon, 307, 670
Combining sentence parts, 56–57
Combining sentences, 54–55
Commas, 656–669
  with adjectives, 658–659
  with adverbs, 658–659
  with appositives, 662–663
  to avoid confusion, 656–657
  with city, state, and country,
    668
  in compound constructions, 354
  in compound predicates, 600
  in compound sentences,
    599–601, 665–666
  with dates, 667
  with direct address, 662–663
  with direct quotations, 664, 676
  with indirect quotations, 665
  with interrupters, 660–661
  with introductory words, 660
  in letters, 669
  in a series, 657–660
  to set off *names*, 662–663
  after *yes, no*, 660
Common nouns, 431–433
Comparisons
  using adjectives, 486–488
  using adverbs, 501–502
  as context clue, 10–11

Complete predicate of a sentence,
  348
Complete sentence, 344–345
Complete subject of a sentence,
  344
Completing applications and work-
  related forms, 316–320
Completion, or fill-in-the-blank
  tests, 296–297
Complex sentences, 607–627, 621
  and clauses, 609–610
  definition of, 608, 611
  and sentence fragments,
    619–620
Compositions, 159–231
  body of, 160, 166–167, 184–185,
    196–197, 218–219, 228–229
  chronological order in, 180–181
  characters in, 178–179
  choosing point of view for,
    182–183
  choosing subjects for, 162–163,
    194–195, 214
  conclusion of, 160–161,
    166–167, 184–185, 196–197,
    218–219, 228–229
  conflict in, 178–179
  definition of, 160–161
  descriptive, 193–201. *See also*
    Descriptive compositions.
  details in, 180–181, 194–195
  development of, 162–163
  dialogue in, 186–187
  explanatory
    how, 203–211
    what, 223–232, 231
    why, 213–221
  final copy of, 172–173, 175
  first drafts of, 166–167, 174–175
    descriptive, 196–199
    explanatory, 134–135, 144–145,
      154–155

narrative, 184–189
first-person point of view in, 182–183
flashback, use of, 180–181, 188–189
general-to-specific organization, 226–227
guidelines for writing, 162–163, 174–175
introduction in, 160–161, 166–167, 184–185, 196–197, 218–219, 228–229
main ideas in, 160–161, 164–165
narrative, 177–191. *See also* Narrative compositions.
narrowing topic for, 194–195
omniscient point of view in, 182–183
opinion in, 213–221
order of importance as method of organization in, 216–217
organizing ideas, 164–165
parts of, 160–161
planning, 178–179, 204–205
plot in, 178–179, 180–181
point of view in, 182–183
pre-writing, 160–165, 174
revision of, 168–169, 175, 190–191, 200–201, 210–221, 230–231
sensory details in, 194–195
setting in, 178–179
spatial order in, 194–195
step-by-step order in, 206–207
third-person point of view in, 182–183
time sequence in. *See* Chronological order.
title for, 170–172
topic sentence in, 160, 214

transitions in, 188–189, 208–209, 218–219
See also Writing, Pre-writing, *and* Transitions.
Compound direct object, 533
Compound object of prepositions, 519, 533
Compound object of verb, 533
Compound predicate, 533, 593, 598
Compound predicate adjective, 533, 534
Compound predicate noun, 536
Compound sentences, 592–606, 621
combining related thoughts, 602–603
commas in, 665–667
or compound predicate, 598–599
definition of, 595–596
diagraming of, 596
punctuation of, 599–601
Compound subjects, 354–356, 533, 578–580
diagraming, 355–356
Compound verbs, 354–356, 533
diagraming, 355–356
Conclusions
in compositions, 160–161, 166–167, 184–185, 196–197, 218–219, 228–229
in paragraphs, 92–93
in reports, 240–241
in speeches, 332, 333
Conflict, in stories, 178–179
Conjunctions, 532–537
in compound constructions, 533
in compound sentence parts, 532–535, 594
in compound sentences, 595–596

coordinating, 533
correlative, 533
definition of, 532–533
subordinating, 610
Context
  clues, 6–13
  definition of, 6
  learning word meanings from
    comparison, 10–11
    contrast, 10–11
    definition, 6–7
    examples, 8–9
    inference, 12–13
    restatement, 6–7
Contractions
  apostrophe in, 674–675
  list of, 674
  negatives, 508–509
  n't not included in verb, 383,
    508–509
Cross-reference card, 266
Cumulative review
  capitalization, punctuation,
    spelling, 709–710
  parts of speech, 572–573
  sentence, 628–630
  usage, 590–591

D

Dates
  capitalization of, 637–638
  commas in, 667
Declarative sentences, 346–347
  definition of, 346
  periods in, 346
Definition
  as context clue, 6–7
  in dictionary, 29
  in explanatory *what* paragraph,
    150–153

Demonstrations, 324, 327
Demonstrative adjectives, 485
Demonstrative pronouns, 465–466,
  485–486
Descriptions, 117–127
Descriptive compositions
  ending a description in, 198–199
  first draft of, 196–197
  revising, 200–201
  using sensory details, 194–195
Descriptive paragraphs, 72–73,
  117–127
  first draft of, 124–125
  gathering sensory details,
    118–119
  mood in, 122–123
  revising, 126–127
  using spatial order, 120–121
  using transitional words,
    124–125
Details
  descriptive, in paragraphs,
    86–87, 106–107
  organizing, 88–89
  sensory, 70, 86, 118–119,
    194–195
  in speeches, 330–331
Dewey Decimal System, 262–264
Diagraming, 349–350
  adjectives, 480
  adverbs, 499
  compound sentences, 596
  compound subjects and verbs,
    355
  direct objects, 435
  imperative sentences, 363
  indirect objects, 437–438
  interrogative sentences, 359
  possessive nouns, 445
  predicate adjectives, 483
  predicate nouns, 483
  prepositional phrases, 521–522

questions. *See* Interrogative
  sentences.
subjects in unusual word order,
  356–357
verbs and their subjects,
  349–350
Diagrams. *See* Graphic aids.
Dialogue, 186–187
Dialogue tags, 186–187
Dictionary, 23–33
  abridged, 24
  accent marks in, 28
  alphabetical order in, 24
  abbreviations and symbols in, 24
  antonyms in, 29
  definition of, 24
  definitions in, 29
  entries, information in, 28–33
  entry word, 28
  guide words, 26–27
  irregular verbs in, 395
  meaning, choosing right one,
    31–33. *See also* Context clues.
  origin of word in, 28
  part of speech listed in, 28
  plurals in, 443
  principle parts in, 395
  pronunciation in, 28
  special forms or endings in, 28
  syllables in entries, 28
  synonyms in, 29
  types of, 24
  unabridged, 24
  See also Words *and* Vocabulary.
Directions
  following, 278–279
  giving (in a speech), 324, 326
  for reading forms, 316–320
Direct objects, 384–387, 434–436
  compound, 458–459
  definition of, 385
  diagraming, 435

nouns as, 434–436
predicate words or, distinguishing, 390
pronouns as, 454–455, 458–459
recognizing, 385–388
Direct quotations,
  capitalization of, 641–642
  commas in, 676
  punctuation of, 676–678
Discovery draft. *See* First draft.
does/do, 575
Double negatives, 508

E

Empty sentences, 46–47
Encyclopedia, 268–269
Ending compositions. *See* Conclu-
  sions in compositions; *see also*
  Compositions, conclusions.
Ending sentences in paragraphs,
  92–93
English language
  as a living language, 2–3
  jargon, 40–41
  nonstandard, 36–37
  slang, 38–39
  standard, 36–37
English language words. *See*
  Words.
Entry words in a dictionary, 28
Envelope, addressing, 303–304
Essay tests, 296–297
Examples
  as context clue to meaning of
    word, 8–9
  used to develop a paragraph,
    70–71, 86–87
except/accept, 700
Exclamation mark, or point,
  with exclamatory sentences, 346
  with interjections, 538–540

with quotation marks, 678
Exclamatory sentences
definition of, 346
diagraming, 359
punctuation of, 346
subjects and verbs in, 358–360
Explanatory compositions, 203–231
how, 203–211
revising, 210–211
step-by-step order in,
206–207
using transitional words in,
208–209
what, 223–231
developing a definition,
224–225
first draft of, 228–229
organizing a definition in,
226–227
revising, 230–231
why, 213–221
developing an opinion,
214–215
first draft of, 218–219
organizing an opinion,
216–217
revising, 220–221
using transitional phrases,
218–219
Explanatory paragraphs, 129–157
definition of, 72–73
how, 129–137
explaining a process, 130–131
first draft of, 134–135
revising, 136–137
step-by-step order in,
132–133
transitions in, 134–135
what, 149–157
definition of, 150–151
developing a definition in,
152–153

first draft of, 154–155
organization in, 152–153
revising, 156–157
why, 139–147
definition of, 140
developing an opinion in,
140–141
first draft of, 144–145
organizing an opinion in,
142–143
revising, 146–147
transitions in, 144–145

F

Facts
checking, 250–251
defined, 234, 248
and opinions, 234–235, 252–253
Fiction books, 262
Final copy
of compositions, 172–173, 175
of paragraphs, 103
First drafts
of compositions, 166–167,
174–175, 184–189, 196–199,
208–209, 218–219, 228–229
of descriptive writing, 124–125,
196–199
dialogue in, 186–187
ending sentence in, 92–93
of explanatory writing, 134–135,
144–145, 154–155, 208–209,
218–29
of narrative writing, 112–113,
184–189
of paragraphs, 90–93, 144–145,
154–155
as part of a process, 76–77
of reports, 240–241
transitions in, 188–189

First-person point of view
in compositions, 182–183
in paragraphs, 110–111
Flashback, use of in writing,
180–181, 188–189
Forms, filling out, 316–320
Fragments, 344, 372–374,
619–621
Friendly letters. *See* Letters,
friendly.
Future tense, 392–393

G

General-to specific-order, 88–89,
152–153, 226–227
Geographical names, capitalization
of, 635
Gerunds, 555, 556–557, 560–561,
565
Goals for study, 280–281
Graphic aids, 288–289
Graphs. *See* Graphic aids.
Guidelines for writing composi-
tions, 162–163
Guide cards, 267
Guide words
in dictionary, 26–27
in encyclopedia, 269

H

has/have, 383–384, 575
Heading in letters, 300, 307
hear/here, 701
Helping verbs, 351–354, 383–384,
394, 403
here/there, 489–490
Homograph, 31–32
How compositions, 203–211. *See
also* Explanatory compositions,
how.

How paragraphs, 129–137. *See also*
Explanatory paragraphs, *how.*
Hyphen, 671–672

I

I
and agreement with verbs, 577
capitalization of, 633
with first-person point of view,
110–111, 182–183
ie/ei, 698
Illustrations, 288
Imaginary narrative compositions
(stories), 178–179
Imaginary subjects for paragraphs,
106–107
Imperative sentences
definition of, 346
diagraming, 363
period with, 346
you, as understood subject in, 346,
362–363
Importance of reasons, order of,
88–89, 142–143
Incidents in paragraphs, 70–71
Indenting first line of paragraphs
in letters, 300, 307
Infinitive, 555, 561–566
phrase, 562–564
split, 564–565
Initials
capitalization of, 632
periods with, 653
Indirect objects, 437–438
Inference, drawing word meaning
from, 12–13
Inside address of business letters,
307–308
Interjections, 538–540
Interrogative sentences
definition of, 346

diagraming, 359
question mark with, 346
subjects and verbs in, 358–360
Introductions
  in compositions, 160–161,
    166–167, 184–185, 196–197,
    218–219, 228–229
  in reports, 240–241
  in speeches, 332
Invitations. *See* Letters.
Irregular verbs, 403–418
  agreement with subject,
    575–576
  using a dictionary to find princi-
    pal parts, 395
  and helping verbs, 383–384,
    394–395
  is, are, was, were, 381, 390, 575
  lists of principle parts, 396
  rules for, 394–395
  list of principle parts, 396
  rules for, 394–395
Italics, underlining for, 681
its/it's, 461, 674

J

Jargon, 40–41
Job applications, filling out,
  316–317

K

kind/sort, 490

L

Language
  capitalization of, 638
  to express mood, 122–123

loaded, 258–259
  for special fields, 4–5
lay/lie, 422
lead/led, 701
learn/teach, 420
leave/let, 421
led/lead, 701
legend, 288
let/leave, 421
Letters, 299–315
  of application, 313–315
  business, 307–308
  envelopes, addressing,
    303–304
  friendly, 300–302
  of request, 310–311
  social notes, 305–306
  ZIP code in, 303–304
Library, using the, 261–273
  author card, 265
  call numbers, 262
  classification and arrangement of
    fiction and nonfiction books,
    262–263
  cross-reference card, 266
  Dewey Decimal System, 262
  encyclopedias, 268–270
  subject card, 266
  title card, 266
lie/lay, 422
Linking verbs, 390–392
Listening, 338–339
Logical order in composition,
  See Chronological order, Order
    of importance, Spatial order,
    and Step-by-Step order.
Logical order in paragraphs. *See*
  Chronological order, General-to-
    specific order, Order of
    importance, Spatial order,
    and Step-by-step order.
lose/loose, 701

M

Magazines, as sources, 272
Main clause, 609–610
Main idea
  in compositions, 160–161,
    164–165
  listening for, 338–339
  in paragraphs, 68–69
  in speeches, 332–333
  See also Topic Sentence.
Main verbs, 351–354, 383–384
Maps. *See* Graphic aids.
Matching tests, 294–295
may/can, 423
Mixed Review. *See* end of each
  lesson.
Modifiers. *See* Adjectives, Adverbs.
  Prepositional Phrases.
Mood, in descriptive paragraphs,
  122–123
More/most
  with adjectives, 486–487
  with adverbs, 501–504
Multiple choice tests, 294–295

N

Narrative compositions, 177–191
  choosing point of view in,
    182–183
  dialogue in, 186–187
  first draft of, 184–189
  planning a story, 178–179
  plotting a story, 180–181
  revising, 190–191
  transitions in, 188–189
Narrative paragraphs, 72–73,
  105–115
  choosing point of view in,
    110–111
  chronological order in, 108–109,
    112–113

  developing, 106–107
  first draft of, 112–113
  revising, 114–115
  transitions in, 112–113
Nationalities, capitalization of, 638
Negatives
  definition of, 508
  double, 508
  n't not part of verb, 383, 508
Nonfiction books, 262–267
Nonstandard English, 36–37
Note cards, 236–237
Notes, pre-writing, 106–107,
  164–165
Notes, social. *See* Letters.
Notetaking, 236–237
Nouns, 429–452
  clauses, 616–618
  as compound objects
    of prepositions, 517–518, 519
    of verbs, 519, 533
  as compound subjects, 354–356,
    533
  common, 431–433
  definition of, 430
  as direct objects, 434–436
  as indirect objects, 437–439
  as objects of prepositions,
    517–518
  as objects of verbs, 434–436
  plural forms of, 441–443, 575
  possessive forms of, 444–445
  predicate, 439–441
  proper, 431–433
  in sentence patterns, 546–554
  singular forms of, 441–443, 575
  as subject of the verb, 433–434
no words, *not* words. *See*
  Negatives.
Number of the verb, 575, 576
N LV Adj. sentence pattern,
  550–551

N LV N sentence pattern, 549–550
N V sentence pattern, 546–547
N V N sentence pattern, 547–548
N V N N sentence pattern, 548–549

O

Objective tests, 294–295
Object of the preposition, 517–520
Object of the verb, 384–387
Object pronouns, 454–455, 458–459
Observations, 86, 248–249
Omniscient point of view, 182–183
Opinion
  definition of, 252
  and facts, 214–215, 252–253
  supporting, 216–217, 254–255
  is *why* composition, 214–215
  in *why* paragraph, 140–141
Order of importance, as method of organization, 88–89, 142–143, 216–217
Order of writing
  chronological, 88–89, 108–109, 112–113, 180–181
  general-to-specific, 88–89, 152–153, 266–227,
  importance, 88–89, 142–143, 216–217
  spatial, 88–89, 120–121, 193–194
  step-by-step, 132–133, 206–207
Organizations, capitalization of, 637
Outlines
  capitalization in, 644
  periods in, 653
Outside sources, 234
Overloaded sentences, 50–51

P

Padded sentences, 48–49
Paragraphs, 63–159
  adjectives in, 106–107, 118–119
  anecdotes, use of in, 70–71
  audience of, 82–83
  chronological order in, 88–89, 108–109
  definition of, 64–65
  descriptive, 72–73, 117–127
  details in, 70, 86–87, 106. *See also* Details.
  developing, 70–71, 86–87
  ending sentence in, 92–93
  examples in, 70
  explanatory, 72–73, 129–157. *See also* Explanatory paragraphs.
  facts and statistics in, 70
  final copy of, 103
  first drafts of, 112–113, 124–125, 134–135, 144–145, 154–155
  first-person point of view in, 110–111
  general-to-specific order in, 88–89, 152–153
  incidents in, use of, 70–71
  kinds of, 72–73
  logical order in. *See* Logical order in paragraphs.
  main idea in, 68–69
  narrative, 72–73, 105–115. *See also* Narrative paragraphs.
  order of importance in, 88–89, 142–143
  organizing, 88–89, 142–143. *See also* Order of writing.
  point of view in, 110–111
  purpose of, 82–83
  revising, 76–77, 94–95, 114–115, 126–127, 156–157

sensory details in, 70, 118–119
spatial order in, 88–89, 120–121
step-by-step order in, 132–133
third-person point of view in,
    110–111
time sequence in, 88–89
topic for, narrowing, 80–81
topic sentence in, 68–69, 84–85
transitions in, 112–113,
    124–125, 132–133, 144–145
unity in, 66–67
Participle, 555, 558–561, 565
Participial phrase, 559–560
Parts of speech, 28–29, 538–544
    definition of, 538
    as shown in dictionary entries,
        28
    using words as different,
        540–541
    See also the particular parts of
        speech.
Past participle of verbs, 394–395
Past tense of verbs, 392–393
peace/piece, 702
Period, 652–653
    with quotation marks, 676
Personal observation to attain in-
    formation, 86
Personal point of view. *See* First-
    person point of view.
Phrases and clauses, 609
Phrases, transitional
    in compositions, 188–189
    in paragraphs, 112–113,
        124–125, 132–133, 144–145
piece/peace, 702
Plot in stories, 178–179
Plural forms
    of nouns, 441–443
    of pronouns, 462–463,
        583–584
    of verbs, 575

Poetry lines, capitalization of, 641
Point of view
    first-person, 110–111, 182–183
    omniscient, 182–183
    third-person limited, 182–183
    third-person, 110–111, 182–183
Possessive nouns, 444–445
Possessive pronouns, 454–455,
    461–462
Predicate
    complete, 348
    compound, 354–355, 533,
        593
    definition of, 344
    simple, 348–350, 593
Predicate adjectives, 390, 481–484
    compound, 533
    definition of, 390, 481–482
    diagraming, 483
Predicate nouns, 390, 439–441
    compound, 533
    definition of, 390
    diagraming, 483
Predicate pronouns, 456–457
Predicate words, 390
Prefixes, 18–19
    and spelling, 697
Prepositional phrases, 515,
    520–525
Prepositions, 514–531
    adverbs or, distinguishing,
        525–526
    compound objects of, 519
    definition of, 514–515
    list of, 517
    objects of, 517–520
        nouns as, 517–518
        pronouns as, 518
Present tense of verbs, 392–393
Pre-writing
    as part of a process, 76–77,
        98–99

choosing a point of view,
110–111, 182–183
choosing a subject, 78–79,
140–141, 162–163
for compositions, 162–165
creating mood, 122–123
definition of, 76, 98
for descriptive writing, 118–121,
194–197
developing a definition, 152–153
developing an opinion, 140–141,
214–215
developing a paragraph, 86–87
for explanatory writing,
130–133, 140–143, 150–153,
204–207, 214–217, 224–227
gathering ideas, 86–87,
162–163
gathering sensory details,
118–119
guidelines, 162–163
for narrative writing, 106–107,
178–183
narrowing a topic, 80–81,
106–107
notes, 106–107, 164–165
organizing paragraphs
chronological order, 88–89,
108–109
general-to-specific order,
88–89
order of importance, 88–89,
142–143
spatial order, 88–89, 120–121
step-by-step order, 130–133
stating definitions, 150–151
using sensory details, 194–195
writing a topic sentence,
84–85
Principal parts of verbs, 394–396
principal/principle, 702
Process of writing

pre-writing, 76–77, 98–99. *See
also* Pre-writing.
proofreading, 101
revising, 76–77, 100–101. *See
also* Revising.
steps in, 76–77
writing the first draft, 76–77,
99–100. *See also* First draft.
See also Writing.
Pronouns, 453–477
as adjectives, 484
and antecedents, 462–464
as compound objects of preposition, 519
compound personal, 464–465
definition of, 453
demonstrative, 465–466, 485
indefinite, 468–469, 583–584
interrogative, 466–467
after linking verbs, 456–457
as objects, 454–455, 458–459
of prepositions, 519
of verbs, 458–459
plural, 462–463, 583–584
possessive, 454–455, 461–462
predicate, 456–457
relative, 614–615
singular forms of, 462–463,
583–584
as subjects, 454–457
agreement with verbs,
583–584
with point of view, 110–111,
182–183
substituting nouns, 453
we/us, 459–460
Pronunciation of words, as shown
in dictionary entries, 28
Proofreading, 101
Proper adjectives, 479–481
capitalization of, 479
definition of, 479

Proper nouns, 431–433
  capitalization of, 431
  definition of, 431
Punctuation, 651–691
  accent mark, 28
  apostrophe, 672–676
  to avoid confusion, 656
  colon, 307, 670
  comma, 656–669. *See also*
    Comma.
  in compound sentences, 53–55,
    599–601
  at end of a sentence, 346,
    652–656
  exclamation mark, or point,
    654–655
  hyphen, 671–672
  in letters, 299–315
  period, 652–653
  question mark, 654–655
  quotation marks, 676–681
  semicolon, 600, 669
  and underlining, 681
Purr words, 258–259

Q

Question mark, 346
Questions. *See* Interrogative
  sentences.
quiet/quite, 702
Quotations
  capitalization in, 641–642
  commas with, 676, 644–645
  definition of, 676–677
  direct, 676, 678–680
  divided, 677
  punctuation with, 644–645
Quotation marks, 676–681
  commas with, 676
  in dialogue, 679–680

  with divided quotations, 677
  exclamation marks with, 678
  question marks with, 678
  for titles, 680–681

R

raise/rise, 424
*Readers Guide to Periodical Liter-
  ature,* 272
Reading, 286–287
Real life narrative compositions,
  178–179
Real life subjects for paragraphs,
  106–107
Reference works, 271–272
Regular verbs, 394–395. *See also*
  Verbs.
Relative clauses, 614–615
Religions, capitalization of,
  638
Reports, 233–245
Research, 86, 236–237. *See also*
  Study and research skills.
Restatement, as context clue to
  word meaning, 6–7
Return address on envelope,
  303–304
Revision
  definition of, 76–77
  of compositions, 168–169, 175,
    190–191, 200–201, 210–211,
    220–221
  of descriptive writing, 126–127,
    200–201
  of explanatory writing, 136–137,
    146–147, 156–157, 210–211,
    220–221
  of first drafts, 94–95, 126–127,
    200–201, 220–221
  of narrative writing, 114–115

of paragraphs, 94–95, 100–101,
114–115, 126–127, 136–137,
146–147, 156–157
as part of a process, 76–77,
100–101
of a report, 242–243
rise/raise, 424
Run-on sentences, 374–375

S

s'/'s, 444–445
Salutation in letters, 300, 307
Scanning, 286–287
Schedules for study, 280–281
Semicolon, 600, 669
Senses, as basis for gathering detail, 118–119
Sensory details, 70, 118–119,
194–195
Sentence fragments, 344, 372–374,
619–621
Sentence patterns, 545–554
N LV Adj., 550–551
N LV N, 549–550
N V, 546–547
N V N, 547–548
N V N N, 548–549
Sentences, 43–61, 343–379
by adding single words, 58–59
beginning with *there,* 360–361
capitalization of, 641
combining, 54–55
by adding single words, 58–59
sentence parts, 56–57
complete, 344–345
complete predicate in, 344
complete subject in, 344
complex, 607–627
compound, 53–55, 60–61,
592–606, 621

compound predicate in,
354–355, 533
compound subject in, 354–355
correct use of, 42–51, 344–349
declative, 346
definition of, 44, 344, 594
diagraming, 349–350. *See also*
specific sentence parts.
empty, 46–47
ending, in paragraphs, 92–93
end punctuation in, 346
exclamatory, 346, 358–361
fragments, 344, 372–374,
619–621
imperative, 346, 362–363
interrogative, 346, 358–361
overloaded, 50–51
padded, 48–49
in paragraphs, 64–67
parts of, 344–345
patterns of, 345–354
predicate in, 344–345
punctuation in, 346. *See also*
specific punctuation.
run-on, 374–375
simple, 621
simple predicate (verb) in,
348–349, 593–594
simple subject in, 344–345,
348–349, 593–594
topic, 68–69, 84–85
writing, 43–61
set/sit, 425
Setting in stories, 178
Short-answer tests, 296–297
Signature in letters, 300, 307
Simple predicate (the verb),
348–349
Simple sentences, 354–355, 621
Simple subject, 344–345, 348–349
Singular forms of nouns, 441–443
sit/set, 425

Skimming, 286–287
Slang, 38–39
Snarl words, 258–259
sort/kind, 490
Sources, 250–251
Spatial order
  in compositions, 194–195
  in paragraphs, 88–89, 120–121
  in speeches, 332
  Specific examples in paragraphs,
    70–71, 86–87
Speech, 323–339
  and appearance, 334
  choosing topics for, 328
  evaluating a speech, 338–339
  and eye contact, 334
  formal, 324–325, 328–329,
    332–333
    choosing topic for, 328
    controlling voice, 334
    determining purpose, 328
    gathering information,
      330–331
    identifying audience, 328
    narrowing topic, 328
    organizing information,
      330–331
  and gestures, 334
  guidelines for content, 328–331
  guidelines for presentation,
    334–335, 339
  informal, 324–325, 326–327
    announcements, 324, 326
    demonstrations, 324, 327
    directions, 324, 326
    introductions, 324, 326
  listening to, 338–339
  and posture, 339
  and practice, 336–337
Spelling, 692–708
  and doubling final consonant,
    699

habits for improving, 693–694
ie/ei, 698–699
memory devices, 693, 694
method of attack, 693–694
prefixes, 697
rules for, 695–696
suffixes, 697
words often confused, 700–703
SQ3R study method, 282–283
Standard English, 36–37
State-of-being verbs, 348, 381,
  390–392. *See also* Linking verbs.
Step-by-step order
  in *how* compositions, 206–207
  in *how* paragraphs, 132–133
Stories, writing, 106–107, 178–179
Study and research skills, 275–297
  assignments, understanding,
    276–277
  following directions, 278–279
  graphic aids, 288–289
  reading rate, 286–287
  SQ3R study method, 282–283
  study plans, 280–281
  taking notes, 284–285
  test-taking, 292–297
  time and place to work, 280–281
Subject card, 266
Subject pronouns, 454–457
Subject of the sentence
  agreement with verb, 574–589
  complete, 344
  compound, 354–356
  definition of, 344
  diagraming, 349–350
  in exclamatory, 358–360
  in imperative sentences, 346,
    362–363
  in interrogative sentences,
    358–360
  nouns as, 433–434
  pronouns as, 456–457

simple, 348–349, 593
understood (you), 346, 362–363
in unusual positions, 356–358
of the verb, 348
Subordinate clause, 609–612,
618–619
Suffixes, 20–21, 479, 697
Superlatives
adjectives as, 486–487
adverbs as, 502–503
Syllables
in dictionary entries, 28
dividing words into, 671–672
Synonyms, 14–15, 29

T

Tables. *See* Graphic aids.
Talks. *See* Speech.
teach/learn, 420
Test taking, 292–297
Thank-you notes. *See* Letters.
their/they're 674–675
them/those, 489
there, here, where introducing
sentences, 581–582
Thesis statement, 234
Third-person point of view
in compositions, 182–183
in paragraphs, 110–111
those/them, 489
Time Sequence. *See* Chronological
order.
Title card, 266
Titles
capitalization of, 632–633
of compositions, 170–171
of persons, 632–633
of written works, 680–681
to/too/two, 703
Topic, choosing, 78–79

Topic, narrowing the
for compositions, 162–163
for paragraphs, 78–79
Topic sentences
in compositions, 160–214
in paragraphs, 68–69, 84–85
Transitions
showing chronological order,
112–113, 188–189
in compositions, 188–189,
208–209, 218–219
showing order of importance of
reasons, 218–219
in paragraphs, 112–113,
124–125, 132–133
showing spatial order, 124–125,
193–194
showing step-by-step order,
132–133, 208–209
True-false tests, 294–295
two/to/too, 703

U

Underlining titles for italics, 681
Understood subject (you), 346,
362–363
Unity in paragraphs, 66–67
Using grammar in writing. *See* end
of each lesson.
Using mechanics in writing
capitalization, 650
punctuation, 691
spelling, 708

V

Verb (simple predicate), 348–349
Verbals, 555–574
Verbs, 380–428
action, 381–382

after *there*, 581–582
agreement with subject, 574–577
be, 381, 390
    See also State-of-being verbs, Linking verbs *and* Irregular verbs.
in a clause, 608–611
compound, 354–355
with compound subjects, 578–580
contractions, 383
definition of, 380–382
diagraming, 349–350
using dictionary to find principal parts, 395
direct objects of, 384–387
helping, 351–354, 383–384, 394, 403
in imperative sentences, 362–363
intransitive, 387–389
irregular, 403–418, 383, 394–395, 396
linking, 381, 390–392
main, 351–354, 383–384
in negative contractions, 383, 508–509
number, definition of, 576
object of, 384–387
past paticiple of, 394–395
plural forms of, 575
present part, 394–395
principal parts of, 394–396
regular, 394–395
in sentence patterns, 345–354
separated parts of, 352–353, 383
singular forms of, 575
state-of-being, 348, 381–382, 390–392
subjects of, 348
tenses, 392–393

transitive, 387–389
troublesome, 419–427
using negatives, 508
See also Irregular verbs.
Vertical file, 271–272
Vocabulary, 1–21
    See also Words *and* Dictionary.

W

we/us, 459–460
weather/whether, 703
well/good, 507
whether/weather, 703
who/whom, 467, 614–615
who's/whose, 674, 703
what compositions, 223–231
what paragraphs, 149–159
why compositions, 213–221
why paragraphs, 139–147
Word endings as shown in dictionary entries, 28
Word order and sentence meaning, 545–546
Word parts, 16–21
Words, English language
    antonyms, 14–15, 29
    base, 16–17
    borrowed, 2–3
    clipped, 2
    context clues to meaning of, 6–13
    entry words in dictionary, 28
    as different parts of speech, 540–541
    guide words, 26–27
    homographs, 31–32
    jargon, 40–41
    origin of, 2,
    from people's names, 2
    purr words, 258–259
        snarl words, 258–259

for special fields, 4–5
synonyms, 14–15, 29
slang, 38–39
transitions
  in compositions, 188–189,
    208–209, 218–219
  in paragraphs, 112–113,
    124–125, 132–133
Work-related forms, 319–320
Writing
  choosing a point of view,
    110–111, 182–183
  choosing a subject, 162–163,
    194–195, 214
  compositions. *See* Compositions.
  final copy, 103, 172–173, 175
  first drafts
    of compositions, 166–167,
      174–175, 184–189,
        196–199, 208–209,
          218–219, 228–229
    of paragraphs, 90–93,
      144–145, 154–155
  narrowing a topic, 78–79, 80–81,
    162–163
  paragraphs, 63–159. *See also*
    Paragraphs.

pre-writing, 76–77, 78–89,
  98–99, 162–165, 194–197,
  214–215. See also Pre-writing.
  as a process, 76–77, 98–103
  proofreading, 101
  revision
    of compositions, 168–169,
      175, 190–191, 200–201,
      220–221, 230–231
    of paragraphs, 76–77,
      100–101, 114–115,
        126–127, 136–137,
          146–147, 156–157
  sentences, 43–61
  using combining skills in, 60–61
Written tests, 296–297

Y

you
  as understood subject, 346,
    362–363
  and agreement with verb, 577
your/you're, 674

Z

ZIP code, 303–304

Acknowledgments

Susan A. Schmeltz: For "Paper Dragons" by Susan Alton Schmeltz, from *Cricket*, Vol. 6, No. 7, March 1979.

Photographs

Tom McCarthy/Hillstrom Stock, ii; Alex Webb/Magnum, xviii; Jim Whitmer, 22, 34, 96, 212, 232; James L. Ballard, 42, 176; Normal Morrison/Hillstrom Stock, 52, 298; Jacqueline Durand, 62, 260, 274, 322; Brent Jones, 74, 116, 202, 222; Paul Damen/Click Chicago, 104; Don & Pat Volenti/ Hillstrom Stock, 128, 148; Don Smetzer/Click Chicago, 138, 340; Timothy Eagan/Woodfin Camp, 158; Ray F. Hillstrom, Jr., 192; David Borth/Hillstrom Stock, 246.

Cover

Sinjerli Variation IIA, 1977. Frank Stella. Petersburg Press, London and New York, © Vert Foncé, 1977.

Editorial Credits

Editor-in-Chief: Joseph F. Littell
Editorial Director: Joy Littell
Administrative Editor: Kathleen Laya
Managing Editor: Geraldine Macsai

Director of Secondary English: Bonnie Dobkin
Editors: James M. LiSacchi, Mary Schafer
Associate Editor: Robert D. Shepherd
Associate Designer: Mary E. MacDonald
Assistant Designer: Debbie Costello
Cover Design: Joy Littell, Mary E. MacDonald